Encyclopaedia of

MOTOR-CYCLE SPORT

Encyclopaedia of

MOTOR-CYCLE SPORT

Compiled by

PETER CARRICK

ROBERT HALE LIMITED
LONDON

ST. MARTIN'S PRESS
NEW YORK

First edition 1977
Second edition 1982

ISBN 0 7091 8874 9

Robert Hale Limited
Clerkenwell House
Clerkenwell Green
London EC1

St. Martin's Press, Inc.
175 Fifth Avenue
New York, N.Y. 10010

Library of Congress Catalog Card Number 82-47650

ISBN 0-312-24868-7

Printed in Great Britain by
St. Edmundsbury Press, Bury St. Edmunds, Suffolk.
Bound by Woolnough Bookbinding Ltd., Northants.

Preface

Encyclopaedia of Motor-Cycle Sport is probably the most comprehensive work of reference on the subject ever compiled. The period covered is from the birth of organised motor-cycle racing in the early 1900s to the present day. It is probably unequalled in its extensive coverage of race results through the years.

There are histories of major racing factories; biographies of all star riders, past and present; and full descriptions of the important races. The major events, including the TTs, World Championships and Daytona, receive extensive coverage.

The book leans more towards road racing than other branches of the sport, though the enthusiast will find plenty to interest him in the good coverage given to moto-cross and scrambling, trials, grass track, sprinting, drag racing and world record attempts. Since speedway has developed along independent lines and now occupies a separate place as a major sport, no attempt has been made to give it more than cursory attention, though the reader will undoubtedly find of interest the references to its origins, history and development, together with the tables of the main international results and notes about its major personalities.

Even a book of this size and scope is unable to encompass every facet of such a diverse sport and in attempting to give as broad a perspective as possible, your favourite event, incident, rider or machine may have been omitted, or not dealt with as extensively as you would have liked. Any such shortcomings brought to notice will be carefully filed for consideration in subsequent editions.

Acknowledgements

Sources too numerous to mention individually have been used to compile *Encyclopaedia of Motor-Cycle Sport*, but my thanks are extended to them all. In particular I should like to express my gratitude to *Motor Cycle Weekly*, for research facilities, *Motor Cycle News*, circuit owners and race organisers, the Auto-Cycle Union, RAC and the many motor-cycle clubs who have provided information, and to Charlie Rous, Harry Louis, Jerry Clayton, Bob Currie, Mary Driver and Ted Davis for their suggestions, specialist knowledge (willingly imparted), advice and general comments. Particularly, my appreciation is extended to Vic Willoughby, for his contribution on the technical development of the sport.

My special thanks go to Moira Barron for the formidable job of typing the manuscript and to Sheena Atkinson and Beverley Mortimer for their help.

Illustrations

38 The British team which won the SPEEDWAY Team World Championship for the first time
39 JOCK TAYLOR, sidecar world champion 1980, with passenger Benga Johansson
40 STANLEY WOODS, the most outstanding rider of his time

PICTURE CREDITS

Author and publisher are particularly grateful to *Motor Cycle Weekly* for permission to reproduce the above listed copyright photographs. Individual photographers whose work is represented are: W. Gruber, 1; M. Woollett, 2, 8, 32; Cy Stork, 4; B. R. Nicholls, 5, 9, 13, 23, 24, 39; H. Stansfield, 25; Pippo Terreni, 10, 31; K. Lee, 18; K. Price, 19; Maguire, 20; Alf Weedon, 22; Jan Heese, 30; J. Stoddart, 34; Cecil Bailey, 37.

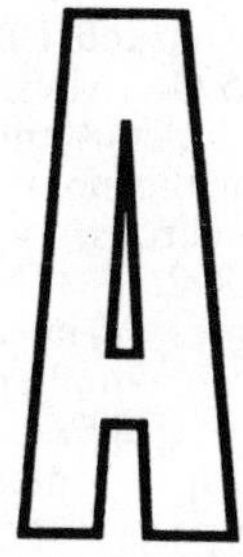

A-CU ROAD RACING STARS

(*See also* BRITISH ROAD RACING CHAMPIONSHIPS)

Forerunner to the British Championships, the A-CU Road Racing Stars were introduced by the Auto-Cycle Union in 1958 to reward consistency of performance in a series of events held throughout the season. Riders scored points in a pre-determined number of national races and at the end of the season, riders in specified categories with most points received A-CU Stars.

1958: S. M. B. Hailwood (125cc), S. M. B. Hailwood (250cc), S. M. B. Hailwood (350cc), A. M. Godfrey (500cc), P. V. Harris (three-wheeler).

1959: S. M. B. Hailwood (125cc), S. M. B. Hailwood (250cc), S. M. B. Hailwood (350cc), S. M. B. Hailwood (500cc), P. V. Harris (three-wheeler).

1960: S. M. B. Hailwood (125cc), S. M. B. Hailwood (250cc), S. M. B. Hailwood (350cc), S. M. B. Hailwood (500cc), W. Boddice (three-wheeler).

1961: D. Shorey (125cc), S. M. B. Hailwood (250cc), P. W. Read (350cc), S. M. B. Hailwood (500cc), C. J. Vincent (three-wheeler).

1962: D. Shorey (125cc), D. Shorey (250cc), D. W. Minter (350cc), D. W. Minter (500cc), W. Boddice (three-wheeler).

1963: D. Simmonds (125cc), T. Phillips (250cc), P. W. Read (350cc), P. W. Read (500cc), C. J. Vincent (three-wheeler).

1964: W. D. Ivy (125cc), D. W. Minter (250cc), J. Cooper (350cc), D. W. Minter (500cc), C. J. Vincent (three-wheeler).

1965: G. Ashton (50cc), W. D. Ivy (125cc), D. Simmonds (250cc), D. W. Minter (350cc), W. D. Ivy (500cc), C. J. Vincent (three-wheeler).

In 1966 the 'stars' system was abandoned and replaced by a British Championship in each machine class. This system continued until 1973, when Star Championships were reintroduced for the 125cc and 250cc categories, the British Championship titles continuing to be won in the over-250cc class solo and in the sidecar categories.

Star Champions in the 125cc and 250cc classes are as follows:

1973: A. Hockley (125cc) and T. Rutter (250cc).

1974: D. Saltwell (125cc) and A. Hockley (250cc).

1975: G. Shirtliff (125cc) and D. Chatterton (250cc).

1976: C. Horton (125cc) and G. Waring (250cc).

1977: L. Carr (125cc) and C. Padgett (250cc).

1978: B. Murray (125cc) and D. Huxley (250cc).

1979: P. Mellor (125cc) and P. Mellor (250cc)

1980: M. Higgins (125cc) and A. Bond (250cc).

1981: P. Mellor (125cc) and P. Wild (250cc).

AERMACCHI

This Italian factory has never won a World Championship, nor a TT, though in the former Kel Carruthers and Renzo Pasolini brought them closest to it. In the 350cc World Championships of 1966 Pasolini was third, with Carruthers in the same position in the same category in 1968. Begamonti gave them a third position in the 1970 500cc World Championship riding an Aermacchi/MV. Aermacchi were taken over by Harley-Davidson in 1960 and in 1970 the factory produced twin-cylinder two-stroke racers as competition to Yamaha. Pasolini rode them with success in 1972 and in the World Championships was second in the 250cc category, only one point behind World Champion Saarinen, and third in the 350cc table.

AGOSTINI, Giacomo

Agostini, fifteen times world champion (end 1981), gained an international reputation during the 1960s and remained to dominate the 350cc and 500cc classes of the World Championships right into the 1970s, one of only three or four riders whose reputations earned in the sensational days of the Japanese domination bridged the two decades, Phil Read being the other outstanding example. Born in 1943 at Lovere, near Bermago, Northern Italy, his first efforts were on a 175cc Morini in Italian domestic road races and in hill climb events. On a works machine borrowed from the Italian factory he entered his first major road race in 1963. In 1964 he became Morini's number one rider and beat Tarquinio Provini to win the 250cc Italian championship. He was signed by the Italian MV concern in 1965 and had immediate success. Having raced nothing bigger than 250cc machines, and in spite of his lack of experience in international competition, he finished the season as runner-up to Mike Hailwood in the 500cc World Championship and only mechanical failure during the Japanese Grand Prix of the same year prevented his winning of the 350cc title. His first Grand Prix victory was in the 350cc West German classic of 1965 at the Nurburgring on an MV-3. He gained his first world championship the following year in the 500cc category during a season dominated by the keen competition between himself and former MV team-mate Mike Hailwood, who during the close season had switched to Honda. He secured the title in the final round of the series, the Italian Grand Prix held at Monza in September. In the World 350cc Championship of 1966, Agostini was runner-up to Hailwood. Since then Agostini has become the most outstanding record-breaker of them all. His reign as 350cc World Champion continued uninterrupted and he won the title every year, 1968-74 inclusive. Having beaten Hailwood to the 500cc championship in 1966, Agostini was to become 500cc World Champion from then until 1973, when he was beaten to the title by MV team-mate, Phil Read. The keen circuit rivalry between Agostini and Hailwood on their powerful MV and Honda machines in 1966-67 quickly became a legend in the sport, his courageous battles against Hailwood and the might of the Japanese factory constituting one of the most thrilling chapters in racing's recent history – and finally denying Honda their one remaining major ambition, the 500cc World Championship.

Agostini competed regularly on the Isle of Man and up to 1973 achieved ten TT victories on the 350cc and 500cc MVs. Later, however, he became a persistent critic of the TT Races, claiming the mountain circuit to be far too dangerous. He did not compete there after 1972.

Agostini, a bachelor, comes from a wealthy family and has three younger brothers. His interest in motor-cycle racing developed when he was nine when his father bought him a Vespa scooter. Two years later he had a Bianchi moped, which he rode in gymkhanas. At 15 he owned two machines, a Parilla which he used for trials and a 175cc Guzzi roadster. Then came the 175cc Morini used for hill climbing and, in 1961, for competing in junior road racing events. Though Agostini's outstanding talent is beyond question, it is also true that much of his success has been achieved during years when there was little real competition for his MV machines. For much of his career he has occupied a lonely role and has gained his successes without the stimulus of close competition, waiting for someone to come along with competitive machinery. His two outstanding season-long battles were in 1966 after Hailwood had quit the MV line-up for Honda, and in 1973 against Phil Read. He was successful against Hailwood in 1966, but was beaten by Read in 1973, losing the 500cc title for the first time in seven years. The most serious threat to his monopoly of the 350cc class came from Jarno Saarinen of Finland riding a Yamaha. Saarinen was runner-up to Agostini in both 1971 and 1972.

Agostini has always been a popular champion and enjoyed great box-office appeal. Handsome and fashionable, he has been in demand as a model and has appeared in films. He made his first appearance on the Isle of Man in 1965, riding MVs in the Junior and Senior events. He was placed third in the Junior and retired in the Senior. He rode in the TTs every year from then until and including 1972. Among an impressive list of achievements are the following:

1. The largest number of World Championship titles (350cc World Champion in 1968, 1969, 1970, 1971, 1972, 1973, 1974 and 500cc World Champion in 1966, 1967, 1968, 1969, 1970, 1971, 1972 and 1975).

2. The only man to be double world champion in five consecutive years (350 and 500cc titles in 1968, 1969, 1970, 1971,

1972).

3. In 1970 he equalled Mike Hailwood's record (achieved in 1966) of 19 Grand Prix wins in a season.

4. Rode the then fastest road race in the world during the 500cc Belgian Grand Prix held on the Francorchamps circuit (8 miles 1,340 yards) near Spa in Belgium. His record time for this 12-lap race was 49 min 5.3 sec at an average speed of 128.506 mph on July 1 1973.

5. Set a new record in October 1972 by winning his thirteenth Italian road race championship with victories in 350 and 500cc races at San Remo. The previous best of 12 titles was held by Tarquinio Provini.

Agostini first lapped the Isle of Man TT circuit at more than 100 mph in 1966 and his record number of 65 100-mph laps is now well ahead of his nearest rival, Mike Hailwood. His achievements on the Isle of Man are as follows:

1965: third place in the Junior;
1966: winner of the Junior and second in the Senior;
1967: second in the Junior;
1968: winner of both the Senior and Junior;
1969: winner of both the Senior and Junior;
1970: winner of both the Senior and Junior;
1971: winner of the Senior;
1972: winner of both the Senior and Junior.

Unlike most top riders Agostini stayed with one make of machine for almost the whole of his career, riding MVs from 1965 up to and including 1973. His discontent with the Italian concern following MV team-mate Phil Read's winning of the 500cc World Championship that year, during which Agostini claimed that as No. 1 rider he was having to ride second-best machines, brought a major shift in his career. After spending most of his career on four-stroke machines Ago signed for Yamaha to contest the classic events of 1974 on 350cc and 500cc two-stroke machines and also the formula 750 events on the new Yamaha 700-four. He was immediately successful with a victory in the United States in the big Daytona 200-mile road race against top American competition and his partnership with Yamaha quickly became the major talking-point in the sport; but he was unable to duplicate the double-class success he had achieved with MV, losing the 500cc title in 1973 and 1974, though retaining the 350cc championship.

Agostini has also won most of the big events in Britain, including Mallory Park's Race of the Year and the Race of the South at Brands Hatch.

He regained the 500cc World Title in 1975 riding for Yamaha and shortly after left international motor-cycle racing for motor sport.

AGUSTA, Count Domenico

This almost legendary Sicilian, who inherited his father's aircraft business in 1927 and founded MV Agusta in 1945 to make motor-cycles, was born in Palermo in 1907 and died in Milan in 1971. In motor-cycle racing Count Agusta had no equal. A dynamic businessman, autocratic boss of Meccanica Verghera Agusta of Gallarate, his passion for the sport was exceptional and his determination to see his factory a world leader almost obsessional. He was an enigma. Seldom attending race meetings, he was both unpredictable and at times unapproachable. A secret kind of man, he kept himself very much in the background, preferring to make his reputation through MV's successes on the track.

Count Agusta was tough, iron-willed and intensely patriotic. Boss of the MV helicopter and motor-cycle firm, he considered racing more of a hobby than a business. It was a hobby which consumed his life and in which he invested heavily. His relentless pursuit of international fame brought MV more successes, including a greater number of world championships, than any other factory. This was his reward. MV's first racer was introduced in 1950 and during the next ten years the firm had collected 82 classic victories in all four solo classes and their machines and riders had won 15 world championships. At the time of the Count's death MV Agusta riders had secured 31 world championships, to which were added 32 manufacturers world championship titles. This was twice that of their nearest rivals, Honda and BMW. In the late 1950s when the European motor-cycle market slumped, the Count's passionate interest kept MV in racing, virtually the only major factory to remain in road racing. His greatest success was undoubtedly MV's denial of the 500cc world championship crown to Honda in 1966 (against such riders as Hailwood and Redman) and again in 1967. They were the only factory successfully to resist Honda domination. A galaxy of star riders represented MV during the Count's lifetime including Agostini, Hailwood, Hocking, Provini, Surtees, Hartle, Ubbiali, Taveri, Sandford and Graham. Succeeding Count Agusta on his death as the boss of MV was the 47-year old surviver of a family of four brothers, Corrado Agusta, who had been with the company all his life. By then it was the second largest manufacturer of helicopters in the world.

AJS

One of the oldest manufacturers of racing motor-cycles and one of a number of British factories which dominated European racing between the wars, AJS had already raced successfully before the outbreak of the First World War, registering a first and second in the Junior TT of 1914. When hostilities ceased they soon became successful in the TTs and on the continent in the 350cc class. They won three Junior TTs in succession – 1920-22.

In 1921 Howard Davies became the first rider to win a Senior TT on a Junior machine (at an average speed of 56.50 mph), and that same year the first three places in the Junior TT were all gained on AJS machinery. Jimmy Simpson created the first Isle of Man lap record at over 60 mph and again at 70 mph in 1924 and 1926 on AJS machines and it was the famous "Cammy Ajays", introduced in 1930, which gave Jimmy Guthrie his first TT victory, in the lightweight class that same year. During this period AJS contested many events on the continent with distinction and success.

The company was named after A. J. Stevens of Wolverhampton whose family founded the firm and built their first motor-cycle in 1897. Their first entry in the TTs was in 1911 with two 98cc side-valve singles, finishing 15th and 16th in the first TT to use the mountain circuit. Cyril Williams' TT win on AJS in 1920 was an outstanding achievement, for he was well over nine minutes ahead of the second-placed rider. Davies' Senior victory on a 350cc AJS in 1921 at a speed of 54.50 mph was an all-time TT record. That year the AJS team had seven entries in the Junior event and six finished, in first, second, third, fourth, sixth and eighth positions, Eric Williams winning at 52.11 mph and Davies, second, setting a lap record of 55.15 mph. Jimmy Simpson joined the team in 1923 and although his outright successes were restricted, he achieved a number of records including his 59.59 mph in the 350cc event of 1923. His 64.54 mph on a 350 in 1924 was the first 60 mph-plus lap to be seen on the Isle of Man. In 1925, on a 500 AJS, Simpson set a lap record of 68.97 mph. In 1926 it was Simpson again lapping at over 70 mph for the first time at 70.43 mph. In 1927 AJS brought in chain-driven ohc singles but they were not successful.

Another distinction achieved by AJS was the very first 100 mph lap speed to be achieved on the Ulster Clady circuit in August 1939 with a 4-cylinder machine ridden by Walter Rusk. Rusk later retired from the race with broken forks. Jimmy Guthrie's victory in the 250 TT of 1930 was significant because he won at a record 64.71 mph on a machine which had been the idea of former Velocette rider Freddie Hicks, who had joined AJS in 1930. This machine, in spite of its successful debut, was not raced again and the AJS concern was taken over by Matchless (later to become AMC Ltd) in 1931. Because of the policy of the Matchless concern, run by two illustrious names in TT racing, Harry and Charlie Collier, AJS machines were soon back in racing but in 1934, with ohc machines which were hardly competitive, AJS found the going hard against the "works" machines of Norton, Velocette and others. A 4-cylinder 500cc V4 machine was introduced in 1935-36 and it was on the water-cooled supercharged V4 that Walter Rusk achieved his over-100 mph record in Ulster. For a number of years following the end of the Second World War, AJS were active in race competition. It was in 1947 that they introduced their famous Porcupine, a racing twin so named because of its unusual cylinder head fins. AJS alone, at this time, seemed to appreciate that the days of the single-cylinder machine were ended in the face of the Italian multis. Les Graham and Jock West were the riders for the Porcupine's first appearance at the TT, though mechanical troubles slowed them down. West, troubled with a slipping clutch, nonetheless made second-fastest lap of the race and finished in 14th position. Graham occupied sixth position at the end of six laps but his chain came off at Governor's Bridge on the last lap and he pushed home to finish in ninth position. The Porcupine was developed over a period of eight years and although achieving notable successes was never able to do very much on the Isle of Man. Best performance there was perhaps in the Senior event of 1949 when Les Graham looked set to win but had a magneto armature spindle shear towards the end of the final lap.

The 500cc twins used in the 1954 TTs by the AJS factory team were technically much different from the original Porcupines but the name persisted. Rod Coleman, Derek Farrant and Bob McIntyre were the riders. In weather conditions which terminated the race at the end of four laps Bob McIntyre occupied fourteenth place. Coleman had been up in fifth place for the first three laps before retiring with a split fuel tank. Rod Coleman did better in the Ulster Grand Prix that year finishing second, 30 seconds behind Ray Amm's Norton in a race which also was shortened because of adverse weather conditions. These events of 1954 were significant for AJS and indeed for the other British factory teams. They witnessed the end of the British factory teams in international competition, including the senior TT, for by this time the Italian 4s were much quicker.

Results:

World Championships:
1949: first in 500cc (L. Graham).
1950: third in 500cc (L. Graham) and third in 350cc (L. Graham).
1951: third in 350cc (W. Doran).
1954: third in 350cc (R. Coleman).
1964: third in 350cc (M. Duff).

TT Races:
1914: first (E. Williams) and second (C. Williams) in Junior.
1920: first (C. Williams) in Junior.
1921: first (H. R. Davies) in Senior, on Junior machine, and first (E. Williams), second (H. R. Davies) and third (T. M. Sheard) in Junior.
1922: first (T. M. Sheard) and second (G. Grinton) in Junior.
1923: second (H. F. Harris) in Junior.
1924: third (H. R. Scott) in Junior.
1925: second (F. A. Longman) in Senior and third (J. H. Simpson) in Junior.
1926: third (F. A. Longman) in Senior and second (J. H. Simpson) in Junior.
1927: third (J. H. Simpson) in Junior.
1928: second (G. E. Rowley) in Senior.
1929: second (W. L. Handley) in Junior.
1930: first (A. J. Guthrie) in Lightweight.
1951: second (W. Doran) in Senior.
1952: third (R. W. Coleman) in Junior.
1954: first (R. Coleman) and second (D. Farrant) in Junior.
1956: second (D. Ennett) in Junior.
1959: first (A. King) in Formula 1 350cc.
1960: third (R. McIntyre) in Junior.
1964: second (P. W. Read) and third (M. A. Duff) in Junior.

In the ten years from 1920 AJS machines also recorded the fastest lap on seven occasions.

AMERICAN MOTOR CYCLISTS ASSOCIATION

The American Motor Cyclists Association is the governing body of motor cycle sport in the United States. Founded in 1924 the AMA for many years held little significance for British and European riders. A disagreement between them and the FIM, and brought about basically by the difference in attitudes in the type of machines to be available for competition, meant that any FICM registered rider risked suspension if he took part in AMA competitions. The AMA felt the interests of motor cycling would be better served if they restricted bikes used in competition to basically sports machines. The FIM disagreed with this policy. For years the sport in America and in Europe went their separate ways. The main difference of that development was in the basic nature of the races themselves. In Britain and elsewhere in Europe Grand Prix races were specialised to the extent of being exclusively road races, while in America the AMA Championship series incorporated many different types of racing, i.e. dirt track racing, run over loose surface circuits over half a mile and a mile, road racing and American-style TT racing, which is a combination of moto-cross and dirt track racing. The AMA left the FIM in the early 1920s. Machine capacity classes developed differently in America. As long ago as the 1930s in America overhead valve and single overhead camshaft engines up to 500cc could race on equal terms with

750cc side-valve V-twins which were then popular with Harley-Davidson and Indian, the major American racing factories. They were happy with a single big machine class and it was not until the 1960s, with the growing popularity of lightweights, that a 250cc class was started. The specialised racing machines used in Europe were ineligible for American events, and before the 1960s there was little road racing taking place in America anyway. Earlier, Manx Nortons prepared by Steve Lancefield and Francis Beart had competed successfully at Daytona (see DAYTONA) for four years before the AMA barred the double overhead camshaft 'featherbed' Norton in 1953.

Another major difference from Europe was that the AMC has always been much more closely related to the country's motor cycle manufacturers and dealers; also the number of championship points to be won at a meeting is geared to the prize money available. One result of this arrangement is that the top riders attend the top events.

With the sport developing on both sides of the Atlantic, and particularly in America where motor cycle racing began to enjoy a boom in the 1960s, the attractions and advantages of transatlantic competition were obvious. A number of attempts were made to settle the differences, but not until the late 1960s was the AMA readmitted to the FIM. With the AMA's re-entry into the FIM came the AMA's decision to lift the capacity limit for their big machine class to 750cc for all types of engines. All this heralded a new era of transatlantic competition with the transatlantic road races in Britain; encouraged the participation of British competitors in events like Daytona; and foreshadowed the establishment of the F750cc and the Super-bikes series. The Daytona event in March 1970 was the first time that European road racing stars and America's top riders competed on level terms.

The AMA National Championships are varied events and American riders have to be extremely versatile to be successful.

Grand National Champions since 1946:
1946: Chet Dykgraff (Norton)
1947: Jimmy Chann (Harley-Davidson)
1948: Jimmy Chann (Harley-Davidson)
1949: Jimmy Chann (Harley-Davidson)
1950: Larry Headrick (Harley-Davidson)
1951: Bobby Hill (Indian)
1952: Bobby Hill (Indian)
1953: Bill Tuman (Indian)
1954: Joe Leonard (Harley-Davidson)
1955: Brad Andres (Harley-Davidson)
1956: Joe Leonard (Harley-Davidson)
1957: Joe Leonard (Harley-Davidson)
1958: Carroll Resweber (Harley-Davidson)
1959: Carroll Resweber (Harley-Davidson)
1960: Carroll Resweber (Harley-Davidson)
1961: Carroll Resweber (Harley-Davidson)
1962: Bart Markel (Harley-Davidson)
1963: Dick Mann (BSA-Matchless)
1964: Roger Reiman (Harley-Davidson)
1965: Bart Markel (Harley-Davidson)
1966: Bart Markel (Harley-Davidson)
1967: Gary Nixon (Triumph)
1968: Gary Nixon (Triumph)
1969: Mert Lawwill (Harley-Davidson)
1970: Gene Romero (Triumph)
1971: Dick Mann (BSA)
1972: Mark Brelsford (Harley-Davidson)
1973: Ken Roberts (Yamaha)
1974: Ken Roberts (Yamaha)
1975: Gary Scott (Harley-Davidson)
1976: Jay Springsteen (Harley-Davidson)
1977: Jay Springsteen (Harley-Davidson)
1978: Jay Springsteen (Harley-Davidson)
1979: Steve Eklund (Harley-Davidson)
1980: Randy Goss (Harley-Davidson)
1981: Mike Kidd (Harley-Davidson)

AMM, W. Ray

Ray Amm was one of the brightest stars of early post-war racing and it is tragic indeed that he was killed at the height of his career, robbing the sport prematurely of one of its greatest advocates. His devotion to racing and his obsession to do well combined to produce many hair-raising rides, but within the short space of four years he nonetheless became perhaps the most famous rider of all from the Dominions.

Ray Amm came to Britain from Southern Rhodesia in 1951 with an insatiable appetite for racing and a driving ambition to gain a place in a works team. Riding his own two Nortons he quickly made an impression and within a year had attracted the attention of Norton chief Joe Craig, who offered him a works contract. A year later Amm became Norton team leader and that same year (1953) he won both the Junior and Senior TTs. He was only the fifth rider to that time to achieve the double in one year. A spectacular and brave rider, Amm on the Norton pushed Geoff Duke on the Gilera so hard in the Senior TT that year (with a record lap at 97.41 mph) that Duke, in an effort to shake off Amm's challenge, overdid things at Quarter Bridge and the Southern Rhodesian went on to win. This was the race in which Les Graham was killed, a tragedy which left a vacancy in the MV line-up which Ray Amm ironically filled: for it was in his first race for the Italian concern that he himself was killed. Amm was not blind to the overwhelming odds which faced Norton during this period from the powerful Italian machines, yet he was doggedly patriotic and chose to remain with the British factory in spite of tempting offers. Against fearsome odds he managed to take the Senior TT of 1954 for Norton and collect runner-up positions in both the 350cc and 500cc World Championships. Later, however, British machines could offer little opposition to the Italian offensive and Amm reluctantly joined MV in 1955. He was tragically killed at Imola, in his first race for the Italian factory. He was 29.

A religious and respected rider, Ray Amm was associated with the experimental kneeler Norton. Raced only once, by Amm, the Southern Rhodesian established a new 350cc lap record at the North West 200, before having to retire on lap three.

TT wins:
1953: Senior (Norton), Junior (Norton).
1954: Senior (Norton).

ANDERSON, Fergus

Fergus Anderson was one of the early British riders who saw the potential of riding regularly on the Continent. Competing in Grand Prix events in the 1950s he formed, along with riders like Ted Mellors and others, what was probably the first 'Continental Circus'. His interest in racing developed as a youngster, for his home backed onto the famous Brooklands circuit in Surrey, England. Before he moved to 'foreign' machines he rode a variety of bikes including Rudge and Velocette. He first competed in the TT Races riding DKW machines in the Senior and Junior races of 1939.

In 1947 he won the 350cc Swiss Grand Prix, that year the Grand Prix d'Europe, on a Velocette. He signed for the Italian Moto Guzzi factory in 1950 and, after finishing second and third in the 250cc World Championships in 1952 and '53, he alerted the Italian factory to the potential in a 350cc version of their highly successful four-valve 250. He became 350cc World Champion on the Guzzi in 1953 – the first World Championship in that class to be won by a non-British machine – and was World Champion again in 1954. Anderson then retired from racing to head Guzzi's competition department, but in 1955 he left on a point of principle. A year later, at the age of 47, he returned to racing and was killed when thrown from his BMW machine at an international meeting in Belgium.

Fergus Anderson was a most respected rider. He lived for many years on the Continent and worked as a journalist in Hamburg. He became well known for his regular 'Continental' column in the British weekly *Motor Cycle*.

ANDERSON, Hugh

One of the most outstanding racers to come from New Zealand, Hugh Anderson's greatest Grand Prix successes were in 1963-65, riding Suzuki machines in the lightweight classes. He was double World Champion in 1963 (50cc and 125cc), captured the 50cc World title in 1964 and the 125cc World title in 1965. He was third in the 125cc class in 1964 and in the 50cc class in 1965. He first competed in the TTs in 1960 on a Norton and with Suzuki has an impressive record 1963-66 as follows: 1963 – winner Lightweight (125) TT and runner up Lightweight (50) TT. 1964 – winner Lightweight (50) TT. 1965 – fifth, Lightweight (125) and runner-up Lightweight (50) TT. 1966 – third in Lightweight (125) and Lightweight (50) TTs.

ANDREW, Mick

Mick Andrew (born 1946) was killed in a road accident in 1970, after making his name in British short circuit racing during the previous three years. He first warranted attention because of his excellent performance in the 1966 Hutchinson 100, and in 1969 he won the event riding a Kuhn Commando. In 1969 he gained the Grovewood Award for the most promising newcomer of the year.

ANGLO-AMERICAN MATCH RACE SERIES

This series of races in which a team of British riders competes against a team of American riders was inaugurated shortly after the Auto-Cycle Union and the American Motor Cyclists Association came together to adopt a common set of regulations for the big Formula 750 machines. The first series was held in 1971 and, sponsored by the BSA-Triumph Group, was restricted on the British side to BSA-Triumph works riders. The British team won, 183 points to 137 points. Top scorers were (Britain) Paul Smart and Ray Pickrell (76 each) and (USA) Dick Mann (46). The 1972 series was not restricted to any particular make of machine and Cal Rayborn (Harley-Davidson) won three of the six races; but despite this Britain won the series, 255 points to 212 points. Top scorers were (Britain) Ray Pickrell (69) and (USA) Cal Rayborn (69). Britain won again in 1973, 416 points to 398 points. Top scorers were (Britain) Peter Williams (84) and (USA) Yvon du Hamel (84).

The 1974 series of matches was sponsored by John Player and the teams were as follows: America – Kenny Roberts (700 Yamaha), Gene Romero (700 Yamaha), Gary Fisher (700 Yamaha), John Long (700 Yamaha), Yvon du Hamel (750 Kawasaki), Art Baumann (750 Kawasaki), Gary Nixon (750 Suzuki), Dave Aldana (750 J P Norton), Reserve – Jim Evans (700 Yamaha). Great Britain – Paul Smart (750 Suzuki), Barry Sheene (750 Suzuki), Stan Woods (750 Suzuki), Peter Williams (750 J P Norton), Dave Croxford (750 J P Norton), Percy Tait (750 Triumph-Three), Mick Grant (700 Yamaha), Barry Ditchburn (700 Yamaha), Reserve – Ron Chandler (750 Triumph-Three). Victory went to Britain yet again, 416 points to 401 points. American Yamaha rider Kenny Roberts won four of the six races. Top scorers were (USA) Kenny Roberts and (Britain) Barry Sheene.

The races are held over Easter on circuits owned by Motor Circuits Development Ltd – Brands Hatch (Good Friday), Mallory Park (Easter Sunday) and Oulton Park (Easter Monday).

Recent Results:

1975: USA 278 points, GB 243 points. Top individual scorers were Dave Aldana (USA) 51 points and Pat Mahoney (GB) 45 points. The opening round at Brands Hatch was cancelled owing to snow on the track.

1976: GB 412 points, USA 384 points. Top individual scorers were Steve Baker (USA) 92 points and Barry Sheene (GB) 77 points.

1977: USA 410 points, GB 379 points. Top individual scorers were Pat Hennen (USA) 83 points, Steve Baker (USA) 82 points and Barry Sheene (GB) 79 points.

1978: GB 435 points, USA 379 points. Top individual scorers were Pat Hennen (USA) 92 points, Kenny Roberts (USA) 79 points and Dave Potter (GB) 74 points.

1979: USA 448 points, GB 352 points. Top individual scorers were Mike Baldwin (USA) 88 points, Randy Mamola (USA) 67 points and Barry Sheene (GB) and Dave Aldana (USA) 63 points each.

1980: USA 443 points, GB 369 points. Top individual scorers were Kenny Roberts (USA) 92 points, Freddie Spencer (USA) 76 points, Randy Mamola (USA) 74 points and Keith Huewen (GB) 59 points.

1981: GB 466 points, USA 345 points. Top individual scorers were John Newbold (GB) 72 points, Dave Potter (GB) 70 points, Dale Singleton (USA) 65 points and Keith Huewen (GB) 60 points.

ANSCHEIDT, Hans-Georg

Anscheidt's greatest successes were recorded in the 1960s when, riding a Suzuki, he became 50cc World Champion in 1966, '67 and '68. Born in 1935 at Konigsberg, East Prussia, Anscheidt began his career in cross country competitions and later gained experience on grass, cinder and sand. His road racing début was on a Kreidler machine, while he was working for the factory in the testing and development department, and he secured the European 50cc championship in 1961 – before the introduction of the World title series. Riding the 15-speed Kreidler two-stroke he was runner-up to Suzuki's Ernst Degner in the 50cc World Championship of 1962, and was second behind Hugh Anderson in 1963. Still Kreidler-mounted he was third behind Anderson (Suzuki) and Bryans (Honda) in 1964. He did not compete in the classics in 1965, but the offer of a contract with Suzuki brought him back and he secured his first world title in the first year – 1966. A versatile rider, Hans-Georg Anscheidt also achieved success in trials and won his first ISDT Gold Medal in 1960. Weighing 9½ stone and only 5ft 2 in tall, his stature was ideal for the racing of 50cc machines.

ARIEL

Ariel machines go back to 1898, but the first Ariel motor bike did not appear until 1902. Ariels entered the TT for the first time in 1911 when a 498cc version finished 13th in the Senior race.

Ariel never supported racing officially, but a number of Ariel specials achieved success. Those prepared by L. W. E. Hartley of Plumstead were well known, in particular the 70 mph guaranteed performance engine from which Hartley eventually obtained 90 mph, exceptional for a side-valve engine of 1926.

Jock West, a famous rider of the time, also achieved notable success on Ariel machines and with a 500cc version in 1926 took many first places and established a number of records on grass tracks.

Ariel won the Maudes Trophy three times: in 1927 when an Ariel sidecar outfit of 557cc capacity covered 5000 miles without an engine stop; in 1928 with a test extending over 22 days and ending with a one-hour speed record test at Brooklands, 10,000 miles in all being covered by 250cc and 500cc models at an average of 20 mph; and finally in 1931 with an involved test of speed, reliability, economy and ease of maintenance.

ARMCO

Armco is a steel beam vehicular guardrail mounted on timber or steel posts. Primarily designed for highways, it is also used on race circuits for spectator protection.

Its main function is to restrain and guide out-of-control vehicles and reduce hazard to other traffic. Originally introduced by the Armco Steel Corporation in USA in 1933 and by Armco Ltd in Britain in 1955, hence the name, but it is no longer exclusively produced by Armco.

ASSEN

The Assen circuit, located by the small town which bears the same name in the north-east corner of Holland, is the established home of the Dutch TT and is one of the most famous Grand Prix circuits in the world. It was created exclusively for motor cycle racing. The present circuit was developed from the former 10.7 mile van Drenthe circuit, on which the Assen Tourist Trophy race was held annually from 1927 to 1955. The last bend, start-finish straight and S-bend of this old course were retained, but the long straights were replaced by a series of corners and curves which makes the present van Drenthe Assen course a firm favourite among riders. The 4¾-mile circuit attracts crowds in excess of 100,000 for the Dutch TT and is the scene of the most carnival atmosphere as Holland celebrates what the country regards as its most important sporting event.

AUSTRIAN GRAND PRIX

The Austrian Grand Prix is run on the 2.63-miles Salzburg circuit, near Salzburg. From 1927–30 it was run at a track near Vienna with many British riders taking part – Jimmy Simpson, Wal Handley, etc. It was reorganized in 1950 and from 1958 was held each year at Salzburg.

Results:

1971: 50cc J. De Vries (Kreidler). 125cc A. Nieto (Derbi). 250cc S. Grassetti (MZ-RE). 350cc G. Agostini (MV). 500cc G. Agostini (MV). Sidecars, Butscher/Huber (BMW).

1972: 125cc A. Nieto (Derbi). 250cc B. Jansson (Maico/Derbi/Yamaha). 350cc G. Agostini (MV). 500cc G. Agostini (MV). Sidecars K. Enders/R. Engelhardt (BMW).

1973: 125cc K. Andersson (Yamaha). 250cc J. Saarinen (Yamaha). 350cc J. Drapal (Yamaha). 500cc J. Saarinen (Yamaha). Sidecars K. Enders/R. Engelhardt (BMW).

1974: 125cc K. Andersson (Yamaha). 350cc G. Agostini (Yamaha). 500cc G. Agostini (Yamaha). Sidecars S. Schauzu/W. Kalauch (BMW).

1975: 125cc P. Pileri (Morbidelli). 350cc I. Kanaya (Yamaha). 500cc I. Kanaya (Yamaha). Sidecars R. Steinhausen/J. Huber (Busch-Konig).

1976: 125cc P. Bianchi (Morbidelli).

350cc J. Cecotto (Yamaha). 500cc B. Sheene (Suzuki). Sidecars R. Steinhausen/J. Huber (Konig).

1977: 125cc E. Lazzarini (Morbidelli). 350cc (race abandoned after eight laps following accident). 500cc J. Findlay (Suzuki). Sidecars R. Biland/K. Williams (Schmid-Yamaha).

1978: 125cc E. Lazzarini (MBA). 350cc K. Ballington (Kawasaki). 500cc K. Roberts (Yamaha). Sidecars R. Biland/K. Williams (TTM-Yamaha).

1979: 125cc A. Nieto (Minarelli). 350cc K. Ballington (Kawasaki). 500cc K. Roberts (Yamaha). Sidecars (conventional B2-A) G. Brodin/B. Gallros (Yamaha) and (prototype B2-B) R. Biland/K. Waltisperg (LCR-Yamaha).

1980: Snow on the Salzburg track caused the Austrian Grand Prix, scheduled for April, to be abandoned.

1981: 125cc A. Nieto (Minarelli). 350cc P. Fernandez (Yamaha). 500cc R. Mamola (Suzuki). Sidecars J. Taylor/B. Johansson (Yamaha).

AUTO-CYCLE UNION

The Auto-Cycle Union (A-CU) is the governing body of motor cycle sport in Britain and the Commonwealth, excluding Canada and Northern Ireland. It is a branch of the Royal Automobile Club and is responsible to the FIM (Federation Internationale Motocycliste), the international federation and top authority of the sport, for the administration of motor cycle racing in the United Kingdom. Founded in 1903 as the Auto-Cycle Club to protect the interests of motor cyclists and to encourage the sport and pastime of motor cycling, the Auto-Cycle Club organised both speed and reliability events and sent teams of British riders to compete in foreign races.

The ACC became the Auto-Cycle Union in 1907 and that same year organised the first of the famous Isle of Man Tourist Trophy races, which became the premier sporting competition in motorcycle racing. Since 1924 the A-CU has existed solely for the purpose of encouraging and controlling the sport. Address: Millbuck House, Corporation Street, Rugby, Warwickshire. Secretary General: Mr. K. E. Shierson.

BAKER, Steve
Frail-looking, bespectacled Steve Baker made an impact on the European road racing scene. At 23 in 1976, he went to Venezuela and won the first round in the Formula 750 world championship, following this with an equally impressive win in the second round at Imola. Baker was in the lead for all except one of the 64 laps of the two-leg race.

Baker, who used to work in a Canadian motor cycle shop, was second at Daytona in 1974 and before moving into world 750cc racing, did well in American events. He rode Yamaha machines and was regarded as one of the most exciting of a crop of new road racers to emerge in the mid-1970s.

Although he tended to disappoint his fans in the later 1970s, and left racing after suffering a number of crashes, there is no denying that at his peak he became one of the most talented riders in the business. He was 750cc World Champion (1977), and runner up in the 500cc World Championship (1977).

BALLINGTON, Hugh Neville 'Kork'
Born in Southern Rhodesia, Ballington raced there and in South Africa before travelling to Britain to compete in Europe. His successes in South Africa included wins over Sheene and Agostini. Wins at Oulton Park, Snetterton, Mallory Park and Brands Hatch were followed by impressive victories in the 250cc and 350cc British Grand Prix at Silverstone in 1977 on Sid Griffith-sponsored Yamahas. When Kawasaki decided they were ready to challenge for the 250cc and 350cc world titles, they signed Kork Ballington as team mate to Mick Grant. He was 250cc and 350cc double World Champion in 1978 on Kawasaki and also scored impressive double wins at the two Donington Park 1978 meetings. He repeated his Grand Prix success by winning the 250cc and 350cc World Championships in 1979.

BANKS, John
One of Britain's top moto-cross riders. John Banks (born 1944) was a BSA rider for six years, with experience of two-stroke scramblers with Dot before that. Banks was runner-up in the world series in 1968 and 1969 and won the 500cc British Championship in 1968-69, 1971 and 1973. In 1973 Banks was the best Briton at the Moto Cross des Nations.

BARCELONA 24-HOURS RACE
One of the most important European long distance events, held annually at Montjuich Park.
Winners since 1969:
1969: S. Canellas/C. Roca (360 Bultaco), 684 laps.
1970: D. Degens/I. Goddard (650 Dresda), 656 laps.
1971: A. Brettoni/S. Angiolini (750 Laverda), 687 laps.
1972: J. Bordons/B. Grau (360 Bultaco), 689 laps.
1973: S. Canellas/B. Grau (860 Ducati), 720 laps.
1974: G. Goudier/A. Genoud (900 Kawasaki), 712 laps.
1975: S. Canellas/B. Grau (905 Ducati), 731 laps.
1976: S. Woods/C. Williams (940 Honda) 747 laps.
1977: C. Huguet/P. Korhonen (997 Honda) 760 laps.
1978: C. Leon/J. C. Chemarin (998 Honda) 763 laps.
1979: C. Leon/J. C. Chemarin (998 Honda) 773 laps.
1980: J. Mallol/A. Tejedo (900 Ducati) 755 laps.
1981: R. Roche/J. Lafond (1000 Kawasaki) 777 laps.

BAUMANN, Art
An American (born California 1944) Art Baumann became the world's fastest officially-timed road racer at 171.75 mph while qualifying for the Daytona 200 of 1972. He achieved this speed on a works 750cc Suzuki. Baumann began motorcycle racing when he was 21 and later scored success riding a 350 Honda. He joined the Yamaha works team in America in 1967 and in 1969, on a 500cc works Suzuki, became the first rider to win an AMA national on a two-stroke.

BELGIAN GRAND PRIX
The traditional home of the Belgian Grand Prix is the 8.8-mile sweeping cir-

cuit at Francorchamps, near Spa in the hilly Ardennes, where even in the early 1960s riders were reaching speeds of well over 120mph. It is the fastest Grand Prix circuit in the world and incorporates considerable gradients and has hairpins at opposing ends – La Source, just before the pits, and Stavelot. The Belgian Grand Prix is one of the earliest classic races and with only two exceptions (at Dinant in 1923 and Floreffe in 1936) has been held every year since 1921 at Francorchamps. In 1921 legendary names like Hassall, Le Vack, Walker and Dixon were contesting the event and that year Hassall won the 500cc class on a Norton with Bert Le Vack (Indian) second and Fred Dixon (Indian) third. The race was run over 188 miles, about twice the distance of more recent races.

In 1979 a new, shorter circuit measuring 4.13 miles was used for the first time, but the occasion was marred by a riders' boycott, with international stars like Kenny Roberts, Virginio Ferrari, Wil Hartog, Barry Sheene, Steve Parrish, Kork Ballington and Gregg Hansford all refusing to ride because they considered the track was too slippery. Banned and fined by the FIM for allegedly masterminding the riders' boycott, Roberts and Ferrari later had the ban and the fines lifted.

Results:

1954: 350cc K. Kavanagh (Guzzi); 500cc G. Duke (Gilera); sidecar E. S. Oliver (Norton).

1955: 350cc W. A. Lomas (Guzzi); 500cc G. Colnago (Gilera); sidecar W. Noll (BMW).

1956: 125cc C. Ubbiali (MV); 250cc C. Ubbiali (MV); 350cc J. Surtees (MV); 500cc J. Surtees (MV); sidecar W. Noll (BMW).

1957: 125cc T. Provini (Mondial); 250cc J. Hartle (MV); 350cc K. R. Campbell (Guzzi); 500cc J. Brett (Norton); sidecar W. Schneider (BMW).

1958: 125cc A. Gandossi (Ducati); 250cc (Not run); 350cc J. Surtees (MV); 500cc J. Surtees (MV); sidecar W. Schneider (BMW).

1959: 125cc C. Ubbiali (MV); 350cc G. Hocking (Norton) (Formula 1 Race); 500cc J. Surtees (MV); sidecar W. Schneider (BMW).

1960: 125cc E. Degner (MZ); 250cc C. Ubbiali (MV); 500cc J. Surtees (MV); sidecar H. Fath (BMW).

1961: 125cc L. Taveri (Honda); 250cc J. A. Redman (Honda); 500cc G. Hocking (MV); sidecar F. Scheidegger (BMW).

1962: 50cc E. Degner (Suzuki); 125cc L. Taveri (Honda); 250cc R. McG. McIntyre (Honda); 500cc S. M. B. Hailwood (MV); sidecar F. Camathias (BMW).

1963: 50cc I. Moroshita (Suzuki); 125cc B. Schneider (Suzuki); 250cc F. Ito (Yamaha); 500cc S. M. B. Hailwood (MV); sidecar F. Scheidegger (BMW).

1964: 50cc R. Bryans (Honda); 250cc M. A. Duff (Yamaha); 500cc S. M. B. Hailwood (MV); sidecar M. Deubel (BMW).

1965: 50cc E. Degner (Suzuki); 250cc J. A. Redman (Honda); 500cc S. M. B. Hailwood (MV); sidecar F. Scheidegger (BMW).

1966: 250cc S. M. B. Hailwood (Honda); 500cc G. Agostini (MV); sidecar F. Scheidegger (BMW).

1967: 50cc H. G. Anscheidt (Suzuki); 250 cc W. Ivy (Yamaha); 500cc G. Agostini (MV); sidecar K. Enders/R. Engelhardt (BMW).

1968: 50cc H. G. Anscheidt (Suzuki); 250cc P. Read (Yamaha); 500cc G. Agostini (MV); sidecar G. Auerbacher/H. Hahn. (BMW).

1969: 50cc B. Smith (Derbi); 125cc D. A. Simmonds (Kawasaki); 250cc S. Herrero (Ossa); 500cc G. Agostini (MV); sidecar H. Fath/W. Kalauch (URS 67).

1970: 50cc A. Toersen (Jamathi); 125cc A. Nieto (Derbi); 250cc R. Gould (Yamaha); 500cc G. Agostini (MV); sidecars Butscher/Huber (BMW).

1971: 50cc J. De Vries (Kreidler); 125cc B. Sheene (Suzuki); 250cc S. Grassetti (MZ-RE); 500cc G. Agostini (MV); sidecar S. Schauzu/W. Kalauch (BMW).

1972: 50cc A. Nieto (Derbi); 125cc A. Nieto (Derbi); 250cc J. Saarinen (Yamaha); 500cc G. Agostini (MV); sidecar K. Enders/R. Engelhardt (BMW).

1973: 50cc J. De Vries (Kreidler); 125cc J. Schurgers (Bridgestone); 250cc T. Länsivuori (Yamaha); 500cc G. Agostini (MV); sidecar K. Enders/R. Engelhardt (BMW).

1974: 50cc G. Thurow (Kreidler); 125cc

A. Nieto (Derbi). 250cc K. Andersson (Yamaha); 500cc P. Read (MV); sidecar R. Steinhausen/K. Scheurer (Konig).

1975: 50cc J. Vanzeebroeck (Kreidler); 125cc P. Pileri (Morbidelli); 250cc J. Cecotto (Yahama); 500cc P. Read (MV); sidecar R. Steinhausen/S. Huber (Konig).

1976: 50cc H. Rittberger (Kreidler); 125cc A. Nieto (Bultaco); 250cc W. Villa (Harley-Davidson); 500cc J. Williams (Suzuki); sidecar R. Steinhausen/S. Huber (Busch).

1977: 50cc E. Lazzarini (Kreidler); 125cc P. Bianchi (Morbidelli); 250cc W. Villa (Harley-Davidson); 500cc B. Sheene (Suzuki); sidecar W. Schwarzel/A. Huber (Aro).

1978: 50cc R. Tormo (Bultaco); 125cc P. Bianchi (Minarelli); 250cc P. Pileri (Morbidelli); 500cc W. Hartog (Suzuki); sidecar B. Holzer/K. Meierhaus (LCR-Yamaha).

1979: 50cc H. V. Kessel (X16); 125cc B. Smith (Morbidelli); 250cc E. Stollinger (Kawasaki); 500cc D. Ireland (Suzuki); sidecar R. Steinhausen/K. Arthur (Yamaha).

1980: 50cc S. Dorflinger (Kreidler); 125cc A. Nieto (Minarelli); 250cc A. Mang (Kawasaki); 500cc R. Mamola (Suzuki); sidecar J. Taylor/B. Johansson (Yamaha).

1981: 50cc R. Tormo (Bultaco); 250cc A. Mang (Kawasaki); 500cc M. Lucchinelli (Suzuki); sidecar R. Biland/K. Waltisperg (Yamaha).

BENELLI

This famous Italian marque first gained prominence in 1939 when Ted Mellors won the Lightweight TT of that year, succeeding in a class which had long been dominated by DKW and Guzzi machines.

The Benelli brothers, who owned the company, had racing ambitions but their development programme was interrupted by the second World War. Ted Mellors had gained his TT victory on a single-cylinder machine and the supercharged water-cooled 4-cylinder 250 which Benelli had built to contest international events was never permitted to demonstrate its ability. The banning of supercharging after the war kept it under covers. Dario Ambrosini brought himself and Benelli fame by winning the 250cc World Championship and also the Manufacturer's Award for Benelli in 1950 on a developed version of the pre-war double overhead camshaft single and against an array of powerful Guzzi machines. When Ambrosini was killed while practising for the French Grand Prix of 1951, Benelli became inactive, but reappeared in international racing in 1959 with new machines ridden by Dickie Dale and Geoff Duke. They achieved a number of successes but were to wilt before the power of the Japanese onslaught on world motor-cycle racing in the early 1960s. In later years Renzo Pasolini was closely associated with Benelli and in 1967 and 1968 completed eight 100 mph laps in the TT races.

Important Achievements:

1949: second in 250cc World Championship (Ambrosini);

1950: World Championship 250cc (Ambrosini);

1951: third in 250cc World Championship (Ambrosini);

1968: second in 350cc World Championship (Pasolini);

1969: 250cc World Championship (Carruthers);

1970: third in 350cc World Championship (Pasolini).

TT achievements for Benelli include Lightweight victories in 1939 (Mellors), 1950 (Ambrosini) and (250cc) 1969 (Carruthers), a second in the Junior event of 1968 (Pasolini) and a second in the Lightweight 250cc event of 1968 (Pasolini)

BENNETT, Alec

Prominent during the period 1922-32 Alec Bennett (born Ireland) did almost the whole of his racing on the Isle of Man, though he won the French Grand Prix four times and the Belgian Grand Prix twice during a remarkable career. He was not a prolific rider, competing in fewer than 30 events during the whole of his career, 18 of which were the Isle of Man TTs. He won the Senior TT in 1922 (Sunbeam), 1924 (Norton) and 1927 (Norton) and the Junior TT in 1926 and 1928 (Velocettes). His race speed of 58.31 mph in his first Senior TT victory in 1922 broke the lap record by almost 4 mph. His success in 1924 was the first victory for Norton in the TT races for 17 years. He won by 87 seconds at an average of 61.64 mph, the first time the TTs had witnessed an average speed in excess of 60 mph. His TT victory of 1926 was the first registered by Velocette. At the time of his retirement, at 32, he had won more TT races than any other rider, in spite of contesting fewer events in the whole of his career than many riders take part in during just one season. His last race was in 1932, after his retirement, when he finished eighth in the Junior TT on a Velocette.

TT Wins:
1922: Senior (Sunbeam). 1924, Senior (Norton).
1926: Junior (Velocette). 1927, Senior (Norton).
1928: Junior (Velocette).

BERGAMONTI, Angelo
Born Italy 1939, Angelo Bergamonti started racing in 1957 on a 175cc Morini. Riding Morinis and Patons he won the Italian 500cc and 250cc Championships in 1967, later racing factory Aermacchis with distinction. He gained recognition from MV Agusta who signed him towards the end of 1971 as support for Agostini in the pursuit of the 1972 World Championships, but only six months later he was killed before the series started. He crashed in heavy rain while chasing Agostini during the 350cc event at a Riccione International meeting and died in hospital at Bologna.

BICKERS, Dave
Britain's most successful and probably the most popular 250cc scrambler, Bickers, a familiar figure in the 1960s in his green sweater and white helmet, began his outstanding career in 1959 when his early mentor and scrambling ace Brian Stonebridge began taking him to the continent to gain experience against European opposition. With the Greeves team he registered his first Grand Prix win in Switzerland in 1960. That year and in 1961 he won the European title (no world titles in those days) riding Greeves. He gave the European title rounds a miss in 1962, after which he found the opposition had stiffened considerably. So for all his outstanding ability he has never won an "official" world title – the world name tag succeeding the "European" in 1963. Bickers won six British Championships (then known as 250 A-CU Stars) and retired from the Grand Prix series in 1969. Dave Bickers comes from Coddenham, Suffolk, where he has a motor cycle business.

BMW
BMW is the abbreviation for the German manufactured motor cycles made by the Bavarian Motor Works in Munich. The firm, originally founded in 1916 to produce engines for the German Air Force, began making motor cycles in 1923 and is immortalised in motor cycle racing history because of its dominance of the sidecar category of the World Championships for almost twenty years from 1954. Their first World Championship was won in 1954 by Wilhelm Noll of West Germany when he moved into a class which since the World Championships began in 1949 had been dominated by the British Norton and the Italian Gilera concerns. Thus began a remarkable record. From 1954 to 1967 inclusive, the World Sidecar Championship was won by BMW machinery, which also gained second and third places in the same championships from 1957 until 1968. BMW regained the World Sidecar Championships in 1969 and retained the title in 1970. In 1972 they again occupied the first three places and were first and third again in 1973.

Although BMW became a phenomenon in the sidecar class, they were also extremely successful in pre-war years in solo events. They started racing in the early 1920s with horizontally opposed twin-cylinder machines which had little success in international competition. Careful development and improvement over a number of years yielded supercharged versions of this flat-twin 500cc machine which, with telescopic front forks and rear springing, had increased speed and reliability. By the late 1930s they were often superior to the, until then, virtually invincible Nortons and Velocettes, and managed to break the British domination of the 500cc solo class. On the continent BMW successes were many and Jock West, in 1937 and 1938 won the Ulster Grand Prix on a BMW. George Meier became the first foreign rider on a foreign machine (BMW) to win the Senior TT. That was in 1939.

The outstanding low-speed torque and reliability of the BMW makes it ideal for sidecar racing and it is in this class that the factory concentrated after the Second

World War. With superchargers banned in post-war years, BMW could never match their pre-war successes in solo racing. Most of their international honours have been won by German riders. Pre-war, BMW was also extremely active in the record-breaking world and Ernst Henne's world land speed solo record of 174 mph which was made on a supercharged BMW in 1937 stood for 14 years.

Results
World Sidecar Championships:
1954: first (Noll).
1955: first (Faust), second (Noll) and third (Schneider).
1956: first (Noll) and second (Hillebrand).
1957: first (Hillebrand), second (Schneider) and third (Camathias).
1958: first (Schneider), second (Camathias) and third (Fath).
1959: first (Schneider), second (Camathias) and third (Scheidegger).
1960: first (Fath), second (Scheidegger) and third (Harris).
1961: first (Deubel), second (Scheidegger) and third (Strub).
1962: first (Deubel), second (Camathias) and third (Scheidegger).
1963: first (Deubel); second (Camathias) and third (Scheidegger).
1964: first (Deubel), second (Scheidegger) and third (Seeley).
1965: first (Scheidegger), second (Deubel) and third (Auerbacher).
1966: first (Scheidegger), second (Deubel) and third (Seeley).
1967: first (Enders), second (Auerbacher) and third (Schauzu).
1968: second (Auerbacher) and third (Schauzu).
1969: first (Enders) and third (Auerbacher).
1970: first (Enders), second (Auerbacher) and third (Schauzu).
1971: second (Schauza) and third (Butscher).
1972: first (Enders), second (Luthringshauser) and third (Schauzu).
1973: first (Enders) and third (Schauzu).
1974: first Butch-BMW (Enders) and third (Schauzu).

BONERA, Gianfranco
Born Monza, Italy, 1946, Bonera made his race début on a 125cc Aermacchi in 1971 and that year finished fourth in the Italian Junior 125cc championships. In 1972 he was Italian 500cc Junior Champion. He won the 500-Kms event in Rome on a 500cc Suzuki. Bonera became one of the first private owners of the new 350cc air-cooled, two-stroke twin cylinder racing Harleys and in his Grand Prix début in the autumn of 1973 in Yugoslavia he finished third (500cc), gaining fourth place on the same machine in the follow-up Czech Grand Prix. He seemed set to join Harley-Davidson as a full team member but at the start of 1974 he found himself without a firm contract. He was set to buy a couple of Yamahas when MV offered him a contract to race as number two to 500cc World Champion Phil Read. Bonera accepted and made his début for MV at Modena on March 19, 1974. He was an instant success with MV, gaining second place in the 500cc world championship at his first attempt. He won the Italian Grand Prix, was second in Austria, Finland and Czechoslovakia, third in France and fourth in Sweden and Holland. It was a remarkable performance which made Bonera a rider unequalled at the time for his rapid rise to fame.

Modest, with a growing confidence, Gianfranco Bonera has the ability to **learn a race circuit extremely quickly. In the latter half of the 1970s, however, his form was less rewarding while riding Suzuki machinery. Recent 500cc World Championship positions: 1977 – 6th; 1978 – 26th. In the F750 World Championship he was 4th in 1978 and 5th in 1979, both years on Yamaha.**

Before switching to motor cycle racing Bonera was a cycle champion, a heavy crash in 1968 bringing five years of track and road racing to an end. Three years later, having in the meantime ridden a roadster motor cycle, he decided to go racing again, but this time on motor cycles.

BORET BROTHERS
One of the most promising sidecar road-racing teams in Britain in the early 1970s, Gerry and Nick Boret took third place in the sidecar TT of 1972 in only their second appearance on the Isle of Man with their chisel-shaped Renwick Developments outfit, and were British sidecar champions in 1973. Gerry had raced sidecars in the early 1960s, but

retired in 1968. Nick's interest in sidecar racing inspired Gerry to return and they teamed together for the first time in 1969. Their original outfit was a Triumph-powered RGM, but after a year the Triumph was replaced by a 1000cc Vincent V-twin. The wedge-shaped Konig-powered outfit for which the Boret brothers were quickly to become known, was first raced in mid-1970. Contesting a number of Grand Prix events in 1973 they showed promise before mechanical problems forced retirements in a number of rounds. The Borets' unusual outfit was designed and built by John Renwick. The chassis weighed only 45lbs and the outfit had a wheelbase of 60in and a track of 36in. All three wheels were quickly detachable. The 680cc Konig four-cylinder two-stroke engine was claimed to give a top speed of 150 mph. They retired from racing at the end of 1976.

BRANDS HATCH
Brands Hatch motor cycle road racing circuit is situated 20 miles south east of London on the A 20, near Farningham. It consists of a Grand Prix circuit (2.65 miles) and a club circuit (1.24 miles). It is used for international, national and club racing and is owned by Motor Circuit Developments Ltd, who also own Mallory Park, Oulton Park and Snetterton. The circuit has been built out of undulating meadow land and a natural amphitheatre which was first used for cycle racing and pace making. By 1928 it was being used by motor cycles as a grass track circuit. It became probably the most famous grass track circuit of its time in Britain. At the end of the second World War and with the growing popularity of motor-cycle road-racing, plans were made to convert Brands into a premier road racing circuit. Grass racing ended there in 1949 and the first road race was held during Easter 1950 and attended by 35,000 people. John Surtees, who was later to become so closely associated with Brands Hatch and to become the unofficial "King of Brands", made his début at the circuit on his 500 Vincent Grey Flash in 1951 Improvements, extensions, and developments have continued over the years. The full international GP circuit was completed in 1960 and Mike Hailwood won all four solo classes in the opening meeting in July. The venue has developed into one of the most popular stadiums for motor cycle racing in the country. It is also used for car racing.

After John Surtees retired from motor-cycle racing Derek Minter was acclaimed the new unofficial "King of Brands". When the Brands Hatch management, seeing the commercial value in the "King of Brands" title, held a feature race to establish an official "King" for the first time in 1965, Minter was successful in winning the race and so made the title his officially. The "King of Brands" event has since become a featured attraction at the circuit and until 1973 was held at the important Good Friday meeting. In 1973 the "King of Brands" event was changed to the Spring Bank Holiday Monday International Meeting, the Good Friday meeting at Brands by then earmarked for the Anglo-American series. Later, the King of Brands title was awarded to the rider who achieved best performances in the programme's three major races.

Popular features of the circuit are Druids Hill Bend, South Bank Bend, Pilgrims Drop, Hawthorn Hill and Bend, Portobello Straight (renamed Derek Minter Straight), Westfield Bend, Dingle Dell, Stirling's Bend and Clearways. The circuit was improved for 1976.

Brands Hatch held the first motor cycle event ever to be shown publicly on television in Britain, a grass track meeting in 1974.

King of Brands title holders: Derek Minter (1965), Bill Ivy (1966), Ron Chandler (1967), Dave Croxford (1968), Peter Williams (1969), Pat Mahoney (1970), Brian Kemp (1971), Barry Sheene (1972 and 1973), Barry Ditchburn (1974), Barry Ditchburn (1975), Dave Potter (1976), Barry Sheene (1977), Clive Padgett (1978), Dave Potter (1979), Stan Woods (1980), Dave Potter (1981).

Address: Brands Hatch Circuit Limited, Fawkham, Nr Dartford, Kent, DA3 8NG.

BREEDLOVE, Craig
More famous for his attacks on the world land-speed record on four wheels, Breedlove held the record five times between 1963 and 1970. In 1973 he turned his attention to the motor cycle outright speed record and at the Bonneville Salt Flats, Utah, survived a 400-mph crash when his rocket-powered motor cycle left the ground. Use of the

parachutes ripped away large sections of the machine, which made a three-point landing. He was attempting to set fourteen new motor-cycle records when the crash occurred.

BRELSFORD, Mark

An American rider of outstanding talent. Brelsford was the top amateur in AMA racing in 1968 and joined Harley-Davidson on his graduation to expert status in 1969. That year he was eighth in the AMA's top ten listings, graduating to seventh in 1970 and again 1971. Mark Brelsford (born 1949) had his big success in 1972 when he became Grand National Champion. That year he brought Harley-Davidson's new XR750 alloy engine its first success, in the Louisville half-miler.

BRIGGS, Barry

One of the most successful and popular speedway riders of all times, Barry Briggs of Christchurch, New Zealand, has ridden in turn for Wimbledon, New Cross, Southampton and Swindon. He has been World Champion four times (including twice in Sweden in 1964 and 1966), runner-up three times, and third on three occasions. He won the British Riders' Championship five times in succession – 1965-69. His first World Championship victory was in 1957 at Wembley when he beat the then reigning champion, Ove Fundin, in a run-off. The next year he won the title with maximum points. He was title holder again in 1964 and 1966. Briggs received sponsorship from the Czechoslovakian Jawa factory and was the first rider to race their Eso machine in Britain. Briggs received the MBE in 1973.

BRITISH EXPERTS TRIAL

To qualify in this important classic event run each year by the Birmingham MCC it is necessary to be a former 'Expert' winner or to have gained a specified minimum of points in the previous year's national trials. Sammy Miller has by far the best record. In 1965 he became the first rider to win the British Expert four times and he has since won it in 1968.

Results:

1950: solo W. Nicholson; sidecar H. Tozer.
1951: solo T. U. Ellis; sidecar C. V. Kemp.
1952: solo J. V. Brittain; sidecar H. Tozer.
1953: solo J. V. Brittain; sidecar F. Wilkins.
1954: solo W. Nicholson; sidecar F. Darrieulat.
1955: solo J. V. Smith; sidecar A. J. Humphries.
1956: solo J. V. Smith; sidecar F. Darrieulat.
1957: solo G. L. Jackson; sidecar F. Wilkins.
1958: solo G. L. Jackson; sidecar F. Wilkins.
1959: solo S. H. Miller; sidecar F. Wilkins.
1960: solo W. Wilkinson; sidecar W. C. Slocombe.
1961: solo G. L. Jackson; sidecar P. Wraith.
1962: solo S. H. Miller; sidecar R. J. Langston.
1963: solo J. V. Smith; sidecar C. A. Morewood.
1964: solo S. H. Miller; sidecar R. J. Langston.
1965: solo S. H. Miller; sidecar R. J. Langston.
1966: solo S. Ellis; sidecar R. J. Langston.
1967: No trial.
1968: solo S. H. Miller; sidecar A. Morewood.
1969: solo J. Harrison; sidecar R. Bradley.
1970: solo M. Rathmell; sidecar A. Morewood.
1971: solo R. Edwards; sidecar R. Round.
1972: solo M. Rathmell; sidecar R. Round.
1973: solo C. Smith; sidecar A. Lampkin.
1974: solo M. Wilkinson; sidecar J. Mathews.
1975: solo M. Wilkinson; sidecar C. Dommett.
1976: solo R. Shepherd; sidecar C. Dommett.
1977: solo M. Lampkin; sidecar A. Clarke.
1978: solo M. Lampkin; sidecar A. Clarke.
1979: solo J. Reynolds; sidecar A. Clarke.
1980: solo M. Rathmell; sidecar A. Clarke.
1981: solo P. Cartwright; sidecar J. Gaskell.

BRITISH MOTOR CYCLE RACING CLUB

The British Motor Cycle Racing Club (known as Bemsee) is a non-territorial club. It was founded in 1909 with Brooklands as its home and is the oldest club in the world formed solely for road racing. It started life as a small private club, but after the second World War was formed into a limited company. Twelve meetings a year are organised for club members at Snetterton and Brands Hatch. The club is famous for its organisation of the important Hutchinson 100 meetings (see separate entry) which were held every year at Silverstone from 1949 to 1965, after which the meeting was transferred to Brands Hatch.

Address: British Motor Cycle Racing Club, Bemsee House, 30 Dartnell Road, Croydon, Surrey. Secretary: Barbara Bailey.

BRITISH ROAD RACING CHAMPIONSHIPS

(*See also* A-CU ROAD RACING STARS)

Run on lines similar to those of the World Championship the British Road Racing Championships under the auspices of the Auto-Cycle Union take place on home circuits and are a series of races held throughout the season in which riders collect points related to their success. This national competition in 1966 succeeded the A-CU Road Racing Stars, a similar competition which had been inaugurated in 1958. At the same time the old style British Championships title decided at one International meeting was scrapped. The new-style British Championships continued as detailed until 1973 when there was a reversal in part to the old-style star system. The "stars" were revived in the 125cc and 250cc class, British Championships being awarded in a solo and a sidecar classification. The two categories for 1975, for instance, were as follows: solo – over 250cc and not over 1000cc; sidecar – over 350cc and not over 1000cc. The competition was open to drivers holding 1975 National or International Competition Licences issued by the A-CU, Scottish A-CU or MCU of Ireland. Rounds were held at six meetings with points allocated at each meeting as follows: first (15 pts), second (12 pts), third (10 pts), fourth (8 pts), fifth (6 pts), sixth (5 pts), seventh (4 pts), eighth (3 pts), ninth (2 pts) and tenth (1 pt).

Winners of the British Road Racing Championships since inception are as follows:

British Championships (*one meeting*)

1960: S. M. Hailwood (ultra lightweight), S. M. Hailwood (lightweight), R. McIntyre (Junior), R. McIntyre (Senior), P. V. Harris (sidecar).

1961: P. H. Tait (ultra lightweight), S. M. Hailwood (lightweight), J. Hartle (Junior), D. Minter (Senior), P. V. Harris (sidecar).

1962: H. R. Anderson (50cc), D. F. Shorey (125cc), D. Minter (250cc), D. Minter (Junior), D. Minter (Senior), C. J. Seeley (sidecar).

1963: H. R. Anderson (50cc), H. R. Anderson (125cc), T. Robb (250cc), P. W. Read (Junior), D. Minter (Senior), C. J. Seeley (sidecar).

1964: H. R. Anderson (50cc), F. Perris (125cc), P. W. Read (250cc), M. Duff (Junior), D. Minter (Senior), C. J. Vincent (sidecar).

1965: C. J. Vincent (50cc), D. A. Simmonds (125cc), M. Duff (250cc), D. Shorey (Junior), W. D. Ivy (Senior), C. J. Vincent (sidecar).

British Championships (*series of meetings*)

1966: R. Scivyer (125cc), P. Inchley (250cc), J. Cooper (350cc), J. Cooper (500cc), O. Greenwood (Sidecar).

1967: M. Carney (125cc), D. Chatterton (250cc), D. Croxford (350cc), R. Chandler (500cc), O. Greenwood (sidecar).

1968: J. Curry (125cc), J. Cooper (250cc), A. Barnett (350cc), D. Croxford (500cc), P. Brown (sidecar).

1969: G. Ashton (50cc), C. Mortimer (125cc), D. Browning (250cc), P. Mahoney (350cc), D. Croxford (500cc), C. Vincent (sidecar).

1970: F. Whitway (50cc), B. Sheene (125cc), S. Machin (250cc), D. Chatterton (350cc), P. Williams (500cc), C. Vincent (3-wheeler).

1971: B. Sheene (125cc), S. Machin (250cc), T. Rutter (350cc), D. P. May (500cc), P. Tait (740cc), C. Vincent (3-wheeler).

1972: S. Machin (125cc), S. Machin (250cc), M. Grant (350cc), J. Harvey (500cc), D. Potter (750cc), N. Hanks (3-wheeler).
1973: D. Croxford (solo), G. Boret (sidecar).
1974: S. Woods (solo), M. Hobson (sidecar).
1975: R. Marshall (solo), M. Hobson (sidecar).
1976: S. Parrish (solo), D. Greasley (sidecar).
1977: R. Marshall (solo), B. Hodgkins (sidecar).
1978: S. Manship (solo), D. Jones (sidecar).
1979: K. Huewen (solo), D. Greasley (sidecar).
1980: B. Marks (solo), R. Dixon (sidecar).
1981: B. Smith (solo), J. Taylor (sidecar).

BRITISH WORLD BEATER
In the last fifteen years a number of attempts have been made to give British Grand Prix road racing a world beating machine, but without success. There were plans in 1965 for a Velocette-BRM World Championship machine to be financed from the proceeds of the Manx Lottery. Then Dr Josef Ehrlich, in 1966, announced work on a new power unit to form the basis of a revolutionary 180 mph 500cc two-stroke racing multi to challenge the Grand Prix monopoly of MV. Later during the decade Weslake announced their ambitions to produce a world beater for Britain; but none of these ambitious projects has so far succeeded in its objective.

BROOKLANDS
Brooklands holds a legendary place in British motor-cycle racing history. This outstanding 2.767-mile banked concrete circuit was the idea of motoring sportsman H. F. Locke-King and constructed to a design by Colonel H. C. L. Holden. It was opened in 1907. For more than 30 years it was the background to hundreds of races, record attempts and testing by British motor-cycle manufacturers. There were three main courses: the complete outer circuit or full course (2.767 miles); a short course using the Finishing Straight but not the Home Banking (2.616 miles); the Mountain Course using only the Home Banking and the Finishing Straight (1.17 miles). Later a simulated road course called the Campbell circuit was introduced and used anti-clockwise. There was also a Test Hill with gradients to the extent of 1 in 4, sheds, workshops and similar facilities.

Brooklands provided the only means on the British mainland for the long hours of testing of new ideas, and to this extent played a significant part in the development of British motor-cycle racing during the early 1900s. Situated near Weybridge, Surrey, Brooklands re-opened after the First World War in 1920 and remained in use until the outbreak of the Second World War. Much of Brooklands became the site for an aircraft factory for Vickers-Armstrong and it was never again used seriously as a race circuit, though some sections of the concrete banking still remain, now well over-grown. The first official motor-cycle race to take place at Brooklands was on Easter Monday 1908. It was a two-lap event with 24 competitors on machines of all sizes up to V-twins of 1000cc. W. E. Cook won on an NLG Peugeot twin, averaging 63 mph. When the British Motor Cycle Racing Club was formed in 1909 Brooklands was its natural home and remained the club's headquarters until 1939. This club instituted the Brooklands Gold Star, a yellow metal award, which was presented to club members who at one of the club's meetings lapped the Outer Circuit at 100 mph or more. The first of some 200 Gold Stars awarded went to Bert Le Vack in 1922.

Many records were established at Brooklands, among the most significant being a new land speed two-wheel record by Claude Temple on a 996cc British Anzani in 1923. He raised the record to 108.45 mph. Noel Pope (1909 - 1971) established the all-time Brooklands lap record for the Outer Circuit at 124.51 mph on 4th July 1939. He was riding a Brough Superior powered by a supercharged 996cc V-twin JAP engine Pope also captured the all-time sidecar record at 106.6 mph. The race lap record for the Outer Circuit was set up by Eric Fernihough (1905 - 1938) at an average speed of 123.588 mph on 28th July 1935. He was riding a Brough Superior powered by an unsupercharged 996cc V-twin JAP engine. Both Pope and Fernihough represented the UK. Vintage enthusiasts make periodic pilgrimages to what remains of the once-famous

Brooklands circuit.

BROUGH SUPERIOR

Prominent in the years between the wars, Brough is a name linked inseparably with all the legends of British motor cycle racing: Brooklands; the early speed events; and such early gladiators of the sport as Freddie Dixon, Bert Le Vack and Eric Fernihough. Most of Brough's racing successes were achieved at Brooklands. In the early 1920s their creator George Brough made fastest-time-of-the-day in 51 out of 52 events while Le Vack, Baragwanath and Dixon achieved notable success in the 200-mile solo and sidecar races. Baragwanath and Dixon were the first riders, and for a time the only riders, to have won a Brooklands Gold Star for lapping with a sidecar at 100 mph at a British Motor Cycle Racing Club meeting. Brough Superior also gained the distinction of producing the first side-valve machine to lap Brooklands at 100 mph, in 1922.

Brough Superiors were also successful in their attempts at maximum speed records beginning in 1924 when Le Vack twice set new figures for solo and sidecar and just a few weeks later improved his performance to 119.74 mph (solo) and 100.33 mph (sidecar), thus taking a sidecar outfit over the 100 mph for the first time during official timing.

JAP-engined Brough Superior machines brought more fame in world record attempts to Le Vack in 1929 and Eric Fernihough in 1937, both riders capturing the ultimate record. After the war Bob Berry made a number of unsuccessful record attempts at Pendine Sands and Noel Pope broke a number of records as a prelude to an attempt on the world's fastest, scheduled for 1939 but abandoned because of the war. After the war Pope took a fully-enclosed Brough to Bonneville Salt Flats in the USA to attack the world's fastest record, but he crashed the machine and had to abandon the attempt.

BROWN, George

George Brown (born 1912) was a motor-cycle road-racer before turning to sprinting in which he gained outstanding success and numerous world records on his famous 994cc Nero and 1147cc Super Nero Vincent-powered machines. Only his loyalty to Vincent HRD, for whom he was then chief tester and much concerned with development, is said to have eliminated his consideration for a place in the famous works Norton team of the early 1950s. He joined the Vincent company in 1934 and is said to have reached 140 mph while testing competition Vincents on public roads. After retiring in the Senior TT after Les Graham crashed, (1953) and crashing at Cadwell Park and Eppynt, Brown retired from road racing to concentrate on sprints and hill climbs, an activity which he later pursued with considerable success. In more than 21 years of competition he gained countless world and national records. He retired in 1967, at 55 years of age, the upper limit imposed by the FIM for an international licence, but continued to compete in national events. Among his many records were the World Kilometre sidecar title gained in 1960 at a speed of 98.98 mph and the World One Kilometre solo record gained in 1961 at a speed of 108.74 mph. He retired from international competition with an outstandingly successful three days at Greenham Common, near Newbury, in November 1966 by claiming seven world and nine national records.

As early as 1965 Brown, who ran a motor cycle business in Stevenage, Hertfordshire, clocked a one-way speed of 190 mph at Chelveston, only 34 mph short of the world land speed record and set his last records in 1971 at over 165 mph when he was 59 years old. That year he suffered a heart attack and retired from competitive racing. The original streamlined, but unsupercharged Nero machine which enabled Brown to secure his first World Records, in 1960, and only a year later was timed at 187 mph, is still in existence (1981), along with his equally famous Super Nero, built in 1965.

George Brown is considered by most authorities to have been Britain's greatest post-war record breaker, and acknowledged as the father-figure of the record-breaking world. He sustained tremendous enthusiasm for the sport and was to achieve many outstanding successes on his record-breaking Vincents and on a 250cc Ariel and in 1967, he held 10 world and 20 national records; by 1972 he held the remarkable total of 13 world and national records (see below) and six national-only records. His declared ambition was to reach 200 mph on two wheels.

1964: flying kilo (1000cc class) 172.642 mph; standing $\frac{1}{4}$ (1300cc sidecar class) 152.840 mph; flying $\frac{1}{4}$ (1000cc class) 10.283 sec.
1965: standing $\frac{1}{4}$ (1000cc class) 10.311 sec.
1966: standing $\frac{1}{4}$ (1000cc sidecar class) 11.806 sec; standing kilo (1000cc class) 19.152 sec; standing kilo (1000cc sidecar class) 21.927 sec; standing kilo (1300cc sidecar class) 21.625 sec; flying kilo (1000cc sidecar class) 158.356 mph; flying kilo (1300cc sidecar class) 149.644 mph; standing mile (1000cc class) 28.032 sec; standing mile (1000cc sidecar class) 30.346 sec; standing mile (1300 cc sidecar class) 31.057 sec; flying $\frac{1}{4}$ (1000cc class) 189.334 mph.
1967: standing mile (1300cc class) 27.979 sec.
1969: flying mile (1300cc class) 111.438 mph.
1970: flying mile (1300cc sidecar class) 124.437 mph; flying mile (1300cc sidecar class) 128.234 mph.
1971: flying mile (1300cc class) 165.51 mph.

The outstanding reliability of Brown's Nero machines was the basis of their combined success over more than twenty years of competition. The original Nero was an all-purpose machine. It was primarily a racer though it had to be good enough for sprinting and hill climbing since Brown had ambitions in all three fields. In 1950 he had Nero fitted with a Velocette swinging arm rear suspension and AJS telescopic front forks and the machine, though hardly used for racing, proved effective in hill climbs. In 1960, with sprinting fast developing into a keenly competitive and specialised sport, Nero had to become a more specialised machine. Traction was improved by lengthening the wheel base, Avon specialist tyres were fitted and altogether the machine was lowered. Streamlined, but not supercharged, the machine in this basic form brought George Brown his first world records in 1960. Nero's performance peak for the quarter mile was said to be 10.01 seconds and 19.2 seconds for the standing start kilometre and was timed at 187 mph as far back as 1960. Brown's other famous sprint machine, the 1147cc Super Nero, was built in 1965 and was the big capacity counterpart to the original Nero. Brown also competed successfully with a blown 1000cc machine. George Brown died in February 1979.

BRYANS, Ralph

Bryans (born Northern Ireland 1948) was a racing star of the 1960s when Japanese interest brought huge investment into the sport. Only six years after his racing début he was a World Champion in 1965, riding Honda to success in the 50cc class. He first raced in the Irish event, Tandragee 100, and won his class on a 197cc Ambassador Villiers. On a Norton he finished second on handicap in the Skerries 100 of 1961 and in 1962 was placed 9th in the 350cc Ulster Grand Prix. In the early years Bryans took part in almost all branches of motor cycle sport, but decided to concentrate on road racing in 1962. His big chance came in 1963 when he signed for Bultaco after a couple of test rides in Spain. Only two months later Honda, after Jim Redman had been impressed by the Ralph Bryans potential, offered a much bigger contract and Bultaco sportingly released him.

In his first year with Honda Bryans won four Grands Prix and was second in the 50cc World Championship behind Hugh Anderson. It was a remarkable achievement since he had not before raced on many of the Grand Prix circuits. His impressive début for Honda was consolidated the following year when he secured the 50cc World Championship. He was second in 1966. His successes included first in 1966 and second in 1964 in the 50cc TT.

World Champion:
1965: 50cc (Honda).

TT Wins:
1966: 50cc (Honda).

BSA/BSA-TRIUMPH

For almost fifty years from the turn of the century BSA were the world's biggest manufacturer of motor cycles yet they had no works road-racing machines. They did, however, support trials and scrambles extensively and derived much publicity from this involvement. With modified roadsters BSA first competed at the TTs in 1913, but from six starters only one finished, in 17th position. BSA returned to the TT in 1921 with works machines designed specifically for racing but were unsuccessful. All six retired with valve or piston failure. As a result race development stopped and except for a few private entries during the 1920s, BSA became conspicuously absent from the circuits, and for 20 years from 1930 no BSA machine of any sort, works or privately sponsored, was entered in the TT. BSA revived an interest in racing when Wal Handley riding a 500cc Empire Star at 102 mph won a race at Brooklands in 1937 producing a fastest lap of 107.57 mph.

This success led to the introduction of the BSA Gold Star in 1938. Handley's works-prepared racer ran on alcohol fuel and was fitted with iron head and barrel, but the Gold Star engine was announced with an all-alloy top half, and after the war it reappeared with plunger rear-springing and telescopic forks. The 350cc and 500cc Gold Stars proved to be superb competitive machines, being produced for road racing, trials and scrambles.

As a clubman's racer it was outstanding, winning the 350cc Clubman's TT on the Isle of Man annually from 1949 to 1956; the 500 version won in 1954, 55 and 56. On BSA Gold Stars many top road racers of the future were to gain their experience including Bob McIntyre, Phil Read and Derek Minter.

BSA almost introduced a works special racer in 1953, a horizontal single-cylinder 250 with double overhead camshafts and four valves. Geoff Duke, the proposed rider, tested the prototype and considered it had great potential, being good enough to contest the 250 World Championship against Guzzi and NSU, the chief opposition of the time. It was said to be superior to a 350 works Norton. Designed by Doug Hele, the engineer behind BSA's much later 750 successes, the 250 Grand Prix BSA was never raced (the BSA top brass apparently wanting much firmer assurances of early success than Hele could possibly give).

In the 1960s BSA machines gained more road racing success than ever before through the efforts of private entrants, and in the sidecar class Chris Vincent was particularly outstanding. The 650 twin became fundamental to the British sidecar class, but seven times British Champion Chris Vincent, despite his record of success, suffered from the lack of factory interest and support. In moto-cross the role of BSA, with the outstanding success of Jeff Smith, is well known.

The growing importance of production and F750-type road racing, and the opening up of competition in America, stimulated BSA's interest. By this time the British motor cycle industry had weathered a number of traumatic experiences, culminating in the BSA – Triumph merger. The potential had been demonstrated in 1969 when two American-prepared BSA three-cylinder Rocket 3 machines ridden by Yvon Du Hamel and Dick Mann, at speeds in excess of 120 mph, set a number of records in the 750cc class of the AMA's stock-machine class. In 1971 the BSA-Triumph Group, largely through the American BSA Co. Inc. and for the first time in many years, embarked on an extensive racing programme, not in Grand Prix events, but in AMA competition. With an eye on the vast American market, where the potential for large capacity road machines was huge, the publicity and glamour of road racing success at events like the Daytona 200 had enormous value. At Daytona, in 1971, there was an impressive total of ten riders on 750cc 3-cylinder BSA and Triumph machines. They finished in the first three places; and at the Ontario, California classic, John Cooper won an impressive victory in his first attempt, riding a 750cc BSA-3. In 1972, however, came the news of a racing cut-back and that there would be no BSA-Triumph racing team that year, though the intention was for the American side of Triumph to continue in racing. The merger of ailing and loss-making BSA with Norton came in 1973 with the establishment of Norton Villiers Triumph, with Dennis Poore, who had earlier rescued AJS and Norton from bankruptcy, in charge. In 1975, however, after a workers' co-operative had been set up at the firm's Meriden factory, the home of Triumph machines, Government cash aid was actively and urgently solicited to keep the firm in business.

The BSA/Triumph 750-3 cylinder machines were first bench-tested in 1969, the engine giving almost 80 bhp. The racing success of the 650 Bonneville twin formed a good base for further development and the 750-3 cylinder, which had existed for some time, looked ripe for racing development. With the revision in regulations for AMA racing confirming 750cc for ohv engines for 1970 providing the impetus required, the factory produced six racing machines for Daytona that year. Though the machines had plenty of power, reliability and handling were questionable. But in 1971, the BSA-threes came through with impressive results. In addition to Daytona and Ontario, they secured the Coupe d'Endurance, the Le Mans Bol d'Or, and at home won the 750cc British Championship, the Thruxton Formula 750, the F750 TT, Hutchinson 100, Thruxton 500-miler, the Superbike Championship and the Race of the Year and Race of the South events at Mallory Park and Brands Hatch respectively.

BULTACO

This famous Spanish marque with headquarters in Barcelona is more famous for its success in trials (particularly through the achievements of Irishman Sammy Miller) than in road racing, though it has achieved a measure of distinction in the latter. In the World Championships of 1968 Ginger Molloy of New Zealand came third in the 125cc category on a Bultaco. A year earlier a Bultaco machine won the Production 250cc TT. Through the veteran racer Angel Nieto and the Spanish rider Ricardo Tormo, Bultaco came back strongly in the 50cc World Championship, Nieto taking the title in 1976 and 1977, and Tormo in 1978 and 1981.

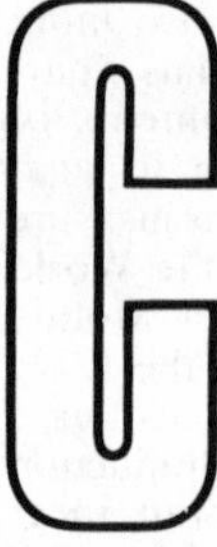

CADWELL PARK
Cadwell Park, used for International, National and Club racing in addition to moto-cross, is situated seven miles north-west of Horncastle on the A 153, and five miles south-west of Louth, in Lincolnshire. The main circuit is 2.25 miles and there is a 1.5 mile club circuit. Address: Charles Wilkinson, Cadwell Park, Cadwell Manor, Louth, Lincolnshire.

CALDARELLA, Benedicto
Benedicto Caldarella (born Argentina) is one of the few South American riders to make an impact on international motorcycle racing. He is particularly remembered for his strong challenge to Mike Hailwood in a series of dynamic rides on works Gilera 4s in the mid-1960s. In the United States Grand Prix of 1964, for instance, he stayed close to Hailwood for fourteen laps before gearbox trouble ended his challenge.

CAMATHIAS, Florian
This famous Swiss sidecar pilot caused a great many problems for the German sidecar racers during the late 1950s and early 1960s. He was also a brilliant designer and tuner of racing sidecar outfits. Born in 1924, he gained his first Grand Prix win in Holland in 1958, though he had already made his mark before then, finishing fifth in the World Championships in 1956 and third in 1957. In 1958 he was runner-up in the World Championships and came nearest to the title the following year when he ended the season with the same number of points as the German ace Walter Schneider, the latter gaining the title after first and second placings had been counted.

Camathias and fellow-Swiss Fritz Scheidegger were virtually the only non-German sidecar racers to make any impact in the Grands Prix during the late 1950s and early 1960s. With his British-style 'right-hand drive' outfit and his privately prepared engines, Camathias was a constant source of embarrassment to the German BMW factory and their unofficial works team. He was seriously injured at Modena in 1961, but in 1962 was once again runner-up in the World Championship with his BMW-powered Florian Camathias Special. He was second again in 1963, but at Brands Hatch in October 1965 his outfit went off the road and Camathias was killed.

CAMPBELL, Keith R.
Keith Campbell was the first Australian to win a World Championship, a distinction he achieved in 1957 when he beat Bob McIntyre and Liberati to take the 350cc crown. Campbell's early riding in Australia was on a 498cc AJS and his progression to road racing came mainly through scrambling. In 1951, on his first trip to Europe, he entered the Junior Manx Grand Prix but came off just before Verandah, suffering a broken thumb and lacerated face. A determined and uninhibited character, he later won the South Australian 350cc Championship. Back in Europe during 1955, he gained a number of important victories and was signed by Guzzi in late 1956. His World Championship was won on the Guzzi. Campbell attended the TTs in 1957 (Guzzi) and 1958 (Norton). 1957 – fifth in the Senior and second in the Junior, 1958 – retired in the Senior and seventh in the Junior.

CARRUTHERS, Kel
Born 1938 in Australia, Kel Carruthers rode with outstanding success there on a factory-loaned 250 Honda-4 and his own Nortons, before coming to Europe in 1965. His major distinction in Europe came in 1969 on a works Benelli-4, when he won the 250cc World Championship and the 250cc TT. His TT victory in 1969 was the first by an Australian for 13 years (K.T. Kavanagh) and the first success for the Benelli factory on the Isle of Man since 1950. He won the 250cc TT again in 1970, on a Yamaha. In both TT victories he also established fastest laps. He left Europe for the United States in 1970, linking with Californian road racer and Yamaha dealer, Don Vesco. After winning the 250cc event at Daytona he travelled to Europe to compete in World Championship events. He finished in

second place in both the 250cc and 350cc categories, behind Rod Gould and Giacomo Agostini respectively.

In 1971, again riding Don Vesco's Yamahas, he won six of the seven American Motor Cycle Association 250cc races, becoming the first non-American to win an AMCA Championship race. This was at Atlanta, Georgia. He was second on a 350cc Yamaha to John Cooper in the Ontario classic of 1971. Kel Carruthers, who retired from racing in 1974 to concentrate on running the Yamaha racing team in America, was the first motor-cycle racer to win major honours in Australia, Europe and America.

World Championship wins:
1969: 250cc (Benelli).
TT Wins:
1969: 250cc (Benelli).
1970: 250cc (Yamaha).

CASTLE COMBE

This well known motor-cycle racing circuit, situated five miles north-west of Chippenham on the B 4039, became a race track in 1950 and was used for national and club meetings. The 1.84 mile circuit was under the control of Motor Circuit Developments for the last two years of its life. It was used for motor-cycle racing for the last time in 1972. In a bid to keep racing going at Castle Combe, Motor Circuit Developments sent local residents a four point questionnaire, but despite this and a recommendation at the end of a six day public enquiry that racing should be allowed to continue the circuit was closed to motor cycle racing. It was due to host a motor-cycle race meeting again towards the end of 1981.

CECOTTO, Johnny

A new racing sensation burst on to the European Grand Prix scene in 1975 in the form of Johnny Cecotto, a curly-haired, fun-loving 19-year-old from Venezuela. Almost unheard of outside his own country, Cecotto grabbed all the headlines when he won both the 250cc and 350cc events at his debut Grand Prix at the Paul Ricard circuit in France in the opening round of the 1975 World Championships.

He went on to prove it was no fluke – winning again in West Germany (350cc), Italy (350cc), Belgium (250cc) and Finland (350cc). It was an exceptional, sustained performance which gave him the 350cc World Championship, against a serious challenge from many established riders including Agostini, at his first attempt. He was also fourth in the 250cc class. In August 1975 Yamaha signed him to a full works contract for 1976.

Cecotto was born in the Venezuelan capital of Caracas in January 1956 of Italian parents. His garage-owning father, a former Venezuelan champion on a Manx Norton, bought Johnny a 750-Honda 4, on which he had his first races. He was then offered the use of an ex-works 750cc Kawasaki and his form on this machine led to an offer from the Venezuelan Yamaha importer, Andres Ippolito, who became Cecotto's sponsor/manager.

Cecotto, who was Venezuelan 1000cc champion in 1973 and 1974, began studying mechanical engineering, but gave this up following his outstanding European successes, which led to official factory support from Yamaha.

America's Daytona event witnessed the Cecotto style for the first time in 1974, when he finished 35th on a 350cc Yamaha! A year later he qualified for the front row of the grid and finished in third place. In 1976 he became at 20 the youngest winner of the Daytona 200 at a record speed of 108.77 mph, lapping all his rivals.

Johnny Cecotto has great crowd appeal and is an exciting rider. Riding Yamaha, Cecotto was 350cc World Champion in 1975 and F750 World Champion in 1978.

CHATTERTON, Derek

Derek Chatterton made his debut as a road racer when he was sixteen. Born in 1945 he comes from Lincolnshire and was producing some good performances by 1966 when he raced into third place behind such established names as Phil Read and Mike Duff on works Yamahas in the 250cc Hutchinson 100. He gained distinction by becoming the first rider to win the British 250cc and 350cc titles on two-stroke machinery, preparing the machines himself. He was 250cc British Champion in 1967 and 350cc British Champion in 1970, both astride Yamahas. Among a number of victories was that over Agostini in the 1000cc race at Cadwell Park in September 1971. His first appearance in the TTs was in 1968, riding Mondial in the lightweight (125), when he retired, and a Yamaha in the the Junior (placed 10th).

CLERMONT-FERRAND
The traditional home of the French Grand Prix, Clermont-Ferrand is one of the most beautiful of the classic circuits and is situated in the mountains of the Auvergne. It is said to be built on the rock of a long-extinct volcano. Similar to the Nurburgring because of its many bends and mountain track, the surface is good, though with the longest straight only 650 yd it is very much a rider's circuit. It has plenty of tight bends and numerous gradients. Five miles long, it was first used in 1960. (*See also* FRENCH GRAND PRIX.)

COLLINS, Peter
At 20 years of age Collins (born Heatley, Cheshire) in 1974 became the first ever English rider to win the European Speedway Championship. This distinction he achieved at Wembley on 31st August. Other major successes in 1974 for this talented rider included British League Riders' Champion, member of Britain's successful World Team Cup squad, World Finalist, World Championship qualifying round winner and a British League record: 29 matches, 117 rides, 322 total points with a calculated match average of 11.01. After his outstanding 1974 season Collins was being hotly tipped to become the first Englishman to become World Champion since Peter Craven's success in 1962. This distinction he achieved in 1976 and, at 22 years old, he became the youngest World Speedway Champion for 21 years.

CONTINENTAL CIRCUS
This is the popular name for the small group of riders who regularly compete in the series of European Grand Prix events. Origins of the continental circus were established soon after the end of the first World War when the Grands Prix in France, Belgium and Holland attracted increasing numbers of British road racers. In the 1950s increasing commercial interest and sophistication in the sport increased the importance and emphasis of the continental circus which probably reached a peak in the late 1950s, and in the 1960s with riders like Hailwood, Ivy, Redman, Read and others forming an elite corps of riders with lucrative works contracts contesting a full and arduous Grand Prix programme.

CONTINENTAL AND US RIDERS
After a decade when British and Commonwealth riders on non-British machinery dominated the road racing World Championships, American and Continental riders gained the ascendancy in the 1970s. Prominent at the beginning of the 1980s were Kenny Roberts, Randy Mamola and Mike Baldwin (USA), Virginio Ferrari, Franco Uncini, Marco Lucchinelli, Walter Villa, Graziano Rossi, Paolo Pileri, Pierpaolo Bianchi and Eugenio Lazzarini (Italy), Wil Hartog, Boet Van Dulmen and Henk Van Kessel (Holland), Philippe Coulon and Michel Frutschi (Switzerland), Christian Sarron, Michel Rougerie, Patrick Fernandez, Patrick Pons, Jean-François Balde and Olivier Chevallier (France), Anton Mang (Germany) and Angel Nieto and Ricardo Tormo (Spain).

CONTROL OF THE SPORT
As mentioned elsewhere the FIM is responsible for motor sport internationally, and the A-CU is the largest and most influential body in the British Isles. It has 20 territorial clubs and more than 500 affiliated clubs. In Scotland the sport is controlled by a national club of the A-CU, the Scottish A-CU, Kippilaw, Torphichen Street, Bathgate, West Lothian, and in Ireland, both north and south, the sport is the responsibility of the Motor Cycle Union of Ireland, 11 Glen Crescent, White Abbey, Newtownabbey, Northern Ireland, which has direct affiliation to the FIM.

COOPER, Frederick
Fred Cooper (born London 1924) and one of Britain's most successful motorcycle sprint racers, remains most famous for his attempts to reach 200 mph on his twin-engined 1300cc Triumph powered Cyclotron in 1968 and 1969. The 200 mph was a qualifying time which Cooper had to reach to gain substantial financial backing from the *Daily Express* in an attempt on the outright world motor cycle speed record, then held officially by American Bill Johnson at 224.57 mph, though Bob Leppan, in his Gyronaught projectile, had raised the record unofficially to 245.667 mph in 1966. At the time Cooper already held two world

records – the one mile standing start and the 500cc quarter mile – and was later to average 194 mph over the kilometre at Elvington to give him the world record for a 1300cc machine.

Cooper's first scheduled attempt to reach 200 mph at Fairford never took place because unexpected difficulties arose during efforts to secure the use of the runways. At Honington in June 1968 he clocked 185 mph before a rear crank shaft sheared on his sixth and final run. A third and final attempt scheduled for Duxford airfield in Essex in March 1969 never took place because of bad weather, though it is extremely doubtful if Cooper could have reached a qualifying time on a runway only 1½ miles long.

In 1972 Fred Cooper was 48 years old and still actively interested in speed records. In September that year he became the fastest ever motor-cyclist in Britain on the basis of a two way average, his speed of 189.87 mph for the Flying Quarter Mile at the NSA's records weekend at the Concorde base at Fairford in Gloucestershire giving Cooper his third national record; he already held the kilometre and mile records. This latest record, made on his famous Cyclotron, included a first run at 193 mph. He also became only the second man (Alf Hagon being the first) to top 200 mph in Britain when he reached 200.4 mph in 1972.

Fred Cooper's famous sprint machine was the 1,267cc Vee-four Triumph-powered Cyclotron, with 71 x 80mm engine, 180-degree crank spacing, supercharged and coupled by helical gears. Cyclotron in world record breaking form would have undergone considerable change, had Cooper reached that Bonneville-qualifying 200 mph. Extensive streamlining would have been necessary and the basic layout of the projected world record-breaker would be patterned on the long, low, streamliners of Bill Johnson and Bob Leppan which then held the world outright record officially and unofficially. Later the 80mm-stroke crankshafts originally fitted were replaced by standard cranks giving an 82mm stroke, increasing the total capacity to 1,299cc and compression from 8 to 1 to 8½ to 1.

Cooper never reached the qualifying 200 mph and therefore did not achieve his ambition of an attempt at the outright motor-cycle world record at Bonneville in the USA.

COOPER, John H.

John Cooper's racing career extended over almost 20 years and his greatest achievements were during the three years before his retirement. Known for most of his racing life as a successful private rider, Cooper had to wait until 1971 before securing his first major factory contract. Riding a 750cc BSA-3 he won the Champion Spark Plug Classic (and £6,000) in Ontario, California, in 1971 at his first attempt. Earlier, on the same machine, he had scored his second successive victory in Mallory Park's International Race of the Year, this time beating Giacomo Agostini on the 500cc MV. After 30 laps of the 1.35 mile Leicestershire circuit Cooper won by three-fifths of a second from Agostini.

John Cooper, tall and bespectacled, was born in Derby in 1938 and first raced in 1954 when he was 16 on a 197cc James. His first major victory was at the Scarborough International in 1961. He was a prolific racer in the 1960s becoming British Champion on four occasions: 350cc (1964/66), 500cc (1966), 250cc (1968). He almost retired in 1969 following a fall at Cadwell Park, but the Yamsel machine, a 350cc hybrid consisting of a Yamaha engine in a modified Seeley frame, was responsible for maintaining his interest and bringing him further success. Out of 23 races with the Yamsel he won 18.

John Cooper has always been closely associated with Mallory Park which was regarded as his home circuit. He first won the *Race of the Year* there in 1965, and won it twice more, in 1970-71. His most outstanding successes came in 1971 and 1972 with BSA-Triumph. He registered 15 firsts, 6 seconds, and 10 thirds – plus 14 fastest laps including four lap records. Other important wins included the Race of the South at Brands Hatch in 1971, achieved against strong opposition including Agostini on the MV, and the *Motor Cycle News* Superbike Championship in 1972. He was voted Man of the Year by readers of *Motor Cycle News* in 1970 and 1971 (with the most votes ever in the competition to that time). After his dramatic success in the Ontario event he was offered a contract with Norton, but preferred to stay with BSA/Triumph. He finally joined Nortons in 1973 but virtually retired from racing after breaking a leg at Brands Hatch that year.

John Cooper spent most of his long career without a factory contract and for this reason did not compete seriously in classic events. Noted for his outspoken comments, he was a strong critic of the TT races, claiming the rewards for competing and winning were in no way related to the importance of the race, the additional revenue the Isle of Man authorities received from the racing, or the dangers the course imposed. John Cooper became distinctive by the 'moon eyes' painted on his crash helmet, an idea adopted early in his career.

COTTON
This British machine, made by E. Cotton (Motor Cycles) Ltd of Gloucester, was raced with success in 250cc British events by Derek Minter in the 1960s. The firm was founded by Bill Cotton in 1919 and revived by Monty Denley and Pat Onions in 1954. Cottons first appeared in the TT results in 1923 when Stanley Woods won the Junior event. In 1924 Cotton machines were second in the lightweight and second and third in the ultra lightweight TTs. Second places in both classes were recorded in 1925 and in 1926 Cottons were one, two and three in the lightweight TT. Cottons were also strong at Brooklands and in a final blast of success at the famous circuit a 250cc Cotton ridden by Eric Fernihough and C. K. Mortimer broke 12 world records from four to twelve hours in 1935.

In 1978 the first machine was produced by the new Cotton/EMX Company – a 250cc moto-cross bike.

CROFT AUTODROME
Used for National and Club racing. Length of circuit is 1.75 miles. The circuit is situated seven miles south of Darlington. Address: Croft Autodrome, Croft, Darlington, Co. Durham.

CROXFORD, Dave L.
Born London 1940, Dave Croxford was British Champion three times before riding for the John Player Norton team. He won the Thruxton 500 miler for JPN, probably their finest performance. Big and brave, and a natural morale booster in any team, Croxford began racing when he was 18 first as a sidecar passenger, but by 1962 was riding a Manx Norton successfully, before moving on to G50 Matchless and 7R AJS machines, By this time he was contesting the home circuits regularly. A brief retirement was followed by outstanding success. In 1967 he rode second to Peter Williams in the 350cc event at Mallory Park and that same year gained his first British Championship in the 350cc class. He was 500cc Champion in 1968 and 1969. He first rode for John Player Norton on an F750 in October 1972 and gained the solo British Championship for them in 1973. His first appearance in the TT Races was in 1965, his best performance that year being 11th in the Senior on a Matchless.

CRYSTAL PALACE
The Crystal Palace motor-cycle race circuit was situated on Anerley Hill, Sydenham, in the grounds of the old Crystal Palace, and was only 1.39 miles in length and almost rectangular. It was the only motor-cycle race circuit in London. Doubts about its future were first expressed in 1971 and it was last used for motor-cycle racing in 1972.

CZ
CZ is a Czechoslovakian factory famous for its success in scrambling (motocross) and in speedway. Their motocross success began in 1957 with the conversion of a 175cc trials model and during that year, three of the factory's trials riders began competing in motocross. A couple of years of machine development followed before, in 1959, CZ finished second in the Czech National Championships. Inspired by this performance they moved seriously into European competition with new models in 1960 but found Jawa opposition too formidable. Steady progress was made over the next few years, with riders like Vlastimil Valek and Karel Pilar and with improved machinery. By the end of 1963 Valek had brought CZ into second position in the World Championship and the factory was producing a number of replica models for other riders. It was in 1963 that Joel Robert, after riding a "Starmaker" Greeves, switched to CZ and the following year (1964), in the 250cc Belgian GP, he brought the Czech factory their first really significant victory and went on to win the world title. Within another year CZ had dominated the 250cc scene. By this time Russia had moved into motocross and their team was riding CZ machines, Victor Arbekov won the world 250cc title that year, with Robert second – both on CZ machines.

CZ had not been inactive in the 500cc class and in 1963 Pilar contested this category with a 260cc CZ, winning the Czech title. Larger machines followed this encouraging start and it was not long before the great names of motocross, including the East German Paul Friedrichs, and Britain's Dave Bickers, were riding CZ 350cc models. Later came 400cc and new 250cc machines.

CZECHOSLOVAKIAN GRAND PRIX

The Czechoslovakian Grand Prix is run on the Brno circuit in Moravia. This circuit was originally 11.06 miles but in 1963 it was shortened to 8.66 miles. Though much smaller than the Isle of Man TT course, it shares its characteristics, winding through villages and hollows and up a small mountain. There is a friendly community atmosphere about this Grand Prix with spectators camping in the surrounding woods. The first World Championship meeting was held in Czechoslovakia in 1965. The circuit was modified for 1975 and measures 6.79 miles. Plans were announced in 1978 for further modifications to the Brno track incorporating a long circuit (2.98 miles) and a short version (2.12 miles).

Results:

1965: 125cc F. G. Perris (Suzuki); 250cc P. W. Read (Yamaha); 350cc J. A. Redman (Honda); 500cc S. M. B. Hailwood (MV).

1966: 125cc L. Taveri (Honda); 250cc S. M. B. Hailwood (Honda); 350cc S. M. B. Hailwood (Honda); 500cc S. M. B. Hailwood (Honda).

1967: 125cc W. D. Ivy (Yamaha); 250cc P. W. Read (Yamaha); 350cc S. M. B. Hailwood (Honda); 500cc S. M. B. Hailwood (Honda).

1968: 125cc P. W. Read (Yamaha); 250cc P. W. Read (Yamaha); 350cc G. Agostini (MV); 500cc G. Agostini (MV).

1969: 50cc P. Lodewijkx (Jamathi); 125cc D. A. Simmonds (Kawasaki); 250cc R. Pasolini (Benelli); 350cc G. Agostini (MV); 500cc G. Agostini (MV).

1970: 50cc A. Toersen (Jamathi); 125cc G. Parlotti (Morbidelli); 250cc K. Carruthers (Yamaha); 350cc G. Agostini (MV); sidecars K. Anders/W. Kalauch (BMW).

1971: 50cc B. Sheene (Suzuki); 125cc A. Nieto (Derbi); 250cc J. Drapal (Yamaha); 350cc J. Saarinen (Yamaha); sidecars S. Schauzu/W. Kalauch (BMW).

1972: 125cc B. Jansson (Maico); 250cc J. Saarinen (Yamaha); 350cc J. Saarinen (Yamaha); 500cc G. Agostini (MV); sidecars K. Enders/R. Engelhardt (BMW).

1973: 125cc O. Buscherini (Malanca); 250cc D. Braun (Yamaha); 350cc T. Lansivuori (Yamaha); 500cc G. Agostini (MV); sidecars K. Enders/R. Engelhardt (BMW).

1974: 50cc H. van Kessel (Van Veen Kreidler); 125cc K. Andersson (Yamaha); 250cc W. Villa (Harley-Davidson); 500cc P. W. Read (MV); sidecar W. Schwarzel/K. Kleis (Konig).

1975: 125cc L. Gustafsson (Yamaha); 250cc M. Rougerie (Harley-Davidson); 350cc O. Buscherini (Yamaha); 500cc P. W. Read (MV); sidecar W. Schwarzel/A. Huber (Konig).

1976: 250cc W. Villa (Harley-Davidson); 350cc W. Villa (Harley-Davidson); 500cc J. Newbold (Suzuki); sidecar H. Schmid/M. Martial (Yamaha).

1977: 250cc F. Uncini (Harley-Davidson); 350cc J. Cecotto (Yamaha); 500cc J. Cecotto (Yamaha); sidecar R. Steinhausen/W. Kalauch (Busch-Yamaha).

1978: 50cc R. Tormo (Bultaco); 250cc K. Ballington (Kawasaki); 350cc K. Ballington (Kawasaki); sidecar A. Michel/S. Collins (Seymaz-Yamaha).

1979: 125cc G. Bertin (Motobecane); 250cc K. Ballington (Kawasaki); 350cc K. Ballington (Kawasaki); sidecar BZA R. Biland/K. Waltisperg (Schmid Yamaha).

1980: 125cc G. Bertin (Motobecane); 250cc A. Mang (Kawasaki); 350cc A. Mang (Kawasaki); sidecar R. Biland/K. Waltisperg (Yamaha).

1981: 50cc T. Timmer (Bultaco); 250cc A. Mang (Kawasaki); 350cc A. Mang (Kawasaki); sidecar R. Biland/K. Waltisperg (Yamaha).

DANIELL, Harold L

Harold Daniell was one of the legendary few British riders who dominated racing on the Isle of Man during pre-second World War years. Although his successes were significant and important, it is obvious that the war came at a most inopportune time in his career and robbed him of many more almost certain victories. He won the Senior TT in 1938 and when racing resumed on the island, won the Senior again in 1947 and 1949.

Born in London in 1910, Daniell was a friendly jovial character. Plump, bespectacled, he began racing in the 1930s at places like Brooklands and Donington. He won the 1933 Senior Manx Grand Prix which brought him works rides for AJS, which were not noted for their success; he was happier on the Lancefield-Nortons which he had ridden earlier. He rode a works Norton for the first time in 1938 and won the Senior TT by 55.2 seconds from Stanley Woods, after establishing a 91 mph lap – the first time in the history of the TT that the course had been lapped in under 25 minutes. It was an astonishing race which brought Harold Daniell immortality in the racing world for Daniell had never won a TT before, yet Woods, whom he beat, had already notched up a record nine victories. The record lap stood until 1950. Daniell is also remembered as originator of the term 'featherbed' to describe Norton's revolutionary frame on which, as Norton team leader, he did so much testing.

Harold Daniell retired from racing in 1951 and died at 57 in 1967.

TT wins:

1938: Senior (Norton).
1947: Senior (Norton).
1949: Senior (Norton).

DANIELS, Bruce

Successful on a BMW in long distance production machine racing between 1959 and 1961. Bruce Daniels began racing in 1954 on a 500cc International Norton. Subsequent rides on a 500cc Gold Star and then a 500cc Manx Norton brought him recognition at British short circuits, but it was in long distance events that he was to become most successful, being a member of teams which won the Thruxton 500 and the Barcelona 24 hour race in 1959, was second at Barcelona in 1960 and won the 1000 kilometre race at Silverstone in 1961.

DAVIES, Howard R.

Famous as the designer, builder and rider of his own HRD machines Howard Davies is also remembered for his performance in the Senior TT of 1921 when he became the first, and so far only, Senior TT winner on a 350cc machine. The distinction also goes to AJS on which Davies produced an average 54.50 mph to win. After riding a Sunbeam in the TT of 1914, Davies rode AJS machines from 1920 until 1923, but apart from 1921 when he was second in the Junior as well as winner of the Senior, he suffered five retirements. A switch to OEC in 1924, in which he retired in both the Senior and Junior events, was the prelude to the riding of his own HRD machines in 1925, 26 and 27.

The remnants of his once famous business were later acquired by Philip J. Vincent.

Results:

1925: second in the Junior, and first in the Senior.
1926: retired in the Senior.
1927: retired in the Senior.

DAYTONA 200

In the mid-1970s the Daytona 200 was the premier road race in the world, certainly from the manufacturers' point of view; an outstanding prestige event and a showcase for the vast American market. Although it has a history going back more than 35 years, it is only since the late 1960s that it has become significant for European motor-cycle racers. The strong appeal of Daytona begins with the circuit itself, which is an enclosed race bowl with bankings at either end allowing speeds of up to 180 mph on motor cycles to be recorded there. The bankings slope at 31 degrees. The Daytona 200 is important because it is the first event of the

American international season and gives an initial opportunity to see new machinery developed during the close season and promising new star riders. Also contributing to the importance of Daytona, more particularly from the manufacturers' point of view, is the fierce demands the race makes on machines! For a rider the course is simple and easy to learn, but the stresses on engines and frames, with additional considerations like tyre wear, reliability and fuel consumption, are probably greater at Daytona than at any other circuit. It is probably the most heavily advertised and sales promoted motor-cycle race in the world. Generally held in brilliant sunshine it presents an exciting spectacle. The presence of top riders from America and from Britain and the continent was virtually guaranteed because of the high rewards offered. In 1973 for instance this 200-miler offered £14,000 in prize money, £2,100 in lap money and nearly £15,000 in contingency awards making a total of over £30,000. The trend towards 750cc road racing towards the end of the 1960s combined with the reinstatement of America within the FIM to give a new dimension to Daytona. The AMA lifted the capacity limit to 750cc for all types of engines, encouraging the participation of British and European works teams. This development tempted Mike Hailwood back to motor cycle racing and in 1970 he joined Americans Jim Rice and Dave Aldana in a new BSA works team. Over-heating problems cost the BSA-Triumph team the race and Dick Mann was the winner on a factory Honda.

Qualifying speeds at Daytona reached more than 150 mph for the first time in 1969 when Yvon Duhamel went round at 150.5 mph. In 1972 Californian Don Emde won the 200 mile Classic on a private 350cc R3 Yamaha entered by dealer, Mel Dinesen. It was the first time a two-stroke had won in the 35-year-history of the race.

The Daytona Classic, which normally runs of course to 200 miles, was reduced in 1974 to 180 miles because of the energy crisis. It was Agostini's first public appearance as World Champion since he left MV for Yamaha. In the Daytona 200 pit-stops are crucial and the big 750s have to stop twice. In 1974 Yamaha dominated with 71 out of 101 entries and the race also attracted a record total of 40 non-USA entries. For the 1974 event a chicane was introduced in the back straight. Winner Agostini's average of 105.01 mph was a record and beat the previous best set by Dick Mann (BSA) in 1971. The 1974 Daytona was an outstanding triumph for Agostini and the new TZ750 Yamaha. It was the Italian's first race on a Yamaha, his first on a two-stroke machine and his first race in the United States. For Yamaha, the TZ750 had to prove itself at Daytona, though the 500cc-4 versions had been raced successfully in Europe the previous year and the 700s had seen service later in both the United States and Japan. Agostini's impressive win gave Yamaha their third victory in as many years, though Don Emde's success in 1972, as previously mentioned, was astride a privately-entered machine.

Though of comparatively recent importance for Britain, the Daytona 200 has a long and interesting tradition. Popular in the early 1900s for its speed events and the world's first car drag race held on the beach, Daytona, in Florida, became famous as the venue for repeated World Land Speed records made by drivers like Sir Malcolm Campbell and Sir Henry Segrave during the 1930s. A beach-road circuit was later constructed there and the first motor cycle event held in 1937. By this time the AMA, who since 1931 had been organising a 200-mile motor cycle race at a couple of locations in the USA, were attracted to Daytona and persuaded the promoters to transfer their event to Daytona. That was in 1937 and it was the start of the Daytona 200.

This first Daytona 200 in 1937 had 98 entries riding for a winner's stake of £140 in a total purse of £340. This initial beach course was used from 1937-41 inclusive and then again after the war for one year (1947). Because of development in the area the course was shifted for 1948, but still on the beach. The circuit was increased to 4.2 miles. It was on this course that the event was successfully contested by the Norton factory from 1949 to 52. They won the event for four consecutive years and in 1949 so dominated the race that Norton riders finished first, second and third. The American authorities later banned the successful over-the-counter Norton racers, even though they had been in competition with American Harley-Davidson and Indian machines of 750cc. The last Daytona 200 to be staged on this beach course was in 1960. Thereafter it was transferred to the new Daytona International Speedway run by Bill France, a former Daytona garage owner and stock car racer, and from then its stature and prestige grew enormously.

In recent years the nearest British riders have come to victory was in 1971 when both Mike Hailwood and Paul Smart were impressive before retiring. In the later 1970s, however, Daytona lost much of its prestige and failed to attract as many top riders as in previous years, principally because of autocratic circuit-owner Bill France's refusal to pay start money according to FIM rules. In 1978 the Daytona 200 lost its status as a round in the F750 World Championship.

The first woman to qualify for the Daytona 200 was American rider Gina Bovaird, in 1980.

Daytona Winners (Old Circuit):
1937: Ed Kretz (Indian);
1938: Ben Campanale (Harley-Davidson);
1939: Ben Campanale (Harley-Davidson);
1940: Babe Tancrede (Harley-Davidson);
1947: Johnny Spiegelhoff (Indian);
1948: Floyd Emde (Indian);
1949: Dick Klamfoth (Norton);
1950: Billy Mathews (Norton);
1951: Dick Klamfoth (Norton);
1952: Dick Klamfoth (Norton);
1953: Paul Goldsmith (Harley-Davidson);
1954: Bobby Hill (BSA);
1955: Brad Andres (Harley-Davidson);
1956: John Gibson (Harley-Davidson);
1957: Joe Leonard (Harley-Davidson);
1958: Joe Leonard (Harley-Davidson);
1959: Brad Andres (Harley-Davidson);
1960: Brad Andres (Harley-Davidson).

Daytona Winners (New Circuit):
1961: Roger Reiman (Harley-Davidson) 69.25 mph;
1962: Don Burnett (Triumph) 71.981 mph;
1963: Ralph White (Harley-Davidson) 77.678 mph;
1964: Roger Reiman (Harley-Davidson) 94.833 mph;
1965: Roger Reiman (Harley-Davidson) 90.041 mph;
1966: Buddy Elmore (Triumph) 96.582 mph;
1967: Gary Nixon (Triumph) 98.227 mph;
1968: Cal Rayborn (Harley-Davidson) 101.290 mph;
1969: Cal Rayborn (Harley-Davidson) 100.882 mph;
1970: Dick Mann (Honda) 102.691 mph;
1971: Dick Mann (BSA) 104.737 mph;
1972: Don Emde (Yamaha) 103.358 mph;
1973: Jarno Saarinen (Yamaha) 98.178 mph;
1974: Giacomo Agostini (Yamaha) 105.010 mph;
1975: Gene Romero (Yamaha) 106.45 mph;
1976: Johnny Cecotto (Yamaha) 108.77 mph;
1977: Steve Baker (Yamaha) 108.95 mph;
1978: Kenny Roberts (Yamaha) 108.39 mph;
1979: Dale Singleton (Yamaha) 107.69 mph;
1980: Patrick Pons (Yamaha) 107.55 mph;
1981: Dale Singleton (Yamaha) 108.52 mph.
1982: Graeme Crosby (Yamaha) 109.13 mph.

DEARDEN, Reg

One of the most prominent private sponsors in the sport, Reg Dearden was closely associated with the Isle of Man and with Norton machines. A rider of only moderate success, it was as a sponsor that he became best known. It was on Nortons provided by Dearden that Gary Hocking achieved the success which led him to a place in the MV team in 1960, and Les Graham was on a Dearden-sponsored Velocette when he eclipsed works entries to win the Swiss Grand Prix in the early 1950s. He also sponsored Fergus Anderson on a Velocette. Born 1907, Reg Dearden died in January 1972.

DE COSTER, Roger

One of the most successful moto cross specialists De Coster (born Belgium) won his first World Championship in 1971. He was World Champion again in the next two years. In 1974 he also won the lucrative American Trans-AMA moto cross championship. He was 500cc World Champion again in 1975 and 1976 to give him a total of five world titles.

DEGENS, Dave

Degens was first successful as a short-circuit road racer and at the peak of his career was approaching the status of men like John Cooper (as he was at that time) and perhaps even Derek Minter. He also gained a number of distinctions in long distance events. His career began in 1959 at Thruxton and he was soon winning regularly on his Gold Star. After a short spell in the army, he was sponsored by Geoff Monty. Others who backed him at various times were Sid Lawton, Steve Lancefield, Paul Dunstall and Tom Arter. He almost secured a coveted Honda works contract in the 60s when team rider Alan Shepherd was injured, but the machine he should have ridden in the TT had been wrecked in the French GP and there was no ride available. In 1965 and 1966 he won the 500-miler at Thruxton on a Triumph Bonneville prepared by Lawton and the Barcelona race on a Dresda Triton. With Rex Butcher he registered the first all-British victory in this classic event.

After an enforced layoff of two years Degens returned to racing and concentrated on long distance events. With Ian Goddard in 1969 he led the famous Barcelona 24-hour race for seven hours before a couple of broken chains and other problems dropped them back to take sixth place. In 1970, again with Goddard, he won the famous Barcelona event riding one of his own Dresda models. He thus became the first British rider to win the Barcelona marathon twice on British machinery. (*See also* DRESDA).

DEGNER, Ernst

Degner (born Silesia 1931) was an MZ racing star, finishing third for East Germany in the 125cc World Championship of 1960 and second in the same class in 1961. He may well have won the championship that year for he was leading at the time of the Swedish Grand Prix. In a sensational move at that meeting, however, Degner decided to defect to Western Europe and went to live in West Germany, later making his home in Britain. In an effort to secure the title Degner borrowed an EMC machine from Joe Ehrlich, but in the final round, in South America, the machine failed and Tom Phillis took the title on a Honda. Afterwards he joined Suzuki and won their first 50cc TT and the World title in 1962. He retired at the end of 1965 after being badly burned in a crash in the Japanese Grand Prix.

DERBI

Unknown in racing circles before the later 1960s, this Spanish factory, unlike other Spanish manufacturers who turned to moto cross and trials, concentrated on Grand Prix racing and became famous between 1968 and 1972 when they won five road-race World Championships (individual) and four manufacturers' road-race World Championships. Angel Nieto was the one rider closely associated with Derbi's success and became Spain's first world champion. He gained the 50cc World Championship for them in 1969, 1970 and 1972 and was second in 1971. With the same rider, Derbi gained double World Championships in 1972, Nieto adding the 125cc title which he had also won in 1971. He had been second in the 125cc World Championship in 1970.

Derbi, owned by Don Simeon Rabassa, first made bicycles, then switched to motor cycles, concentrating on the light models for the home market. Their first successful 50cc racer, with a five-speed gearbox and an output of 9bhp, won a three-hour race at Castellon. Derbi's first major victory was achieved by Australian Barry Smith at the 1966 Austrian Grand Prix. The East German Grand Prix of 1969 saw Nieto, on a Derbi machine, score his first World Championship victory. When Derbi retired from World Championship racing at the end of 1972, Nieto signed for the Italian Morbidelli concern, though he continued to race Derbis in Spanish National Championship meetings.

DEUBEL, Max

This talented German was the second man to win the World Sidecar Championship four times (Eric Oliver being the first) and the only rider to win it four times in succesion – 1961 to 1964. In 1962 he achieved the first sidecar lap on the Isle of Man at over 90 mph. He retired in 1966.

DIRT TRACK RACING

Dirt Track Racing is an important and popular branch of motor-cycle sport in the United States. Races take place on mile ovals with lap speeds averaging 90 mph and more than 120 mph by no means uncommon down the straights. Broadsiding (a feature of the events) the British big twins and Harley-Davidson V-twins, which are the most popular machines in this kind of competition, requires a great deal of skill and courage since the track surfaces, though not tarmac, are often "baked" almost as hard because of the long American summers. The AMA Championship includes a number of these dirt track events, which are also called TTs, in the USA.

In Britain Dirt Track Racing is the old name for Speedway.

DITCHBURN, Barry
Son of successful grass-track rider Harry Ditchburn, son Barry rode Ilford dealer Ted Broad's Yamahas for four seasons from 1970 and had his most successful season in 1974. In the Race of Aces in August he set the first-ever 100 mph lap at the Snetterton circuit, was third in the John Player Grand Prix at Silverstone, figured in the Transatlantic road races and was declared BP Superman of the Year. He also triumphed in the Thruxton 500 miler in company with Kork Ballington. Later, Ditchburn gained prominence as a member of the British Kawasaki team, but his works contract was not renewed for 1978 and he switched to riding Yamaha machinery.

DIXON, Freddie W.
Freddie Dixon was a motor cycle racing ace of the 1920s and a member of the band of riders who competed both before and after the First World War. He is most particularly noted for being the only rider to win both a solo and sidecar TT. His sidecar win was in 1923 with a Douglas outfit. His solo victory was astride an HRD in the Junior TT of 1927. Dixon (born Stockton-on-Tees 1892) took part in local hill climbs when seventeen and entered his first TT in 1912 on a local machine called a Cleveland. After the war he rode Indian machines until 1923, his best performance being second in the Senior of 1921. When the sidecar TT was introduced in 1923 Dixon was delighted, having already built himself a successful hill-climb outfit. He won that first sidecar TT from Graham Walker at 53.15 mph. In the sidecar TT of 1924 Dixon set the fastest lap at 53.24 mph, but had to retire. In 1925 he again produced the fastest lap at 57.18 mph before being forced to retire. Following a disagreement with Douglas he switched to solo riding in 1927, winning the Junior TT and finishing sixth in the Senior, both on HRD. He retired from motor cycle racing in 1929 and died in 1957.

DKW
This famous German factory has always been known for the production of two-stroke machines and introduced its first racer, a 175cc water-cooled model, in 1926 from a factory at Zschopau. Until then they had concentrated on racing machines which were really tuned production engines in special frames. By the 1930s, heavily financed by the German Government, they were challenging strongly in the 250cc and 350cc classes. By 1936 DKW were beginning to make an impact on the Isle of Man and that year, in the lightweight class, A. Geiss was third and Stanley Woods made the fastest lap at 76.20 mph. The following year a DKW machine was again third in the lightweight TT, a prelude to Ewald Kluge's success in 1938 when he won the class and also set up the fastest lap. Kluge was more than ten minutes faster than the next rider, S. Wood on an Excelsior, and improved the existing lap record by almost 3 mph – 57 sec. Kluge's 250 was a water-cooled two-stroke with three pistons, a rotary valve and just one sparking plug. It was an extremely fast, if incredibly noisy, machine.

After the war DKW (standing for Dampf Kraft Wager) machines were made in West Germany and in the 350cc class their three-cylinder two-strokes, which had been introduced in 1952 and were on the Isle of Man in 1953, were extremely competitive to the reigning Guzzi factory by 1955. This model was air-cooled and had the engine set across the frame. It had been designed deliberately as a lightweight with weight-saving a major priority. It was a machine noted particularly for its exceptional rate of acceleration. This machine produced 42bhp and although it made little impact in the TT, it was far more successful on the continent. In 1955 A. Hobl rode a DKW into third place in the 350cc World Championship and was second in the same class the following year.

DONINGTON PARK
Famous pre-war, Donington is remem-

bered as the first of the modern type of road racing circuits built on private lands. The first meeting took place at Easter 1931 and the last, an international event, in August 1939. During the war and for some time afterwards, Donington was under the control of the army. Later a number of attempts were made to reintroduce racing at the circuit and in 1966 Motor Circuit Developments showed considerable interest, but plans were later shelved.

Situated in Leicestershire, some 10 miles from Derby and just off the M1, Donington Park was bought by Tom Wheatcroft in the early 1970s with the object of converting it once more into a racing circuit. Opposition however came from the Leicestershire County Council, on the grounds of air safety (since the circuit adjoins the main runway of the East Midlands Airport) and from other bodies including the Castle Donington Parish Council and local preservation societies. To help the fight for the re-establishment of the circuit, a Donington Park Racing Association was formed as an action group and a public enquiry was arranged for early in 1974.

Big crowds attended motor cycle racing events at Donington. There were 20,000 spectators at the first meeting and 35,000 at the 1934 meeting there. The original loose surface of 1931 was converted into tarmac in 1932 and the circuit slightly extended for 1934. A long distance Grand Prix was held in 1935.

The 3.2-mile circuit was used for the first time in 1938 when Maurice Cann on a 500cc Norton set up a lap record of 72.21 mph. Also riding a Norton, Harold Daniel improved on this at a special lap-record attempt at a Dunlop Jubilee meeting. His speed was 77.48 mph. At the final meeting at Donington, held a few days before the outbreak of war, Freddie Frith won the 350 and 500cc events. Lap record: Harold Daniel (Norton) 77.48 mph in August 1938.

Tom Wheatcroft was finally successful in overcoming objections to the re-establishment of the circuit for racing and the first international meeting at the new circuit took place in July 1978, watched by a record crowd of 30,000. It has since become a major circuit.

DOUGLAS

Started in the early 1900s from Bristol, the Douglas company's first products were horizontally-opposed engines of 350cc capacity intended to be fitted into cycle frames, but they quickly moved into the production of genuine motor cycles. With a market for Douglas bikes established, the firm at once turned to racing, their first successes being achieved prior to World War 1 when, in 1911, a Douglas took the Lands End to John O'Groats record in 39hr 40min. In 1912 they were first and second in the Junior TT and won the 350cc class of the Spanish TT. In 1913 Douglas machines were first, second and third in the Spanish TT, fourth in the 350cc class of the French Grand Prix and on the Isle of Man were second in the Junior TT.

Douglas racing machines were powered by engines with mechanically operated side valves, magneto ignition, two-speed gearboxes and final drive to belt. Just before the outbreak of war they experimented with a complex arrangement of double primary chains and two gear controls, giving four speeds from a two-speed gearbox. Their racing successes, however, had virtually vanished by 1914.

In 1920 Douglas introduced a new ohv racing engine, but at the TT races that year it proved unreliable. In spite of modifications, results were again disappointing on the Isle of Man in 1921, but in the French Grand Prix, second and third places were gained in the 350cc class. In 1922 Cyril Pullin rode a 500cc Douglas over a half-mile course at an electrically-timed 100.06 mph – the first time a 500cc motor cycle had exceeded 100 mph in Britain. There was a seventh place that same year in the Senior TT.

Significant development work took place between seasons and produced new, more graceful machines which were to become famous as being among the most handsome racing motor cycles ever built up to that time. Their performance matched their looks and in 1923 Douglas won the Senior TT at 55.55 mph (Tom Sheard) while Jim Whalley made the fastest lap at 59.74 mph. Seven other Douglas machines finished, in 6th, 8th 10th, 13th, 15th, 23rd and 24th positions. Douglas machines also finished third and fifth in the Junior TT and there were numerous other successes at Brooklands and on the Continent.

In 1924, Dixon took third place on a solo Douglas in the Senior TT and in 1925 Len Parker won the sidecar TT, the last to be held before its abandonment for more than 22 competitive years.

Douglas is remembered as one of the early companies to use road racing seriously as a means of research.

With the introduction of dirt-track racing (later to become speedway) into England in 1927, most manufacturers were quick to adapt sports and racing models to the needs of this fast-growing sport and Douglas did this with considerable success. For a number of years they were the biggest name and were famous in this sport almost all over the world.

Douglas last competed officially in the TT races in 1932, though privately-entered Douglas machines for several years thereafter continued to race at Brooklands, Donington and various sand-racing venues. After the war several Douglas machines were raced in the Clubman's TT, but gained little success.

DRAG RACING

(*See also* SPRINTING)

The origins of drag racing go back to 1923 on the promenade at Brighton when two riders set off together in a half mile race. Such races were labelled 'drags' – a sport which later was to become very popular in America where special strips were set up for the sport. Drag racing in Britain really began in 1964 when American stars came over for the first Drag Festival. Another major boost for the sport was the opening of the Santa Pod Raceway in Bedfordshire, a special drag strip, in 1966. More recently a drag racing course was set up at Crosland Moor, in Yorkshire, and the sport has also taken place at Silverstone and Snetterton. America's Tom "TC" Christenson is recognised as the world's greatest drag racer and in 1974 achieved the first eight-second run for the standing quarter mile in England at Silverstone. After a qualifying 9.56 seconds run he clocked 8.45 seconds with a terminal speed of 169 mph on his 1500cc double-engined Norton 'Hogslayer'.

Drag race meetings in England are held by the National Drag Racing Club and the British Drag Racing and Hot Rod Association. Drag racing is a more commercial form of sprinting and, unlike sprinting, is based on riders racing against each other and not just against the clock. Unlike FIM-controlled sprint records, which are the average of two timed runs, one in each direction and within a certain time limit, drag racing speeds are established one way only and after only one run.

DRESDA

This specialist machine, Triumph powered, is produced by Dresda Autos Ltd of London and in racing was made famous in the 1960s by British short circuit road racer Dave Degens, who owns the firm.

DUCATI

This famous racing factory from Italy won its début race, the 125cc Swedish Grand Prix, in 1956. Their successful single cylinder machine, the product of designer Ing Taglioni, was the first in the history of motor cycle racing to have an engine with desmodromic (positively-operated cams used to close the valves as well as open them) valves. In 1958 Ducati works riders won three of the season's major 125cc international events and in the Italian Grand Prix of that year took the first five places to dispose of a powerful challenge from their Italian rivals, MV. In 1959 the factory won the 125cc Ulster Grand Prix to give Mike Hailwood his first Grand Prix victory. Larger 250cc twins, one of which was for Hailwood, and a 350cc machine were introduced, but the factory retired from racing shortly afterwards.

Results:

A. Gandossi was second in the 125cc World Championship of 1958. M. Hailwood was third in the 125cc World Championship of 1959. Ducati machines were ridden by winners of the 250cc production TTs of 1969 and 1970.

DUHAMEL, Yvon

This French-Canadian rider, born in 1941, made his reputation on the American circuits. Though only 5ft 1in tall he quickly gained a following for his courageous and forceful riding. He is known as the wild man of American road racing and also as 'superfrog' because of his ability on a race machine and his French-Canadian descent. Winner of the 250cc race at Daytona in 1968 and 1969 on Yamaha, he made his British début in the 1970 Race of the Year, finishing tenth on a 350cc Yamaha. He won the

Talladega 200, America's fastest road race, in 1971 (108.46 mph) and 1972 (110.441 mph), riding a Kawasaki. In 1973 he was the joint highest scorer (with England's Peter Williams) in the Anglo-American Match Race series and in 1974 captained the 'American' team.

Duhamel comes from Quebec and began racing on the half-mile dirt tracks over North America, coupling this with winter racing on ice. For a number of years he was the winner of major championships in both sports. He visited Daytona for the first time in 1966 with a 500cc BSA, but made no impact until 1968 when he finished eighth.

He signed a contract with Kawasaki in 1971, at which point he began to concentrate seriously on road racing. He has competed increasingly in Europe in anticipation of Kawasaki bringing out a really competitive 500cc racer, on which he would then hope to make an all-out assault on the World Championship, but the opportunity did not arrive before the French-Canadian was past his peak as an international racer.

DUKE, Geoffrey E.

An outstanding champion, Geoff Duke's smooth, impeccable style brought him four world titles when with Norton and three more after switching to the Italian Gilera. He is generally accepted as the first of the modern-style racers and is given credit for the introduction of one-piece leathers. His interest in motor cycles developed from his first machine (of which he shared ownership with a friend), bought when he was only thirteen. At sixteen he owned an ancient 175cc Dot. Two years later he went into the army and eventually became a despatch rider, being chosen later for the army's team. After demobilisation in 1947 he bought a 350cc BSA and went to work for the firm as a tuner for their trials machines. His competition career began as a member of the BSA trials team and after his obvious skills had been noticed by the Irish rider Artie Bell, Duke switched to a job at Norton. His road racing début, at the comparatively late age of 26, in 1948, was on a 350cc Norton in the Manx Grand Prix. He was out in front before a split oil tank forced his retirement.

His ambitions were now solidly directed towards road racing and 1949 was a significant year. He won the Senior Clubman's race on the Isle of Man at a record 82.97 mph, won the Senior Manx GP and finished second in the Junior event. Norton were convinced of his potential and he joined the works team, winning almost all the races he entered that year. In his first TT, in 1950, he won the Senior at a record speed of 92.27 mph, with a record lap of 93.33 mph, and was second in the Junior. In 1951 he did even better, capturing both the Senior and Junior TTs, establishing the fastest lap in each class, and won almost every classic event, taking the world title in both the 500cc and 350cc classes. He was the first rider to hold both titles in one year and for his contribution to motor cycle racing, received the OBE, the second rider to be so honoured (the first was Freddie Frith in 1950). In 1952 Duke again took the 350cc World Championship and also the Junior TT.

During this period Duke was finding his single cylinder Nortons increasingly outpaced by the extremely fast multis from Italy like the Gilera. Reluctant to change to foreign machinery, and as an outlet for his frustrations, he switched to car racing in 1953 and drove an Aston Martin DB 2, though with little success. He was tempted back to bike racing with an offer of a works contract from Gilera, thus beginning the second part of this outstanding racer's career.

He captured the 500cc World Championship for Gilera in 1953, repeating his success in 1954 and again in 1955. He was second in the Senior TT of 1954 and won the event in 1955. Although there was still much racing left in Duke, circumstances dictated that we had seen the best of his talents. There was disappointment for his fans in 1956 when, following his support for riders in a dispute over starting money at the Dutch TT, he found himself suspended by the FIM and therefore missed a number of classic rounds. A formidable threat to Duke's superiority was also looming large in the form of John Surtees, much more potent opposition since switching to MV. The two giants clashed only once in 1956, Surtees finishing best after Duke broke down. In the Ulster that year Duke crashed in the wet and was not able to score his first championship points until the final round, the Italian Grand Prix at Monza, which he won. The following year (1957) a crash at Imola kept him out of four of the six Classic events. Then came the shock withdrawal from racing of Gilera, Guzzi and Mondial, the dominant forces in world championship racing.

Perforce, the greatest racing days of Geoffrey Duke were over, for while the sport struggled painfully to recover from the Italian withdrawal, the number of available works contracts had diminished; but Duke continued to ride. He rode a BMW in 1958; then switched back to a Norton for 1959. In 1960 he tried car racing again, but following a crash in Sweden in September 1961, he announced his retirement from racing.

Geoff Duke's brilliant riding brought him a total of six motor cycle World Championships, five TTs and numerous International Grands Prix. He was supremely stylish and rode with consumate ease. His smooth, unobtrusive style belied his absolute mastery and it was his extreme skill, plus the roadholding of the 'featherbed' Norton, which enabled him to win two of his 500cc World titles against the powerful multicylinder Gileras. He also had an intuitive 'feel' for machines and Duke's suggestions and advice to both Norton and Gilera, made important contributions to the business of machine modifications and adaptations.

Geoffrey Duke came back into the news in 1963 with his enterprising attempt to break the monopoly of MV in the 500cc World Championship. With virtually no opposition, MV had collected the title almost unchallenged for five years. In an effort to break the run and to inject more interest in the championships, Duke formed *Scuderia Duke*, persuaded Gilera to loan him the outstandingly successful 1957 Gileras, and with Derek Minter and John Hartle (and later Phil Read) signed as riders, he attempted to take the world crown from MV. But he was unsuccessful. He was also in the news in 1966 when his name was linked with plans for the building of a Velocette-BRM World Championship machine financed by funds from the Manx lottery but, unfortunately, it did not materialise.

World Championship wins:
1951: 350cc (Norton) and 500cc (Norton).
1952: 350cc (Norton)
1953: 500cc (Gilera
1954: 500cc (Gilera)
1955: 500cc (Gilera)

TT wins:
1950: Senior (Norton)
1951: Senior (Norton) and Junior (Norton)
1952: Junior (Norton)
1955: Senior (Gilera)

DUNDROD

This well known circuit in Northern Ireland, situated near Belfast and in existence since 1925, became the home of the Ulster Grand Prix in 1953 after the demise of the Clady circuit the previous year. It has plenty of bends and some gradients and one particularly acute right-hand hairpin. Ridden clockwise, the circuit is 7.4 miles long and although it has been criticised by a number of riders, remains Ulster's leading road racing circuit. After the start/finish the course develops through Rushyhill, Leathemstown Corner, Leathemstown Bridge, Irelands' Corner, Budore, Jordans Cross, Wheelers Corner and Hairpin.

In 1971 the Grand Prix House, built in 1965 by voluntary labour with £2500 worth of materials donated by Gallahers, who have been closely associated with the Ulster circuit, was wrecked as a result of a bomb explosion.

DUNSTALL DOMIRACER

The Dunstall Domiracer is a development of a British-built Norton machine created by the Paul Dunstall organisation of London. Norton's original Domiracer, derived from their road-going Dominator, had its début on the Isle of Man in 1961 and, ridden by Australia's Tom Phillis, secured third place in the Senior class, establishing the first-ever 100 mph lap by a pushrod engine.

DUTCH TT

The first Dutch TT to be run under that title was in 1955 on the $4\frac{3}{4}$-mile Drenthe circuit at Assen in the north east corner of Holland, though its predecessor, the Assen Tourist Trophy, had been staged on a longer 10.27 mile circuit since 1927. The present circuit, which twists and bends, is a severe test of a rider's skill and is one of the most popular of Grand Prix circuits. The Dutch TT, which always takes place on a Saturday in June and is the Grand Prix event to follow the Isle of Man TT, every year attracts a vast crowd in excess of 100,000 and the whole atmosphere is exciting and spectacular. It is a carnival occasion with thousands of spectators arriving in the small town on Friday evening, filling cafes and bars and restaurants. It is generally considered to be Holland's most important sporting occasion.

The first post-war meeting on the former longer Drenthe circuit was held in September 1946 and was restricted that year to Dutch riders. There was a crowd of 80,000. The 500cc event was won by Piet Knijnenburg on a BMW. The following year the Dutch TT was again a full scale classic and took place on its traditional date in June. The Germans were unable to take part because of the FIM ban which lasted until their readmission in 1951, and the 1947 race was a fight between Britain and Italy with Artie Bell (Norton) winning the 500cc event at 84.53. Bell repeated his success the following year in a race which saw the end of the British domination for, a Geoff Duke victory in 1951 apart, Italian Gilera and MV machines took the 500cc Dutch TT every year from 1949 to 1965. By 1951 so popular had the event become that a crowd estimated to be more than 150,000 saw Velocette's monopoly of the 350cc event broken by Bill Doran on an AJS.

The first 100 mph lap was achieved in 1952, though way back in 1939 only bad weather prevented Dorino Serafini on a supercharged Gilera from gaining this distinction. In 1952 it finally came the way of Umberto Masetti on a Gilera. A record lap of 105.42 mph in 1954 was destined to stand for all time to the credit of Geoff Duke and Gilera, for it was the last time the old course was used. The new course, which retained the last bend, start-finish straight and S-bend, but incorporated an exciting series of twists and bends in place of the former long straights, came into use in 1955. John Surtees' four consecutive wins riding an MV in the 500cc event from 1956-59 established a record. A 125cc event was introduced in 1948, a sidecar event in 1955, and a 50cc event in 1962. For fourteen years the remarkable BMW won the sidecar event.

In the 1974 Dutch TT new lap records were established in five of the six classes: 125cc – Nieto (Derbi) 89.01 mph; 250cc – Roberts (Yamaha) 92.70 mph; 350cc – Agostini (Yamaha) 94.22 mph; 500cc – Agostini (Yamaha) 95.80 mph; sidecars – Enders/Engelhardt (Busch BMW) 85.61 mph. Agostini also created a new race record in the 500cc event at 93.91 mph.

Results:

1947: 350cc P. Goodman (Velocette); 500cc A. Bell (Norton).

1948: 125cc D. Renooy (Eysink); 350cc K. Bills (Velocette). 500cc A. Bell (Norton).

1949: 125cc N. Pagani (Mondial); 350cc F. Frith (Velocette); 500cc N. Pagani (Gilera).

1950: 125cc B. Ruffo (Mondial); 350cc A. Foster (Velocette); 500cc U. Masetti (Gilera).

1951: 125cc G. Leoni (Mondial); 350cc W. Doran (AJS); 500cc G. Duke (Norton).

1952: 125cc C. Sandford (MV); 250cc E. Lorenzetti (Guzzi); 350cc G. Duke (Norton); 500cc U. Masetti (Gilera).

1953: 125cc W. Haas (NSU); 250cc W. Haas (NSU); 350cc E. Lorenzetti (Guzzi); 500cc G. Duke (Gilera).

1954: 125cc R. Hollaus (NSU); 250cc W. Haas (NSU); 350cc F. Anderson (Guzzi); 500cc G. Duke (Gilera).

1955: 125cc C. Ubbiali (MV); 250cc L. Taveri (MV); 350cc K. Kavanagh (Guzzi); 500cc G. Duke (Gilera); sidecar K. Faust (BMW).

1956: 125cc C. Ubbiali (MV); 250cc C. Ubbiali (MV); 350cc W. Lomas (Guzzi); 500cc J. Surtees (MV); sidecar F. Hillebrand (BMW).

1957: 125cc T. Provini (Mondial); 250cc T. Provini (Mondial); 350cc K. Campbell (Guzzi); 500cc J. Surtees (MV); sidecar F. Hillebrand (BMW).

1958: 125cc C. Ubbiali (MV); 250cc T. Provini (MV); 350cc J. Surtees (MV); 500cc J. Surtees (MV). sidecar F. Camathias (BMW).

1959: 125cc C. Ubbiali (MV); 250cc T. Provini (MV); 350cc R. Brown (Norton); 500cc J. Surtees (MV); sidecar F. Camathias (BMW).

1960: 125cc C. Ubbiali (MV); 250cc C. Ubbiali (MV); 350cc J. Surtees (MV); 500cc R. Venturi (MV); sidecar P. V. Harris (BMW).

1961: 125cc T. Phillis (Honda); 250cc M. Hailwood (Honda); 350cc G. Hocking (MV); 500cc G. Hocking (MV); sidecar M. Deubel (BMW).

1962: 50cc E. Degner (Suzuki); 125cc L. Taveri (Honda); 250cc J. Redman

(Honda); 350cc J. Redman (Honda); 500cc M. Hailwood (MV); sidecar F. Scheidegger (BMW).

1963: 50cc E. Degner (Suzuki); 125cc H. Anderson (Suzuki); 250cc J. Redman (Honda); 350cc J. Redman (Honda); 500cc J. Hartle (Gilera); sidecar M; Deubel (BMW).

1964: 50cc R. Bryans (Honda); 125cc J. Redman (Honda); 250cc J. Redman (Honda); 350cc J. Redman (Honda); 500cc M. Hailwood (MV); sidecar C. Seeley (BMW).

1965: 50cc R. Bryans (Honda); 125cc M. Duff (Yamaha); 250cc J. Redman (Honda); 350cc J. Redman (Honda); 500cc M. Hailwood (MV); sidecar F. Scheidegger (BMW).

1966: 50cc L. Taveri (Honda); 125cc W. Ivy (Yamaha); 250cc M. Hailwood (Honda); 350cc M. Hailwood (Honda); 500cc J. Redman (Honda); sidecar F. Scheidegger (BMW).

1967: 50cc Y. Katayama (Suzuki); 125cc P. Read (Yamaha); 250cc M. Hailwood (Honda); 350cc M. Hailwood (Honda); 500cc M. Hailwood (Honda); sidecar K. Enders (BMW).

1968: 50cc P. Lodewijkx (Jamathi); 125cc P. Read (Yamaha); 250cc W. Ivy (Yamaha); 350cc G. Agostini (MV); 500cc G. Agostini (MV); sidecar J. Attenberger (BMW).

1969: 50cc B. Smith (Derbi); 125cc D Simmonds (Kawasaki); 250cc R. Pasolini (Benelli); 350cc G. Agostini (MV); 500cc G. Agostini (MV); sidecar H. Fath (Urs).

1970: 50cc A. Nieto (Derbi); 125cc D. Braun (Suzuki); 250cc R. Gould (Yamaha); 350cc G. Agostini (MV); 500cc G. Agostini (MV); sidecar G. Auerbacher/H. Hahn (BMW).

1971: 50cc A. Nieto (Derbi); 125cc A. Nieto (Derbi); 250cc P. Read (Yamaha); 350cc G. Agostini (MV); 500cc G. Agostini (MV); sidecar H. Owesle/Kremer/Rutterford (Munch/Fath/Urs).

1972: 50cc A. Nieto (Derbi); 125cc A. Nieto (Derbi); 250cc R. Gould (Yamaha); 350cc G. Agostini (MV); 500cc G. Agostini (MV); sidecar K. Enders/R. Engelhardt (BMW).

1973: 50cc B. Kneubühler (Van Veen Kreidler); 125cc E. Lazzarini (Privioccetti); 250cc D. Braun (Yamaha); 350cc G. Agostini (MV); 500cc P. Read (MV); sidecar K. Enders/R. Engelhardt (BMW).

1974: 50cc H. Rittberger (Kreidler); 125cc B. Kneubühler (Yamaha); 250cc W. Villa (Harley-Davidson); 350cc G. Agostini (Yamaha); 500cc G. Agostini (Yamaha); sidecar K. Enders/R. Engelhardt (Busch BMW).

1975: 50cc A. Nieto (Kreidler); 125cc P. Pileri (Morbidelli); 250cc W. Villa (Harley-Davidson); 350cc D. Braun (Yamaha); 500cc B. Sheene (Suzuki); sidecar W. Schwarzel/A. Huber (Konig).

1976: 50cc A. Nieto (Bultaco); 125cc P. Bianchi (Morbidelli); 250cc W. Villa (Harley-Davidson); 350cc G. Agostini (MV); 500cc B. Sheene (Suzuki); sidecar H. Schmid/J. Martial (Yamaha).

1977: 50cc A. Nieto (Bultaco); 125cc A. Nieto (Bultaco); 250cc M. Grant (Kawasaki); 350cc K. Ballington (Yamaha); 500cc W. Hartog (Suzuki); sidecar R. Biland/K. Williams (Schmid-Yamaha).

1978: 50cc E. Lazzarini (Kreidler); 125cc E. Lazzarini (MBA); 250cc K. Roberts (Yamaha); 350cc K. Ballington (Kawasaki); 500cc J. Cecotto (Yamaha); sidecar W. Schwarzel/A. Huber (Fath).

1979: 50cc E. Lazzarini (Kreidler); 125cc A. Nieto (Bultaco); 250cc G. Rossi (Morbidelli); 350cc G. Hansford (Kawasaki); 500cc V. Ferrari (Suzuki); sidecar R. Biland/W. Waltisperg (Yamaha).

1980: 50cc R. Tormo (Kreidler); 125cc A. Nieto (Minarelli); 250cc C. Lavado (Yamaha); 350cc J. Ekerold (Yamaha); 500cc J. Middleburg (Yamaha); sidecar J. Taylor/B. Johansson (Yamaha).

1981: 50cc R. Tormo (Bultaco); 125cc A. Nieto (Minarelli); 250cc A. Mang (Kawasaki); 350cc A. Mang (Kawasaki); 500cc M. Lucchinelli (Suzuki); sidecar A. Michel/M. Burkhard (Yamaha).

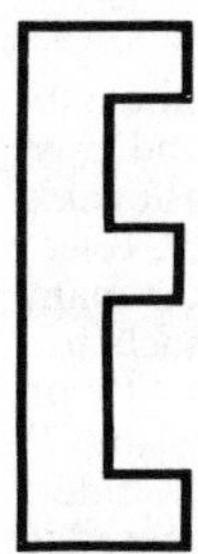

EAST GERMAN GRAND PRIX

With the partition of Germany following the end of the Second World War the pre-war German Grand Prix was abandoned and eventually replaced by the West German Grand Prix (see separate entry) and the East German Grand Prix. The East German Grand Prix was awarded World Championship status for the first time in 1961.

Results:

1958: 125cc E. Degner (MZ); 250cc H. Fügner (MZ); 350cc L. Taveri (Norton); 500cc R. H. Dale (BMW); sidecar W. Schneider (BMW).
1959: 350cc J. G. Hempleman (Norton).
1960: 125cc E. Degner (MZ); 250cc J. G. Hempleman (MZ); 350cc J. A. Redman (Norton); 500cc J. G. Hempleman (Norton); sidecar F. Camathias (BMW).
1961: 125cc E. Degner (MZ); 250cc S. M. B. Hailwood (Honda); 350cc G. Hocking (MV); 500cc G. Hocking (MV).
1962 50cc J. Huberts (Kreidler); 125cc L. Taveri (Honda); 250cc J. A. Redman (Honda); 350cc J. A. Redman (Honda); 500cc S. M. B. Hailwood (MV).
1963: 125cc H. R. Anderson (Suzuki); 250cc S. M. B. Hailwood (MV); 350cc S. M. B. Hailwood (MV); 500cc S. M. B. Hailwood (MV).
1964: 125cc H. R. Anderson (Suzuki); 250cc P. W. Read (Yamaha); 350cc J. A. Redman (Honda); 500cc S. M. B. Hailwood (MV).
1965: 125cc F. G. Perris (Suzuki); 250cc J. A. Redman (Honda); 350cc J. A. Redman (Honda); 500cc S. M. B. Hailwood (MV).
1966: 125cc L. Taveri (Honda); 250cc S. M. B. Hailwood (Honda); 350cc G. Agostini (MV); 500cc F. Stastny (440 Jawa-CZ).
1967: 125cc W. D. Ivy (Yamaha); 250cc P. W. Read (Yamaha); 350cc S. M. B. Hailwood (Honda); 500cc G. Agostini (MV).
1968: 125cc P. W. Read (Yamaha); 250cc W. D. Ivy (Yamaha); 350cc G. Agostini (MV); 500cc G. Agostini (MV).
1969: 50cc A. Nieto (Derbi); 125cc D. A. Simmonds (Kawasaki); 250cc R. Pasolini (Benelli); 350cc G. Agostini (MV); 500cc G. Agostini (MV).
1970: 50cc A. Toersen (Jamathi); 125cc A. Nieto (Derbi); 250cc R. Gould (Yamaha); 350cc G. Agostini (MV); 500cc G. Agostini (MV).
1971: 50cc A. Nieto (Derbi); 125cc A. Nieto (Derbi); 250cc D. Braun (Yamaha); 350cc G. Agostini (MV); 500cc G. Agostini (MV).
1972: 50cc T. Thimmer (Jamathi); 125cc B. Jansson (Maico); 250cc J. Saarinen (Yamaha); 350cc P. W. Read (MV); 500cc G. Agostini (MV).

For economic reasons the East German authorities did not apply to be included in the World Championships after 1972.

EHRLICH, Dr Joseph

Dr Joe Ehrlich is an engine designer and well known as the builder of the 125cc EMC road race challenge to the Japanese in the early 1960s. In 1962 at Silverstone, **Derek Minter, Mike Hailwood and Rex** Avery finished first, second and third on EMC machines in the Hutchinson 100. Ehrlich designed his first two-stroke engine in 1934 in Austria and came to Britain in 1937 to work with Harland and Wolf. He had experience with DKW and also with the East German MZ factory. In 1948 he produced a 350 split single which was raced by Les Archer and the following year produced a twin piston 125. With Minter, Hailwood and Avery, Ehrlich achieved notable success, and provided a serious threat to the Japanese Honda concern. In 1962 Ehrlich's EMCs held almost every 125cc lap record in this country. In 1965 Ehrlich, as an individual, was unable to compete with the amount of money the Japanese were devoting to the development of their machines and he retired from racing, though he returned two years later with a 125cc twin. He was involved in the late 1960s in an exciting proposal to build a

British world beater, an ambition which was never fulfilled, and in 1974 he once more made the headlines with plans for the building of his own 650cc three-cylinder two-stroke engine.

ENDERS, Klaus

Klaus Enders was born in 1937 and has been synonymous with world championship sidecar racing throughout the whole of his career. Enders, from West Germany, first won the sidecar World Championship in 1967 on a BMW outfit. He was successful again in 1969 and in 1970, 1972, 1973 and 1974. His first appearance in TT results is in 1967 when he was second with the BMW in the 500cc sidecar event. He won the 500cc sidecar TT in 1969 establishing the fastest lap at 92.54 mph. He repeated his success in 1970 again registering the fastest lap at 93.79 mph. He set an absolute race lap record of 24 minutes – 94.32 mph – in 1968. His success in the TTs has alternated with mechanical failures. In 1969 he led the 500cc sidecar TT all the way to win, producing the fastest lap at 92.54 mph. At 37, in 1974, it was reported that Enders retired from racing following what was described as a long disagreement with his sponsor Gerhardt Heukerot and with Dieter Busch, who built his outfits and prepared the special BMW engines he used. Enders' six world titles is the best performance recorded in the sidecar class.

World Championship wins:
Sidecar class in 1967, 1969, 1970, 1972, 1973 (all BMW) and 1974 (Busch BMW).

TT wins:
1969: sidecar 500 (BMW).
1970: sidecar 500 (BMW).

ESO

This racing machine, which became popular and successful in speedway and grass track events, came from Czechoslovakia and was later taken over by Jawa. It was the great Barry Briggs who, after many years' devotion to JAP machines, switched to Eso and won his first title on that machine in 1966. By 1968 possibly 75 per cent of the world's speedway riders were using Eso machinery. It appeared to combine successfully exceptional power, outstanding durability and great reliability.

EXCELSIOR

An early British machine famous, and remembered, for its success in the TTs of 1929 and '33, both in the lightweight event. Inspired by the successful Rudge machine of the day, the winning Excelsior of 1933 was an experimental four-valve two-carburettor machine with the valves radially disposed. Ridden by Sid Gleave the machine secured a surprise victory (for it had gone virtually direct from the test bench to the Isle of Man), at a record 71.59 mph, with a fastest lap at 72.62 mph. The earlier victory of 1929 was established by S. A. Crabtree. Though Excelsior were not to repeat their Isle of Man success they were second in 1936 (H. G. Tyrell-Smith), second in 1937 (S. Woods), second (S. Woods), and third (H. G. Tyrell-Smith) in 1938 and third (Tyrell-Smith) in 1939. With the resumption of the TTs in 1947 Excelsior were to achieve just two more placings in the results: third in 1947 (B. Drinkwater) and 1948 (D. St. J. Beasley).

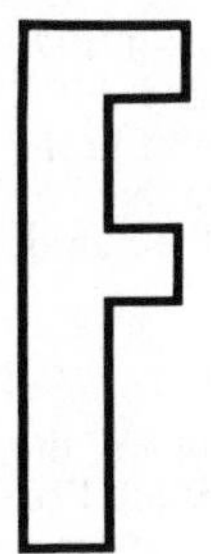

FATH, Helmut
An outstanding name in world sidecar racing, Helmut Fath's notable career divides quite separately into two parts: the years before his serious racing accident in 1961, when he rode BMW machinery, and his come-back years when he piloted his own Urs outfit. Remarkably, in both parts he became World Champion. Born in 1929, this talented West German rider first appears in the world ratings in 1958 when he was third in the Championships on the BMW. Two years later he reached his peak when he became the World Champion of 1960 and also took the sidecar TT at a race average of 84.1 mph, establishing the fastest lap at 85.79 mph. He looked poised to consolidate his international reputation when a serious accident at the Nurburgring in 1961 put him out of racing.

He did not return until 1967, but then with a new machine, the Urs. He had planned his come-back as early as 1963 but was unable to persuade BMW to provide him with parts for a BMW outfit. Undeterred, and with the help of colleagues in West Germany, he started to design a new machine and the Urs was the result. Designed, built and developed by Fath and his supporters, it was a double overhead camshaft unit with fuel injection, a four-cylinder home-built machine which, after a number of disappointments with retirements at a number of circuits in the early part of 1967, brought him the World Title (gained at the expense of BMW) in 1968. He almost repeated his success the following year, but crashed in Finland in a non-championship race. This allowed Klaus Enders to take the title by the narrow margin of five points.

World Championship wins:
Sidecar class, 1960 (BMW) and 1968 (Urs).

TT wins:
1960, sidecar (BMW).

FERNIHOUGH, Eric
An outstanding speed and sprint man of pre-war days, Eric Fernihough started his racing career in the days of Brooklands and created a sensation there in 1935 when, in his first season riding an unsupercharged Brough twin, he smashed the outer-circuit lap record at an incredible 123.58 mph, dispossessing the long-experienced Noel Pope of the record. Although he rode in the TT and in long distance trials, it was as a record breaker that 'Ferni' was to become most famous, his greatest achievement being the capturing of the official World Speed Record for Britain from Germany's Ernst Henne in 1937. He held it for but six months and was to die in an effort to win back the record for Britain.

Physically, temperamentally and intellectually, Eric Fernihough looked nothing like the 'brand image' of a speed ace. Pale, slim and bespectacled, he was outstanding as a tuner and development engineer, yet his approach to record breaking was perforce unscientific, even by the standards of his day. His enormous courage was beyond question. He disliked a lot of streamlining and made his world record attempts with various types of fairing developed, as one authority put it, 'on a suck-it-and-see basis'. Fernihough raced in the days before sponsorship and he was unable to solicit much support from an industry which appeared to be remarkably unmoved by his efforts to give Britain the prestige of the 'World's Fastest' title. So on a Brough Superior-JAP, the basis of which had been given to him by George Brough, he went ahead just the same. Without sponsorship he was unable to afford the specialist help and facilities required for a world record attempt, so he did most of the work himself, often by guesswork, generally by trial and error, and without knowing whether his machine had the basic power or the aerodynamic ability to make a sensible attempt on the record. Bonneville was out of the question, so he made the 1000-mile journey to Gyon, in Hungary, and with tremendous bravery and riding prowess, willed success out of the most unlikely situation.

His first world record bid was in 1936, and was only partially successful. He

reached 163 mph, 6 mph short of the record, but enough to give him the world's flying mile record. Encouraged, he returned to England and spent the winter of 1936–37 preparing for his second attempt and was back at Gyon in 1937. Practice runs were anything but encouraging and hasty work was necessary. Then, on the narrow and bumpy road, on April 19th, Eric Fernihough brought Britain the official World Speed Record for the first time in seven years, reaching a two-way average of 169.8 mph. His success was short lived. First Taruffi and then Henne made new records within seven months, so in 1938 Fernihough went back to Gyon to try again. At what was estimated to be a speed of about 180 mph the Brough veered off course and although 'Ferni' stayed on for some 200 yards, the crash which was to end his life came when the machine struck an intersecting track. Largely unacknowledged during his lifetime, Fernihough's memory fared better and a plaque commemorating his racing exploits was mounted in the clubhouse wall at Brooklands in 1939 and was later presented to his widow when Brooklands itself became just a memory.
World Land Speed Record Holder (169.8 mph), 1937.

FIM
This is the abbreviation for the Fédération Interationale Motorcycliste, the world governing body for motor cycle sport. The organisation came into being in 1904 under the title. Fédération Internationale des Clubs Motorcyclistes. It operates from its headquarters at 19 Chemin William-Barbey, 1292 Chambesy, Geneva, Switzerland.

FINDLAY, Jack
An Australian, Findlay came to Europe in 1958 and in 1967 was fifth in the World Championship on the McIntyre Matchless he acquired for £500 in 1963. By 1968 he had become perhaps the most successful and best private rider in Grand Prix events. In that year he was runner-up on the Matchless to Agostini in the 500cc World Championship. He has been a prolific competitor in the TTs since 1959 and has ridden a variety of machines on the Island including Norton, Matchless, AJS, Bultaco, Honda, Aermacchi, Yamaha and Suzuki. He was third in the Junior TT of 1969, riding Aermacchi, fourth in the Senior of 1970 on a Seeley, and in 1972 in the F750 event he was third on a Suzuki and in the Junior was fourth on a Yamaha. As something of a veteran he won the Senior TT in 1973 on the Suzuki.

FINNISH GRAND PRIX
The Finnish Grand Prix is run on the 3.08 miles Imatra circuit. The Grand Prix coincides with a carnival in the area which surrounds the race with a festive character. The Tampere circuit was used in 1962 and 1963.

Results:
1962: 50cc L. Taveri (Honda); 125cc J. A. Redman (Honda); 350cc T. H. Robb (Honda); 500cc A. Shepherd (Matchless).
1963: 50cc H. C. Anscheidt (Kreidler); 125cc H. R. Anderson (Suzuki); 350cc S. M. B. Hailwood (MV); 500cc S. M. B. Hailwood (MV).
1964: 50cc H. R. Anderson (Suzuki); 125cc L. Taveri (Honda); 350cc J. A. Redman (Honda); 500cc J. J. Ahearn (Norton).
1965: 125cc H. Anderson (Suzuki); 250cc M. Duff (Yamaha); 350cc G. Agostini (MV); 500cc G. Agostini (MV).
1966: 125cc P. W. Read (Yamaha); 250cc S. M. B. Hailwood (Honda); 350cc S. M. B. Hailwood (Honda); 500cc G. Agostini (MV).
1967: 125cc S. Graham (Suzuki); 250cc S. M. B. Hailwood (Honda); 500cc G. Agostini (MV); sidecar J. Attenberger/J. Schillinger (BMW).
1968: 125cc P. W. Read (Yamaha); 250cc P. W. Read (Yamaha); 500cc G. Agostini (MV); sidecar H. Fath/W. Kalauch (Urs).
1969: 125cc D. A. Simmonds (Kawasaki); 250cc K. Andersson (Yamaha); 350cc G. Agostini (MV); 500cc G. Agostini (MV); sidecar K. Enders/R. Engelhardt (BMW).
1970: 125cc D. Simmonds (Kawasaki); 250cc R. Gould (Yamaha); 350cc G. Agostini (MV); 500cc G. Agostini (MV); sidecar K. Enders/R. Engelhardt/W. Kalauch (BMW).
1971: 125cc B. Sheene (Suzuki); 250cc R. A. Gould (Yamaha); 350cc G. Agostini (MV); 500cc G. Agostini (MV); sidecar H. Owesle/P. Rut-

terford (Munch).

1972: 125cc K. Andersson (Yamaha); 250cc J. Saarinen (Yamaha); 350cc G. Agostini (MV); 500cc G. Agostini (MV); sidecar C. Vincent/M. Casey (Munch Urs).

1973: 125cc O. Buscherini (Malanca); 250cc T. Lansivouri (Yamaha); 350cc G. Agostini (MV); 500cc G. Agostini (MV); sidecar K. Rahko/K. Laatikainen (Honda).

1974: 50cc J. van Zeebroek (Kreidler); 250cc W. Villa (Harley Davidson); 350cc J. Dodds (Yamaha); 500cc P. W. Read (MV).

1975: 50cc A. Nieto (Kreidler); 250cc M. Rougerie (Harley-Davidson); 350cc J. Cecotto (Yamaha); 500cc G. Agostini (Yamaha).

1976: 50cc J. van Zeebroeck (Kreidler); 125cc P. Bianchi (Morbidelli); 250cc W. Villa (Harley-Davidson); 350cc W. Villa (Harley-Davidson); 500cc P. Hennen (Suzuki).

1977: 125cc P. Bianchi (Morbidelli); 250cc W. Villa (Harley-Davidson); 350cc T. Katayama (Yamaha); 500cc J. Cecotto (Yamaha).

1978: 125cc A. Nieto (Minarelli); 250cc K. Ballington (Kawasaki); 350cc K. Ballington (Kawasaki); 500cc W. Hartog (Suzuki).

1979: 125cc R. Tormo (Bultaco); 250cc K. Ballington (Kawasaki); 350cc G. Hansford (Kawasaki); 500cc B. van Dulmen (Suzuki).

1980: 125cc A. Nieto (Minarelli); 250cc K. Ballington (Kawasaki); 500cc W. Hartog (Suzuki); sidecar J. Taylor (Yamaha).

1981: 125cc A. Nieto (Minarelli); 250cc A. Mang (Kawasaki); 500cc M. Lucchinelli (Suzuki); sidecar R. Biland/K. Waltisperg (Yamaha).

FORMULA 750

Formula 750 is a class for 750cc machines based on production engine components, and in America it was introduced as a separate category in 1969. In Britain it is of comparatively recent origin, and became established perhaps primarily as a result of closer liaison between racing in Europe and the United States. When the AMA became a fully-fledged member of the FIM in October 1970, efforts were made by the A-CU to arrange a series of races in Britain and America based on the AMA 750cc. It was clear that there was a strong demand in Europe for the FIM to raise the top world championship class from 500cc to 750cc, to bring it in line with the USA. Based on road engines, with strong manufacturers' support, the class was also welcomed in Europe where, since 1969, a number of 750cc-type races had been held. A Formula 750 TT was introduced into the Isle of Man race programme in 1971 and the A-CU made a powerful bid to have Formula 750 racing recognised and accepted by the FIM as an international class. This came to fruition in 1973 with the new FIM Formula 750 Championship. The Silverstone circuit was selected as the venue for the British round. Other rounds were arranged for Italy, United States, France, Finland and West Germany. The new formula, however, ran into a number of teething problems. There were misunderstandings and mistakes, and a number of organisers abandoned F750 events and ran 250cc-750cc open events. This happened at Imola, where the first round of the 1974 FIM series was due to be held. The race organisers abandoned the meeting's championship status and ran instead an open 250cc-750cc event.

After showing immense possibilities, the new Formula 750 class seemed caught up in a number of technicalities and problems, but the promise appeared to have returned in 1974 when the FIM announced that a Formula 1-type World Road Race Championship for Formula 750 road racers would be introduced, probably in 1976. Under newly formulated rules only 25 machines were expected to be homologated compared to 200 (under previous rules) and races would have a minimum distance of 200 miles. A Formula 750 'world' series under the auspices of the FIM was instituted in 1973, but did not acquire official status as a World Championship competition until 1977.

Results:

1973: Barry Sheene (GB) first; John Dodds (Australia) second; Jack Findlay (Australia) third.

1974: John Dodds (Australia) first; Patrick Pons (France) second; Jack Findlay (Australia) third.

1975: Jack Findlay (Australia) first; Barry Sheene (GB) second; Patrick Pons (France) third.

1976: Victor Palomo (Spain) first; Gary Nixon (USA) second; John Newbold (GB) third.

1977: Steve Baker (USA) first; Christian Sarron (France) second; Giacomo Agostini (Italy) third.

1978: Johnny Cecotto (Venezuela) first; Kenny Roberts (USA) second; Christian Sarron (France) third.

1979: Patrick Pons (France) first; Michel Fratschi (Switzerland) second; Johnny Cecotto (Venezuela) third.

Despite strong efforts to promote Formula 750 as the premier racing class, it lost its World Championship status when a working party set up by the FIM to consider the future of World Championship road racing recommended that Formula 750 should disappear after 1979.

FRENCH GRAND PRIX

France has been in the forefront of motorised racing since the earliest days and it is therefore appropriate that the adopted name for the classic races should now be universally known by the French language *Grand Prix*. If not the earliest Grand Prix to be held, the French was certainly among the first and a French Grand Prix would have been held in 1914 but for the outbreak of war. When Grand Prix racing was revived in 1920 the French GP was perhaps the first to be held though it attracted no support from Britain. In 1921 however, with the French Grand Prix run over the famous Le Mans circuit, there was a good entry from Britain and the 'continental circus' was on its way. In the early years of this famous race, different courses over normal roads were used, but in 1966 the five-mile circuit de Montagne d'Auvergne, near Clermont-Ferrand, not used since 1961 became the home of the French Grand Prix for a number of years. Other recent homes of the French Grand Prix include the 2.7 mile Bugatti circuit at Le Mans, used for the first time in 1969, and the Paul Ricard circuit, used for the first time in 1973.

Results:

1951: 250cc B. Ruffo (Guzzi); 350cc G. F. Duke (Norton); 500cc Alfredo Milani (Gilera); sidecar E. S. Oliver (Norton).

1953: 350cc F. K. Anderson (Guzzi); 500cc G. E. Duke (Gilera); sidecar E. S. Oliver (Norton).

1954: 250cc W. Haas (NSU); 350cc P. Monneret (AJS); 500cc P. Monneret (Gilera).

1955: 125cc C. Ubbiali (MV); 350cc D. Agostini (Guzzi); 500cc G. E. Duke (Gilera).

1959: 350cc J. Surtees (MV); 500cc J. Surtees (MV); sidecar F. Scheidegger (BMW).

1960: 350cc G. Hocking (MV); 500cc J. Surtees (MV); sidecar H. Fath (BMW).

1961: 125cc T. E. Phillis (Honda); 250cc T. E. Phillis (Honda); 500cc G. Hocking (MV); sidecar F. Scheidegger (BMW).

1962: 50cc J. Huberts (Kreidler); 125cc K. Takahashi (Honda); 250cc J. A. Redman (Honda); sidecar M. Deubel (BMW).

1963: 50cc H. G. Anscheidt (Kreidler); 125cc H. R. Anderson (Suzuki); 250cc not run, sidecar not run.

1964: 50cc H. R. Anderson (Suzuki); 125cc L. Taveri (Honda); 250cc P. W. Read (Yamaha); sidecar F. Scheidegger (BMW).

1965: 50cc R. Bryans (Honda); 125cc H. Anderson (Suzuki); 250cc P. Read (Yamaha); sidecar F. Camathias (BMW).

1966: 250cc S. M. B. Hailwood (Honda); 350cc S. M. B. Hailwood (Honda); sidecar F. Scheidegger (BMW).

1967: 50cc Y. Katayama (Suzuki); 125cc W. Ivy (Yamaha); 250cc W. Ivy (Yamaha); sidecar K. Enders/R. Engelhardt (BMW).

1968: Cancelled because of national strike in France.

1969: 50cc A. Toersen (Kreidler); 125cc J. Aureal (Yamaha); 250cc S. Herrero (Ossa); 500cc G. Agostini (MV); sidecar H. Fath/W. Kalauch (URS).

1970: 50cc A. Nieto (Derbi); 125cc D. Braun (Suzuki); 250cc R. Gould (Yamaha); 500cc G. Agostini (MV); sidecar K. Enders/R. Engelhardt (BMW).

1971: 50cc J. de Vries (Kreidler); 125cc B. Sheene (Suzuki); 250cc S. Grassetti (MZ); 500cc G. Agostini (MV); sidecar S. Schauzu/W. Kalauch (BMW).

1972: 125cc G. Parlotti (Morbidelli); 250cc P. Read (Yamaha); 350cc J. Saarinen (Yamaha); 500cc G. Agostini (MV); sidecar H. Luthringhauser/Cusnik (BMW).

1973: 125cc K. Andersson (Yamaha);

250cc J. Saarinen (Yamaha); 350cc G. Agostini (MV); 500cc J. Saarinen (Yamaha); sidecar K. Enders/R. Engelhardt (BMW).

1974: 50cc H. Van Kessel (Kreidler); 125cc K. Andersson (Yamaha); 350cc G. Agostini (Yamaha); 500cc P. Read (MV); sidecar S. Schauzu/W. Kalauch.

1975: 125cc K. Andersson (Yamaha); 250cc J. Cecotto (Yamaha); 350cc J. Cecotto (Yamaha); 500cc G. Agostini (Yamaha); sidecar H. Schmid/M. Matile (Konig).

1976: 50cc H. Rittberger (Kreidler); 250cc W. Villa (Harley-Davidson); 350cc W. Villa (Harley-Davidson); 500cc B. Sheene (Suzuki); sidecars R. Biland/K. Williams (Seymaz).

1977: 125cc P. Bianchi (Morbidelli); 250cc J. Ekerold (Yamaha); 350cc T. Katayama (Yamaha); 500cc B. Sheene (Suzuki); sidecar A. Michel/G. Lecorre (Yamaha).

1978: 125cc P. Bianchi (Minarelli); 250cc G. Hansford (Kawasaki); 350cc G. Hansford (Kawasaki); 500cc K. Roberts (Yamaha); sidecar R. Biland/K. Williams (Yamaha).

1979: 50cc E. Lazzarini (Kreidler); 125cc G. Bertin (Motobecane); 250cc K. Ballington (Kawasaki); 350cc P. Fernandez (Yamaha); 500cc B. Sheene (Suzuki); sidecar R. Biland/K. Waltisperg (LCR Yamaha).

1980: 125cc A. Nieto (Minarelli); 250cc K. Ballington (Kawasaki); 350cc J. Ekerold (Yamaha); 500cc K. Roberts (Yamaha); sidecar R. Biland/K. Waltisperg (Yamaha).

1981: 125cc A. Nieto (Minarelli); 250cc A. Mang (Kawasaki); 500cc M. Lucchinelli (Suzuki);sidecar R. Biland/K. Waltisperg (Yamaha).

FRIEDRICHS, Paul

Paul Friedrichs gained fame riding a CZ to become World 500cc Moto Cross Champion in 1966, 1967 and 1968. Twenty-six when he gained his first world title, Friedrichs comes from East Germany. He scored his first Grand Prix win in Czechoslovakia in 1965, finishing the season as runner-up to Jeff Smith in the World Championship of that year. He began his competitive career riding a 125cc MZ and had experience on Simson and ESO machines before joining CZ.

FRITH, Frederick L.

Freddie Frith is one of the legendary names of British motor cycle racing closely identified with the Isle of Man TT races of pre-war and immediate postwar vintage. His career began in the late 1920s when he competed in local grass track meetings near his home in Grimsby. His first attempt at the Junior Manx came in 1930 on a KTT Velocette, when he finished third. Frith made his name as a member of the Norton team riding Manx Nortons for four years prior to the outbreak of war. After the war he rode with success his own 350cc Velocette and later, before Velocette supported racing, teamed with Ken Bills to ride as a two-man Velocette team under the sponsorship of Nigel Spring.

Frith competed in his first TT in 1936 and achieved immediate success. He won the Junior event (also establishing the fastest lap at 81.94 mph) and was third in the Senior, behind Guthrie and Woods. He did even better in 1937, beating Woods to win the Senior and finishing second in the Junior. In the Senior of that year he achieved the distinction of registering the first 90-plus lap in the history of the TT – 90.27 mph.

An accident when practising on his Senior Guzzi prevented Frith from entering the 1947 races on the Island and he had mixed fortunes in 1948. He rode a Triumph in the Senior, but retired; in the Junior he was unbeatable. He repeated his Junior success in 1949 and established the fastest lap in both 1948 and 1949. He retired at the end of 1949 at 39 years of age with an outstandingly successful season, for not only did he win the Junior TT, but he became the 350cc World Champion with outright wins in Switzerland, Holland, Belgium and Northern Ireland, his final ride before retirement. With Les Graham and Eric Oliver, he shares the distinction of being a British rider to win a World Title in the first year of the Championships. After his retirement he was awarded the OBE, the first motor cycle racer to be so honoured.

World Championship wins:

1949, 350cc (Velocette).

TT wins:

1936, Junior (Norton); 1937, Senior (Norton).

1948, Junior (Velocette); 1949, Junior (Velocette).

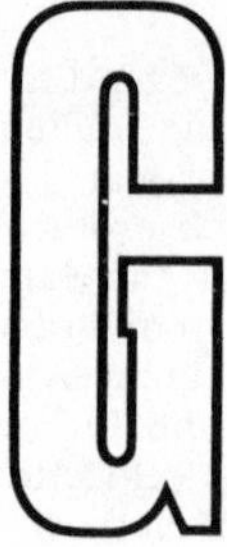

GCR
The General Council Regulations (GCR) are produced by the Auto-Cycle Union. It is to these regulations that all competition events are run.

GERMAN GRAND PRIX
One of the major continental classic events pre-second World War, the German Grand Prix was first held under that title in 1925 on a six-mile circuit on the outskirts of Berlin. The main classes were for machines in the 250cc, 350cc, 500cc, 175cc, 750cc and 1000cc categories, but the last three were regarded as being relatively unimportant and by the early 1930s these events had been taken out of the programme. Only three British riders contested that first event. More were in Germany a year later and while BMW took the first three places in the 500cc event, Jimmy Simpson (AJS) won the 350cc class and Jack Porter (New Gerrard) the 250cc class.

The status of the German Grand Prix was enhanced in 1927 when it moved to the Nurburgring and was also the European Grand Prix. By this time Britain was gaining supremacy, and in 1927 Graham Walker won the 500cc race – which lasted over 5½ hours! Jimmy Simpson (AJS) was the winner of the 350cc event and C. T. Ashby (OK-Supreme) the 250cc race. For the next four years the German Grand Prix was held at the Nurburgring and Britain dominated the event. Because of economic conditions in Germany there was no German Grand Prix in 1932, but in 1933 the event returned to the Avus circuit on the outskirts of Berlin, much changed since the earlier races there. In 1934 the races moved to Sachsenring, near Chemnitz and later the home of the East German Grand Prix. It remained there until the war. The 500cc event in 1934 was tragic. Two Belgian FN riders and a factory rider from Husqvarna were killed. In 1936 the race was the Grand Prix of Europe and 240,000 spectators saw Britain supreme in the three classes. The BMWs were back in competition in 1937, but the tragedy of the 500cc race was the fatal accident to Jimmy Guthrie. He crashed within a mile of the finish while in the lead, and died that same evening. By 1938 the Italian Gileras were beginning to make an impact and were to win the 500cc race the following year in the last pre-war German Grand Prix to be held – less than three weeks before the outbreak of war.

Results:
250cc
1925: C. T. Ashby (Zenith).
1926: J. A. Porter (New Gerrard).
1927: C. T. Ashby (OK-Supreme).
1928: S. A. Crabtree (Excelsior JAP).
1929: S. A. Crabtree (Heck JAP).
1930: L. C. Crabtree (Excelsior JAP).
1931: R. Toricelli (Puch).
1932: No race.
1933: C. Dodson (New Imperial).
1934: H. G. Tyrell Smith (Rudge).
1935: W. Winkler (DKW).
1936: H. G. Tyrell Smith (Excelsior).
1937: E. Kluge (DKW).
1938: E. Kluge (DKW).
1939: N. Pagani (Guzzi).

350cc
1925: A. Maffeis (Maffeis).
1926: J. H. Simpson (AJS).
1927: J. H. Simpson (AJS).
1928: P. Ghersi (Norton).
1929: W. Handley (Motosacoche).
1930: J. Guthrie (AJS).
1931: H. G. Tyrell Smith (Rudge).
1932: No race.
1933: A. Loof (Imperial Python).
1934: J. Simpson (Norton).
1935: W. Rusk (Norton).
1936: F. L. Frith (Norton).
1937: H. L. Daniell (Norton).
1938: J. H. White (Norton).
1939: W. Hamelehle (DKW).

500cc
1925: P. Koppen (BMW).
1926: H. Stelzer (BMW).
1927: G. Walker (Sunbeam).
1928: C. Dodson (Sunbeam).
1929: H. G. Tyrell Smith (Rudge).
1930: G. Walker (Rudge).
1931: S. Woods (Norton).
1932: No race.

1933: F. Stelzer (BMW).
1934: O. Ley (DKW).
1935: J. Guthrie (Norton).
1936: J. Guthrie (Norton).
1937: K. Gall (BMW).
1938: G. Meier (BMW).
1939: D. Serafini (Gilera).

See also EAST GERMAN GRAND PRIX and WEST GERMAN GRAND PRIX.

GILERA, Count
Count Giuseppe Gilera (born Italy 1887) founded the famous factory which had so much road racing success in the 1950s. He died at his Arcore home just outside Milan, at 84 years of age, in November 1971. Gilera started his motor cycle business in 1909 and after steady development his machines, together with those of the MV factory, dominated the larger capacity classes of Grand Prix racing with riders like Geoff Duke and Bob McIntyre. Derek Minter also registered marked success on the Gilera. The Count was actively running the factory until 1970 when it was taken over by his son, Piaggo.

GILERA
Although this Italian factory dominated the road racing scene in the 1950s they first came to prominence in 1937 when Piero Taruffi broke the one-hour record at a speed of 121.23 mph on a fully enclosed, water-cooled, four-cylinder machine and also established a new World Speed Record of 170.5 mph on 21st October, 1937. These performances were the prelude to an intensive racing programme which brought them important victories just before the war and supremacy in the 500cc class in the 1950s. In 1939 Gilera, with Dorino Serafini, won both the German Grand Prix and the Ulster Grand Prix at record speed, beating the formidable BMW machines, and in that year Gilera gained the European Championship.

Gilera returned to racing after the war with magnificent air-cooled four-cylinder machines. These were extremely fast but suffered from poor handling characteristics and a lack of low-speed torque. By 1950 these problems had, to a large extent, been overcome and Umberto Masetti became their first World Champion, in 1950. In the eight years from 1950 until their withdrawal from racing at the end of 1957, Gilera achieved victories in 31 classic events and collected six 500cc solo individual World Championships. Masetti, Duke and Liberati were their main riders.

Gilera also collected many other distinctions. In 1957 Bob McIntyre, riding a Gilera, became the first rider to lap the Isle of Man Mountain Circuit at over 100 mph, at the same time winning both the Junior and Senior TTs of that year. His lap record on the Isle of Man at 101.12 mph was the culmination of three other laps ridden at over 100 mph, and his success was the first double victory in these major races by a foreign factory.

McIntyre had joined the Gilera works team in 1957 and it was in that year at Monza on a Gilera 350 that he broke the one hour record at a speed of 143 mph.

Another prominent British rider to be closely associated with Gilera was Derek Minter. He rode the Gilera to success on many occasions and, along with John Hartle, was involved in a Gilera come-back in 1957. This scheme, the brain-child of Geoff Duke, was intended as an attempt to break the monopoly of the 500cc World Championship by MV, but it proved unsuccessful. During this period, however, Benedicto Caldarella rode the Gilera with success, being faster than the MV4 of Mike Hailwood on a number of occasions and for a while running second to Hailwood in the US Grand Prix of 1964. Since 1957 there have been many rumours and reports of a full-scale come-back by the Arcore factory, but so far none of these has materialised.

The first four-cylinder Gilera was built as early as 1927, but was never raced. The factory's famous Rondine (a twin overhead-cam four) was introduced in 1935 and attacked a number of speed records, reaching 170 mph over the flying kilometre.

Perhaps the most famous Gileras were the "dustbin" streamlined models of the middle and late 1950s raced with so much success by Geoff Duke and Bob McIntyre. The final versions were similar to the pre-war supercharged models, though they were air cooled and had cylinders only slightly inclined. The gear-train drive to the overhead camshafts between the three cylinders was retained. After Duke had signed for Gilera he modified the frame of the four, which from then on had a five-speed gearbox.

Results:
World Championships:
1949: second (Pagani) and third (Artesiani) in 500cc; second (Frigerio) in sidecar.
1950: first (Masetti) in 500cc and second (Frigerio) in sidecar.
1951: second (Milani) and third (Masetti) in 500cc, and second (Frigerio) and third (Milani) in sidecar.
1952: first (Masetti) in 500cc and second (Milani) in sidecar.
1953: first (Duke), second (Armstrong) and fourth (Milani) in 500cc.
1954: first (Duke) in 500cc.
1955: first (Duke) and second (Armstrong) in 500cc.
1956: second (Ferri) in 125cc.
1957: second (McIntyre) and third (Liberati) in 350cc; first (Liberati) and second (McIntyre) in 500cc.
1963: third (Hartle) in 500cc.
World Speed Record - 21st October–28th November, 1937, by P. Taruffi at 170.5 mph at Brescia-Bergamo on 492cc machine.
TT:
1953: third (Armstrong) in Senior.
1954: second (Duke) in Senior.
1955: first (Duke) and second (Armstrong) in Senior.
1957: first (McIntyre) and third (Brown) in Senior; first (McIntyre) and third (Brown) in Junior.
1963: second (Hartle) and third (Read) in Senior; second (Hartle) in Junior.

GILERA COME-BACK (Scuderia Duke)
In 1963 former Gilera works rider Geoffrey Duke formed Scuderia Duke in an attempt to break the MV monopoly of the 500cc World Championship. He managed to obtain an agreement from Gilera for the loan of their outstanding 1957 machines (which since that time had been under dust covers in the firm's Arcore factory), providing he could prove they were still competitive. Tests at Monza showed they were, with speeds around 116–118 mph being recorded. With Derek Minter, John Hartle and Phil Read signed to ride the machines, Duke now attempted to take the title from MV. After a promising start when the Gileras showed impressive speed, the challenge faltered when Minter and Hartle crashed and then Minter had a disagreement with Duke. The results were not forthcoming and a fine enterprising move, which could have added considerable interest and excitement to the 500cc class, sadly fizzled out.

GODDEN, Don
Don Godden (born 13th November, 1936, at Chidworth, Wiltshire) became one of the famous names in grass track racing during the 1960s and 1970s. His career began on a BSA Bantam in 1951 and continued earnestly in 1953. He was awarded the progress cup in 1954. He became British 500cc Champion (1967) and won A-CU Gold Star awards in 1961 (500cc), 1962 (350cc), 1963 (350cc, 500cc), 1965 (500cc) and 1967 (500cc). He was also the first English rider to ice-race in Russia and the first Englishman to compete in European Long Track Championships of which he won the 1969 title in Oslo. He was runner-up in 1967, 1968 and 1970 and became world record holder for grass speed at Cloppenburg, West Germany, in July 1971 at a speed of 126.61 kph. He was British 500cc Champion again in 1972.

GOULD, Rodney Arthur
Rodney Gould (born 1944, Banbury, Oxfordshire), started his career racing a BSA 350cc Gold Star in a Bemsee production event at Silverstone in 1961. He later rode 350cc and 500cc Nortons before switching to Yamaha and gaining a place in the Yamaha factory team. His first season as a full time professional was in 1967. Prominent on both home and Grand Prix circuits during the mid and later 1960s, Gould was also to compete for Yamaha in 500cc, 350cc and 250cc events.

Rodney Gould became 250cc World Champion on a Yamaha in 1970 and took the works Yamaha to second place in the 1972 250cc TT. He retired from racing in October 1972 to take up the position located in Amsterdam of publicity manager for Yamaha in Europe. He later set up a motor-cycle business in Britain in partnership with Mike Hailwood.

World Championship wins:
1970: 250cc (Yamaha).

GRAHAM, R. Les
One of the leading British riders of the immediate pre- and post-war years, Les

Graham was a popular figure and an outstanding rider, particularly on short circuits. His riding career was interrupted by the war, in which he served as a bomber pilot gaining the DFC, but when racing restarted he led the AJS works team. He brought them the 500cc world title in 1949, the year in which the world championships were introduced, riding the temperamental "Porcupine" twin.

In the Senior TT of that year he had a secure lead, but mechanical failure two miles from the end robbed him of the title. He joined MV in 1951 to ride and help develop the fast but unreliable four-cylinder machines. He was second in the 500cc World Championship of 1952, on the MV. He was also second in the Senior TT of that year. In 1953 he won the 125cc TT on an MV, but was killed the following day racing the four-cylinder MV in the Senior event.

World Championship wins:
1949: 500cc (AJS).

TT wins:
1953: 125cc (MV).

GRAHAM, Stuart

Former road racer Stuart Graham is the elder son of the late AJS and MV works rider, Les Graham (see above). Formerly a Suzuki and Honda works rider, Stuart Graham began to concentrate on the classic events in 1966 after experience on a 350 AJS and a 500 Matchless. After mixed fortunes he rode a works Honda in the East German Grand Prix of 1966 finishing fourth. He secured a works contract to race 50cc and 125cc Suzuki machines during 1967. His outstanding rides include second place to Mike Hailwood in the 250 TT of 1966 and victories in the Finnish 125 Grand Prix and 50cc TT of 1967.

TT wins:
1967: 50cc (Suzuki).

GRAND PRIX RACING

Although the TT Races on the Isle of Man were first held in 1907 and the first French Grand Prix had been arranged to take place as early as 1914 (subsequently cancelled because of the intervention of the first World War), motor-cycle Grand Prix racing did not begin in earnest, with a series of events in different countries, until the early 1920s. There was a French Grand Prix in 1920, followed by Belgian and Italian Grands Prix in 1921, and a Swiss Grand Prix in 1922. The first German Grand Prix was held in 1923 to be followed by the Hungarian and Dutch TTs. The 1921 French Grand Prix was held over the famous Le Mans circuit. In these early Grands Prix there were classes for 250cc, 350cc and 500cc machines, though the 500cc class was by far the most popular. Among the British riders to take part in that first Grand Prix were such TT favourites as Bert le Vack on an Indian, Alec Bennett and Tommy de la Hay on Sunbeams, Graham Walker on a Norton and Freddie Edmond on a Triumph, holder at the time of the Senior TT lap record. The French Grand Prix of 1921 was won by Alec Bennett at 59.9 mph, with Tommy de la Hay second. The 1921 Belgian Grand Prix was held over the now famous Francorchamps circuit, near Spa in the Ardennes. British riders on British machines were again dominant on this winding, hilly course. Hubert Hassall (Norton) won by nearly ten minutes from Bert le Vack (Indian) who was almost 14 minutes ahead of Fred Dixon (also on an Indian).

The experience which British riders had gained over the TT course since 1907, and the machine development which had also accrued from racing on the Isle of Man and at Brooklands, proved immensely valuable. The French and Belgian Grands Prix of 1921 are generally recognised as the first big continental races and British machines and riders were first, second and third in each. So far the Senior class was all that had interested Britain but towards the mid-1920s there were good British entries in both 500cc and 250cc events of the French and Belgian events. Again Britain triumphed, with wins for riders and machines in the Senior and lightweight of both the "French" and "Belgian" – an additional bonus being the victory of British rider E. Remington on a Belgian Rush machine (but powered by a British engine) in the 350cc event of the "Belgian". He was the only British rider in this category, which was soon to develop in status far beyond the 250cc class. For British riders particularly the French and Belgian Grands Prix were the main continental events, although Walter Brandish, on a Triumph, had led the 500cc class in an early Italian Grand Prix until he was forced to retire towards the end of the race.

These earlier races were long and gruelling, most of them well in excess of 200 miles and some almost 300. They could last anything from between four to five hours. With the increasing popularity of motor-cycle racing and improved performance of machines, the sport became more organised. Machines which in the beginning had competed together were now rigidly classified into the various cc capacities and race distances were shortened, to give more sight of the racing to the spectator.

The British Norton factory dominated the 500cc and 350cc classes of Grand Prix racing in the early and mid-1930s. In the years leading up to the outbreak of the second World War, Norton's dominance subsided as the German BMW supercharged flat twin 500cc racer brought a strong challenge to the single-cylinder Norton. In the 250cc and 350cc classes the German DKW two-strokes were strong.

Up till now there had been no world championship series of events. Each Grand Prix was a race in itself and did not contribute towards any kind of overall championship. First signs of that came just before the outbreak of War when the FIM, the governing body of motor cycle sport and in those days known as the FICM, organised a European Championship for 1938. The results of eight of Europe's most important races – the Dutch and the Isle of Man TTs, and the Grand Prix of Belgium, Switzerland, France, Germany, Ulster, and Italy – were to count. In the 500cc category Georg Meier took the title riding a German BMW. The 350cc class was won by Ted Mellors riding a Velocette. Ewald Kluge won the 250cc class for Germany on a DKW. Kluge also was acclaimed *Champion of the Year* for scoring more points than any other rider in all classes. By 1939 Norton had virtually retired from racing due to their commitment to the manufacture of machines for military use, and it was the Italians who provided the most serious challenge to Germany. Because of the outbreak of the second World War a scheduled nine races in the Championship Series was reduced to seven, but titles were awarded all the same. Serafini on a four-cylinder, water-cooled, and supercharged Gilera took the 500cc title with five more points than Georg Meier on the BMW. The 350 title went to Hermann Fleischmann on a DKW. Kluge was again the 250cc champion and once more took the outright Championship.

Grand Prix racing in something like its pre-war form was resumed in 1947 with six recognised classic events, although a few international races had taken place in 1946. Even in 1947 there was no recognised championship. There was a reversal to the previous system of running each major race as a separate event. Many of the names of both riders and machines were recognisable from pre-war days. From Britain there were Nortons and Velocettes and an exciting new AJS machine, a prototype pre-war supercharged racer which was completed in a different form at the end of the war and became the world famous "Porcupine". The ban on superchargers immediately at the end of the war had enforced a change of the original conception of the machine. Britain's immediate post-war challenge came from Italy, with Gilera, and another name to become famous during the next decade, Moto Guzzis. Britain's race winning machines were ridden by well-known names like Daniel, Bell, Goodman, and Foster.

The World Championships in the form of a series of Grands Prix were re-instituted in 1949. Before that the classic round consisted (in 1948) of the same six events. The main competition came from Norton, Velocette, AJS, Gilera, and Moto Guzzi.

Almost coincident with the reintroduction of a Championship Series of races (now called World Championship and not merely European) was the emergence of the Italian Gilera machine which during the 1950s was to dominate much of the Grand Prix racing scene. The Gilera multi-cylinder machines, now much faster than the single-cylinder Nortons, were to bring in a new era in Grand Prix racing. The inroads into Grand Prix racing made by the Italians can clearly be seen from the Championship results of 1949. Mondial and Morini completely dominated the 125cc category, Guzzi and Benelli machines were first and second in the 250cc, and the greatest potential threat of all to British domination, Gilera, were second and third in the 500cc class. Only in the 350cc category were British machines and riders dominant, Frith on a Velocette being first, Armstrong on an AJS second, and Foster on a Velocette third. Masetti on a Gilera won the 500cc Championship of 1950 and, Geoff Duke's victory on a Norton in the 500cc of 1951 apart, set the pattern for an Italian domination of this class from 1952 right through until 1973. It was Gilera (except for 1956 when John Surtees won on an Italian MV) until 1957 when they retired from racing and thereafter MV with Surtees, Hocking, Hailwood and Agostini. Britain continued strong in the 350cc class in 1950, 1951 and 1952 but gave way to Guzzi in 1953. Grand Prix racing in the 'fifties, however, was dominated largely by Italy with Germany's NSU factory in the 125 and 250cc categories providing the only real challenge. Germany were supreme in the side-car Grands Prix with the absolute reliability of the BMW outfit. Gilera, Guzzi and Mondial retired from racing in 1957. MV, however, continued to be outstanding. Their record in 1958, 1959 and 1960, is impressive. In these three years they captured every solo World Championship, also registering many seconds and thirds.

Grand Prix racing in the 1960s is remembered for the influence of, and domination by, the Japanese works factories led by Honda. It is generally recognised as the period of the greatest investment in racing, with exotic machinery and lucrative works contracts available for the selected team riders who formed the elite "Continental Circus". Between 1961 and 1967, when Honda retired from full-time racing, they won 137 Grands Prix. In the early 1970s classic racing was dominated largely by Yamaha, Suzuki and MV, with BMW still supreme in the side-car classes. In the later 1970s Suzuki, through riders like Barry Sheene, Tepi Lausivuori, Pat Hennen, Wil Hartog and Marco Lucchinelli, and Yamaha, with Kenny Roberts and Johnny Cecotto, dominated the 500cc class. In the 350cc and 250cc classes Harley-Davidson, Yamaha and then Kawasaki were supreme, while the leading makes in 125cc and 50cc were Bultaco and Morbidelli.

See also TT (Tourist Trophy) Races, World Championships and Technical Development.

GRANT, Mick

One of the brightest and most established of Britain's present day stars, Mick Grant (born 1944) comes from Yorkshire and was a keen scrambler on a 250cc Cotton before concentrating on road racing in 1967 on a 500cc Velocette. On this machine – which it is alleged he also used to ride to and from work – he competed in the Manx Grand Prix of 1969, finishing 44th out of 48 starters. With better machinery the following year Grant, a miner's son, showed his promise and determination in his first TT, finishing 18th in the Junior event on a 350 Padgett Yamaha. Since then he has shown consistently improving form. In the 1971 Junior TT, again on the Padgett Yamaha, he took seventh position with a very creditable ride and moved into the limelight dramatically in 1972 with a string of distinctions: third in the Senior on a Kawasaki, third in the Junior on the Yamaha, and at Scarborough wrote his name into the record books by bringing the John Player Norton team its first victory in the Superbike event at the Oliver's Mount circuit. That same year he was 350cc British Champion on the Padgett Yamaha. Since then he has added considerably to his reputation with superb rides on the Isle of Man in 1973 when he secured second position on the F750cc John Player Norton behind Peter Williams and looked set to win the 500cc event when he stormed into the lead with laps of 104.33 mph and 104.41 mph before crashing on oil left on the road. His luck was also out in the 350cc race when he was forced to retire with clutch trouble after leading and putting up a lap at 105.52 mph. In 1974 Grant was second to Tony Rutter in the Junior TT, second to Charlie Williams in the 250cc, and won a postponed 1000cc Production TT riding a Triumph Trident, his first TT victory. Grant has been sponsored in his professional career by John Davidson. In 1974 and 1975 Grant was a member of the Boyer team Kawasaki.

In 1975 Mick Grant became the fastest TT rider of all time when he shattered Mike Hailwood's absolute lap record with a second lap in the Open Classic TT at 109.82 mph, riding a Kawasaki 750cc machine. He increased his own outright TT lap record in 1977 with a lap at 112.77 mph and again in 1978 with a lap at 114.33 mph, both in the 1000cc Classic and on 750cc Kawasaki machinery. After a successful spell with Kawasaki, Grant was signed by Honda for 1979, prior to their announced return to racing.

GRASS-TRACK RACING

Grass-track racing is a specialised, growing branch of motor-cycle sport rather like speedway, but held on grass. Power sliding (the speedway characteristic of sliding the rear wheel) is also well in evidence in grass track racing. Courses and races are generally short – perhaps six laps of a half-mile circuit – and team competitions, with one Centre competing against another, is a feature of the sport.

Grass-track racing is one of the earliest forms of motor cycle sport. There were numerous meetings taking place in the 1920s but the formation of the Brands Hatch combine in 1932, and the concentration this brought to grass-track meetings, gave the sport a tremendous boost. The Midlands and the North-West were also centres of considerable early activity, the Cheshire Centre being particularly significant. The Southern Centre Championships began in 1947 and the South-east Centre Speed Competitions in 1949. The National Championships were started in 1951. The A-CU introduced their Grass-track Stars Competition in 1962. This gave way to the British Championships in 1965. Jack Surtees, father of motor-cycle and car champion John, was a favourite at Brands Hatch in the 1930s along with another immortal name in motor-cycle sport, Eric Oliver. A favourite venue in the 1930s was at Layham's Farm in Kent where the circuit was on a hillside. Because of this Layham's became known as a mountain grass-track event. In the early days the sport was dominated by riders of the calibre of Vic Challener, Dick Tolley, Harry Teretta, Wally Lock, A. C. Turk and Leo Schweiso. Cyril Roger was the first man to reach a 60 mph lap on the old Brands circuit. Eric Oliver regularly reached speeds of 57 mph-plus on his 500 Oliver Special while Jack Surtees, riding a 1000cc HRD, would travel in excess of 50 mph.

Monty Banks, Sid Jarvis, Lew Coffin and Austin Cresswell were among the stars who dominated the sport in the 1950s to give way later in that decade to riders like Arthur Stuffins, Reg Luckhurst, Arthur Wicken and, of course, later, Don Godden, one of the most outstanding of all grass-track riders. He won his first national title in 1965 and became successful against virtually every top European rider. Ace sprinter, Alf Hagon, was also an effective grass-track racer. He took the 350cc and 500cc national titles in 1954 and achieved this outstanding double success again in 1962. Dave Baybutt, Tony Black and Malcolm Simmons are among other treasured names in the sport.

Although grass-track racing does not generate the international atmosphere nor attract the commercial support to bring it the recognition of road racing, speedway, or even moto-cross, it has plenty of supporters and there has been an encouraging revival of interest in more recent times. It is also an excellent training ground for riders who become prominent in other branches of motor-cycle racing. Sidecar events are now a spectacular part of grass-track racing programmes. Most machines are home-built specials, but since the early days the JAP engine has been the main power source for grass-track solo machines. The British Weslake with 4-valve head has made more recent impact.

Being less commercial than other forms of motor sport, grass-track meetings are generally socially clubby affairs. Minimum width of a grass-track is 25 feet on which no more than four riders can take part in a solo scratch race. More riders are allowed on the basis of one for every extra three feet width of track. For sidecars, half the number permitted for solo machines are eligible.

Results:

A-CU Star Winners

1962: 350cc (D. Godden); 500cc (A. Hagan); sidecar (K. Norcuff).
1963: 350cc (D. Godden); 500cc (D. Godden); sidecar (D. Nourish).
1964: 350cc (D. Godden; 500cc (D. Godden); sidecar (N. Mead).
1965: 350cc (T. Black); 500cc (D. Godden); sidecar (M. Webster).

National Champions:

1951: 350cc (S. F. Mintey); 500cc (R. Tolley); sidecar (C. Smith).
1952: 350cc (S. F. Mintey); 500cc (A. J. Cresswell); sidecar (D. Slate).
1953: 350cc (S. F. Mintey); 500cc (A. J. Cresswell); sidecar (D. Yorke).
1954: 350cc (A. J. Hagon); 500cc (A. J. Hagon); sidecar (W. Evans).
1955: 350cc (D. V. Goodacre); 500cc (M. A. Tatum); sidecar (W. Evans).
1956: 350cc (A. J. Cresswell); 500cc (A. J. Hagon); sidecar (W. Evans).

1957: 350cc (M. A. Tatum); 500cc (M. A. Tatum); sidecar (W. Evans).
1958: 350cc (M. Briggs); 500cc (M. Briggs); sidecar (C. Vincent).
1959: 350cc (A. J. Hagon); 500cc (A. J. Hagon); sidecar (F. French).
1960: 350cc (A. J. Hagon); 500cc (A. J. Cresswell); sidecar (W. Evans).
1961: 350cc (A. J. Hagon); 500cc (D. V. Goodacre); sidecar (W. Evans).
1962: 350cc (A. J. Hagon); 500cc (A. J. Hagon); sidecar (B. W. Rust).
1963: 350cc (A. J. Hagon); 500cc (R. Luckhurst); sidecar (N. Mead).
1964: 350cc (A. J. Hagon); 500cc (R. Luckhurst); sidecar (B. W. Rust).
1965: 350cc (T. Black); 500cc (D. V. Godden); sidecar (D. Hunter).

British Champions:
1966: 350cc (D. Baybutt); 500cc (D. Baybutt); sidecar (D. Lofthouse).
1967: 250cc (F. Watts); 350cc (C. Stewart); 500cc (D. Godden); sidecar (M. Webster).
1968: 250cc (C. Stewart); 350cc (W. Bridgett); 500cc (A. Ross); sidecar (D. Hunter).
1969: 250cc (D. Baybutt); 350cc (C. Pusey); 500cc (B. Maxted); sidecar (J. Miell).
1970: 250cc (M. Price); 350cc (C. Pusey); 500cc (C. Baybutt); sidecar (G. Wheeler).
1971: 250cc (T. Black); 350cc (S. Luck); 500cc (B. Maxted); sidecar (S. Smith).
1972: 250cc (C. Baybutt); 350cc (P. Collins); 500cc (D. Godden); sidecar (C. Taylor).
1973: 250cc (C. Baybutt); 350cc (S. Luck); 500cc (B. Maxted); sidecar (S. Smith).
1974: 250cc (C. Baybutt); 350cc (G. Short); 500cc (C. Baybutt); sidecar (T. Scott).
1975: 250cc (D. Brown); 350cc (C. Morton); 500cc (J. Britcher); sidecar (A. Artus).
1976: 250cc (C. Baybutt); 350cc (J. Britcher); 500cc (B. Maxted); sidecar (T. Scott).
1977: 250cc (M. Nicholson); 350cc (J. Britcher); 500cc (C. Baybutt); sidecar (K. Smith).
1978: 250cc (M. Wadsworth); 350cc (G. Short); 500cc (B. Webb); sidecar 500cc (R. Stoneman); sidecar 1000cc (S. Smith).
1979: 250cc (C. Baybutt); 350cc (C. Williams); 500cc (T. Banks); sidecar 500cc (C. Cardy); sidecar 1000cc (D. Heath).
1980: 250cc (J. Doncaster); 350cc (S. Schofield); 500cc (T. Banks); sidecar 500cc (S. Smith/T. Pye); sidecar 1000cc (S. Smith/T. Pye).
1981: 250cc (D. Baybutt); 350cc (S. Schofield); 500cc (S. Wigg); sidecar 500cc (C. Cardy/A. Morrison); L/H sidecar 1000cc (M. Turrell/T. Strivens); R/H sidecar 1000cc (D. Teasdale/K. Chapman).

A European Championship was started in 1978 and was won by Britain's Chris Baybutt. In 1979 the European Grass-Track Championship was won by Gerald Short.
European Solo Grand Prix:
1980: first W. Stauch (West Germany) 25; second G. Short (GB) 21; third S. Lindblom (Sweden) 21.
1981: first N. Farnish (GB) 24; second B. Leigh (GB) 19; third S. Larsson (Denmark) 17.

European Sidecar Grand Prix:
1980: first O. Bauer/P. Stiglbrunner (West Germany) 15; second E. Walla/E. Starke (West Germany) 13; third M. Datzmann/R. Datzmann (West Germany) 10.
1981: first M. Datzmann/R. Datzmann (West Germany) 15; second H. Pagel/H. W. Kemper (West Germany) 13; third O. Bauer/P. Stiglbrunner (West Germany) 10.

GREENWOOD, Owen
Although Owen Greenwood had earlier successfully competed in many branches of motor-cycle racing, it is for his piloting of the controversial mini three-wheeler against traditional sidecars in the mid to late 1960s that he remains most famous. He was at the centre of one of the biggest sensations of the decade. He built a three-wheeler based on the mini and which looked more like a small racing car than the traditional outfit; yet it contravened no rules. In its original form it incorporated a BMC 1071cc engine and at first created no concern, gaining few distinctions during its first season of racing in 1965. After concentrated development, however, it became virtually unbeatable on home circuits in 1966. An increasing wave of protest thenceforth was levelled at Greenwood and the mini, mainly from other sidecar

riders. It was claimed to be dangerous when competing in races with traditional outfits and to give its owner an unfair advantage. Greenwood claimed that having raced Triumphs successfully he had looked around for a new challenge, and settled upon the idea of building a competitive three-wheeler. Moreover, it was perfectly legal according to the rules. In three seasons the mini-racer brought Greenwood more than sixty victories, two British championships and lap records at numerous home circuits. In spite of increasing protests and the lowering of the capacity limits at certain home circuits imposed specifically to eliminate the mini (to which Greenwood responded by fitting a lower capacity and therefore eligible engine) the machine was never banned; and early in 1968 Greenwood sold the machine for £650, together with its higher and lower capacity engines.

GROVEWOOD MOTOR-CYCLE RACING AWARDS

These awards were instituted by the owners of Brands Hatch, Mallory Park and Snetterton in 1965 for the best non-sponsored British riders on UK circuits. In 1968 the awards were broadened, open from that year to non-factory British and Commonwealth riders. Cash awards are presented to the three riders whom a panel of judges consider to have shown the greatest improvement in performance during the year.

Winners (in order):

1965: Billie Nelson, Ray Pickrell and Brian Burgess.
1966: Charlie Sanby, Nigel Mead and Alan Barnett.
1967: Mick Boddice, Steve Jolly and Rob Fitton.
1968: Alan Barnett, Kel Carruthers and Rod Gould.
1969: Mick Andrew, John Findlay and Tony Rutter.
1970: Steve Machin, Paul Smart and Barry Sheene.
1971: Barry Randle, Percy May and Norman Hanks.
1972: Paul Cott, Dave Potter and George O'Dell.
1973: Phil Haslam, John Newbold and Peter and Ron Hardy.
1974: Malcolm Hobson and Jack Armstrong, Martin Sharpe and Steve Mainship.
1975: Steve Parrish, Ron Haslam and Dick Greasley and Cliff Holland.
1976: Barry Woodland, Roger Marshall and Trevor Iveson.
1977: Kevin Wrettom, Jock Taylor and Steve Wright.
1978: Clive Padgett, Keith Huewen and Kevin Stowe.
1979: Mike Thackwell, Nigel Mansell and Terry Gray.
1980: David Leslie, Richard Trott and Dr Jonathan Palmer.
1981: Pete Wild, Alan Carter and Derek Bailey.

GUTHRIE, A. Jimmy

Guthrie (born 1897) was one of the immortal few who made Britain and Norton supreme in motor cycle racing in the 1930s. Born in Hawick, Scotland, Guthrie was a brilliant rider and an outstanding sportsman. On the Isle of Man he was exceptional and won the TT six times, five on Nortons and once on an AJS. He was also declared winner of the 1935 Senior TT, but after a re-calculation it was announced that he had lost the race by four seconds. Although remembered mostly for his illustrious riding in the TTs Guthrie also captured a number of world records including the World's One Hour record at 114.092 mph on the Montlhery track, near Paris, in 1935, and was highly successful on continental circuits. In 1937, for instance, he was Junior and Senior Champion of Europe.

His first appearance in the TTs was in 1923 when he retired in the Junior race riding a Matchless, though he had made a number of significant appearances at Brooklands and in speed trials. From then until 1931, when he began riding Nortons, his fortunes were mixed. He rode Nortons in fourteen TTs from 1931 to 1937 and was never more lowly placed than fifth, though he had two retirements. He was killed (aged 40) on the last corner and while leading the German Grand Prix of 1937. It would have been his third successive victory in this event.

In 1939 a memorial to this great rider was unveiled on the TT mountain course at "The Cutting" above Ramsay and marks the place where he retired in his last TT, the Senior event of 1937.

TT results:

1923: Junior (Matchless) retired.
1927: Junior (New Hudson) retired and

GIACOMO AGOSTINI races to victory on the remarkable 350 MV in the West German Grand Prix of 1969. Agostini took the 350cc World Championship for seven years running from 1968.

AGO besieged by his home fans at Imola in 1974. The handsome Italian enjoyed a superstar following at all the major circuits.

RAY AMM began racing in Europe in 1951, after leaving Rhodesia. Seen here at the 1952 Senior TT in which he finished third.

4 The paddock at BRANDS HATCH. This picture was at the famous Kent circui the mid-1960s when Dere Minter was 'king'.

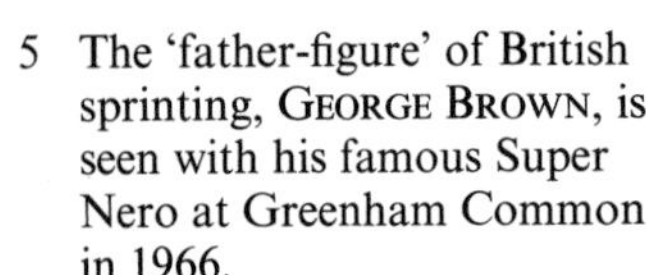

5 The 'father-figure' of British sprinting, GEORGE BROWN, is seen with his famous Super Nero at Greenham Common in 1966.

6 In 1975, in his first year Grand Prix racing, the 1 year-old Venezuelan JOH CECOTTO became the 35(World Champion, the youngest world champio all time. He also finished the following year.

7 A great day for Howard Davies after winning the 1925 Senior TT on his HRD machine at an average speed of 66.13 mph.

8 In the late 1960s the Daytona 200 in the USA was to become the world's most prestigious race. In 1975 Yvon Duhamel on the Kawasaki (No. 17) leads the pack on the first lap.

9 The immaculate style of the legendary GEOFF DUKE on a demonstration ride on the 500cc Gilera four at the Bob McIntyre Memorial meeting at Oulton Park.

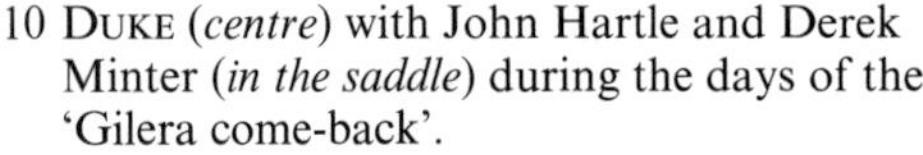

10 DUKE (*centre*) with John Hartle and Derek Minter (*in the saddle*) during the days of the 'Gilera come-back'.

11 ERIC FERNIHOUGH on his record-breaking Brough Superior JAP in 1938. 'Ferni' held the World Speed Record in 1937 at 169.8 mph, but in April 1938 was killed in Hungary while trying to regain the record.

12 Freddie Frith winning the 1949 Junior TT for Velocette. His average speed was 82.15 mph. He also established the fastest lap at 84.23 mph. It was Frith's final TT victory before retirement at 39 years of age, at the end of 1949.

13 The controversial mini-racer of Owen Greenwood, with passenger Terry Fairbrother, at Brands Hatch in the 1960s. In three seasons Greenwood took the mini to more than sixty wins, including two British Championships.

14 A quiet moment at Cesenatico in 1968 for two of the biggest names in motor cycle racing. Phil Read relaxes while Mike Hailwood signs for young admirers.

15 HAILWOOD makes history as he crosses the line to win the Senior TT of 1967. It was his fifth consecutive Senior victory and his twelfth TT win – two more than the 27-year-old record of Stanley Woods.

16 Gary Hocking at the 350cc winner's presentation at the French Grand Prix of 1960. Frantisek Stastny (*left*) was second and John Surtees (*right*) third.

17 In 1961 Honda took the Isle of Man by storm, occupying the first five places in both the 125cc and 250cc TTs. Seen right (*left to right*): Tom Phillis, Luigi Taveri and Mike Hailwood.

18 Famous dragster Norman Hyde takes off on a low nine-second run at the Santa Pod Raceway.

19 A jubilant Bill Ivy salutes the crowd after winning the 'King of Brands' title in 1966. A rider of exceptional skill and daring, he epitomised the 'swinging sixties' cult and attracted an enormous following.

20 The greatest showman and stunt rider of them all. Evel Knievel demonstrates his talents at Wembley in May 1975.

Senior (New Hudson) second.
1928: Senior (Norton) retired, and Junior (Norton) retired.
1930: Lightweight (AJS) first, Junior (AJS) retired and Senior (AJS) retired.
1931: Lightweight (OK) retired, Senior (Norton) second.
1932: Junior (Norton) retired and Senior (Norton) second.
1933: Junior (Norton) third and Senior (Norton) fourth.
1934: Junior (Norton) first and Senior (Norton) first.
1935: Junior (Norton) first and Senior (Norton) second.
1936: Junior (Norton) fifth and Senior (Norton) first.
1937: Junior (Norton) first and Senior (Norton) retired.

GUZZI

Moto Guzzi, to give the factory its full name, entered racing in the early 1920s and withdrew in 1957. Eight world championships and eleven TTs fell to Guzzi machines. The factory, with headquarters at Como, Italy, was consistently renowned for its unique horizontal single-cylinder engine of basic design. Stanley Woods' victory in both the lightweight and Senior TTs of 1935 brought the Italian factory international fame though their machines had in earlier days raced to many continental victories. Guzzi are perhaps most remembered for their vanquishment of the powerful German DKWs in the 1939 250cc German Grand Prix.

After the war Guzzi continued to use the horizontal single-cylinder machine and dominated the 250cc class from about 1947 to 1953. In 1953 they contested the 350cc class with a larger engined machine of the same basic design and won the World Championship in their first year.

This famous Italian company is also remembered for its outstanding technical contribution to the sport. The Guzzi wind tunnel at Mandello del Lario has almost become a part of motor cycle racing folklore. The factory's outstanding experimental and developmental programme gave them a versatility of machines, from their famous singles to V-twins, across-the-frame 3s, in-line 4s and V8 cylinder engines. At one time Guzzi held over 120 international records, mainly as a result of the testing and development of streamlining of machines in the special wind tunnel. Among the many famous riders who rode Guzzi machines with distinction, in addition to Stanley Woods, were Pagani, Cann, Ruffo, Lomas, Anderson, Dale, Kavanagh and Campbell.

Guzzi first competed in the TT Races in 1926. They gained second place in the lightweight of 1927 and had their first TT victory in 1935 when Stanley Woods won both the Senior and lightweight events. This was a sensational victory. Woods made a slow start and was as much as 26 seconds behind leader Jimmy Guthrie's works Norton at the end of six laps. With Woods expected to make a second pit stop, Guthrie looked a certain winner, but Woods gambled on having sufficient fuel, and raced on. He pushed the lap record to 86.53 mph and eventually won by just four seconds. Ruffo won the 250cc World Championship on a Guzzi machine in 1949, the inaugural year of the World Championship Series.

Guzzi returned to competition in 1949, but not to Grand Prix racing. They concentrated on endurance events and on two occasions during that year broke numerous world records at the Monza circuit near Milan.

Guzzi produced many different models, both singles and multis. The first 500cc single was in 1921 and had a horizontal engine, a characteristic of all Guzzi single-cylinder machines. Developments to this first basic machine brought the Italian factory the European Championship of 1924. It was the further development of the 500 which led in 1925 to the first Guzzi 250 which had only two overhead valves.

Guzzi's unconventional machines made a major impact on world competition and between 1953–57 dominated the 350cc championship with their ultra-light flat singles, as a follow-up to their successes in 1949, 1951–2 in the 250cc class.

The man behind the Guzzi success was Giulio Carcano. By reducing the weight, height and width of the flat singles and enclosing them in streamlining, he proved the value of designing the machine as a whole and not concentrating solely on the engine.

Machine Details:

1935: the famous Guzzi twin of 1935 is significant for its victory that year in the Senior TT, the first by a foreign factory since 1911. Ridden by Stanley Woods, this Guzzi was also the first TT winner to incorporate rear springing. Claims for its performance, by 1935 standards, were exceptional: maximum speed of 112 mph, 51 bhp at 7,500 rpm. It weighed 375 lb. This 500cc machine was virtually a "doubled-up" version of the already successful 250 Guzzi – unusual because it was a wide-angle 120° V-twin, with a horizontal front "pot" and the magneto set between the cylinders.

1947–49: these were excellent years for the 250cc Guzzi. They came home first in all three years on the Isle of Man and also won the first 250cc World Championship in 1949. These machines were very similar to the 500 twin ridden with success by Stanley Woods in the 1935 Senior TT. The engine was built in unit with its gearbox and had a horizontal cylinder. It had traditional external flywheel and rear suspension. Drive to camshaft was by shaft and bevel gears. Over the three years the basic design saw little alteration, though in 1949 there were new bottom-leading-link front forks with a large-diameter brake to the front wheel.

1953: the Guzzi-4 of 1953 had an outstanding début and was thereafter a disappointing failure. At Hockenheim in May 1953 Enrico Lorenzetti won at a record average speed of 107.80 mph and Fergus Anderson set up a lap record of 113.27 mph, both on the Guzzi-4. Afterwards little success was achieved. It was an interesting machine and virtually the first "four-in-line" to be raced. In 1954 a full fairing was added and the frame was very similar to the Guzzi 500cc single.

1954–55: Guzzi machines during this period were among the few specially designed to incorporate the full frontal streamlining which was allowed for the first time in 1954. Because of this they soon became known as the "space-frame" Guzzis. Frames and engines were very similar on the 250cc, 350cc and 500cc machines.

1954: Guzzi introduced the astonishing eight-cylinder 500 in 1954 with an engine which consisted of two groups of four cylinders in an open V of 90 degrees. It had a six-speed gearbox. This model developed 65 hp at 1200 rpm and a later version, in 1957, almost 80 hp. Speed was around 174 mph. The Guzzi V-eight was an extraordinary machine, but because of the factory's withdrawal from racing at the end of 1957, its potential was never fully exploited. It was ridden by Dickie Dale in the 1957 TT, finishing fourth though running for most of the race on reduced power.

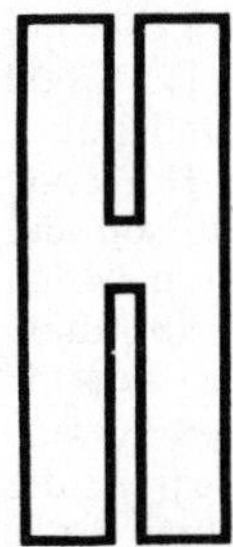

HAGON, Alf

Alf Hagon was outstanding as a sprint and drag racer and record breaker during the 1960s. Hagon, from Leyton, Essex, can be considered one of motor cycling's greatest all-rounders. He began his racing career in 1948 and in addition to speed attempts made a reputation as a speedway and grass-track rider. He was a professional speedway rider for twelve years. In 1962 at the Santa Pod Raceway in Bedfordshire, Hagon became the fastest man in the world on two wheels over the standing quarter-mile. He achieved this outstanding performance on his special 1260cc Hagon JAP and created the record in spite of sustaining a flat tyre during the successful attempt.

Born 1932, bespectacled Alf Hagon took his sprint special to RAF Honington, Suffolk, in September 1968 and there, on a two-mile runway, clocked an officially recorded 206.54 mph. It was the first time in Britain that a motor cycle had reached 200 mph. At the time Hagon was holder of the world standing-start kilo and quarter-mile records. For his successful 200 mph-plus attempt Hagon's supercharged JAP machine was fitted with a gearbox, the gearing was raised and special Dunlop racing tyres were used. His machine was unstreamlined, the best previous speed recorded by an unstreamlined machine being 191.302 mph by Boris Murray on a double-engined Triumph at Bonneville, USA, in 1966. His record for the quarter mile, set up in 1968, was not improved upon until 1974, when Luton's John Hobbs recorded 9.206 sec.

The 1260cc supercharged specialist V-twin JAP on which Hagon was to gain fame was built in 1964 and his first runs over the standing quarter mile were in the high elevens. He soon got down to the high tens, but it took much longer to reach down to around the 10-sec mark. He set 10.117 in early June 1967 and the following month Hagon became the first British rider to break ten seconds for the quarter-mile with a sprint of 9.93 sec at Duxford, Cambs, though since it was not a "time record attempt" the achievement stood as a course record only for Duxford.

In its original form Hagon's JAP was a 1000cc machine, the bore size later being increased from 80mm to 90mm to give 1260cc. It had Hagon's own design frame, a 60-inch wheelbase, JAP speedway cylinder heads and Matchless G50 pistons. Hagon preferred the JAP engine to the Vincent because of its lightness and longer stroke. It weighed about 270 lb.

Alf Hagon was an enthusiastic grass track racer at 15 and won 11 national championships. Later he tried road racing, scrambling, speedway and trials, before gaining fame as a sprint king.

HAILWOOD, S. M. B. (Mike)

Generally accepted as the most outstanding rider of modern times, Mike Hailwood's career in motor cycle racing extended from 1957 until 1969, when he retired to race cars. In the seven years, 1961–67, he won nine World Championships and twelve TTs. During this period he dominated the road racing scene and included in an impressive catalogue of achievements were seven Ulster Grand Prix victories between 1959 and 1967. His performance on the Isle of Man in 1961 during only his fourth visit to the island was exceptional. He won the 125, 250, and 500cc TTs in a week and came close in the Junior event, having to retire 15 miles from home with mechanical trouble. In 1967 he celebrated his tenth year as a TT rider with victories in the Senior, Junior and 250cc lightweight categories, exceeding the record of ten TT victories set up by the great Stanley Woods between the War years. His riding on the Island that week boosted his personal record to 12 TT victories.

Stanley Michael Bailey Hailwood (born Oxford 1940) made his racing début in 1957 on a 125cc MV and during the winter of that year and early 1958 went to South Africa to gain racing experience. He had many successes there. In Europe he quickly made an impact in road racing. At 18 in 1958 he was third, seventh, twelfth and thirteenth in the four solo classes on the Isle of Man and that same year won three out of the four A-CU Road Racing Stars, forerunner of the current British Championships. In 1960 he became the second man to lap the mountain course at over 100 mph on a single cylinder machine only minutes after Derek Minter had become the first. In 1959, when 19 years of age, he registered his first classic win – the 125cc Ulster Grand Prix. In 1966 he set a new absolute mountain course lap record of 107.07 mph as well as becoming the first 250cc rider to establish a race average of more than 100 mph. He also quickly established himself outside Britain and the Isle of Man. As early as 1959 he had reached third place in the 125cc World Championship riding a Ducati and in 1961, at 21 years of age, and in his first full season on a factory machine, he won his first world title, the 250cc championship, on a privately entered Honda-4. On Norton/MV he was second in the 500cc class.

On his first ride on a 500cc MV-4 he won the Italian Grand Prix and, having signed for the Italian factory, rode during 1962 to his first 500cc World Championship. For four years he dominated the 500cc category, becoming world champion again on MVs in 1963, 1964 and 1965. He gained his world honours in 1962–64 with maximum points. In 1965 Hailwood competed in eight of the ten 500cc races counting towards the World Championship and won them all, an outstanding performance. In 1966 he won 19 World Championship races and won at least one World Championship every year from 1961 to 1967.

He established a remarkable double success in 1964 at the Daytona Speed Circuit in Florida. In the morning he broke the World One Hour Speed record at 144 mph and went out again in the afternoon to win the United States 500cc Grand Prix raising the lap record and establishing a race record.

Hailwood was at the forefront of road racing during one of its most scintillating periods, when the Japanese factories were investing huge sums of money in a bid for world recognition. Hailwood was in the vanguard of the exclusive handful of factory riders with lucrative contracts who jet-setted from one Grand Prix to another in one of the most exciting periods in the sport. Son of the rich boss of the biggest motor-cycle dealers in the country who was himself a former motor-cycle racer, Mike Hailwood suffered from his big-money and public school background. Certainly, Hailwood senior bought good bikes for his son and financed a support organisation which was the envy of many less fortunate riders. Although Hailwood was often the target for writers who attributed his success to superior machines, his early rides at British championship meetings on a standard Manx Norton were enough to show his undoubted ability and courage. There is no doubt that he is now accepted as one of the greatest motor-cycle racing stars of all time.

His major triumphs came first as a factory rider for MV, but his relationships with the Italian concern were not always harmonious. It came as no surprise when, after being invincible in the 500cc class on MVs Hailwood signed for Honda in 1966. He thus re-established a relationship between rider and machine which had been successful some five years earlier when, in 1961, he won both the 125cc and 250cc TTs on Honda machines and secured the 250cc World Championship for the Japanese factory.

But his last days with MV were unhappy ones. He could not get the rides he wanted, and the MV factory, sluggish in building new machines, were finding their earlier models less competitive. Honda, in the meantime, had succeeded in achieving every ambition except one, the winning of the 500cc World Championship. They signed Hailwood, the most powerful rider of the time, with this one objective in mind, but for both Honda and Hailwood it was a joint ambition never to be realised. Giacomo Agostini, ironically on the MV, won the World 500cc Championships in both 1966 and 1967 with Hailwood runner-up on both occasions. Hailwood, however, was remarkably successful with Honda bringing them the double (250 and 350) World Championships in 1966 and 1967. Towards the end of the 1960s the big-spending days of Honda and others were at an end and as the era closed Hailwood decided to move out of the bike world to concentrate on motor racing. Some of his greatest rides were against Jim Redman in the East German Grand Prix 250cc duel in 1963 and against team mate Agostini in the 1960s. In 1968 he was awarded the MBE for his services to motor cycle sport.

Nicknamed "Mike the Bike" Hailwood's strong personality often brought brushes with the establishment, factory bosses and other riders and it was his inability to accept mechanical failures which led to his break with MV. A brilliant rider and a shrewd tactician, he was perhaps the most dazzling personality during the most glamorous period in the sport.

World Championship wins:
1961: 250cc (Honda).
1962: 500cc (MV).
1963: 500cc (MV).
1964: 500cc (MV).
1965: 500cc (MV).
1966: 350cc (Honda) and 250cc (Honda).
1967: 350cc (Honda) and 250cc (Honda).

TT wins:
1961: Senior (Norton), 250cc (Honda) and 125cc (Honda).
1962: Junior (MV).
1963: Senior (MV).
1964: Senior (MV).
1965: Senior (MV).
1966: Senior (Honda) and 250cc (Honda).
1967: Senior (Honda), Junior (Honda) and 250cc (Honda).

In what was perhaps the most astonishing and dramatic come-back in the history of the sport, Hailwood, then 38, returned to motor cycling in a limited way, visiting the Isle of Man again in 1978. On an 860cc Ducati he won the Formula 1 race at a race average of 108.512 mph, establishing the fastest lap at 110.627 mph. He also won at Mallory Park on the same machine. He returned to the Isle of Man again to race for what he said would definitely be the last time in 1979 and showed outstanding talent and flair by scoring a runaway win in the Senior race – his fourteenth TT victory. He also set a new class record at 114.02 mph, only 3.2 seconds outside the then absolute record set by Mick Grant on a 750cc Kawasaki in 1978.

Mike Hailwood died on Monday, 23 March 1981, in Birmingham Accident Hospital, from head injuries sustained in a road accident when his car was in collision with a lorry in Warwickshire, only a few miles from his home, two days before, on Saturday, 21 March. His nine-year-old daughter Michelle was killed instantly in the crash, though his son David escaped with cuts and bruises. Mike's brilliant racing career on bikes and in cars had won him the MBE and GM.

HANSFORD, Gregg
Riding works Kawasakis prepared by Neville Doyle, the blond Australian scored tremendous success over several seasons in Australia, New Zealand and the Far East before being persuaded to compete internationally. An outstanding performance at Daytona was followed by victory over Steve Baker at Mosport in Canada in 1977 in the Formula 750cc World Championship. In his first serious season of Grand Prix racing in 1978, Hansford finished second in the 250cc class and third in the 350cc class of the World Championships, on Kawasaki. He continued to ride for Kawasaki in 1979 and again finished second in the 250cc and third in the 350cc classes of the World Championships.

HARLEY-DAVIDSON
Harley-Davidson is an American racing factory with headquarters at Milwaukee, Wisconsin, USA. Over many years they have operated an extensive programme of racing in AMA road racing and at dirt track competitions. In more recent years Harley-Davidson have also had world outright speed ambitions and they set up a new record in 1970 when Cal Rayborn reached 265.492 mph at Bonneville. The machine was a specially designed V-twin overhead. The AMA Championship went to Harley-Davidson in 1969 after which they lost it until 1972 when it was won for them again by Mark Brelsford. Harleys have been noted for running a fairly large factory team and in 1972 had six expert riders and one junior, and because of the variety of events which make up the AMA Championship, some 30 machines of varying types had to be prepared for events for these riders.

At one time the factory held 14 official Bonneville speed records and has broken dozens of others over the years.

Harley-Davidson's racing history began in 1908 when the Federation of American Motorcyclists (predecessor of today's American Motorcycle Association) scheduled its Endurance Run for 29th June in the Catskill Mountains of New York. The 61 entrants lined up at the start included Walter Davidson, the lone Harley-Davidson rider. In the first day of running, the rough terrain of the mountains took its toll. Fifteen riders had dropped out by the end of the first day but Davidson was still going strong. He was well up in the standings when the 46 remaining riders started the second day to circle the 180 miles around Long Island to Brooklyn. Repeating his performance of the day before, Davidson again outclassed the field and was awarded a unique winning score. A week later Davidson set the FAM economy record, 188.234 miles per gallon, when he covered 50 miles of hilly territory on Long Island on one quart and one ounce of fuel.

At this time the policy of Harley-Davidson was to build no special racing machines. The only Harley-Davidson "racers" were stock machines ridden by private owners. In 1914 the Harley-Davidson Racing Department was established and the factory continued strongly in competitions, winning many events until 1917, when the US entered the war and racing halted.

When racing was resumed after the war, Harley-Davidson continued to win races at a phenomenal rate. Road races and endurance races alike were dominated by stock racing machines produced by Harley-Davidson.

In 1920 Harley-Davidson captured the first four places at the Ascot track in Los Angeles; the first five at the South American Tourist Trophy Race and won overwhelmingly at Dodge City, Sheepshead Bay and other major events. In the same year both the stock and racing engines set speed records at Daytona Beach. In 1921 Harley-Davidson riders won eight out of eight National Championship races.

Through the hectic racing years of the early 1920s both dealer and privately entered motor-cycles supplemented the factory teams by entering races the factory teams missed. In 1937 Harley-Davidson set a new speed record of 136.183 miles per hour at Daytona. Though American racing was suspended during World War II, the big races and their leaders remained the same when the racing action was resumed after the war. In 1947 Harley-Davidson won the National TT, the National Miniature TT, and Nationals at Richmond, Springfield and Milwaukee. Seven of the top ten riders at Daytona were on Harley-Davidson machines.

The early 1950s brought a new concept to National motorcycle racing – the naming of a National Champion based on a point system applying to American Motorcycle Association sanctioned National races. In 1954, Joe Leonard, on a Harley-Davidson, became the first National Champion under this system. Harley-Davidson riders also finished second and third in the Championship ratings.

For four years from 1958 Carroll Resweber dominated American motorcycle racing on a Harley-Davidson to become the most successful rider of the period with absolute supremacy. Resweber's greatest year was probably 1961, when he won 98 per cent of all the races he entered.

The "Indianapolis 500" of motorcycle racing is the annual 200-Mile National Championship Race at Daytona International Speedway. The first 200-Mile National Championship Race for motorcycles was held on this course in 1961, and Harley-Davidson took first place four times in the first five years.

In 1968 Cal Rayborn on a Harley-Davidson registered a record average speed of 101.29 mph at Daytona, after being the first rider in Daytona history to lap the entire field of competitors and the first to average over 100 mph for the entire race.

The start of the vast American organisation, Harley-Davidson, began in 1902 when craftsman Bill Harley combined with pattern maker Arthur Davidson to begin work on a motor cycle. The prototype was unsuccessful, so they began again in a 10ft by 15ft wooden shed in the Davidson's family backyard in Milwaukee. Fifty motor cycles were produced in 1906 and the company was incorporated in 1907. Production went up: 150 machines in 1907; in 1917 18,000. The company in 1960 acquired a 50 per cent share in the Italian Aermacchi company of Farese, following a search for a supplier of smaller capacity models to supplement the Harley-Davidson range.

Harley-Davidson was later owned by AMF Inc., the giant organisation which operates in the recreational and leisure field. In 1981 AMF sold Harley-Davidson to the firm's former management team led by Vaughn Beals.

The rider most associated with Harley-

Davidson in the World Championships – and the most successful – is the Italian Walter Villa. On Harley-Davidson, Villa captured the 250cc World Championship in 1974, 1975 and 1976 and the 350cc World Championship in 1976.

HARRIS, Peter (Pip) Valentine
Prominent British sidecar racer, Harris entered his first event, a grass track meeting, in 1946. He turned to road racing in 1948, combining with grass track, but gave up the latter in 1949. He rode Norton and Matchless outfits before turning to BMW in 1959. He entered the TTs from 1954 to 1967 (except 1962, 64 and 66) and never finished lower than fourth though had several retirements. He was second in 1956 (Norton) and 1960 (BMW) and third in 1955 (Matchless) and 1961 (BMW).

HARTLE, John
John Hartle's racing career began at Scarborough's Olivers Mount circuit in 1954 and it was at Scarborough, 14 years later, that it ended when this distinguished rider from Chapel-en-le-Frith was fatally injured while accelerating up the steep hill after negotiating the Mere hairpin and following a collision with John Blanchard. He was an astonishingly dedicated and courageous rider and continued to race after surviving a number of serious crashes. Following his début in major competition at Scarborough in 1954, Hartle secured a place in the Norton works team and he later had works rides on a regular basis for MV and Gilera. Always closely linked with Isle of Man racing, he first rode in the TTs in 1955 on a Norton, being sixth in the Junior and 13th in the Senior. In 1956 he was third in the Junior and second in the Senior. In 1957 he joined former Norton team mate John Surtees on on MV and rode the famous Italian machines that year in the TTs and also in 1958, 59 and 60. In 1958, on the MV, he became only the second rider to lap the Isle of Man circuit at over 100 mph, was second to Surtees in the Junior TT of 1959, and in 1960 he won the Junior TT and was second in the Senior, all on MV. Riding Gilera machines in 1963 he was runner up in both the Senior and Junior events. In 1960 he won the Ulster Grand Prix. This impressive performance had been achieved despite serious crashes – at Scarborough in 1961, when injury kept him out of racing for almost two years; and in 1964 at Imola, when a fractured skull and other injuries forced a temporary retirement of a further two years. In 1963 he had been signed by Geoff Duke as a member of his Scuderia Duke team in the former Gilera rider's brave attempt to break the MV monopoly of the 500cc World Championship and on the 1957 Gileras, Hartle consistently lapped Monza during tests at around 116 mph.

Hartle returned to racing in 1967, quickly recapturing form. Among numerous victories were the Hutchinson 100 and the 750cc Production TT, and he secured third place on his Matchless in the 500cc World Championship behind Agostini and Hailwood. He crashed twice on the Isle of Man in 1968 and later that year came the fatal Scarborough meeting.

HASLAM, Phil
One of Britain's most promising road racers of the early 1970s, Haslam, from Langley Mill, Notts, was killed while in the lead in the 500cc race at Scarborough's Oliver's Mount circuit in July 1974. He was 24. In 1973 Haslam became the first man to achieve a 100 mph lap in the Manx Grand Prix. His record lap was 103.15 mph. He was killed during his first season as a professional.

HASLAM, Ron
Popular British rider in the 1980s. 'Rocket' Ron's triumphs in 1981 included wins in the TT Formula 1 and the Classic race in the Ulster Grand Prix, two wins at Donington, and victory in the new Streetbike Series.

HELE, Doug
One of the most significant development engineers in British racing, Doug Hele's contemporary fame results from his role as BSA/Triumph development engineer, but in earlier years Hele's work with the pushrod engine was largely responsible for making it significant in racing. His Norton Domiracer, built in 1961, gave Tom Phillis third place in the Senior TT of that year and was the first pushrod machine to lap the Mountain course at 100 mph. At Triumph he became responsible for preparing factory machines for Daytona, TT and other major circuits and achieved remarkable success. The Triumph Bonneville, which he de-

veloped, captured the first production machine 100 mph lap (Malcolm Uphill riding) in 1969, and that year secured the Production Machine TT, the Thruxton 500-miler and the FIM Coup d'Endurance.

Doug Hele will always be noted for his close association with John Cooper in a number of victories shortly before the latter's retirement and culminating in the success of Cooper in the American Ontario 250-miler in 1971 at his first attempt.

HENNE, Ernst
Ernst Henne was one of the most prolific record breakers of all time, setting up world speed records no fewer than seven times in just eight years and all on BMW machines. No other land speed record breaker can remotely match his performance in the number of times he took the record. At 21 years of age and already dedicated to motor cycle racing, Henne was operating a motor cycle dealership in Munich when his potential on a racing cycle was spotted by BMW. He joined them in 1926 and in 1929 made his first and successful attempt on the world outright speed record. On 19th September, 1929, he rocketed over a mile stretch of the Ingoldstadt-Munich road at 134.68 mph on a 750cc BMW. Henne returned to the same track in 1930, after the Englishman Joe Wright had bettered his previous record by some 3 mph, and by the smallest of margins recaptured the record for BMW. Although Wright later that same year advanced the record by as much as 13 mph. Henne was not to be beaten. Two years later, at the Tat track in Hungary, he improved on Wright's performance, taking the record at 152 mph on a 735cc BMW. Between 1932–1936 Ernst Henne was supreme. He pushed up the record four times – from 152 mph in November 1932 to 169 mph in October 1936. After first Fernihough (169.5 mph in 1937) and then Taruffi (170.5 mph in 1937), Henne came back in November 1937 and at the Darmstadt course in Germany raised the record to 173.67 mph. It was the last prewar record and was not improved upon until 1951, when fellow German Herz reached 180 mph. By this time Henne was too old for record breaking.

Henne, a quiet, serious individual, was born in Bavaria in 1904 and in addition to his record breaking, for which he was most famous, took part in a variety of motor-cycle sports for the BMW factory, including trials, road racing and hill climbs. He will always be noted for the streamlined helmets he wore before full fairings were added to his record breaking machines. The period during which Henne was active witnessed much change in machinery used for these world record attempts, from fairly traditional looking motor cycles to the beginning of fully enclosed streamlining.

HENNEN, Pat
Pat Hennen holds the distinction of being the first American to win a World Championship round. Riding a Suzuki 4, and after a major battle against Giacomo Agostini and Tepi Lansivuori, he won the 500cc Finnish Grand Prix in 1976.

HERRON, Tom W.
One of the few Irish riders to be a success in Britain and on the Continent as well as in Ireland in such races as the NW 200 and the Skerries, Herron was born in Lisburn, Northern Ireland. He started racing in 1965 and continued to improve despite a number of bad accidents. He competed in several World Championship races in 1974 and in 1975 was third in the Junior TT on a Yamaha. In 1976 Herron was fourth in both the 250cc and 350cc World Championships, and in 1977 finished runner-up to Katayama for the 350cc world title. That year he came second in the Senior TT behind Phil Read. A hard-riding, hard-living personality, Herron joined the works Suzuki team in 1979 and seemed on the verge of the really big-time when, lying fourth in the 500cc World Championship, he was tragically killed that year after crashing on the last lap of the 1000cc race at the North West 200 in Ulster in May. He was 30.

HOCKING, Gary
With fine examples set by Ray Amm and then Jim Redman and Paddy Driver, Gary Hocking left Southern Rhodesia to take European racing by storm and entered his first TT in 1959, finishing twelfth in the Junior event on a Norton. The very next year, having switched to MV, he was second in the 125, 250 and 350cc classes of the World Championship and in 1961 gained both the 500cc and 350cc World Titles. In 1962 he won the Senior TT and was second in the Junior. It was a meteoric rise in a devastating career which was to end as dramatically as it had begun and prospered. His bike

career closed after squabbles with MV, after which he switched to car racing and was killed in 1962 while practising for the Natal Grand Prix.

Born in Wales, Hocking went to Southern Rhodesia with his parents and started racing at 17 in Bulawayo in grass track meetings. He progressed to a 250cc Velocette, then had a Triumph Tiger 110 and a 350 Manx Norton. Once in Europe he was soon in the headlines. He finished sixth in his very first race – the 500cc class of the 1958 Dutch TT no less – and at the Nurburgring he ran John Hartle close on the mighty MV. He beat the MV and Hartle in the French Grand Prix of 1959 and also that year, this time on an MZ at the Swedish Grand Prix, he was superior to Carlo Ubbiali and the MV in the 250 event. It was Hocking's first Grand Prix victory. He later signed for MV and almost brought them the world title in 1960. He won the TT that year on only his second time in the Isle of Man. A tough, determined character, Gary Hocking's relationships with Mike Hailwood when both were riding MVs became somewhat strained and his upsets with the MV factory bosses were well known. But in spite of these situations he was able to ride with outstanding success and in 1962 broke John Surtees' TT lap record with a speed of 105.75 mph.

Results: Double World Champion (350 and 500cc classes) in 1961. Second in the 350, 250 and 125cc classes of the World Championship in 1960 and third in the 250cc World Championship of 1959.

TT Races: Winner of the Senior and second in the Junior TT in 1962, winner of the lightweight (250) TT and second in the lightweight (125) TT in 1960, and second in the Junior TT of 1961.

HONDA

In the 1960s the Japanese dominated Grand Prix motor-cycle racing with Honda the most dynamic and successful factory. Enormous investment backed their bid for world-wide domination and during nine outstanding years of international competition they achieved 16 world championships and approaching 140 classic victories.

After racing in Japan, Honda, with headquarters in Tokyo, moved into Europe in 1959, competing in the 125cc TT on the Isle of Man. They were the first Japanese factory to race in Europe. Their six-speed twins were much admired as beautiful examples of engineering, but ridden by Japanese riders unfamiliar with the Isle of Man circuit, they failed to achieve individual honours, though Honda collected the Manufacturers Team Award in the lightweight category with a sixth, seventh and eleventh position. In 1960 they signed Australians Tom Phillis and Bob Brown, competing without much success in the 125cc and 250cc events on the Isle of Man and at a number of continental classics. It was in 1960 that the outstanding Rhodesian Jim Redman, later to become team manager during Honda's most successful years, had his first ride for the Japanese factory. He was fourth that year in the 250cc world championship. In 1961 MV had virtually retired from racing and Honda seized the opportunity to press their claim for domination. Luigi Taveri signed for them and both Redman and Phillis had their contracts renewed. Brown had been killed in 1960. Machines were also given to Bob McIntyre and Mike Hailwood The effort was well rewarded. Phillis won the 125cc world championship and Hailwood became 250cc world champion. Hailwood also captured the 125cc and 250cc TT events.

In 1962 Honda invested heavily in new machinery and riders. The early-season 350cc entries were enlarged 250s and it was not until later in the season that Redman rode the first fully-blown 350cc Honda. With beautifully-prepared machines Honda contested all except the 500cc and sidecar world championships. By this time Tommy Robb had also been signed as a team rider. Redman won the world 250cc and 350cc classes and Taveri took the 125cc title. On the Isle of Man Taveri won the 125cc TT, though Redman was second to Derek Minter in the 250cc event who, ironically, was entered on a privately-prepared Honda. In the Junior TT Tom Phillis crashed and was killed.

After the massive effort of 1961 and 1962, Honda cut back slightly in 1963, though managed still to collect the Junior 350cc and lightweight 250cc TTs through Jim Redman, who also secured the World Championship crown in both categories. They did not compete in the 50cc World Championship of 1963 and their 125cc machines were slower than the Suzuki of New Zealand's Hugh Anderson.

Honda spent lavishly again for the 1964 season, producing a new four-cylinder 125cc machine and also a six-cylinder 250cc racer. In the world championship Taveri became 125cc champion, Redman lost the 250cc crown to Phil Read on the remarkably fast Yamaha, though he was again world champion in the 350cc category. On the Isle of Man Honda dominated, collecting 1st, 2nd and 3rd places in the 125cc TT and winning the 250cc and 350cc events.

Honda distinctions from then until their official effective retirement from racing at the end of the 1967 season are as follows:

1965

World Championships

50cc (Ralph Bryans): 350cc (Jim Redman). Also second in 50cc and third in 250cc.

TT Races

50cc (Luigi Taveri): 250cc (Jim Redman): 350cc (Jim Redman). Also second in 125cc.

1966

World Championships

125cc (Luigi Taveri); 250cc (Mike Hailwood); 350cc (Mike Hailwood). Also second and third in 50cc, third in 125cc, third in 250cc and second in 500cc.

TT Races

50cc (Ralph Bryans); 250cc (Mike Hailwood); 500cc (Mike Hailwood). Also second in 50cc and second in 250cc.

1967

World Championships

250cc (Mike Hailwood); 350cc (Mike Hailwood). Also third in 350cc and second in 500cc.

TT Races

250cc (Mike Hailwood); 350cc (Mike Hailwood); 500cc (Mike Hailwood). Also third in 250cc.

Honda left Grand Prix motor cycle racing with a supreme record with which only the vintage years of Norton could remotely compare. Their huge investment, dedication and lavish support-system for their riders and machines gave the sport a new dimension. Since their departure there have been repeated rumours of their return to full-scale racing, but so far the rumours have been without foundation. Honda ambitions seemed turned more to the United States and in the early 1970s they began to take part in important United States events like the Daytona races. They have also been active in a bid to capture the outright world motor-cycle speed record with their mighty Honda Hawk projectile which reached 286.56 mph on the Bonneville Salt Flats in 1972, making it at that time unofficially, the fastest two-wheel vehicle on earth.

In spite of Honda's phenomenal success in Grand Prix racing in the Sixties one important objective eluded them, the 500cc World Championship. It was principally to achieve this prestigious aim that they signed Mike Hailwood to a substantial contract, but after a season of outstanding battles with Agostini on the MV, Hailwood found the big Honda insufficiently reliable. Honda were perhaps most successful in the 350cc class where they collected the world championship six years in succession, 1962 to 1965 with Jim Redman and 1966 and 1967 through Mike Hailwood. Redman, with a total of six world titles on the Japanese machines, was Honda's most successful rider. Hailwood brought Honda the distinction of being the first factory in motor cycle history to win all four races at a Grand Prix meeting. This occurred at Brno in Czechoslovakia in 1966. Hailwood won the 250, 350 and 500cc races and Honda mounted Taveri won the 125cc event. Honda produced new race machines for the first time in almost a decade in 1976, for factory-backed competition in long distance races.

Included in Honda's impressive list of distinctions were 18 world titles in the manufacturer's category.

After much speculation and rumour, Honda announced plans for a £2½ million return to Grand Prix road racing in 1979 after a number of years of successful competition in endurance racing, but their initial machines (the NR500) were hardly competitive. They announced plans for a further attempt in 1982, this time with two-stroke machinery, and signed World Champion Marco Lucchinelli to the richest contract in the history of motor-cycle racing.

Machine Notes

The early 125cc Honda was a sophisticated machine with two cylinders, overhead cam, four valves per cylinder and twin ignition, but produced only limited power against the MV single, and in 1960 Honda undertook a complete rebuilding job. New models were a two-cylinder 125 and a 250-4, with the twin overhead-cam controlled by a central gear train. Development work brought Honda success in 1961. This 250 racer of 1961 was Honda's first really successful model. Power was 45 bhp at 14,000 rpm. With the introduction of the 50cc world championship in 1962 Honda produced a twin overhead-cam single with four valves geared to 10 hp at 14,000 rpm for a speed of 87 mph, but it was inferior to the Suzuki two-stroke. Redman's first success in the 350cc category was in 1962 on a bored out 250 to 285cc. In 1964 Honda introduced a new four-cylinder 125, revving to 16,000 and with an eight-speed gearbox. Speed was reckoned to exceed 124 mph. In the 250 class, a development of the existing design, lighter and lower, started the season and, faced with keen competition from Yamaha, a new six-cylinder design was introduced. In 1965 a new twin-cylinder machine gave Honda (Ralph Bryans) the 50cc title but in the 125 and 250cc classes Honda struggled. For the Japanese Grand Prix of that year they introduced a five-cylinder 125. This exceptional machine had eight speeds and revved at 20,000 rpm, and helped Honda reach their peak in 1966; they won all five solo manufacturers' world titles. Their new 250 machine was a six-speed, six-cylinder model timed at the TT at 143 mph, and the powerful Honda 500-4 introduced for Hailwood had a top speed of 168 mph. Its handling never matched its power and Hailwood was often ill at ease with it. At the start of 1967 Honda dropped out of the 50 and 125cc classes. Hailwood, however, had a new 297cc six-cylinder machine, introduced at the West German Grand Prix in May, and on this he easily secured the 350cc world title.

HUSQVARNA

A Swedish make of motor cycle hailing from the town of that name, Husqvarna have been one of the most prominent and prolific machines in moto cross, taking eleven individual world championships, 1962–78. The factory began making motor cycles in 1903 and from 1931 to 1936 were prominent in road racing. Husqvarna machines appeared regularly in the Isle of Man TTs and in European road-racing classic events. Unsuccessful on the Island, their powerful OHV V-twin was ridden with success by Stanley Woods in Swedish events. By 1936, however, the factory's participation in road racing was in sharp decline. In 1960 a modified version of a single cylinder overhead valve 500cc roadster machine first produced in 1936, ridden by Bill Nilsson, brought Husqvarnas their first 500cc world moto cross championship. In the early 1950s 175cc Husqvarnas took a prominent role in the International Six Days and other trial events.

In moto cross Rolf Tibblin became the Champion of Europe in 1959 on a 250cc Husqvarna. When Torsten Hallman joined the company it was the prelude to an impressive run of successes. He brought the Swedish make the 500cc moto cross title in 1962 and 1963 and was Champion of the World in 1962, 1963, 1966 and 1967. In 1969 Aberg won the first of his two 500cc world titles on Husky two-strokes. In British Championship events Husqvarna have been prominent. On a 400cc Husqvarna Bryan Goss became the first private owner to win the British 500cc moto cross title. Alan Clough was British 250cc Champion in 1967 riding a Husqvarna and Bryan Wade, Vic Eastwood and others have ridden Husqvarna successfully. Ridden by Bryan Wade and Andy Robertson this outstanding Swedish machine achieved the double British Championship in 1972. Heikki Mikkola gained the world 500cc Moto Cross Championship in 1974 and the 250cc class in 1976, both on Husqvarna.

HUTCHINSON 100

In the early days of British motor-cycle racing the Hutchinson 100, organised by the British Motor Cycle Racing Club (Bemsee), was one of the most important road race events. Discounting the TT Races on the Isle of Man, the Hutchinson 100 is England's oldest road race meeting, dating back to the days of Brooklands in 1925. The first Hutchinson 100, so named because it was organised in conjunction with the Hutchinson Tyre Company and was run over 100 miles, was a handicap event and until the outbreak of the second World War took place on the outer circuit at Brooklands. It was later reshaped as a road race. With the closure of Brooklands, the Hutchinson 100 was run in 1947 and 1948 at Dunholme Lodge RAF station, near Lincoln. It transferred to Silverstone in 1949 and then moved to Brands Hatch in 1966, being run in an anti-clockwise direction. The huge silver Mellano Trophy (donated originally by A. V. Mellano of the Hutchinson Tyre Company) is presented to the rider whose average speed in a race beats the existing lap record for that class by the greatest margin, or is nearest to the lap record.

Mellano trophy winners at Brands Hatch
1966: H. Anderson.
1967: J. Hartle.
1968: P. Read.
1969: G. Auerbacher.
1970: K. Enders.
1971: P. Williams.
1972: D. Potter.
1973: B. Sheene.
1974: P. Williams.
1975: B. Sheene.
1976: B. Sheene.

After 1976 the Hutchinson 100 was cancelled and the Mellano Trophy was reduced to a club meeting on the reversed Brands Hatch long circuit. Too many meetings of international status in Britain and increasing costs were blamed for the demise of what was once reckoned to be the principal short circuit meeting in the British season.

I

IMOLA
Home of the Italian Grand Prix in recent years and generally regarded much more of a rider's circuit than Monza. Equally famous for the Italian 200-mile race inaugurated in 1972. Situated near Rimini on the Adriatic coast, the prestige and importance of Imola has increased in recent years with the development of the 200-miler as a major event. In spite of the Italian moto-cross Grand Prix being held only forty miles away, the 1973 Imola 200-miler attracted 80,000 spectators, 10,000 more than the previous year. The Imola meeting became Europe's leading road race, attracting an international entry. The Imola circuit is 3.19 miles and for the 1974 200-miler two chicanes were added, as a precaution following the deaths of Saarinen and Pasolini at Monza in 1973.

INDIAN
This famous American machine was prominent in international racing during the early days of motor-cycle sport. Indians were ridden with success at Brooklands and a notable victory there was that of Indian rider Jake de Rosier of the USA over Britain's legendary Charlie Collier (Matchless) in 1911. Only a week earlier de Rosier had shattered three world records on the tough 994 Indian. On the Isle of Man, Indian machines took the first three places in the Senior TT of 1911 – the first foreign factory to win a TT. In the outright speed world Indians were significant in the early years. American Ed Walker is credited with 103.5 mph (the first in excess of 100 mph) on a 994cc Indian twin at Daytona Beach in 1920, though there appears some doubt about it being officially authenticated. The Indian company was originally noted for pedal cycles but in 1900 George M. Hendee, the manufacturer, became associated with Oscar Hedstrom, and in 1911 the first Indian motor cycle was produced, a $1\frac{1}{2}$ hp single-cylinder machine which weighed only 98 lb.

INTERNATIONAL/ BRITISH NATIONAL RECORDS
The regulations governing attempts at International and British National records are set out in a special booklet issued by the Auto-Cycle Union.

INTERNATIONAL CUP RACES
These were early attempts in France to bring about organised motor cycle racing; as *Motor Cycle* put it, "likely to become as important an affair in connection with the motor cycle pastime as the Gordon-Bennett cup race for motor cars". The first took place in 1904 and was organised by the Auto-Cycle Club de France. A British team took part but was hopelessly outclassed, though the race was written into the history books of the sport more for its almost total lack of organisation and poor sportsmanship than for its racing. So bad was the running of the race that the results were declared void. The following year the International Cup Race was under the organisation of the newly constituted Federation Internationale des Clubs Motorcyclistes and was a success, establishing the authority of the FICM, predecessor of the present FIM. The rules of the International Cup Race restricted machines to a weight limit of 110 lb and encouraged machines with big engines in light, spindly frames and with thin wheels and tyres. A British team again took part but were once more outclassed. It was because the British riders of the day, backed by the Auto-Cycle Club, so disliked the rules and the running of the International Cup Race that they looked earnestly for an alternative of their own. They wanted a road race of major importance for *touring machines* and found a possible venue where a planned race could be held on actual roads in the Isle of Man. It was from this beginning that the TT races were born.

INTERNATIONAL SIX-DAYS TRIAL
The International Six-Days Trial was started in England in 1913 and was based on Carlisle. It grew out of a national six-days trial promoted by the A-CU. It takes place once a year over, as its name implies, six days and is now held in a

different country each year. It is perhaps the most important event in the trials calendar and although rewarding the best individual performers with gold, silver and bronze medals, remains essentially a team event with riders from many countries competing in six-man teams for the Premier World Trophy and four-man teams for the Silver Vase. Countries enter one team for the World Trophy but may enter two teams for the Silver Vase. There are also manufacturers and club team contests.

The ISDT is quite unique and very different from the normal sporting trial. Although in common with other trials it began from the basis of reliability it developed quite differently from other events and is now an inter-nation competition based purely on time over a 1000-mile course and in a number of cross-country speed, braking and acceleration tests. In this way it is perhaps now more like moto cross or the major international car rallies. The event is made up of special timed stages, over which riders must keep to a minimum speed.

For both riders and machines the ISDT is incredibly tough and many competitors fail to complete the course. Run over rugged terrain which includes rough mountain and forest tracks as well as normal roads, marshes, streams, mud, rocks and ruts, it is extremely exhausting for riders and fiercely demanding on machines for, over the six days, no part of the machine other than tyres may be changed. Machines are not limited by capacity though power alone would be a disadvantage. Lightness and, in particular, handling are all important in cross-country conditions.

The ISDT, which was originally run with road machines, has embraced a number of changes over the years, including the introduction of special tests, more arduous cross-country sections, shorter daily routes. Riders in the inter-nation contest were at one time obliged to use machines manufactured in their own country, but this rule was abandoned after 1970. Early teams included a sidecar combination, an arrangement later abandoned. The Silver Vase contest was introduced in 1924 for up to three-man teams using any machines.

The "world" interest in the ISDT and the prestige it has acquired makes it an event of great interest to the motor cycle factories and on an increasing basis have official teams competed – Bultaco, Ossa, MZ, Puch and others.

In the early post-war ISDTs Britain did well and in spite of strong competition from Czechoslovakia won the world trophy from 1948 to 1951, and again in 1953. But that, sadly, was the last British success (end 1975). It must be said that non-competitive machinery reduced Britain's chances in the years since 1953 and the abandoning of the rule whereby teams were obliged to compete on machines built in their own country, was therefore welcomed in Britain. In 1974 the British team for the World Trophy competed on Jawas, but only David Jeremiah of South Wales, out of 36 British competitors, completed the 1038-mile course without losing a single mark and thereby earned a Gold Medal.

Interest in trials in the USA has increased enormously in recent times, a development which has not gone unnoticed by the main manufacturers of trials machines who rightly see a vast sales potential in the USA for their machines.

In 1974 the ISDT took place in Italy over a tough course. Fourteen countries entered their six-man teams for the World Trophy. They were Belgium, Czechoslovakia, Canada, France, East Germany, Holland, Italy, Britain, Poland, Russia, Sweden, Switzerland, USA and West Germany. In addition Austria, Finland and Spain were represented in the 19 Silver Vase teams. It is perhaps the most international of all motor cycle events.

Britain's World Trophy team for the 1974 ISDT was: Mick Bowers (250cc Jawa), Ernie Page (250cc Jawa), Vic Allan (350cc Jawa), Andy Robertson (350cc Jawa), Dave Jeremiah (360cc Jawa), John Pease (360cc Jawa), Reserve – Dave Smith (360cc Jawa). The team manager was Ken Heanes. The fiftieth ISDT took place on the Isle of Man in 1975.

Results:

1947: Trophy – Czechoslovakia; Vase – Czechoslovakia.
1948: Trophy – Britain; Vase – Britain.
1949: Trophy – Britain; Vase – Czechoslovakia.
1950: Trophy – Britain; Vase – Britain.
1951: Trophy – Britain; Vase – Holland.
1952: Trophy – Czechoslovakia; Vase –

Czechoslovakia.
1953: Trophy – Britain; Vase – Czechoslovakia.
1954: Trophy – Czechoslovakia; Vase – Holland.
1955: Trophy – Germany; Vase – Czechoslovakia.
1956: Trophy – Czechoslovakia; Vase – Holland.
1957: Trophy – Germany; Vase – Czechoslovakia.
1958: Trophy – Czechoslovakia; Vase – Czechoslovakia.
1959: Trophy – Czechoslovakia; Vase – Czechoslovakia.
1960: Trophy – Austria; Vase – Italy.
1961: Trophy – West Germany; Vase – Czechoslovakia.
1962: Trophy – Czechoslovakia; Vase – West Germany.
1963: Trophy – East Germany; Vase – Italy.
1964: Trophy – East Germany; Vase – East Germany.
1965: Trophy – East Germany; Vase – East Germany.
1966: Trophy – East Germany; Vase – West Germany.
1967: Trophy – East Germany; Vase – Czechoslovakia.
1968: Trophy – West Germany; Vase – Italy.
1969: Trophy – East Germany; Vase – West Germany.
1970: Trophy – Czechoslovakia; Vase – Czechoslovakia.
1971: Trophy – Czechoslovakia; Vase – Czechoslovakia.
1972: Trophy – Czechoslovakia; Vase – Czechoslovakia.
1973: Trophy – Czechoslovakia; Vase – America.
1974: Trophy – Czechoslovakia; Vase – Czechoslovakia.
1975: Trophy – West Germany; Vase – Italy.
1976: Trophy – West Germany; Vase – Czechoslovakia.
1977: Trophy – Czechoslovakia; Vase – Czechoslovakia.
1978: Trophy – Czechoslovakia; Vase – Italy.
1979: Trophy – Italy; Vase – Czechoslovakia.
1980: Trophy – Italy; Vase – West Germany.
1981: Trophy – Italy; Vase – Italy.

ITALIAN GRAND PRIX
One of the earliest classic events, the Italian Grand Prix was established in the years immediately following the end of the first World War. The Italian Grand Prix of 1921 included only one British entry, but by 1924 British interest in the Italian was sufficient for Jimmy Simpson to be first home on his AJS in the 350cc class. By 1925 the Italian Grand Prix, though still not seriously considered by the majority of British racers, who preferred to concentrate for obvious reasons of distance and expense on the French and Belgian GPs, was attracting more attention and Jock Porter (New Gerrard) won the lightweight class in an Italian Grand Prix which that year constituted the first Grand Prix of Europe. Monza, the famous circuit near Milan, is the traditional home of the Italian Grand Prix, although the famous circuit at Imola has been extensively used. The newly constructed 3.26-mile circuit of Mugello, near Florence in the north of Italy, was used for the first time in 1976.

Results:
1950: 125cc G. Leoni (Mondial); 250cc D. Ambrosini (Benelli); 350cc G. E. Duke (Norton); 500cc G. E. Duke (Norton); sidecar E. S. Oliver (Norton).
1951: 125cc C. Ubbiali (Mondial); 250cc E. Lorenzetti (Guzzi); 350cc G. E. Duke (Norton); 500cc Alfredo Milani (Gilera); sidecar Alb. Milani (Gilera).
1952: 125cc E. Mendogni (Morini); 250cc E. Lorenzetti (Guzzi); 350cc W. R. Amm (Norton); 500cc R. L. Graham (MV); sidecar E. Merlo (Gilera).
1953: 125cc W. Haas (NSU); 250cc E. Lorenzetti (Guzzi); 350cc E. Lorenzetti (Guzzi); 500cc G. E. Duke (Gilera); sidecar E. S. Oliver (Norton).
1954: 125cc G. Sala (MV); 250cc A. F. Wheeler (Guzzi); 350cc F. K. Anderson (Guzzi); 500cc G. E. Duke (Gilera); sidecar W. Noll (BMW).
1955: 125cc C. Ubbiali (MV); 250cc C. Ubbiali (MV); 350cc R. H. Dale (Guzzi); 500cc U. Masetti (MV); sidecar W. Noll (BMW).
1956: 125cc C. Ubbiali (MV); 250cc C. Ubbiali (MV); 350cc L. Liberati (Gilera); 500cc G. E. Duke (Gilera); sidecar Alb. Milani (Gilera).

1957: 125cc C. Ubbiali (MV); 250cc T. Provini (Mondial); 350cc R. McG. McIntyre (Gilera); 500cc L. Liberati (Gilera); sidecar Alb. Milani (Gilera).

1958: 125cc R. Spaggiari (Ducati); 250cc E. Mendogni (Morini); 350cc J. Surtees (MV); 500cc J. Surtees (MV).

1959: 125cc E. Degner (MZ); 250cc C. Ubbiali (MV); 350cc J. Surtees (MV); 500cc J. Surtees (MV).

1960: 125cc C. Ubbiali (MV); 250cc C. Ubbiali (MV); 350cc G. Hocking (MV); 500cc J. Surtees (MV).

1961: 125cc E. Degner (MZ); 250cc J. A. Redman (Honda); 350cc G. Hocking (MV); 500cc S. M. B. Hailwood (MV).

1962: 50cc H. G. Anscheidt (Kreidler); 125cc T. Tanaka (Honda); 250cc J. A. Redman (Honda); 350cc J. A. Redman (Honda); 500cc S. M. B. Hailwood (MV).

1963: 125cc L. Taveri (Honda); 250cc T. Provini (Morini); 350cc J. A. Redman (Honda); 500cc S. M. B. Hailwood (MV).

1964: 125cc L. Taveri (Honda); 250cc P. W. Read (Yamaha); 350cc J. A. Redman (Honda); 500cc S. M. B. Hailwood (MV).

1965: 125cc H. Anderson (Suzuki); 250cc T. Provini (Benelli); 350cc G. Agostini (MV); 500cc S. M. B. Hailwood (MV); sidecars F. Scheidegger (BMW).

1966: 50cc H. G. Anscheidt (Suzuki); 125cc L. Taveri (Honda); 250cc S. M. B. Hailwood (Honda); 350cc G. Agostini (MV-Agusta); 500cc G. Agostini (MV-Agusta).

1967: 125cc W. Ivy (Yamaha); 250cc P. Read (Yamaha); 350cc R. Bryans (Honda); 500cc G. Agostini (MV-Agusta); sidecars G. Auerbacher/B. Nelson (BMW).

1968: 125cc W. Ivy (Yamaha); 250cc P. Read (Yamaha); 350cc G. Agostini (MV-Agusta); 500cc G. Agostini (MV-Agusta).

1969: 50cc P. Lodewijkx (Jamathi); 125cc D. A. Simmonds (Kawasaki); 250cc P. Read (Yamaha); 350cc P. Read (Yamaha); 500cc A. Pagani (Linto).

1970: 50cc J. De Vries (Kreidler); 125cc A. Nieto (Derbi); 250cc R. Gould (Yamaha); 350cc G. Agostini (MV-Agusta); 500cc G. Agostini (MV-Agusta).

1971: 50cc J. De Vries (Kreidler); 125cc G. Parlotti (Morbidelli); 250cc G. Marsowszky (Yamaha); 350cc J. Saarinen (Yamaha); 500cc A. Pagani (Linto/MV-Agusta).

1972: 50cc J. De Vries (Kreidler); 125cc A. Nieto (Derbi); 250cc R. Pasolini (Aermacchi); 350cc G. Agostini (MV-Agusta); 500cc G. Agostini (MV-Agusta).

1973: 50cc J. De Vries (Kreidler); 125cc K. Anderson (Yamaha); 350cc G. Agostini (MV-Agusta).

1974: 50cc H. van Kessel (Van Veen Kreidler); 125cc A. Nieto (Derbi); 250cc W. Villa (Harley-Davidson); 350cc G. Agostini (Yamaha); 500cc G. Bonera (MV); sidecar K. Enders/R. Englehardt (BMW).

1975: 50cc A. Nieto (Kreidler); 125cc P. Pileri (Morbidelli); 250cc W. Villa (Harley-Davidson); 350cc J. Cecotto (Yamaha); 500cc G. Agostini (Yamaha).

1976: 50cc A. Nieto (Bultaco); 125cc P. Bianchi (Morbidelli); 250cc W. Villa (Harley-Davidson); 350cc J. Cecotto (Yamaha); 500cc B. Sheene (Suzuki).

1977: 50cc E. Lazzarini (Kreidler); 125cc P. Bianchi (Morbidelli); 250cc F. Uncini (Harley-Davidson); 350cc A. North (Yamaha); 500cc B. Sheene (Suzuki).

1978: 50cc R. Tormo (Bultaco); 125cc E. Lazzarini (MBA); 250cc K. Ballington (Kawasaki); 350cc K. Ballington (Kawasaki); 500cc K. Roberts (Yamaha); sidecar R. Biland/K. Williams (Beo-Yamaha).

1979: 50cc E. Lazzarini (Kreidler); 125cc A. Nieto (Minarelli); 250cc K. Ballington (Kawasaki); 350cc G. Hansford (Kawasaki); 500cc K. Roberts (Yamaha).

1980: 50cc E. Lazzarini (Kreidler); 125cc P. Bianchi (MBA); 250cc A. Mang (Kawasaki); 350cc J. Cecotto (Yamaha); 500cc K. Roberts (Yamaha).

1981: 50cc R. Tormo (Bultaco); 125cc G. Bertin (Sanvenero); 250cc M. Massimiani (Ad Majora); 350cc J. Ekerold (Bimoto); 500cc K. Roberts (Yamaha).

IVY, W. D.
Born in Kent on 27th August, 1942, Bill Ivy raced British machines on his home circuit of Brands Hatch for early sponsors in 1959 and early 1960 seasons. In 1966 he signed a contract with Yamaha and a short but meteoric rise to world acclaim followed.

Ivy's first racing was on a 50cc Itom sponsored by Chisholms of Maidstone in 1959 and that same year at Brands Hatch he captured the lap record for the short circuit. He raced for Geoff Monty before moving on in 1965 to Tom Kirby for whom he rode AJS and Matchless machines. He won the British Championship title for the first time in 1965. He turned full time professional that year and in 1966 took the King of Brands title away from Derek Minter. His first win for Yamaha was in the Spanish Grand Prix of 1966 and from then on his sensational career was on the way. Ivy became one of the exclusive band of "circus" riders which typified the 1960s when Honda, Yamaha and Suzuki brought a new dimension to the sport with vast investments and big contracts for the top riders. Ivy, though only 5 ft 3 in tall and weighing 9½ stone, could handle big machines well but it was on Yamaha 125cc and 250cc machinery that he had his greatest international triumphs. He won the world 125cc Championship for Britain on a Yamaha in 1967 and on the Isle of Man he won the 125cc TT in 1966 and the 250cc TT in 1968. He was a colourful, flamboyant character with a fearless style. He epitomised the swinging sixties cult. The climax of Ivy's career came in 1968 and in the duels he had with Yamaha teammate Phil Read – a row which involved the riding to team orders and which culminated in one of the major sensations of the period. Ivy and Read openly squabbled amid protests and counter-protests. Read ignored orders and became World Champion in both the 125cc and 250cc classes; Ivy, just missing both titles, announced his retirement from racing. He returned in 1969, however, with a contract to ride for Jawa. He was killed while practising for the East German Grand Prix at Sachsenring.

Ivy's spectacular technique and sheer bravery brought him many distinctions, particularly on the Isle of Man, where he registered two incredible performances in 1968, perhaps his most outstanding year. In the lightweight event he raised the lap record to an outstanding 105.51 mph, superior to Mike Hailwood's previous 250cc record by more than 12 seconds. That same year he became the first man to lap the Isle of Man course at over 100 mph on a 125cc machine. In all Ivy recorded eight 100 mph and over laps during his TT career. At both the Italian and Ulster Grands Prix of 1968 he won the 125cc and 250cc races. During his short, sensational career Bill Ivy was seldom out of the headlines and he gained a reputation as something of a hell-raiser with outspoken comments, involvement in off-track scuffles and swift reaction to official mumbo-jumbo. Any over-emphasis of these aspects of his character, however, do him less than justice. Those who knew him best said he was kindly and sensitive and there is no denying that he was one of the most exciting and successful riders of all time. The memory of the still lamented Bill Ivy is maintained through challenge races held annually at Brands Hatch.

World Championships:
1967: 125cc (Yamaha).

TT wins:
1966: 125cc (Yamaha).
1968: 250cc (Yamaha).

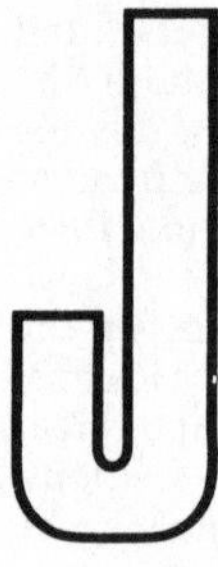

JAPANESE GRAND PRIX

Significant in the 1960s when Japanese factory-sponsored works teams made an all-out assault in classic racing, the Japanese Grand Prix has been held on the Suzuki circuit, which belongs to Honda, and Fisco.

Results:

1963: 50cc L. Taveri (Honda); 125cc F. G. Perris (Suzuki); 250cc J. A. Redman (Honda); 350cc J. A. Redman (Honda).
1964: 50cc R. Bryans (Honda); 125cc E. Degner (Suzuki); 250cc J. A. Redman (Honda); 350cc J. A. Redman (Honda).
1965: 50cc L. Taveri (Honda); 125cc H. R. Anderson (Suzuki); 250cc S. M. B. Hailwood (Honda); 350cc S. M. B. Hailwood (MV).
1966: 50cc Y. Katayama (Suzuki); 125cc W. D. Ivy (Yamaha); 250cc T. Hasegawa (Yamaha); 350cc P. W. Read (Yamaha).
1967: 50cc M. Itoh (Suzuki); 125cc W. D. Ivy (Yamaha); 250cc R. Bryans (Honda); 350cc S. M. B. Hailwood (Honda).
1968: Cancelled.

JAWA

This machine was brought to the attention of the British road-racing public in 1969 when the dynamic Bill Ivy, who only months before had announced his retirement following squabbles with Phil Read in the Yamaha team, signed to ride for the factory. The Czechoslovakian company had been racing without success for a couple of seasons, but in 1969 with the Japanese factories out of racing and Ivy contracted, Jawa prospects looked bright. On the 350cc two-stroke, Ivy showed brilliant form in the Dutch TT and led the race from Agostini, before mechanical trouble slowed him down and he finished second. The measure of success which Jawa might have achieved with Ivy was never revealed because it was in the same year that Ivy lost his life on the Jawa while practising for the East German Grand Prix at Sachsenring.

Jawa have been dominant in moto cross, winning the 250 world moto cross title and the International Six-Days Trial.

JEFFERIES, A. T.

Jefferies, a Yorkshireman born 1948, began racing in 1969 and won his first important race at Scarborough in 1970. He raced in the TTs both years, his best placing being fifth in the 750 Production TT of 1969 on a Triumph. He achieved much success in the Island in 1971, winning both the Junior TT on a Yamsel and the Formula 750 TT (the first to be held) on the 750cc Triumph. He was also second in the 750cc Production TT on a Triumph Trident. He has since figured prominently in 750cc racing. He was third in the F750 TT on the Triumph in 1973.

JOHN PLAYER NORTON

The combination of John Player sponsorship and Norton machines began in 1972 when John Player decided they required an outlet which had seen very little activity from other tobacco companies yet had a very large following.

The team for 1972 was: Phil Read, Peter Williams, Tony Rutter (last race Cadwell 14th May), Jody Nichlos (one ride at Silverstone 13th August), Mick Grant (first race Mallory, 11th June to end of season), Dave Croxford (only race was on F750 Paris, 22nd October).

The team for 1973 was John Cooper (last race Brands 20th April), Peter Williams, Dave Croxford (who joined the team for the F750 at Brands on 20th April and with Williams rode Production JPN all season), and Mick Grant (Isle of Man and Scarborough) and who was also loaned JPN for Oulton Park Anglo-American races 23rd April. In 1973 a number of long distance events were also contested as follows: *Barcelona* – Dave Croxford/Peter Williams; *Bol d'Or* – Dave Croxford/Peter Williams and Rex Butcher/Barry Scully. *Thruxton 500 miler* – Dave Croxford/Percy Tait and Rex Butcher/Norman White.

The main successes of the JPN machines were as follows: Scarborough

September 1972 – Mick Grant (first); Thruxton 500 mile October 1972 – Dave Croxford and Percy Tait (first); Rex Butcher and Jim Harvey (second); Brands Hatch October 1972 – Phil Read (first) and Peter Williams (third); John Player Transatlantic Trophy Easter 1973 – Peter Williams (four wins and highest point scorer); Cadwell Park May 1973 – Peter Williams (first overall); Isle of Man TT June 1973 – Peter Williams (first) and Mick Grant (second); runner-up (equal to points of winner) in Motor Cycle News F750 superbike Championship – Peter Williams.

Development had been achieved say JPN by two important factors (*a*) giving the team money which Norton would not otherwise have had, enabling them to produce better bikes in power, handling, and braking and in other departments where they could afford to develop their ideas; examples are monocoque chassis and alloy wheels; (*b*) John Player provided a new "all-mod cons" transporter and additional tools in order to make the lives easier for the mechanics, enabling them to spend more time on the machines. It is certainly true that John Player injected much needed enthusiasm and money into motor-cycle racing, giving the whole scene a more colourful look and bringing added publicity for the sport both in the Easter Anglo-American match series and the Silverstone International, as well as through the John Player Norton team itself.

John Player discontinued their sponsorship of the works Norton team for 1975, but continued for a time to support both the Silverstone Grand Prix and the Trans-Atlantic Match Race Series.

Team manager of JPN was Frank Perris, a sucessful racing motorcyclist of the 1960s, who joined JPN team on its formation in 1972. The JPN team headquarters were at Thruxton.

KATAYAMA, Takasumi

Although Japan conquered the world with their machines from Honda, Suzuki, Yamaha and, later and to a lesser degree, Kawasaki, the country has not been a world force when it comes to producing riders. From the inception of the World Championships in 1949 there has not been a Japanese title holder (to 1975), but showing excellent potential in 1973 to do well in Europe was Katayama with an easy victory in the road race at Fuju, 100 miles north-west of Tokyo. Katayama (born 1951) contested the World Championships in 1974 and finished fourth on a Yamaha in the 250cc class. As Yamaha works rider in Japan, Katayama won the Japanese 250cc title in 1972 and the 350cc title in 1973. On his first visit to England he won the 250cc race at Silverstone and broke the lap record formerly held jointly by Saarinen and Gould. Katayama was 350cc World Champion in 1977 and was runner-up to Kork Ballington in 1978, riding Yamaha.

KAWASAKI

A Japanese make of machine made in Tokyo, and prominent in the late 1960s and early 1970s, Kawasaki was the fourth Japanese manufacturer to enter international competition. Their first appearance was at the Japanese Grand Prix of 1965 where the factory presented an array of 125cc two-stroke fours and water-cooled twins fitted with two rotary valves. But racing was extremely competitive and with Suzuki and Yamaha still active in the sport, Kawasaki found the going hard. By 1969 much of the Japanese involvement had disappeared and Dave Simmonds, on a Kawasaki on loan from Japan, won the 125cc World Championship easily in spite of his machine being four years old. In 1970, a Kawasaki machine, ridden by Ginger Molloy, came second in the 500cc World Championship. In the TT races, Dave Simmonds won the 125cc event of 1969 on a Kawasaki, establishing the fastest lap at 92.46 mph. He also established the fastest lap, again on the Japanese machine, in 1970 at 90.90 mph. Kawasaki later moved with outstanding success into Formula 750 racing with their H2-R three-cylinder two strokes. It was the Seeley-frame version of this machine which carried Paul Smart to a £12,000 Ontario victory in 1972 and brought him second place in the 1972 Race of the Year at Mallory Park and victory in the Superbike race at the same meeting. It was on the standard-frame Kawasaki that Yvon Duhamel won America's fastest road race, the Talladega 200, at a record breaking average of 110.44 mph. On this machine he at one point in 1973 held every motor cycle speed record on the circuit up to a distance of 200 miles.

Kawasaki's best performances in the World Championships have come through factory riders Kork Ballington and Gregg Hansford. Ballington secured both the 250cc and 350cc World Championships in 1978 and 1979. Hansford, also in 1978 and 1979, was runner-up in the 250cc series and finished the season in third place on the 350cc Kawasaki. Kawasaki also took the 250cc World Title in 1980 and the 250cc and 350cc Championship in 1981, all through the West German rider Anton Mang.

KIRBY, Tom

One of Britain's leading sponsors in the post-war years, Tom Kirby (born 1923) supported road racing, grass track and scrambles riders during his 25 years of sponsorship. Among the forty riders he at one time sponsored were Mike Hailwood, Phil Read, Alan Barnett, Mike Duff, Paddy Driver, Bill Ivy, Pat Mahoney and Alf Hagon. He is a retired director of Bemsee. His most successful years as a sponsor were 1960-65. In 1965 his G50s finished first, second and third in Brands Hatch Race of the South, ridden by Hailwood.

KNIEVEL, Evel

A former traditional motor-cycle racer, Evel Knievel turned to stunt riding and became a multi-millionaire and something of a living legend in the USA by specialising in flying leaps over rows of motor cars and lorries. An outstanding showman, Knievel's greatest feat came in the autumn of 1974 when he attempted to leap nearly a mile over the 600-ft Snake River Canyon in Idaho in his Sky Cycle Z-2. It was a failure, but perhaps the most sensational failure in the history of stunt riding, for the attempt was accompanied by a mass of publicity across the world. One of the parachutes on the Sky Cycle opened prematurely and the machine and its pilot were carried into the canyon. Fortunately the machine came to rest on a shelf some twenty feet above the waters at the foot of the canyon. Knievel was shaken, but unhurt except for bruising.

Born in 1949 Knievel is a self-confessed ex-jailbird and was said to have courted his wife by kidnapping her on three different occasions. He is the ultimate in flamboyance and in the process of making more than 300 motorcycle jumps has broken more than 100 bones. His appearances at such venues as the vast Astrodome in Texas have attracted as many as 99,000 people. He does his daring leaps on a Harley-Davidson machine. His ambition to leap over a canyon came in 1966 when he set his sights on the Grand Canyon, but permission for him to attempt it was not forthcoming from the various authorities concerned. He settled for the Snake River Canyon as second best.

LAMPKIN BROTHERS
Famous in trials and scrambles the Lampkin brothers have an impressive record.

Arthur (born 1939) won the Scott Trial in 1960 and 1961 (when he was best on observation and fastest on time) and was successful again in 1965. Other successes include runner up in the moto cross European series (1961), later to become the world championships; A-CU Scrambles Stars in 1959 (500cc) and 1961 (250cc); member of Britain's winning Trophee des Nations team in 1961-62 and the winning Moto Cross des Nations team in 1966; winner of the Scottish Six-Days Trial (1963) and the British Experts sidecar category (1973).

Alan Raymond Charles (Sid) Lampkin (born 1945) achieved a finishers certificate in the Scott Trial of 1961 and won both the Scott and the Scottish Six Days in 1966.

Harold Martin Lampkin (born 1951) was second in both the British and European title series of 1972 and became British Trials Champion in 1973. He also won the newly-formed World's Trials Championship in 1975.

LANSIVUORI, Teuvo
This Finnish road racer began to claim European and international recognition in 1973 and had sufficiently established his reputation that when fellow Finn Jarno Saarinen was tragically killed at Monza in May that year he was Yamaha's natural choice as replacement. Because of the death of Saarinen, who was a close friend of Lansivuori, the latter almost retired from racing, but decided to continue and accepted the Yamaha team offer. Teuvo Lansivuori began racing in Finland in 1963, his first experience being at an ice race meeting. He later rode a Husqvarna race machine and made his grand prix debut on a 125cc Montesa in 1968. His first appearance in England was at Silverstone in 1972. In 1973 he was second behind Braun in the 250cc World Championship and was also second in the 350cc category, close behind Agostini. His debut on the works Yamaha 4 was at the Mallory Park September meeting in 1973, when he crashed. Nine months later, again at Mallory, he won the 500cc event against a determined bid from world champion Phil Read.

Results
1973: second in 250cc and 350cc world championships;
1974: third in 500cc world championships.
1976: second in 500cc world championships.

LAWWILL, Mert
A Harley-Davidson team racer since 1965, Mert Lawwill of Tiburon, California, is established as one of the most prominent professional motor-cycle racers in the United States, proficient at most types of United States racing – half mile, mile, short track, road race and TT (steeplechase). He was Grand National Champion in 1969. In 1971, while competing in a TT National, Lawwill crashed, injuring a hand. After several operations and a winter to recuperate, he returned to racing in 1972 and on a new XR-750 Harley-Davidson racer, outpaced a strong opposition to win at the Columbus, Ohio half-mile.

LEPPAN, Bob
American Bob Leppan (born 1938) of Detroit, became the fastest man in the world on two wheels in 1966 when he piloted his Gyronaut X-1, a 1300cc double-engined Triumph-powered special, across Bonneville Salt Flats at 245.6 mph. The record, endorsed by the AMA but not recognised by the FIM stood until 1970 (*see* World Land Speed Records).

LOMAS, W. (Bill) A.
A rider of outstanding merit, Bill Lomas, rather like John Surtees, was not one of the most popular of champions and often he alienated public opinion by his forthright and outspoken comments. Best known for his successes with the Italian Moto Guzzi factory, Bill Lomas was never without a factory contract in his

six-year professional career and was so much a part of Guzzi that when they retired in 1957 he decided to quit as well.

He first became interested in motor cycle sport at fourteen and his first event was a grass track meeting on a Chater Lea shortly after the end of the war. In 1946 he bought a 350 JAP engine, worked it into a Royal Enfield frame and did well with it at Cadwell Park, the major centre for a time after the war. He was Cadwell champion in the 250, 350 and 500cc classes from 1948 to 1950. Early in his career Lomas was also a useful trials rider with James, reaching a fourth position in the Scottish Six Days Trial and a third in the British Experts. His big break into road racing came in 1950 when he joined Bob Foster and the Velocette works team. He remained with Velocette for two years. Thereafter he rode for AJS, NSU and MV. Then came 1955 and his introduction to Guzzi. It was to be his most outstanding year. He was due to ride AJS machines in the Senior and Junior TTs and although the British factory insisted he should not ride MVs in the lighter classes he decided to ignore their instructions. AJS withdrew his rides and he was left with no machinery for the Senior and Junior events. Hearing of his availability Fergus Anderson offered him rides on the 350 and 500cc Guzzis. In a remarkable sequence of events Lomas went on to win the Junior race and was seventh in the Senior. He also won in the 250 on the MV and was placed fourth in the 125. Guzzi had seen enough of the Lomas style to continue offering him rides and he repaid their confidence in him by securing for them the 350cc World Championship. With a full Guzzi contract for 1956, he again secured the 350cc World Championship that year. He retired at 29 in 1957. Lomas rode in the TTs from 1950 to 1956, except for 1953.

World Championships:
1955: 350cc (Guzzi).
1956: 350cc (Guzzi).

TT wins:
1955: 250cc (MV), and Junior (Guzzi).

LONG DISTANCE ROAD RACES

Long distance road races have been part of motor-cycle sport from the earliest times. Recognised among the most important events of this kind are the French Bol d'Or at Le Mans, the Barcelona event at Montjuich and the Spa 24-hour in Belgium, while in Britain there was the Thruxton 500-miler. As the World Grand Prix championships became more and more dominated by Yamaha in the early-mid 1970s, manufacturers began taking a greater interest in long distance events which, as a result, began to grow in importance. The FIM run a Coupe d'Endurance series of races each year, decided on performance in a number of long distance events. Included in this series is the important Liège 24-hours race, won in 1974 by C. Chemarin and G. Debrock (860 Honda) with 288 laps at 105.01 mph average. In 1975 the Bol d'Or, the most important marathon event, qualified for the FIM series. Previously it had been ruled ineligible because its regulations allowed prototypes and engines up to 1000cc. Until 1975 these machines were not permitted in the FIM series.

FIM Coupe d'Endurance results:
1978: *Liège 24 Hours:* J. Buyaert/J. Luc (Honda); *Misano:* C. Leon/J.-C. Chemarin (Honda); *Nurburgring:* C. Leon/J.-C. Chemarin (Honda); *Barcelona 24 hours:* C. Leon/J.-C. Chemarin (Honda); *Bol d'Or 24 hours:* C. Leon/J.-C. Chemarin (Honda); *Brands Hatch:* C. Williams/S. Woods (Honda).
1979: *Le Mans:* C. Leon/J.-C. Chemarin (Honda); *Assen:* C. Huguet/H. Moineau (Kawasaki); *Nurburgring:* C. Leon/J.-C. Chemarin (Honda); *Barcelona:* C. Leon/J.-C. Chemarin (Honda); *Spa:* J. Luc/J. Buyaert (Honda); *Mettet:* G. Green/P. Blaawboer (Suzuki); *Bol d'Or:* C. Leon/J.-C. Chemarin (Honda); *Brands Hatch:* C. Huguet/H. Moineau (Kawasaki).

The FIM Endurance Series was granted world status for 1980 and because the FIM adopted restrictive TT Formula 1 rules for the series, some events, notably the Bol d'Or, did not figure as a championship race.

Results
1980: *Assen:* M. Fontan/H. Moineau (Honda); *Nurburgring:* C. Leon/J.-C. Chemarin (Honda); *Osterreichring:* J.-B. Peyre/P.-E. Samin (Suzuki); *Barcelona:* J. Mallol/A. Tejedo (Ducati); *Suzuka:* W. Cooley/G. Crosby (Suzuki); *Liège:* M. Fontan/H. Moineau (Honda); *Misano:* C. Huguet/R. Hubin (Kawasaki).

Endurance World Champions

1980: 1. M. Fontan/H. Moineau (Honda).
2. C. Huguet (Kawasaki).
3. H. Dahne (Honda).

1981: 1. R. Roche (Kawasaki).
2. J. Lafond (Kawasaki).
3. C. Huguet (Kawasaki).

LUTHRINGSHAUSER, Heinz

Famous sidecar racer from West Germany, Luthringshauser (born 1931) lost his left leg in a car accident in 1961 and has both gear change and brake controls on the right side of his successful BMW outfit. He began racing as a speedway rider in 1949 and after switching to sidecar events began concentrating on road racing with his BMW outfit in 1957. He entered his first TT in 1961 and had his best year in 1974 when he won the 500cc TT and was second in the 750cc event.

LYDDEN CIRCUIT

Lydden Circuit was designed by and built under the personal supervision of the owner, Mr William Chesson, upon a site previously used since 1957 for motor-cycle grass-track racing and later for stock-car racing. As such, it was already well known to thousands of race fans when, after 18 months of preparation, the surfaced track measuring ¾ mile was opened by Derek Minter on 4th April 1965. In that first year, one kart, three motor cycles and seven car race meetings were held; numbers which increased with each successive year. In June 1967 the track was lengthened to its present distance of one mile. This was accomplished by the addition of an elongated hairpin bend, giving it its now familiar shape of a boomerang, with a large sweeping bend at one end and a sharpish hairpin at the other.

The popularity of Lydden Circuit as a motor sports centre for south-east Kent and a venue for Clubman's motor-cycle road-racing was growing and 1967 also saw the introduction of what was to become an annual contest. Called, 'The Lord of Lydden' event the winner of a designated meeting (280–1000cc class) became the 'Lord of Lydden' and holder of the handsome oak trophy for one year. Many of today's well known riders 'cut their teeth' on the Lydden track, as is evidenced by the names on the shield: 1967 Charlie Sanby; 1968 Dave Croxford; 1969-70 Martyn Ashwood; 1971-72 Dave Potter; 1973 Pat Mahoney; 1974 Pat Mahoney; 1975 Pat Mahoney; 1976 Neville Frost; 1977 Kevin Wrettom; 1978 Ivor Morgan; 1979 Kevin Richards; 1980 Andy Belsey; 1981 Tony Harris.

A "first" at Lydden was the staging of international grass track racing in 1968. With an all star line-up of riders it brought together for the first time at Lydden the then reigning World Speedway Champion, Ivan Mauger; four times World Champion, Barry Briggs; European Champion, Don Godden; and the legendary Alf Hagon, in addition to foreign stars. So successful was this that in following years first two then three meetings per year were held. The track was modified by the addition of shale on the bends, to provide a surface suitable for both speedway and grass track riders and thus 'Speedtrack' was born.

Later, on 1st March 1970 another milestone was reached, with the staging of Lydden's first international moto cross meeting. World Champion Bengt Aberg made the long trip from Sweden to match the best that Britain could offer – John Banks, Vic Allan, Dave Nicoll, Vic Eastwood, 'Badger' Goss, Andy Roberton, Malcolm Davis and Jim Aird – and beat them all.

Address:

William Mark Holdings Ltd, 71 West Street, Sittingbourne, Kent.

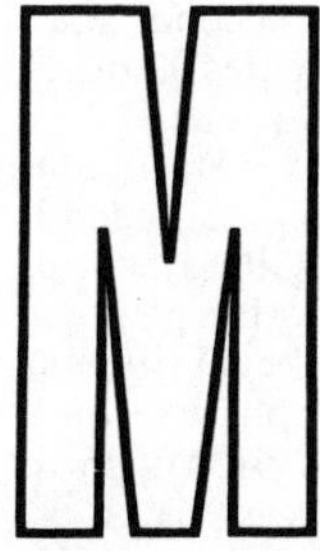

MACHIN, Steve
Machin's first important wins came in 1968 at Cadwell Park on a Bultaco. Born 1945, he began racing in 1965 on a Triumph Tiger Cub. Much success in British events has been achieved on his self-prepared Yamahas. Double British Champion in 1972 (250cc and 125cc), he was British 250cc Champion in 1970 and 1971. He was second in the 250cc A-CU Star competition in 1974.

McINTYRE, R.McG.
A thoughtful and dedicated racer, Bob McIntyre (born Glasgow 1928) gained early success on the race circuit in 1952. He combined short circuit racing at home with events on longer circuits abroad and was successful at both. Although he had factory rides, he spent much of his time as an independent entrant and is remembered for his long and successful association with Joe Potts, the Scottish tuner. He was an AJS works rider in 1954 and became Gilera team leader in 1957, a year in which he won both the Junior and Senior TTs and registered that first ever 100 mph lap. Although Gilera had virtually retired from racing in 1957, McIntyre took a 350cc Gilera 4 to Monza for a final record-breaking attack on the world's one hour motor cycle record. He created a new world record at a speed of 141 mph, a record which was to last until 1964, when Hailwood was fractionally faster at Daytona on the MV. At 33 years of age and at the peak of his career McIntyre crashed a five-speed experimental Norton at Oulton Park in August 1962 and died as a result of his injuries.

"Bob Mac", as he was affectionately known, was assessed by many observers as the finest rider never to win a world championship. He began motor cycle riding on a 500cc 16 H Norton, 1931 model which cost him just £12. He later turned to scrambling, winning a number of club events. His first road race was in a public park at Kirkcaldy and he entered his first amateur event on a borrowed 350cc BSA Gold Star.

His debut on the Isle of Man was in 1952 when he took second place in the Senior Manx Grand Prix on a Junior machine. On a Norton he gained second place in the Junior TT of 1955 and raced to an incredible 99 mph-plus lap in the Senior TT of 1958. His first TT wins were on Gilera machines in the Senior and Junior races of 1957. He is also remembered for his magnificent racing of production Norton and AJS machines against the power of the works MVs in the Senior and Junior TTs of 1959.

McIntyre, though one of the most gifted riders of his day, was always happier riding as a private entrant than as a member of a factory team, in spite of his outstanding success as the Gilera team leader in 1957. After being loaned Honda machines for 1961 he joined the Honda team in 1962. Quietly determined as a man and as a rider, McIntyre came nearest to a world title with Gilera in 1957 (second in both the 350cc and 500cc classes) and with Honda in 1962 (second in the 250cc class). In 1957 he only needed to win at Monza to gain the 500cc World Championship crown, but he was unwell and could not ride.

Bob McIntyre is most remembered as the first TT rider to lap the Isle of Man course at over 100 mph. This historic milestone was on 7th June 1957 and he achieved the distinction on a red and white Gilera. He took 3 hr 2 min 57 sec in this epic senior TT ride, over 8 laps of the TT circuit, and won the race at an average of 98.99 mph. His outstanding performance included four laps at over 100 mph.

A dedicated rider and well respected in the sport, the "Flying Scotsman" was also a sensible rider, never willing to take unnecessary risks, and never rode faster than was necessary to win.

TT wins:
1957: Senior (Gilera) and Junior (Gilera).
1959: Formula 1 500 (Norton).

MAICO
A West German motor-cycle factory which specialises in the production of moto-cross machines. The man mainly

responsible for Maico's racing effort is Gunther Schier, who joined the factory in 1966. The Maico factory was extremely successful in German moto cross before entering international competition seriously.

MALLORY PARK
For many years home of the richest motor-cycle road race in Britain, Mallory Park was opened in April 1956. It is situated near Leicester, in attractive grounds, and has a circuit of 1.35 miles which can be lapped in under a minute. There is also a 1-mile club circuit and the venue is used for International, National and club racing. It is a complex, varied course incorporating many famous bends, from the enormous sweep of Gerrards to the extreme tightness of Shaw's Corner. Other well known sections are Devil's Elbow and the Esses. There were strong rumours in 1973 that Mallory Park was to close as a race circuit, but at that time no firm decision was announced. Mallory Park's Race of the Year is held annually towards the end of the season with the traditional 1,000 guineas going to the winner. John Cooper has always been closely associated with Mallory and won the big event there first in 1965. For the first time, in 1974 the Race of the Year event was staged over two days. In 1979 the race was switched to Oulton Park, and was run over 20 laps of the Cheshire circuit – a distance of over 55 miles. However, it returned to Mallory Park for 1980.

The Race of the year is no longer the richest event and Mallory Park has lost some status in more recent years.

Race of the Year Results:

1958 (40 laps): first, John Surtees (500 M.V, 84.45 mph); second, Bob Anderson (500 Norton); third, Bruce Daniels (500 Norton).

1959 (40 laps): first, Bob McIntyre (500 Norton, 86.09 mph); second, Bob Anderson (500 Norton); third, Mike Hailwood (500 Norton).

1960 (40 laps): first, Mike Hailwood (500 Norton, 86.32 mph); second, Terry Shepherd (500 Norton); third, Ron Langston (500 Matchless).

1961 (40 laps): first, Gary Hocking (500 MV, 87.72 mph); second, Mike Hailwood (500 Norton); third, Alan Shepherd (500 Matchless).

1962 (40 laps): first, Derek Minter (500 Norton, 86.35 mph); second, Alan Shepherd (500 Matchless), third, John Cooper (500 Norton).

1963 (40 laps): first, Mike Hailwood (500 MV, 89.12 mph), second, Derek Minter (500 Gilera), third, Alan Shepherd (500 Matchless).

1964 (40 laps): first, Mike Hailwood (500 MV, 87.09 mph); second, John Cooper (500 Norton); third, Derek Minter (500 Norton).

1965 (30 laps): first, John Cooper (500 Norton, 80.52 mph); second, Phil Read (254 Yamaha); third, Bill Ivy (500 Matchless).

1966 (30 laps): first, Giacomo Agostini (500 MV, 88.87 mph); second, Bill Ivy (250 Yamaha); third, Mike Duff (250 Yamaha).

1967 (30 laps): first, Mike Hailwood (297 Honda, 91.31 mph); second, Giacomo Agostini (500 MV); third, Phil Read (250 Yamaha).

1968 (30 laps): first, Mike Hailwood (297 Honda, 82.16 mph); second, Giacomo Agostini (500 MV); third, Barry Randle (500 Norton).

1969 (30 laps): first, Giacomo Agostini (500 MV, 91.21 mph); second, Ken Redfern (750 Norton); third, Dave Croxford (750 Kuhn Norton).

1970 (30 laps): first, John Cooper (350 Yamsel, 89.81 mph); second, Phil Read (250 Yamaha); third, Paul Smart (750 Triumph-3).

1971 (30 laps): first, John Cooper (750 BSA-3, 91.5 mph); second, Giacomo Agostini (500 MV); third, Ray Pickrell (750 BSA-3).

1972 (30 laps): first, Jarno Saarinen (350 Yamaha, 92.44 mph); second, Paul Smart (750 Kawasaki); third, John Cooper (750 Triumph-3).

1973 (35 laps): first Phil Read (500 MV, 92.59 mph); second, Peter Williams (750 John Player Norton); third, John Dodds (350 Yamaha).

1974 (40 laps): first, Barry Sheene (750 Suzuki); second, Phil Read (500 MV); third, Stan Woods (750 Suzuki).

1975 (40 laps): first Barry Sheene (750 Suzuki); second Dave Aldana (750 Suzuki); third Mick Grant (750 Kawasaki).

1976: (40 laps): first, Steve Baker (750 Yamaha); second, Barry Sheene (540 Suzuki); third, Pat Hennen

(500 Suzuki).

1977: (40 laps): first, Pat Hennen (700 Suzuki); second, Mick Grant (750 Kawasaki); third, Dave Potter (750 Yamaha).

1978: (40 laps): first, Barry Sheene (650 Suzuki); second, Wil Hartog (500 Suzuki); third, Kenny Roberts (750 Yamaha).

1979: (20 laps): first, Kenny Roberts (750 Yamaha); second, Barry Sheene (680 Suzuki); third, Jeff Sayle (750 Yamaha).

1980: (40 laps): first, Randy Mamola (Suzuki); second, Barry Sheene (Yamaha); third, Dave Potter (Yamaha).

1981: (40 laps): first, Graeme Crosby (Suzuki); second Barry Sheene (Yamaha); third, Kork Ballington (Kawasaki).

MAMOLA, Randy

This young, talented American racer created a sensation on British and European circuits during 1980. The young Californian, appearing as a works Suzuki rider, crowned a magnificent European season by winning the Race of the Year at Mallory Park. He finished second in the 500cc World Championships of 1980 and 1981 and undoubtedly is one of the major talents for the 1980s.

"MAN OF THE YEAR" COMPETITION

This popular annual poll is organised by the British weekly newspaper, *Motor Cycle News*. Readers are invited to vote for their most popular motor-cycle racer. It was inaugurated in 1958 and won that year by John Surtees. From small beginnings it has grown into an important event among riders and (to 1974) has been won twice in consecutive years on only two occasions – John Surtees (1958-59) and John Cooper (1970-71).

The Competition is open to all branches of motor-cycle sport.

Winners:

1958: first, John Surtees; second, Mike Hailwood; third, Bob McIntyre; fourth, Derek Minter.

1959: first, John Surtees; second, Mike Hailwood; third, Bob McIntyre; fourth, Arthur Lampkin.

1960: first, Dave Bickers; second, John Surtees; third, Mike Hailwood; fourth, Sammy Miller.

1961: first, Mike Hailwood; second, Dave Bickers; third, Chris Vincent; fourth, Gary Hocking.

1962: first, Derek Minter; second, Dave Bickers; third, Mike Hailwood; fourth, Sammy Miller.

1963: first, Mike Hailwood; second, Dave Bickers; third, Alan Shepherd; fourth, Phil Read.

1964: first, Jeff Smith; second, John Cooper; third, Phil Read; fourth, Mike Hailwood.

1965: first, Bill Ivy; second, Mike Hailwood; third, John Cooper; fourth, Jeff Smith.

1966: first, Giacomo Agostini; second, Mike Hailwood; third, Barry Briggs; fourth, Peter Williams.

1967: first, Mike Hailwood; second, Giacomo Agostini; third, Phil Read; fourth, Bill Ivy.

1968: first, Helmut Fath; second, Phil Read; third, Mike Hailwood; fourth, Giacomo Agostini.

1969: first, Rod Gould; second, Phil Read; third, Giacomo Agostini; fourth, John Banks.

1970: first, John Cooper; second, Phil Read; third, Paul Smart; fourth, Ivan Mauger.

1971: first, John Cooper; second, Phil Read, third, Barry Sheene, fourth, Giacomo Agostini.

1972: first, Ray Pickrell; second, Jarno Saarinen; third, Paul Smart; fourth, John Cooper.

1973: first, Barry Sheene; second, Phil Read; third, Peter Collins; fourth, Peter Williams.

1974: first, Phil Read; second, Barry Sheene; third, Peter Collins; fourth, Dave Croxford.

1975: first, Barry Sheene; second, Mick Grant; third, Phil Read; fourth, Barry Ditchburn.

1976: first, Barry Sheene; second, Peter Collins; third, Mick Grant; fourth, Phil Read.

1977: first, Barry Sheene; second, George O'Dell; third, Mick Grant; fourth, Peter Collins.

1978: first, Mike Hailwood; second, Barry Sheene; third, Kenny Roberts; fourth, Kork Ballington.

1979: first, Barry Sheene; second, Ron Haslam; third, Graham Noyce; fourth, Kenny Roberts.

1980: first, Jock Taylor; second, Barry Sheene; third, Dave Potter; fourth, Gerry Dunlop.

1981: first, Ron Haslam; second, Barry Sheene; third, Marco Lucchinelli; fourth, Neil Hudson.

MANN, Dick

Prominent American racer for some twenty years, Dick Mann, (born 1934) won the AMA Championship in 1963 and 1971, and was second in 1959, 1964 and 1965. He won the Daytona 200 in 1970 (Honda) and in 1971 (BSA). Mann began riding professionally in 1954 and his name first appeared in the American top ten placings in 1957. An extremely versatile rider, he appeared regularly in the top ten placings and was ranked tenth in 1973 although 39 years of age.

MANX GRAND PRIX

The Manx Grand Prix is a series of races held annually on the Isle of Man specifically for competitors who have not ridden previously in an international race, nor have been the holder of any world motor-cycle record. It is a less commercial counterpart to the professional Tourist Trophy races. In the early years of the TT, amateur and professional riders competed against one another on both individually sponsored and factory sponsored machines, but as the sport developed it became more specialised and there grew a need for a series of races in which the more amateur rider would not be compelled to compete with works sponsored riders against whom there was obviously a very remote chance of doing well.

The idea for this breakaway series of races came from members of the Manx Motor Cycle Club and, with the agreement of the Auto-Cycle Union, they arranged the Manx Amateur Motor Cycle Road Race which was later changed to the Amateur TT.

The first race which was to become the Manx Grand Prix took place in 1923 and the month of September was chosen to help extend the holiday season in the Isle of Man. Providing an additional incentive at the time for the establishment of these amateur races was the obvious disagreement which existed between the Isle of Man authorities and the Auto-Cycle Union. This came to a head in 1921 when the Auto-Cycle Union announced their intention to accept an invitation to hold the 1922 TT meeting in Belgium. Although these differences were settled, it is obvious that the establishment of the amateur races was at that time kept in mind as a substitute for the TTs, should the Auto-Cycle Union decide to remove them from the island.

The first amateur TT was run on 20th September 1923. Twenty-nine riders on 500cc machines and four on 350cc machines took part, all running simultaneously over five laps of the TT course. Among the machines competing were Sunbeams, Scotts, Nortons, Triumphs; machines which were equipped with large tanks, larger saddles, separate lubricating tanks and straight-through exhausts with fishtails. Winner was Len Randles on a Sunbeam at a speed of 52.77 mph. Half the entries completed the race. Randles also won the 1924 event at a speed of 56.71 mph. The races during these first two years were restricted to standard stock models, but for the third Amateur TT race regulations permitted the use of any type of machine. Winner was Sub Lieut H. G. Dobbs SRN, at a speed of 59.97 mph. He rode a Norton. The race distance was increased in 1926 to six laps. The number of starters went up to 56. This race was won by Rex Adams on an AJS. In 1927 the regulations stipulated the use of only standard stock models once more and the entries totalled 75. By this time riders from overseas were competing. Percy Hunt from Didsbury, Manchester, was the winner.

In 1928 the 350cc and 500cc machines were separated into different races. For the Junior event there were 26 starters, the winner being Harry Meageen on a Rex Acme. The Senior class was won by Percy Hunt who completed the six laps at a record speed of 69.94 mph – 8 mph faster than any previous winner. He also became the first amateur rider to reach a 70-mph lap, setting the lap record at 71.05. The quality of this performance in an amateur event can be gained from a comparison with the existing TT lap record set up in 1927 by Stanley Woods. Hunt's achievement was two seconds faster.

The Manx Grand Prix races title was introduced because of the ambiguity of the rules affecting these first amateur races. In 1929 there was a good deal of criticism that many of these "amateur" riders were taking bonuses from manufacturers and it was admitted by stewards that several reprimands had been handed out to riders. Some riders admitted to receiving cash handouts from oil and fuel companies but defended their actions by declaring that oil and fuel were not accessories within the meaning of the supplementary regulations and they were therefore committing no offence. It was agreed by the stewards that the wording of the regulations was ambiguous. The first double winner of the races came about because of this storm. The Senior race winner of 1929 was D. J. Potts, but he was later disqualified along with 20 other riders, the trophy going to Norman Lea, who had also won a controversial victory in the Junior event and therefore became the first double winner of these races.

There was so much dispute and controversy surrounding the 1929 races that it was to be the end of the "amateur" TT in that form and by 1930 new regulations had been drafted. In the Junior event of 1929 Meageen on a Rex-Acme was first across the line. Less than two miles from the end, however, the throttle wire on his machine broke and he pushed his machine home. There was some doubt whether a rider was permitted to push his machine – but the stewards decided he was – and then there came a second protest which alleged that Meageen had "received outside assistance" when a well-wishing spectator had given him a push to help him get going after the throttle wire had broken. The stewards agreed he had received help and he was disqualified leaving Lea the winner.

After the end of the Senior event of that year (1929) there was such a storm of protest about riders receiving money that the A-CU instituted an official enquiry. The result of the enquiry, announced more than three months later, declared a "state of affairs which must be classed as disgraceful", and the A-CU suspended, or recommended the suspension, of 21 riders and excluded them from any awards they might have won in the 1929 races. J. D. Potts, winner of the Senior, was included in the list of suspended riders and forfeited his victory. Eric Lea, in an astonishing situation, became therefore the official winner of both the Senior and Junior events, though on time he had been second in each category.

After such a scandal it was obvious that the rules were in need of a good deal of tidying up and the Auto-Cycle Union, in a strong effort to get this done, turned down an application from the Manx Motor Cycle Club to run Senior and Junior road races in 1930 restricted wholly or partially to amateur riders or private owners. The Union and the Club agreed that something must be done, the latter going away to draft new rules. These new regulations stipulated that the competitor must be one who, at the time of entry and for five years preceding the date was domiciled in Great Britain, Northern Ireland or the Irish Free State, the Channel Isles or the Isle of Man. They also stipulated that the competitor, since 1920, must not have been entered as a rider or reserve rider in any international race – a list of which was specified in a lengthy schedule; and that since 1920, the entrant had not been the holder of any world motor-cycle record. These rules were duly approved by the Auto-Cycle Union and a permit was granted to hold the first Manx Grand Prix races in September 1930. This new structure for these races, which had no definition of amateur to create problems, removed the controversy and quickly increased its support. In 1930 entries totalled 101. By 1934 they had risen to 129. In 1958 they were up to 314 (for three events). This rapid development made certain changes necessary. A separate 250cc class was added to the programme in 1934 though there had been an award for the fastest 250 rider in previous Junior races.

Because of the lack of commerical interest, the Manx Grand Prix has always been noted more for riders than machines, and it has been accepted for many years as a nursery for the rider with ambitions to make a name for himself in professional motor-cycle racing.

In the early days of the "amateur" races, and in an effort to keep out commercialism, riders were listed in the official programme with the prefix "Mr", and no mention was made of the make of machine a rider was using, though engine capacities were specified. Many famous TT riders were first featured in the programme of the Manx Grand Prix, including such illustrious names as Harold Daniell, Freddy Frith OBE, Bob McIntyre and Denis Parkinson.

Results:

1923: 500 and 350cc L. Randles (Sunbeam) 52.77 mph; 350cc K.

Twemlow (New Imperial) 52.46 mph.

1924: 500 and 350cc L. Randles (Sunbeam) 56.71 mph; 350cc R. C. Brown (Sunbeam) 54.20 mph.

1925: 500 and 350cc H. G. Dobbs (Norton) 59.97 mph; 350cc J. Morton (New Gerrard) 57.75 mph.

1926: 500 and 350cc R. D. Adams (AJS) 58.46 mph; 350cc W. A. Empsall (Velocette) 52.00 mph.

1927: 500 and 350cc P. Hunt (Norton) 57.66 mph; 350cc S. Gates (Velocette) 51.87 mph.

1928: Senior P. Hunt (Norton) 67.94 mph; Junior W. H. T. Meageen (Rex Acme) 61.58 mph.

1929: Senior E. N. Lea (Norton) 64.02 mph; Junior E. N. Lea (Velocette) 65.24 mph.

1930: Senior E. R. Merrill (Rudge) 69.49 mph; Junior D. J. Pirie (Velocette) 61.63 mph.

1931: Senior J. M. Muir (Norton) 71.79 mph; Junior D. J. Pirie (Velocette) 69.59 mph.

1932: Senior N. Gledhill (Norton) 67.32 mph; Junior J. H. Carr (New Imperial) 69.27 mph.

1933: Senior H. L. Daniell (Norton) 76.98 mph; Junior A. Munks (Velocette) 74.14 mph; lightweight R. Harris (New Imperial) 66.47 mph.

1934: Senior D. J. Pirie (Norton) 79.19 mph; Junior J. H. White (Norton) 75.59 mph; lightweight W. D. Mitchell (Cotton) 63.49 mph.

1935: Senior J. K. Swanston (Norton) 79.62 mph; Junior F. L. Frith (Norton) 76.02 mph; lightweight R. Harris (New Imperial) 68.56 mph.

1936: Senior A. Munks (Norton) 78.88 mph; Junior A. Munks (Velocette) 73.93 mph; lightweight D. Parkinson (Excelsior) 65.68 mph.

1937: Senior M. Cann (Norton) 81.65 mph; Junior M. Cann (Norton) 76.23 mph; lightweight D. Parkinson (Excelsior) 69.68 mph.

1938: Senior K. Bills (Norton) 84.81 mph; Junior K. Bills (Norton) 78.76 mph; lightweight D. Parkinson (Excelsior) 71.05 mph.

1946: Senior E. Lyons (Triumph) 76.73 mph; Junior K. Bills (Norton) 74.18 mph; lightweight L. W. Parsons (Rudge) 65.11 mph.

1947: Senior E. E. Briggs (Norton) 78.338 mph; Junior E. E. Briggs (Norton) 74.644 mph; lightweight A. Munks (Moto Guzzi) 70.632 mph.

1948: Senior D. G. Crossley (Triumph) 80.628 mph; Junior D. Parkinson (Norton) 78.197 mph; lightweight R. H. Dale (Moto Guzzi) 73.368 mph.

1949: Senior G. E. Duke (Norton) 86.063 mph; Junior W. A. C. McCandless (Norton) 81.820 mph.

1950: Senior P. E. Romaine (Norton) 84.123 mph; Junior D. G. Crossley (AJS) 82.589 mph.

1951: Senior D. E. Bennett (Norton) 87.05 mph; Junior R. H. Sherry (AJS) 82.61 mph.

1952: Senior D. K. Farrant (Matchless/AJS) 88.65 mph; Junior R. McIntyre (AJS) 85.73 mph.

1953: Senior D. Parkinson (Norton) 89.68 mph; Junior F. M. Fox (Norton) 84.73 mph.

1954: Senior G. R. Costain (Norton) 80.95 mph; Junior D. Ennett (AJS) 86.33 mph.

1955: Senior G. B. Tanner (Norton) 91.38 mph; Junior G. B. Tanner (Norton) 88.46 mph.

1956: Senior J. Buchan (Norton) 90.83 mph; Junior J. Buchan (Norton) 88.54 mph.

1957: Senior W. A. Holmes (Norton) 91.43 mph; Junior W. A. Holmes (Norton) 89.13 mph.

1958: Senior W. J. Washer (Norton) 92.94 mph; Junior A. Shepherd (Bancroft/AJS) 89.08 mph.

1959: Senior E. B. Crooks (Norton 94.87 mph; Junior P. C. Middleton (Norton) 88.73 mph.

1960: Senior P. W. Read (Norton) 95.38 mph; Junior E. F. H. Boyce (Norton) 90.04 mph.

1961: Senior E. Minihan (Norton) 93.69 mph; Junior F. Reynolds (AJS) 81.28 mph.

1962: Senior P. J. Dunphy (Norton) 91.83 mph; Junior R. P. Dawson (AJS) 89.02 mph.

1963: Senior G. A Jenkins (Norton) 96.10 mph; Junior P. J. Darvill (AJS) 92.48 mph.

1964: Senior S. G. Griffiths (Matchless) 96.27 mph; Junior D. Williams

(MW Special) 92.54 mph; lightweight G. A. Keith (Greeves) 86.19 mph.

1965: Senior M. Uphill (Norton) 89.69 mph; Junior M. Uphill (AJS) 91.22 mph; lightweight D. Craine (Greeves) 88.37 mph.

1966: Senior T. Dickie (Matchless) 94.30 mph; Junior G. B. Buchan (Norton); lightweight R. G. Farmer (Aermacchi) 86.20 mph.

1967: Senior J. Guthrie (Norton) 94.98 mph; Junior J. J. Weatherall (Norton) 83.22 mph; lightweight B. A. Ball (BA Special) 81.35 mph.

1968: Senior J. Findlay (Norton) 90.14 mph; Junior J. Findlay (Norton) 89.85 mph; lightweight F. Whiteway (Suzuki) 88.52 mph.

1969: Senior G. J. Daniels (Cowles Matchless) 93.43 mph; Junior R. G. Duffty (Aermacchi) 92.31 mph; lightweight A. J. S. George (Yamaha) 90.63 mph.

1970: Senior R. Sutcliffe (Cowles Matchless-Metisse) 94.41 mph; Junior C. Brown (Beart Aermacchi) 93.74 mph; lightweight A. Steele (Dugdale Yamaha) 90.44 mph.

1971: Senior M. G. A. Rollason (351 Yamroll) 94.42 mph; Junior S. B. Moynihan (Lawton Aermacchi) 91.17 mph; lightweight C. I. Williams (Dugdale Yamaha) 93.99 mph.

1972: Senior D. Hughes (Arter Matchless) 93.66 mph; Junior D. K. Huggett (Lawton Aermacchi) 95.56 mph; lightweight P. Carpenter (Yamaha) 95.06 mph.

1973: Senior P. Reid (Yamaha) 96.89 mph; Junior P. Haslam (Pharaoh Yamaha) 99.42 mph; lightweight D. Arnold (Walker Yamaha) 97.23 mph.

1974: Senior B. Murray (Dugdale Maxton Yamaha) 93.28 mph; Junior B. Murray (Dugdale Maxton Yamaha) 96.10 mph; lightweight E. Roberts (Dugdale Maxton Yamaha) 90.35 mph.

1975: Senior S. McClements (Crawford Yamaha) 101.042 mph; Junior W. Dinham (Yamaha) 101.24 mph; Lightweight A. Jackson (Yahama) 96.59 mph.

1976: Senior L. Trotter (Crooks Suzuki) 98.47 mph; Junior J. Lindsay (Yamaha) 101.30 mph; Lightweight D. Shimmin (Yamaha) 99.07 mph.

1977: Senior S. Davies (Yamaha) 100.48 mph; Junior K. Riley (Yamaha) 102.63 mph; Lightweight D. Hickman (Maxton Yamaha) 99.951 mph.

1978: Senior G. Linder (497 Suzuki) 102.28 mph; Junior S. Ward (347 Padgett Yamaha) 100.33 mph; Lightweight C. Paterson (247 Yamaha) 96.25 mph.

1979: Senior C. Watts (500 Suzuki) 105.27 mph; Junior C. W. Watts (500 Suzuki) 105.58 mph; Lightweight C. Law (Yamaha) 101.78 mph.

1980: Senior G. Johnson (Yamaha) 103.43 mph; Junior M. Kneen (Yamaha) 103.94 mph; Lightweight S. Williams (Yamaha) 99.31 mph.

1981: 750cc D. East (Suzuki) 106.26 mph; Junior D. Broadhead (Yamaha) 105.91 mph; Lightweight G. Cannell (Cotton) 103.19 mph.

MATCHLESS

The first Matchless motor cycle was produced by the legendary Charles and Harry Collier in 1899. They mounted the engine over the front wheel in the style of their predecessors, but later moved it to behind the saddle tube and then beneath the steering head in the inclined position.

Both Charles and Harry raced their machines successfully at the Canning Town Cycle Track, and Matchless machines were also entered in the International Cup Races. In 1905 Harry finished second in the Auto-Cycle Club's eliminating trials for the Cup Races held on the Isle of Man and was the only British rider to finish in the race. The following year the brothers were first and second in the eliminating race and Harry finished third in the International Cup Race itself, the first time a British machine had achieved notable success in an international event of this kind.

The Matchless design for the International Cup Race was the first British V-twin. In the first TT races of 1907 Charlie Collier won the singles category and Harry rode the fastest lap. A year later Charlie Collier's Matchless was beaten into second place by Jack Marshall's Triumph, but Harry won the TT in 1909 and Charlie in 1910.

The Colliers had used the JAP engine considerably and in 1912 they co-operated with the JAP concern to produce an engine specifically for the Matchless. In the years immediately preceding the first World War, Matchless machines lost much of their winning touch, though they won the 1000cc class of the Brooklands six-hour race.

Matchless machines were far less prominent in racing in the years following the war. Some Matchlesses were raced on the Isle of Man in the mid-1920s without success, though a specially-prepared model won the Hutchinson 100 race in 1928 at Brooklands at a speed of 93.52 mph. It was also on a Matchless that famous TT rider Jimmy Guthrie made his debut.

Later, the Matchless motor cycle became popular for many years in trials and scrambles, and reappeared in the Isle of Man in the Clubman's races.

MAUGER, Ivan Gerald
Born in Christchurch, New Zealand, in 1940, Ivan Mauger is the only speedway rider to have won three successive world titles (1968, '69 and '70) and his total of four such wins up to 1975 has been equalled by only one other rider, Barry Briggs, and bettered by only one, Ove Fundin. He first started riding speedway machines in New Zealand in 1956, coming to Britain a year later. After a disappointing two years he returned to New Zealand, but was tempted back by an offer from Newcastle, for whom he rode in 1963 and '64. He rode for Belle Vue from 1969 – 72 when he moved to Exeter. He led these teams to league championships in 1964, 1970-72, and 1974.

Ivan Mauger has appeared in ten world finals since 1966 and in addition to winning four times, he has been second on three occasions, third once and fourth on two occasions. In 1971 and again in 1972 Mauger won the world 1000-metre sand-track title, was runner up in 1974 and 1975 and has been successful in numerous Continental long-track events. He has won most of the honours the sport has to offer.

Mauger is a rider of outstanding talent, consistency and versatility and has a well-earned reputation for particularly strong starts. He is said to have made more money from speedway than any other rider. In 1976 Ivan Mauger received the MBE, only the second rider in the 48-year English history of the sport to be so honoured and the first while still active in league racing. In 1979 he became the first rider to win six speedway world championships.

MIKKOLA, Heikki
In 1974 Heikki Mikkola became Finland's first-ever moto-cross 500cc World Champion and only the second Finn to win a world title in motor cycle racing, the late Jarno Saarinen being the first, in road racing, in 1972. Mikkola made his world championship debut in 1970 on a 250cc Husqvarna and that year was fourth in the world series, gaining third place in 1971. He moved into 500cc competition in 1972. His World Championship in 1974 robbed Belgian star Roger De Coster of the distinction of being the first man to win four moto-cross world titles in succession. Having won the title in 1971, 1972 and 1973, De Coster was second in 1974. Mikkola switched to the 250cc class for 1976 and gained the title. Back in 500cc moto-cross for 1977, after switching to Yamaha, he once more gained the world title and repeated his success in the class in 1978.

MILLER, Sammy
Belfast-born Samuel Hamilton Miller is generally acknowledged as the greatest of all trials riders. Miller reversed the usual trend of graduation to road racing through other branches of the sport. Instead, he moved from road racing, where he achieved many notable successes, to concentrate on trials riding, competing seriously on the way in grasstrack events and scrambling. Miller (born 1935) was a member of the Italian works Mondial team in 1956 and 1957. He won many events in Ireland, was third behind Sandford and Provini (both also on Mondials) in the 250cc World Championship of 1957, and on a 250cc NSU won the North-West 200 in 1957 and 1958. As a road racer he competed in the TTs in 1956, 1957 and 1958 on NSU, CZ, Ducati and Mondial machinery in the lightweight, 125cc and 250cc classes. His best performances were two fourth places, in 1957 (Mondial) and 1958 (Ducati), both in the 125cc TT. He decided to concentrate on trials riding in

1958 and quickly set about breaking just about every record possible. His outstanding list of successes include 11 British titles, scored in successive years, two European titles, and he has been winner of the British Experts' six times, the Scottish Six Days five times and the Scott seven times. In 1970 in the Scott he won both premier and veteran's awards.

Many of Miller's great successes were achieved on the famous 500cc Ariel, but at the end of 1964 he left BSA, signed for Bultaco and successfully mastered the switch to a 250cc two-stroke while retaining his postion at the top of the trials world. Miller effectively quit top competition in 1970 though remained with Bultaco until late 1973. He was very much involved in designing and developing the Bultaco Sherpa machine which led to the near-Spanish monopoly in trials machines. In 1974 he signed a two-year contract with Honda to help produce a trials machine and run a team of riders in top class events.

MINTER, Derek W.
One of the most outstanding short circuit road racers of all time, Derek Minter (born 1932 in Kent) was at his peak in the early 1960s. At Brands Hatch he was supreme and became the local hero. When John Surtees gave up motor cycles for car racing, the Brands Hatch crowd adopted Minter as his successor as their uncrowned king. He secured the title officially when Brands organised an annual King of Brands race for the first time in 1965. On that day, against world-class opposition works riders Mike Hailwood, Bill Ivy and Phil Read, Minter won the King of Brands, 350cc and 500cc events and established the fastest lap of the day at 88 mph. He failed to retain the King of Brands title in 1966, having to retire with engine trouble, and was unsuccessful again in 1967. He retired from racing in October that year.

Minter was affectionately known as "The Mint". His career began when he started competing in Trials during his National Service in 1951/52 and he was later sponsored during his early road races by local garages near his home close to Canterbury in Kent. His first appearance at Brands Hatch was on a 500cc BSA Gold Star, when he finished mid-way down the field. In 1957 he entered events at Brands Hatch, Crystal Palace and Snetterton on 350cc and 500cc Nortons. It was in 1958 that he went to Holland and Belgium for the first time, gaining a third and fourth place in the Dutch TT and a fourth in the Belgian GP. He turned full-time professional in 1958 and in the early 1960s was Britain's leading privateer, racing regularly at all the home circuits, in the Dutch and Isle of Man TTs, the Belgian GP, and occasionally in more distant events.

Like most riders, Minter rode various machines during the early days, among them BSA, Ducati, Bianchi, MV and EMC, and later he had a season on Seeley Matchless and AJS. It was riding the works Cotton, however, and, particularly, his own Nortons, often tuned by Ray Petty, and the Italian Gilera that he had his greatest successes. Notable victories on Norton were over John Surtees on the powerful MV at Brands Hatch in 1958, and the 100-mph lap in the 1960 Senior TT, the first-ever by a single-cylinder British machine. On the Gilera his outright lap record of 90.34 mph at Brands Hatch in 1963 stood for five years, before being bettered by sixth-tenths of a second by Mike Hailwood; and he beat John Surtees lap record at Monza at a speed of 120.75 mph, recognised by Minter himself and many others as being one of his greatest achievements.

In a professional career spanning seven years, Minter created lap and race records at almost all the British circuits and his distinctions were many. Reputed for his bad starts and storming finishes, his best year was 1962 when he scored probably his most outstanding victory, in the 250cc TT. As a non-works rider on a privately-entered one-year-old Honda, he eclipsed the heavily-financed Honda team with their latest, more sophisticated machines. In 1963 Minter broke his own lap record at Oulton Park at a speed of 92.86 mph to become the first rider to win the 500cc British Championship three years running. He was British Champion twice more in successive years, establishing a record of being British Champion on five occasions. In 1962 he also won the important 1000 guineas race at Mallory Park, the richest race in Britain, and was voted "Man of the Year".

Minter had a classical, compact style and rode with immaculate ease. His exceptional technique made him supreme on the tight-cornered short circuits of

Britain, though he was less successful on the fast, straight circuits abroad where his single-cylinder Nortons were barely competitive against the multi-cylinder works machinery of the regular Grand Prix racers.

He is also remembered, along with John Hartle and Phil Read, as one of the riders chosen by former champion Geoff Duke in the latter's enterprising move in 1963 to break the monopoly of MV in the heavier classes. Duke obtained permission to use the former record-breaking Gilera machines and secured the services of the three star riders, but the brave attempt failed.

Doggedly individualistic, Minter was always frank and outspoken. He found it difficult to submit to the discipline of being a works team member, preferring to ride as a free lance concentrating on the home circuits. For these reasons he was too seldom seen on works machinery and took too little part in Grand Prix racing, though his talent qualified him for both. His potential in full-scale international racing was therefore never fully realised, though he was generally accepted as one of the most skilful riders of his day.

TT wins:
1962, 250cc (Honda).

MOLLOY, 'Ginger'
Famous New Zealand rider who was prominent on the continental circus scene in the 1960s. He later became domiciled in New Zealand and had a great deal of success with Kawasakis.

MONDIAL
This famous Italian factory which specialised in small-capacity machines made its greatest impact in motor-cycle racing between the years 1949 and 1957 when, along with Gilera and Guzzi, they announced their retirement. In the three years 1949-51 Mondial machines and riders won the 125cc Manufacturers' and Individual World Championships. Their superbly built double-overhead camshaft machines, produced by Alfonso Drusiani, were far superior to anything opposing them in the 125cc category and were even faster than many of the then current 250 and 350cc machines. During this three year period they underwent remarkably little change mechanically, though the fairings were extended to develop streamlining. The extent of Mondial's success in the 125cc category was responsible for lifting the prestige of this class, which until their success had been viewed by many factories with distinct amusement. In 1952 they were eclipsed by the speedier MV. In 1956 new and beautifully streamlined 125 and 250cc machines of greater power were introduced and the following year gave Mondial the Manufacturers World Championships and the individual World Championships in both categories.

Carlo Ubbiali, the outstanding Italian rider, was probably the most important racer to be associated with Mondial. Before riding for MV he brought them the 125cc World Championship in 1951. Other famous names to bring success for Mondial were Pagani, Ruffo, Provini and Sandford, who gave Mondial their only 250cc World Championship, in 1957, and after their retirement Mike Hailwood rode a privately entered Mondial with distinction.

Results World Championship:
1949: 125cc (Pagani).
1950: 125cc (Ruffo), also second (Leoni) and third (Ubbiali).
1951: 125cc (Ubbiali), also second (Leoni) and third (McCandless).
1952: second in 125cc (Ubbiali).
1957: 125cc (Provini) and 250cc (Sandford), in the 250cc class second (Provini) and third (Miller).

TT Races:
1951: lightweight 125cc (McCandless), also second (Ubbiali) and third (Leoni).
1952: lightweight 125cc TT, – second (Ubbiali) and third (Parry).
1955: lightweight 125cc TT, – third (Lattanzi).
1957: lightweight 250cc (Sandford) and lightweight 125cc (Provini).

MONTJUICH
The Montjuich circuit at Barcelona is famous as a Grand Prix circuit and also for the 24-hour event, the first all-British win there in the latter being in 1965 when Dave Degens with Rex Butcher rode the Dresda Triton to victory. Degens also won this famous Barcelona 24-hour race with Ian Goddard in 1970 when both were virtually retired from regular racing. Montjuich, situated in the Montjuich Park, is a road circuit of 2.37

miles with a variety of corners and set in beautiful surroundings.

24-Hours Race results

1974: A. Genoud (France) and G. Goudier (Switzerland) on Kawasaki.
1975: S. Canellas and B. Grau (France) on Kawasaki.
1976: S. Woods and C. Williams (GB) on Honda.
1977: C. Huguet (France) and P. Korhonen (Finland) on Honda.
1978: C. Leon and J.-C. Chemarin (France) on Honda.
1979: C. Leon and J.-C. Chemarin (France) on Honda.
1980: J. Mallol and A. Tejedo (Spain) on Ducati.
1981: R. Roche and J. Lafond (France) on Kawasaki.

MONTY, Geoff

Geoff Monty is one of a small group of British sponsors who were active in the 1960s and 1970s. A former rider, Monty won a number of races on his 250 GMS push-rod single machine. Bob Anderson was the first rider to be sponsored by him. Other riders to be sponsored by Monty included John Blanchard, Gordon Bell, Dave Degens, Tony Godfrey, Bill Ivy, Bob McGregor, Tommy Robb, Alan Shepherd, Ray Pickrell and Kevin Cass.

MONZA

Monza is indisputably one of the most famous centres for motor-cycle racing in the world. Its high speed banked course has been used on numerous occasions for world record attempts but grand prix racing takes place over a more natural 3.57 mile track which has five principle bends. Ridden clockwise Monza, which is situated just a few miles from Milan, has been the home of the Italian Grand Prix for many years. In more recent times Monza has been heavily criticised for the state of the circuit and its dangers. Britain's Ray Pickrell, at Monza in 1970 to attack the 750cc ten kilometre, 100 kilometre and one hour world records set by Guzzi the year before, said the track was so badly pitted and holed that racing there was like scrambling at 150 mph. Serious doubts about its future as a road racing circuit were passionately expressed following a particularly disastrous period in 1973 when first Jarno Saarinen and Renzo Pasolini were killed during the 250cc Italian Grand Prix and, seven weeks later, three more Italian riders were killed. But improvements were made and it later held Grand Prix races.

MORBIDELLI

This Italian factory was unknown until the early 1970s when it began competing in the 125 and 350cc Grand Prix. In 1972 Angel Nieto from Spain, who had previously experienced success with the Spanish Derbi factory, signed for Morbidelli when Derbi withdrew from the classic scene.

Morbidelli took the 125cc World Championship in 1975 (Paulo Pileri) and dominated this class in 1976 – first (Pierpaolo Bianchi), second (Eugenio Lazzarini), fourth and fifth. In 1977 they took both the 125cc (Bianchi) and 250cc (Marco Lega) world titles. In 1979 Angel Nieto secured the 125cc World Championship for them.

MORINI

This Italian factory has been intermittently involved in motor-cycle road racing since the first Morini racing machine, a 125 single two-stroke, won the Italian Championship in 1948. Development continued and in 1963 Tarquinio Provini, riding a Morini, ran Honda close in the 250cc class of the World Championships. Provini was only two points short of Redman, the championship being decided in the final round. Morini, in the process, proved that a single-cylinder 4-stroke could still run the multi-cylinder close.

Results World Championships:

1949: 125cc second (R. M. Margi) and third (U. Masetti).
1952: 125cc third (E. Mendogni).
1963: 250cc second (T. Provini).

MORTIMER, Charles

Born in 1949 Charles Mortimer became a Yamaha works rider in 1971. He was presented with the opportunity of a "one off" ride in the TT of that year and impressed factory officials by winning the 125 TT. Charles's father, Charles Senior, was noted for his school for motor-cycle racers and for three years from 1965 Charles junior was one of the instructors at the school. His father gave him early sponsorship. Charles junior won his first race, at Brands Hatch, in 1966, just a year after he began racing. He won the 1970

250cc Production TT on a Ducati. He followed his "debut ride" success in the 1971 125cc TT with victory again in the same race in 1972 and that year was third in the 125cc world championship.

Results:
1973: Second in 125cc World Championship.
1974: Winner F750 TT and third lightweight 250cc TT.

MOTO CROSS

See also SCRAMBLING.

Moto Cross (under its British name of scrambling) originated at Camberley in Surrey in 1924 when a number of enthusiastic clubmen wanted to organise a Southern Trial based on the well-known Yorkshire Scott trial, but without the observed sections which the Scott, along with all trials, included. With no official means of recognition for such an event, the Auto-Cycle Union disapproved of the idea in that form. If it did not include observed sections then it could not be termed a trial, they explained. The enthusiasts went ahead just the same, and as the event was to take place over some of the roughest, toughest ground available, one of them innocently remarked that it would be a scramble. The word and the term were born. That first race had 80 starters and almost half retired.

It was not until after the second World War however that scrambling developed into a specialised sport of immense popularity. Before then moto cross (known as scrambling) was confined to England and was dominated by outstanding all-rounders like Len Heat, Alfie West, and Graham Goodman. It became popular on the continent after the war and with the sport taking strong root there the Moto-Cross des Nations was inaugurated in 1947. France, Holland, Belgium and England competed, each with a five-man team on 500cc machines, but only the three best placed riders gained points contributing to the team effort. The Moto-Cross des Nations became an annual event. Britain's major challenge in the beginning came from Belgium, but in the 1950s Britain were the unqualified leaders with riders like Les Archer and Brian Stonebridge. As the Belgium challenge faded Sweden became prominent and in 1955 secured the title for the first time. It was the prelude to a long and hard fought struggle between British and Swedish riders which extended over many years. Britain were to recapture the title in 1956 and retained it in 1957. Sweden were successful the following year. In 1967, when Holland staged the 21st birthday meeting of the Moto-Cross des Nations, Britain won a convincing victory with the team of Dave Bickers, Jeff Smith, Arthur Lampkin, Vic Eastwood and Keith Hickman. It was Britain's fifth consecutive win in the competition and their 15th victory in the 21 years. A similar event for 250cc machines was created in 1961 under the title Trophee des Nations and run under similar rules. Sweden was prominent in the early years.

Among British riders who became famous in moto-cross were the Rickman brothers, Vic Eastwood, Jeff Smith and Dave Bickers and of the continental riders possibly the best known in the 1960s was Joel Robert. Team racing is the yardstick of the Moto-Cross des Nations.

The present formula was established in 1963. Riders contest two races, points being awarded to all riders who finish. The nation with the three highest scorers in each race is the winner. It is not sufficient therefore for an individual alone to be successful. For instance, Robert won both races in 1964 but his Belgian team did not collect the title. Moto cross as a sport became exceptionally popular in France in the post-war years, principally through the efforts of a businessman, Roland Poirier, who commercialised the sport by staging meetings on the outskirts of Paris. It is now perhaps the most international of all motor-cycle sports, and was exceptionally popular in the 1950s to 1970s, when it became a great attraction on television.

A European Championship for machines up to 500cc was first organised by the FIM in 1952. The first European Moto-cross Champion was Victor Leloup of Belgium on an FN machine. Britain's first European Champion was John Draper riding a BSA in 1955. In 1957 a European Championship was established for 250cc machines and the existing 500 European Championship was up-graded to World status, the 250cc Championship also becoming the World Championship in 1962. There are now twelve Grand Prix in each class taking place in Europe each year. Crowds vary enormously from

3,000 to 100,000. Two of the greatest scramblers ever to ride for Britain were Jeff Smith and Dave Bickers. Riding a BSA machine, Smith became World Champion for the first time in 1964, and developed his exceptional technique as a result of his skill in earlier trials riding. Bickers, riding for the Greeves team, won his first European title in 1960. Moto-cross has very much a European flavour and there is a multiplicity of men and machines sharing the honours from various countries. In Britain too moto-cross can attract good attendances. Hawkstone Park, for instance, probably the country's most famous circuit, has seen attendances of over 70,000. This circuit, $1\frac{1}{4}$ miles long, and situated between Shrewsbury and Whitchurch, is noted for its dust.

Some of the most famous names in Moto-cross racing are Ralph Tiblin, Bill Nilsson and Sten Lundin from Sweden, Jeff Smith of course, Auguste Mingels, Paul Friedrichs of East Germany, Torsten Hallman, the Russian Arbekov, the exceptional Joel Robert and Bengt Aberg. The first big new star of the early 1970s is Roger De Coster (Belgium) who took the 500cc World Championship in 1971-73.

The first pre-war machines to be used for moto cross were of 500cc capacity and over, and were basically road machines, development and specialisation only coming when the war was over and European competition became a reality. It was something of a landmark when Les Archer won the European Championship in 1956 on a single overhead camshaft Norton developed from a race machine. Until then moto cross had been dominated by the four-stroke inverted singles from Norton, Matchless, BSA and the Belgian factory, FN. The early years of the World Championship (500cc) saw the names of AJS, Husqvarna, Monark and Nino prominent, but Jeff Smith's first victory in 1964 was on a 420cc BSA and the four-stroke BSA was to continue honourably in moto cross for years. While the 500cc class was to witness an increase in the cc of moto cross machines over the years, there was also a significant reduction in weight. Too much power, however, is a handicap in moto cross where the difficulties of handling would be disastrously increased.

Husqvarna, CZ, Jawa, Greeves, Bultaco, Maico, and Montesa all became well known for their moto cross machines along with Suzuki who first produced a really competitive machine in 1969, winning their first World Championship in 1971. Nowadays, unlike pre-war and immediate post-war years, the moto cross bike is a highly specialised machine, light yet strong, powerful in the right ranges, and carefully and precisely tuned. The frame is vital and apart from being light and strong, is required to be rigid, yet flexible enough to stand the exceptional rigours of cross country competition. It is only necessary to see a snatch of moto cross to realise how vital suspension is, for the machine has to absorb a constant series of shocks over a period of perhaps 45 minutes. Riders take a hammering too and need to have exceptional physical stamina as well as courage and specialised riding ability.

The sport is now very popular in the USA where, in recent years, Honda have made significant inroads as a prelude, many believe, to greater European involvement.

Results

500cc European Champions:

1952: Victor Leloup (Belgium) FN.
1953: Auguste Mingels (Belgium) FN.
1954: Auguste Mingels (Belgium) FN.
1955: John Draper (Britain) BSA.
1956: Les Archer (Britain) Norton.

500cc World Champions:

1957: Bill Nilsson (Sweden) AJS.
1958: Rene Baeten (Belgium) FN.
1959: Sten Lundin (Sweden) Monark.
1960: Bill Nilsson (Sweden) Husqvarna.
1961: Sten Lundin (Sweden) Monark.
1962: Rolf Tiblin (Sweden) Husqvarna.
1963: Rolf Tiblin (Sweden) Husqvarna.
1964: Jeff Smith (Britain) BSA.
1965: Jeff Smith (Britain) BSA.
1966: Paul Friedrichs (East Germany) CZ.
1967: Paul Friedrichs (East Germany) CZ.
1968: Paul Friedrichs (East Germany) CZ.
1969: Bengt Aberg (Sweden) Husqvarna.
1970: Bengt Aberg (Sweden) Husqvarna.
1971: Roger De Coster (Belgium) Suzuki.
1972: Roger De Coster (Belgium) Suzuki.
1973: Roger De Coster (Belgium) Suzuki.

1974: Heikki Mikkola (Finland) Husqvarna.
1975: Roger De Coster (Belgium) Suzuki.
1976: Roger De Coster (Belgium) Suzuki.
1977: Heikki Mikkola (Finland) Yamaha.
1978: Heikki Mikkola (Finland) Yamaha.
1979: Graham Noyce (Britain) Honda.
1980: André Malherbe (Belgium) Honda.
1981: André Malherbe (Belgium) Honda.

250cc European Champions:
1957: Fritz Betzelbacher (West Germany) Maico.
1958: Jaromir Cizek (Czechoslovakia) CZ.
1959: Rolf Tibblin (Sweden) Husqvarna.
1960: Dave Bickers (Great Britain) Greeves.
1961: Dave Bickers (Great Britain) Greeves.
1962: Torsten Hallman (Sweden) Husqvarna.

250cc World Champions:
1963: Torsten Hallman (Sweden) Husqvarna.
1964: Joel Robert (Belgium) CZ.
1965: Victor Arbekov (Russia) CZ.
1966: Torsten Hallman (Sweden) Husqvarna.
1967: Torsten Hallman (Sweden) Husqvarna.
1968: Joel Robert (Belgium) CZ.
1969: Joel Robert (Belgium) CZ.
1970: Joel Robert (Belgium) Suzuki.
1971: Joel Robert (Belgium) Suzuki.
1972: Joel Robert (Belgium) Suzuki.
1973: Hakan Andersson (Sweden) Yamaha.
1974: G. Moisseev (USSR) KTM.
1975: Harry Everts (Belgium) Puch.
1976: Heikki Mikkola (Finland) Husqvarna.
1977: Gennady Moisseev (Russia) KTM.
1978: Gennady Moisseev (Russia) KTM.
1979: Hakan Carlqvist (Sweden) Husqvarna.
1980: Georges Jobe (Belgium) Suzuki.
1981: Neil Hudson (Great Britain) Yamaha.

750cc European Sidecar Champions:
1971: Rikus Lubbers (Holland) Norton-Wasp.
1972: Robert Grogg (Switzerland) Norton-Wasp.
1973: Lorenz Haller (Switzerland) Honda-Wasp.
1974: Robert Grogg (Switzerland) Norton-Wasp.
1975: Ton Van Heugten (Holland) Yamaha Wasp/Hagon.
1976: Robert Grogg (Switzerland) Norton-Wasp.
1977: Robert Grogg (Switzerland) Norton-Wasp.
1978: Robert Grogg (Switzerland) Norton-Wasp.
1979: Emil Bollhalder (Switzerland) Yamaha-EML.

World Sidecar Champions:
1980: Reinhardt Bohler/Siegfried Müller (West Germany) Yamaha.
1981: Ton Van Heugten/F. Hurkmans (Holland) Yamaha Wasp.

125cc European Champions:
1973: André Malherbe (Belgium) Zundapp.
1974: André Malherbe (Belgium) Zundapp.

125cc World Champions:
1975: Gaston Rahier (Belgium) Suzuki.
1976: Gaston Rahier (Belgium) Suzuki.
1977: Gaston Rahier (Belgium) Suzuki.
1978: Akira Watanabe (Japan) Suzuki.
1979: Harry Everts (Belgium) Suzuki.
1980: Harry Everts (Belgium) Suzuki.
1981: Harry Everts (Belgium) Suzuki.

Moto-Cross des Nations:
1947: Great Britain (Nicholson, Rist, Ray).
1948: Belgium (Jansen, Cox, Milhoux).
1949: Great Britain (Lines, Manns, Scovell).
1950: Great Britain (Draper, Hall, Lines).
1951: Belgium (Leloup, Jansen, Meunier).
1952: Great Britain (Stonebridge, Ward, Nex).
1953: Great Britain (Archer, Draper, Ward).
1954: Great Britain (Ward, Stonebridge, Curtis).
1955: Sweden (Nilsson, Lundin, Gustafsson).
1956: Great Britain (Smith, Ward, Draper).
1957: Great Britain (Smith, Curtis, Martin).
1958: Sweden (Nilsson, Gustafsson, Lundell).

1959: Great Britain (D. J. Rickman, Smith, Draper).
1960: Great Britain (D. J. Rickman, Curtis, Smith).
1961: Sweden (Nilsson, Tibblin, Lundell).
1962: Sweden (Tibblin, Johansson, Nilsson).
1963: Great Britain (D. J. Rickman, D. E. Rickman, Smith).
1964: Great Britain (Smith, D. J. Rickman, D. E. Rickman).
1965: Great Britain (D. J. Rickman, Smith, Eastwood).
1966: Great Britain (Bickers, D. J. Rickman, Lampkin).
1967: Great Britain (Smith, Bickers, Eastwood).
1968: Russia (Shinkarenko, Petushkov, Pogrebniak).
1969: Belgium (De Coster, Geboers, Robert).
1970: Sweden (Aberg, Hammergren, Johansson).
1971: Sweden (Aberg, Hammergren, Johansson).
1972: Belgium (De Coster, Robert, van de Vorst).
1973: Belgium (De Coster, van Velthoven, Geboers).
1974: Sweden (Aberg, Andersson, Kring).
1975: Czechoslovakia (Barborovsky, Novacek, Velky).
1976: Belgium (De Coster, Rahier, Everts, van Velthoven).
1977: Belgium (De Coster, van Velthoven, Malherbe, Mingeb).
1978: Russia (Moisseev, Kavinov, Khudiakov, Korneev).
1979: Belgium (De Coster, Everts, Malherbe, van den Broeck).
1980: Belgium (Malherbe, Jobe, Vromans, van den Broeck).
1981: United States (Sun, La Porte, O'Mara, Hansen).

Trophee des Nations:
1961: Great Britain (Bickers, Smith, Lampkin).
1962: Great Britain (Bickers, Smith, Lampkin.
1963: Sweden (Hallman, Forsberg, Loof).
1964: Sweden (Hallman, Jonsson, Petterson).
1965: No result, meeting nul and void.
1966: Sweden (Hallman, Petterson, Tornblom).
1967: Sweden (Hallman, Pettersen, Eneqvist).
1968: Sweden (Aberg, Hammargran, Bonn).
1969: Belgium (De Coster, Geboers, Robert).
1970: Belgium (De Coster, Geboers, Robert).
1971: Belgium (De Coster, Geboers, van Velthoven).
1972: Belgium (De Coster, Robert, Velthoven).
1973: Belgium (De Coster, Geboers, van Velthoven).
1974: Belgium (De Coster, Everts, van Velthoven).
1975: Belgium (De Coster, Everts, van Velthoven).
1976: Belgium (De Coster, Rahier, Everts, van Velthoven).
1977: Belgium (De Coster, van Velthoven, Everts, Malherbe).
1978: Belgium (De Coster, Rahier, Everts, van Velthoven).
1979: Belgium (De Coster, Everts, Malherbe). Van den Broeck was in the team but broke a leg in practice.
1980: Belgium (Malherbe, Jobe, Everts, Vromans).
1981: United States (La Porte, O'Mara, Sun, Hansen).

MOTOR CIRCUIT DEVELOPMENTS LIMITED
Motor Circuit Developments Limited is a commercial company which controls a number of British circuits: Brands Hatch, Snetterton, Mallory Park and Oulton Park.

MV AGUSTA
MV Agusta have one of the most outstanding records of any factory in motorcycle racing. The first MV (Meccanica Verghera) racing machines were introduced in 1948 and were 125cc two-strokes which did well in national events. The first MV four-strokes appeared in 1950 and during the next decade the famous Italian factory competed in all four solo classes, winning 82 classic events and 15 world championships.

Although they had significant successes in their first years in other classes it is the MV's domination of the 500cc class which was to become such a significant part of racing history. After two years of painstaking development MV's first major successes in this class were registered in 1952 after the British rider and former AJS team rider Les Graham joined the factory. Their victories that year in the Spanish and Italian Grands Prix and their second place in the 500cc TT were preludes to a concerted effort on the world championship in 1953, an attempt which had to be relinquished with Graham's death in the Senior TT of that year. Until that time Les Graham had been responsible for much of the development work on the four-cylinder racers which he had been contracted to ride. A similar situation arose in 1954-55. MV signed Southern Rhodesian Ray Amm in their efforts to gain the Championship but in his first race for them, at Imola, he was killed. 1956-57 were perhaps the most significant years for the MV concern. During this period they signed former Norton works rider John Surtees and towards the end of it their main opposition in the 500cc class, Gilera and Guzzi, withdrew from racing. After that for some years they were virtually invincible in the two larger solo classes.

Similar outstanding success was achieved in the two lightweight categories, principally through the brillince of the Italian rider, Carlo Ubbiali. In the 1950s they gained 42 classic victories and won 8 World Championships in these categories. MV's success in the lightweight classes was gained in the face of fierce opposition and as a result much development work was concentrated into making the 250cc MV singles and twins faster, and indeed they were at one time faster and perhaps more reliable than the 350cc four-cylinder MVs. The astonishing success of MV can also be related to the TT races. Although they did not compete until 1951, by 1973 they had registered more Isle of Man victories than any other manufacturer excluding Norton, who had had machines in the TTs every year since the inception of the TT Races in 1907. The absolute domination of the 500cc class began with the retirement of major competitors like Guzzi and Gilera in 1957. No other factory came up with any serious challenge to the Italian marque and it was left to semi-sponsored and private entries to make up the opposition, but always it was inadequate.

MV's brilliant record has been superficially undermined because of the lack of competition and an academic argument has continued since those days concerning the ability of MV to have secured their invincible position, had there been serious competition. A counter argument suggests that MV would have reacted to the challenge, as they did in the 125cc and 250cc classes in the earlier 1950s when they were successful against extremely stiff opposition. Indeed, in 1957 when MV remained alone in the international competition and gained their victories cheaply, the Italian factory could have been satisfied with the existing single, but they nonetheless produced a 250 based on the coupling of two 125ccs and it was this machine, with an ultimate speed of 137 mph, which brought them the world titles in 1956 and 1960. From 1958 MV supremacy is evident from the world records: first in all four solo classes, second in the 350 and 500cc classes: first in all four classes again in 1959 and yet again in 1960. It was not until 1961, once the Japanese had fixed their sights on the world classics, that MV began to face real competition.

From 1957, first in both the 350 and 500cc classes and then in the 500 category, MV were unassailable. First Mike Hailwood and then Giacomo Agostini carried MV to success after success, the latter brushing aside a spirited Honda challenge in 1966, right through until the early 1970s when the next big challenge to the Italian factory came from Yamaha, who, having conquered almost everything in the 250 class with their extremely fast two-strokes, extended their interest to the larger capacities. Even so a remarkable twist of fate ensured MV World Championships in these two categories when they appeared to be most vulnerable in 1973. After many years of outstanding success with Yamaha, Phil Read switched to MV to compete in the 500cc class. Agostini had one of his worst starts ever to the season and as his luck improved little as the season wore on it was left to Read to take over the mantle for MV and retain for them the 500cc World Championship in 1973. Read repeated his success in 1974, giving MV an unprecedented continuous run-through of 500cc World Championships from 1957 – seventeen years. Agostini took the 350cc World title for MV in 1973.

MV machines first appeared in the results of the TT in 1952 when Les Graham was second in the Senior race and Cecil Sandford brought them their first victory, in the 125cc TT of the same year. From then on the Italian factory were regularly among the results with 1958, 1959, 1960 the vintage years.

An impressive list of star riders have ridden MV machinery over the years including Les Graham, Cecil Sandford, who secured their initial significant victories in 1952 (the 125cc World Championship and 125cc TT), Carlo Ubbiali, Bill Lomas, Dickie Dale, Ray Amm, John Surtees, who led the team in 1956 and won the World 500cc Championship, John Hartle, Tarquinio Provini, Gary Hocking, Mike Hailwood, Giacomo Agostini of course, Phil Read and Angelo Bergamonti.

In the 350cc World Championships only Honda have provided any opposition in the sixteen years, 1958-1967, denying MV the title in 1962-1967. **Yamaha won the title in 1974 and 1975, by which time the reign of MV Agusta was at an end.**

Machine development

The first MV four-stroke in 1950 was a 125cc single with a twin-overhead cam driven by a cascade of pistons. A developed version of this design brought MV their first world title in 1952, but it was inferior to NSU in 1953. A new 125cc MV in 1954 brought the first series of wins. The first 250-class MV was a "developed" 125 and in 1958 the engine capacity was increased to 249cc. The MV 250 based on two 125s was introduced in 1959. The original MV 500-4 was a conventional engine with a double overhead cam four with cylinders to the road, and shaft drive, the latter giving way to a chain in 1952. The machine had power but was less than satisfactory in handling. The frame was modified first by Les Graham and then by John Surtees. In 1966, facing a strong Honda challenge, MV produced a completely new three-cylinder machine with twin overhead cam and a much improved frame. By 1969 the 500 MV-3 had four valves per cylinder and was capable of 168 mph. The 350 MV, a smaller version of the 500, was competitive until 1972. In 1973, facing strong competition from Yamaha, MV gave Agostini a new four-cylinder 350 which the Italian rode for the first time in May that year at the Austrian Grand Prix. With a seven speed gearbox, it had a 52mm bore and a 40.4mm stroke and produced 69 bhp at a maximum 15,000 rpm. MV's latest star rider, Phil Read, gained his first grand prix win for the Italian factory in the third round of the 500cc championship at Hockenheim in 1973. It was on an over-bored 350 and this was the 430cc four-cylinder forerunner to the full 500-4 which Read raced to secure the World Championship for 1973 in Sweden. It was an aircooled four-stroke with a claimed power output of 80 bhp at 14,000 rpm.

MZ

This famous racing factory from East Germany took over the well-known DKW factory at Zschopau when Germany was partitioned after the war, continuing the latter's concentration on the making of two-stroke machines. By 1958 MZ (Motorraderwerke Zschopau) were producing extremely fast 125 and 250cc two-strokes which, incorporating novel disc valves, were already challenging the four-stroke machines in the smaller classes. The factory achieved a number of important Grands Prix successes in 1959 with Gary Hocking riding in 250cc events and Ernst Degner competing in the smaller categories. In the same year Luigi Taveri finished second in the 125cc TT. Degner was also second in the 125cc World Championships of 1961. Although the factory did produce higher capacity machines for competition in the 350cc class, they met with little success and remain noted for their competition in, particularly, the 125cc category. In 1964 Alan Shepherd rode MZ to second place in the lightweight 250cc TT. In the earlier years the potential of MZ machinery was never fully exploited, because of their inability to offer contracts to top riders, and in the early 1960's when they could, they faced the might of Japanese competition. Walter Kaaden headed their racing department during the factory's most successful years.

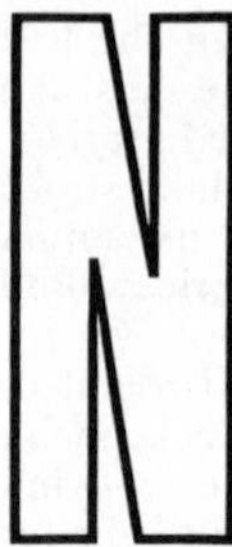

NELSON, Billie

From Eckington, nr Sheffield, Nelson (born 1942) died following a crash in the Yugoslav Grand Prix in September, 1974. He had been racing on the continent for ten years and was a member of the small group of riders making up the regular continental circus. Nelson began racing as a passenger to sidecar expert Charlie Freeman and later combined this with solo racing on Manx Nortons. He is also remembered for his association with Helmut Fath, for whom he rode passenger prior to a crash in Finland in 1969 (after which he retired from sidecar racing) and whose experimental four-cylinder two-stroke he also rode in the 500cc class.

NEWBOLD, John

A young British rider, John Newbold (born 1953) won his first race as a schoolboy grass track rider at Ripley in 1968, when only fifteen. He moved into road racing in March 1971 and after average success in club meetings during 1972 had a good year in 1973, helped and encouraged by former racing star John Cooper. He comes from Nottinghamshire. In 1974 he won the 350cc International Trophy meeting at Oulton Park on a Yamaha. Newbold's big break came at the end of 1974 when it was announced that he would be joining Barry Sheene and Stan Woods in the Suzuki GB team for 1975 to ride mainly 750cc machines. Newbold's best international placing was third in the FIM Formula 750 Prize in 1976.

NIETO, Angel

This exciting road racer from Madrid, Spain, made a remarkable impact in international competition from 1969 to 1972. After he secured the 50cc World Championship at the Yugoslav Grand Prix in 1969 he was accorded a hero's welcome on his return to Barcelona, for never before in the history of motor-cycle racing had a Spaniard won a world title. Nieto (born 1947) at 22 years of age, was also the youngest 50cc rider to win the world title. Described both as temperamental and high-spirited, Nieto started racing at 13 on a second hand 50cc Derbi, and by 1961 was so determined to make a career out of racing that he had found his way to the famous Bultaco factory in Barcelona and got himself a job in their racing department. With Bultaco well-shod for riders there was no chance of Nieto obtaining rides so he moved to the racing department of Derbi and in 1962 he raced machines loaned by the factory. He was only 16 in 1963 when he became a full blown works rider, and following unsuccessful outings on Ducati machines and in a test for Bultaco, Derbi provided him with 50cc and their new 125cc vee-twin two-stroke machines. Nieto won both classes of the Spanish Championship and in 1968 was providing real competition in Grand Prix events for Hans Georg Anscheidt. He collected his first world title in 1969 in the 50cc category, repeating his success the following year, when he was also second in the 125cc class. The positions were reversed in 1971 (second in the 50cc class and winner of the 125cc title) and in 1972 he crowned four years of success with a double world championship. He was only the tenth rider to become a double world champion. With five world championships in four years, Derbi withdrew from Grand Prix racing at the end of 1972, leaving Nieto without a ride, though he agreed to ride Derbi machines in national events in Spain, in which Derbi retained their interest. He joined Morbidelli for world championship rides in 1973 and was seventh in the 125cc World Championship.

After a disappointing 1974 season with Morbidelli, Nieto bought a Van Veen Kreidler used successfully in 1973 and 1974 by Henk van Kessel and Jan de Vries, and recaptured the 50cc World Title in 1975. He gained further world titles in 1976, '77, '79, '81 (Bultaco and Minarelli).

World Champion:
1969: 50cc (Derbi).
1970: 50cc (Derbi).
1971: 125cc (Derbi).
1972: 50cc (Derbi) and 125cc (Derbi).
1975: 50cc (Kreidler).
1976: 50cc (Bultaco).
1977: 50cc (Bultaco).

1979: 125cc (Minarelli).
1981: 125cc (Minarelli).

NIXON, Gary
One of the most popular racers in America. Gary Nixon was born on 25th January 1941 at Anadarko, Oklahoma. His first race machine was a 165cc Harley-Davidson, from which he progressed to drag races where he achieved his first win in 1956 on a 650cc Triumph. His first factory machines were 500cc Triumphs, in 1963. His early victories included the 1960 Santa Fe Short Track, Chicago, on a 200cc Triumph Tiger Cub, 1963 AMA National Road Race at Windber, Pennsylvania, on a factory 500cc Triumph. Among his outstanding distinctions are AMA No. 1 in 1967 and in 1968, and in 1968 he became the first rider to win the 200-miler *and* the 100 mile lightweight race at Daytona in the same year. He has won over 300 races as a professional.

NORTH WEST 200
This famous race in Londonderry, Northern Ireland, is the fastest in the United Kingdom, the lap average speed of 119.83 mph being set up on 16th May 1981 by Joey Dunlop on an 1100cc Honda with a fastest lap of 121.06 mph of the 9.714 mile circuit. The course includes the Portstewart-Coleraine-Portrush public roads.

Results 1974
750cc J. Williams (Yamaha); 500cc J. Williams (Yamaha); 350cc J. Williams (Yamaha); 250cc R. McCullough (Yamaha). Williams set a new lap record of 115.80 mph.

1975
750cc M. Grant (Kawasaki); 500cc M. Grant (Kawasaki); 350cc C. Williams (Maxton Yamaha); 250cc D. Chatterton (Chat Yamaha).
New outright lap record (May 1975) by Mick Grant at 122.62 mph.

1976
750cc P. H. Tait (Suzuki); 500cc M. Sharpe (Spartan); 350cc R. McCullough (Yamaha); 250cc I. Richards (Yamaha).

1977
N-W 200 Superbikes J. Williams (Yamaha); 750cc M. Grant (Kawasaki); 500cc J. Williams (Suzuki); 350cc R. McCullough (Yamaha) and T. Rutter (Yamaha); 250cc T. Rutter (Yamaha).

1978
N-W 200 Superbikes T. Rutter (Yamaha); 750cc T. Herron (Yamaha); 500cc J. Newbold (Suzuki); 350cc T. Rutter (Yamaha); 250cc T. Herron (Yamaha).

1979
1000cc J. Dunlop (Yamaha); 500cc. T. Rutter (Suzuki); 350cc T. Rutter (Yamaha); 250cc B. Jackson (Yamaha); Match Race J. Dunlop (Yamaha).

1980
1000cc K. Huewen (750 Yamaha); 500cc M. Grant (Suzuki); 350cc C. Williams (Yamaha); 250cc G. McGregor (Cotton).

1981
N-W 200 J. Dunlop (Honda); 500cc C. Williams (Yamaha); 350cc D. Robinson (Yamaha); 250cc S. Tonkin (Yamaha).

NORTON
Norton is one of the most famous names in international motor cycle racing and certainly the most successful British factory ever to take part in the sport. The firm's founder was James L. Norton and although a Norton machine is credited with victory in the twin-cylinder class in the first TT Races in 1907, the machine was privately entered by Rem Fowler and was powered by a French Peugeot engine. It was not until approaching the middle 1920s that Norton began to make any great impact on the sport. Bert Denly created a one hour record three times with a final figure of 85.58 mph in 1923, and in 1924 Alec Bennett brought Norton their first official TT victory in the Senior TT at 61.64 mph. In 1924 Norton also took the sidecar race with a 588cc machine piloted by G. H. Tucker. This was the start of Norton's outstanding success in road and track racing and record attempts, and which was to culminate in their domination of motor cycle racing in the 1930s.

Their successes in the TT races were legion and they competed with outstanding merit on all the European Grand Prix circuits. In addition, it can be claimed with little fear of contradiction, that Norton have supported racing over a longer period than any other factory. From almost the beginning of the century until the mid-1950s, except for the two World Wars, Norton have been active in a positive way in the sport. Overall, no other factory can compare with their record.

During their illustrious reign Norton machines and riders took 17 world championships, more than 30 TTs, 46 Manx Grands Prix and countless continental Grands Prix and other important international events all over the world. The vintage Norton year of 1924 also witnessed successes in the Belgian, French, Ulster and Spanish Grands Prix, the Spanish 24-hour race, the Italian Circuit de Cremona and among many others, the Brooklands 200-mile solo and sidecar events. In all Nortons collected 123 first places, compared with the 85 achieved by their nearest rivals, Douglas. A year later, in 1925, Jimmy Norton, the founder of the firm, died after a long illness at the age of 56, and therefore did not see Norton's golden years which followed. Up to 1927 Norton had won four 200-mile races at Brooklands and 11 classics. Norton entered record breaking with relish and in 1927 Bert Denly took the hour record at 100.58 – the first 100 mph for an hour to be achieved by any motor cycle. In 1930 Norton again pushed up the hour record to 110.8 mph and four years later Norton yet again, with Guthrie, improved it to 114 mph.

Such was Norton's dominance on the Isle of Man that following Tim Hunt's 350/500 TT "double" of 1931, it was achieved again by Stanley Woods in 1932 and 1933 and by Jimmy Guthrie in 1934. In 1933 and again in 1950, almost as a swan song, Nortons occupied the first three places in both the Senior and Junior TTs.

Norton's outstanding success is inseparable from that of their development engineer and team manager during their most important years, Joe Craig. It was Craig who developed the famous Norton singles and combined his ingenious engineering skill with the selection of fine riders for the Norton team. The Norton racing organisation which was supreme in the 1930s and in the post-war years until the early 1950s had no equal. Jimmy Guthrie, Jimmy Simpson, Stanley Woods, Freddie Frith, Harold Daniel, Geoff Duke, Ray Amm, John Surtees and Bob McIntyre were just a few of the star riders to gain everlasting fame on Norton machines. The level of consistent performance over many years was exceptional. On the Isle of Man Norton machines brought a number of important milestones including the first 80-mph lap (Jimmy Simpson 1931) and the first 90-mph lap (Freddie Frith 1937).

Norton's racing machines were always closely related to the firm's standard machines and they concentrated over the years in developing their comparatively simple single-cylinder engines while other foreign factories, and principally Gilera, were concentrating on extremely fast multi-cylinder machines. For a time the reliability and the extremely good handling of the Norton singles was more than good enough for the Italian challenge, but only for so long. By the early 1950s the new multi-cylinder machines were taking over and in the Senior TT of 1955 Norton lost the title for the first time in eight years. Norton machines, which had been outstanding in world competition since the end of the war and which had been up to this point modified pre-war machines, were simply not good enough to meet the challenge. Instead, as had been expected, of meeting this multi-cylinder challenge with a new multi-cylinder machine, Norton introduced in 1950 a completely new single-cylinder racer which was to become famous the world over as the Norton "Featherbed". Rex McCandless of Belfast was the mastermind behind the "Featherbed". Its introduction, combined with the signing by Norton of Geoff Duke as a works rider, almost brought them the 500cc World Championship in 1950. Other Norton riders for 1950 were Bell, Lockett and Daniell. Duke won the 500cc TT of 1950 shattering by 2.33 mph the pre-war average speed and lap record set by Daniell at 91 mph. This year indeed saw a battle of the 500cc giants for in addition to Norton who were being fiercely challenged by Gilera, MV Augusta contested the 500cc class for the first time in a Grand Prix. Although Norton, by courtesy of Duke, just missed the individual World Championship they won the Manufacturer's World Championship in 1950. A combination of Joe Craig, Bill McCandless, who had invented the new frame, and the riding of Duke, had kept Norton very much at the top of 500cc world motor cycle racing and brought them outstanding success in 1951. Geoff Duke brought the Norton factory the 350cc and 500cc World Championships in 1951 and, for good measure, Eric Oliver won the sidecar

World Championship on a Norton.

But it was a last ditch battle from Norton. Gilera, Guzzi and MV were the big new forces in motor cycle racing and having invested heavily in the production of fast multi-cylinder machines looked round for the world's best riders. Gilera's gaze settled on Duke and eventually they signed him for the 1953 season. By this time Duke, who brought Nortons the 350cc World Title in 1952 but found the single cylinder Norton simply not fast enough for the Gilera of Masetti, could see no hope of a competitive multi-cylinder Norton being developed, and so reluctantly accepted Gilera's offer to ride for the Italian factory in 1953. 1954 was to be the last year of the big-time support of the classics by Norton. After that Norton machines were ridden successfully by many privately sponsored riders, with the Australians Bob Brown and Jack Ahern, along with John Hartle, Mike Hailwood, Frank Perris and Phil Read reaching the world championship listings in the following ten years.

Norton's technical standards were set by the founder of the firm who was successful as an engineer producing machines for other designers. He had produced his first ohv engine in 1902, but difficulties in the supply of materials led to his concentration on the more reliable side-valve engine. In 1920 the Norton 490 side-valve machine, an early version of the famous 16H, secured second place on the Isle of Man and it also was successfully raced at Brooklands. Norton, their race machines based very much on standard design, continued with this policy over the years, relying on developing comparatively simple single cylinder machines. While opposing factories built more powerful engines, Norton's outstanding advantage was their superior handling and steering and this brought the factory such success that they relied too much for too long on these qualities for their victories, when they could have given more concentration to developing a more powerful engine. Had it not been for the banning of supercharging and the enforced use of "pool" petrol in the years 1946–49, Norton's dominance would have waned sooner. In 1950 the famous "Featherbed" was introduced and it was far superior in handling and road holding to other machines. It enabled Norton to stay at the top until 1952, with the help of Geoff Duke and others, but when Duke left Norton to race the powerful four-cylinder Gilera, the writing was on the wall. Ray Amm filled the Norton vacancy and did exceptionally well in keeping the Norton singles competitive with a determined effort to extract more speed and with the help of streamlining. With Gilera having gained the ascendancy by the mid-1950s Norton had to respond, if respond they would, with a new four cylinder machine, and reports suggested such an engine was being developed: but it never materialised, for after 1954 there was no further "works" racing from Norton. Production of the successful Manx Norton continued until 1962 and was ridden with success, following painstaking work by private tuners, for years to come. Improved by brilliant engineers like Ray Petty, Steve Lancefield and Francis Beart, these Manx racers were able to achieve power outputs in some cases superior to the original factory versions. Mike Hailwood and Derek Minter were among riders who rode such machines with outstanding success.

In 1962 the Norton factory was taken over by AMC Ltd of London and became re-established under the Norton-Villiers banner in 1966. The Norton name came back forcefully into racing in 1972 with the formation of the John Player Norton team with its ambitions in Formula 750 racing. (*See also* John Player Norton.) In 1974 Norton were in the news with the development of a streamliner to attack the World motorcycle speed record.

Results:

World Championships

1949: sidecar (Oliver); also third in sidecar (Vanderschrick) and in 250cc (Mead).

1950: sidecar (Oliver); also third in sidecar (Haldemann) and second in both 350cc (Duke) and 500cc (Duke).

1951: 500cc (Duke); 350cc (Duke) and sidecar (Oliver); also second in 350cc (Lockett).

1952: 350cc (Duke) and sidecar (Smith); also second (Armstrong) and third (Amm) in 350cc, third in 500cc (Armstrong) and third sidecar (Drion).

1953: sidecar (Oliver); also second (Smith) and third (Haldemann) in

sidecar and third (Amm) in 350cc.
1954: second (Amm) in 500cc; second (Amm) in 350cc, and second (Oliver) and third (Smith) in sidecar.

TT Races
1920: second (Brown) in Senior.
1923: second (Black) in Senior; second (Walker) and third (Tucker) in sidecar.
1924: Senior (Bennett).
1925: third (Bennett) in Senior; second (Taylor) and third (Grinton) in sidecar.
1926: Senior (Woods).
1927: Senior (Bennett).
1930: third (Simpson) in Senior.
1931: Senior (Hunt) and Junior (Hunt); also second (Guthrie) and third (Woods) in Senior and second (Guthrie) in Junior.
1932: Senior (Woods) and Junior (Woods); also second (Guthrie) and third (Simpson) in Senior.
1933: Senior (Woods) and Junior (Woods); also second (Simpson) and third (Hunt) in Senior and second (Hunt) and third (Guthrie) in Junior.
1934: Senior (Guthrie) and Junior (Guthrie); also second (Simpson) in Junior.
1935: Junior (Guthrie); also second (Rusk) and third (White) in Junior and second (Guthrie) and third (Rusk) in Senior.
1936: Senior (Guthrie) and Junior (Frith); also third (Frith) in Senior and second (White) in Junior.
1937: Senior (Frith) and Junior (Guthrie); also third (White) in Senior and second (Frith) and third (White) in Junior.
1938: Senior (Daniell); also third (Frith) in Senior and third (Frith) in Junior.
1939: third (Frith) in Senior and second (Daniell) in Junior.
1940–46: No contest.
1947: Senior (Daniell); also second (Bell) in Senior.
1948: Senior (Bell); also second (Doran) and third (Weddell) in Senior and third (Bell) in Junior.
1949: Senior (Daniell); also second (St. J. Lockett) in Senior and third (Bell) in Junior.
1950: Senior (Duke) and Junior (Bell); also second (Bell) and third (St. J. Lockett) in Senior and second (Duke) and third (Daniell) in Junior.
1951: Senior (Duke) and Junior (Duke); also third (McCandless) in Senior and second (St. J. Lockett) and third (Brett) in Junior.
1952: Senior (Armstrong) and Junior (Duke); also third (Amm) in Senior and second (Armstrong) in Junior.
1953: Senior (Amm) and Junior (Amm); also second (Brett) in Senior and second (Kavanagh) in Junior.
1954: Senior (Amm) and sidecar (Oliver); also third (Brett) in Senior and third (Keeler) in Junior.
1955: second (McIntyre) in Junior and second (Boddice) in sidecar.
1956: second (Hartle) and third (Brett) in Senior; third (Hartle) in Junior; and second (Harris) and third (Boddice) in sidecar.

NORTON VILLIERS
When Norton were absorbed into AMC Limited in 1962 racing ceased and production of the successful Manx Norton ended. Not until after AMC had run into financial difficulties and Norton had been restructured under the Norton-Villiers name in 1966 did Nortons move dramatically into racing once again. The new racing policy was constituted on the old concept of race machines based on standard design, rather than the production of highly expensive prestige machines far removed from standard design. With the increasing popularity of Formula 750 racing, Norton-Villiers launched a full-scale assault in Formula 750 and Production machine events in 1972, a team of riders entering all the major international events. This effort attracted support from John Player and the John Player Norton race team was formed (*see* JOHN PLAYER NORTON). Sponsorship from John Player continued until and including 1974. In 1974 Norton-Villiers (which by now had absorbed the loss-making BSA-Triumph group under the new title Norton-Villiers-Triumph – *see* BSA and BSA-TRIUMPH) were said to be investing heavily on a new 750cc water-cooled vertical twin racer which would likely also form the basis of a production unit to replace the outdated Commando design. In 1975 there was news that the first racing

machine to be built by the Norton factory since the Manx went out of production in 1962 would be on sale early in 1975 to be known as the Norton-Thruxton Club Racer.

NORTON VILLIERS TRIUMPH
(*See* NORTON VILLIERS).

NURBURGRING
One of the most famous racing circuits in the world, the Nurburgring is situated close to Koblenz in West Germany, and is possibly the most complicated course in Europe. For some years the German Grand Prix was run on the south loop to give a lap distance of 4.7 miles but in 1970 the north loop was used for the first time since 1958. When, in 1968, the West German Grand Prix returned to the Nurburgring for the first time since 1965, five of the six short lap records were broken, the 50cc record being equalled. Total distance of the Nurburgring is now 14.19 miles and it includes a large number and variety of bends, corners, gradients, bridges, cambers and surface changes, making it an extremely demanding course and a stern test of riding skill. The course is bordered by trees or ravines and is regarded highly by both riders and spectators. (*See also* WEST GERMAN GRAND PRIX.)

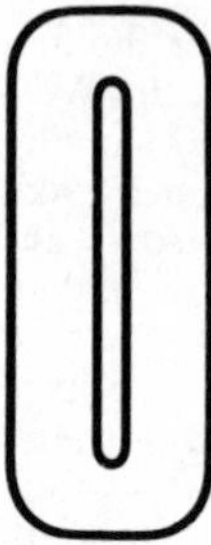

O'DELL, George
At 32 years of age, this Hemel Hempstead racer made history when he became World Sidecar Champion in 1977, the first Britisher to take the title since Eric Oliver had last won it in 1953. Moreover, O'Dell did it without winning a single Grand Prix – yet his performance was so consistent that he gained most championship points. He is also down in the TT record books, having notched the first ever 100 mph sidecar lap, recording 102.80 mph.

Breaking his leg three times and suffering mechanical problems in the following two years kept O'Dell out of the limelight in 1978 and 1979, but he made a determined comeback in 1980.

George O'Dell's life ended tragically on Monday, 23 March 1981, the day of Mike Hailwood's death, in a house blaze in Hemel Hempstead, Hertfordshire. The former World Sidecar Champion had held his estranged wife and three relatives at gunpoint for half an hour until police persuaded him to let his wife go. He later set fire to the house and died in the inferno that followed. The siege drama came only weeks after his second wife had left him and only a week after doctors had warned him that another crash could paralyse him.

OLIVER, Eric S.
One of Britain's greatest sidecar aces, Eric Oliver rode solo machines and sidecars with success before concentrating on the latter after the 1939–45 war, becoming the first ever World Champion sidecar driver in 1949. He gained the world title three times in the next four years and was runner-up in 1954. He was an outstanding exponent of sidecar technique, winning no fewer than eighteen world title three times in the next four years and was runner-up in 1954. He was an outstanding exponent of sidecar techfearless when piloting his phenomenal Norton/Watsonion combination, first rode in the TT Races in 1937 and competed regularly in solo races until 1954, when he won the first sidecar TT held since 1925 at an average speed of 68.87 mph and a fastest lap of 70.85 mph. He is credited with introducing the Kneeler sidecar outfit generally used today. He retired in the 1950s and died in 1981.
World Champion: sidecars 1949, 1950, 1951, 1953 (Nortons).
TT wins: 1954, sidecar (Norton).

ONTARIO
One of the most notable motor-cycle race circuits in the USA, the Ontario Speedway in California is the venue for the famous classic event which counts towards the American Motor Cycle Association's Championship. The race was won in 1972 by Britain's Paul Smart on a Kawasaki. He collected £12,000, earned at the rate of £70 per minute of racing. It was won in 1973 by Yvon Du Hamel and in 1974 by Gene Romero. The Ontario race is decided on two legs or heats and an aggregate is taken of the two. In 1974 the first leg was over 35 laps and the second leg over 25 laps. Romero's victory represented the first time the Californian event had been won by an American.

OULTON PARK
Racing at Oulton Park, near Tarporley, Cheshire, started in 1953. The course at the beginning was $1\frac{1}{2}$ miles and was later extended to 2.761 miles. It is an interesting course with a number of corners and good climbs and descents combining with high-speed stretches. The course is situated in natural parkland. Old Hall Corner, Cascades, Esso, Knicker Brook and Druids are some of the famous features of this course.

Oulton Park is used for international, national and club racing. In 1979 it was used for the first time for the prestigious Race of the Year, previously held at Mallory Park. Results of the Race of the Year 1979 were: first, Kenny Roberts (750 Yamaha); second, Barry Sheene (680 Suzuki); third, Jeff Sayle (750 Yamaha).

Address: Cheshire Car Circuit Ltd., Oulton Park, Little Budworth, Tarporley, Cheshire.

PARKINSON, Denis

The rich, Yorkshire-accented voice of Denis Parkinson is known to thousands of enthusiasts for his comments on television scrambles broadcasts. Parkinson (born 1915) has spent most of his life in a motor-cycle environment and started racing when he was 13 in grass-track handicap events. Later came five victories in the Manx Grand Prix, in which race he made his debut in 1932 when he finished 29th in the Junior. His wins were in 1936 (Lightweight), 1937 (Lightweight), 1938 (Lightweight), 1948 (Junior), and 1953 (Junior). He retired from racing in 1954. For more than 25 years he assisted the BBC with their TT broadcasts and was responsible for the regular televising of scrambles, starting with ITV in 1957.

PASOLINI, Renzo

Renzo Pasolini died, along with Jarno Saarinen, in an appalling crash at Monza in May, 1973. He was on the verge of what was potentially a brilliant career. Pasolini, the son of a racer and record breaker, was born in 1939 and began competitive racing in long distance trials and moto cross. He worked at the Aermacchi factory in Italy and soon found his way into the racing department. His first outing on a road racing Aermacchi was, ironically, at Monza when he was given the opportunity to test machines. In 1962, after completing his national service, Pasolini raced a 175cc Aermacchi as a junior and by 1964 was a member of the factory team. His third place in the 350cc World Championship table in 1966 was a most creditable performance. Riding the single cylinder Aermacchi four-stroke, only Hailwood and Agostini on multi-cylinder racers were placed higher. He joined Benelli to ride four-cylinder machines and achieved a number of successes. He came close to the 250cc World Championship but a crash while practising for the West German Grand Prix upset his hopes.

"Paso" returned to Aermacchi in 1971 to ride new twin-cylinder, two-strokes intended for 350cc and 250cc events. In 1972 he reached a close second place in the 250cc World Championship and was third in the 350cc class. But for mechanical problems with the air-cooled Harley-Davidson (Aermacchi by this time having linked with Harley-Davidson), he might have taken the 250cc championship. During the 1972 season Pasolini began racing the Harley-Davidson alloy XR-750 road racers in the new European Formula 750 class. In October he raced the same machine for the first time in his career in the United States at the 1972 Ontario, California race, finishing third overall. His European race record in 1972 was 9 wins, 12 second place finishes and 6 thirds.

Renzo Pasolini was highly successful in his home country and his achievements included the 250cc and 350cc Italian Championships.

He often raced against Agostini on the powerful MV and gave good performances. He beat Ago for the 1973 350cc Italian title riding a 1972 racer and on one of the new Harley-Davidson water-cooled models he set a new record lap at Monza in the 350cc race before being forced out with machine problems. Though small and of quiet disposition, the bespectacled Italian made no secret of his declared ambition to win a world championship – an ambition he never fulfilled.

PERRIS, Frank G.

Canadian born Frank Perris (born Toronto 1931) moved to England in 1938 and first took an interest in motor cycle racing in 1949 when his father took him to see the TT races. He later bought and raced an old Velocette. In 1956 he rode in the works AJS team and after racing Ray Petty Nortons successfully, signed for Suzuki, joining Hugh Anderson and Ernst Degner in the Japanese factory team. He had a significant win in the 125cc class of the Japanese Grand Prix in 1963, against many of the world's top racers including Jim Redman on a Honda. Perris retired from racing in 1966 following an outing on a 500 Gilera four, after leaving the Suzuki team at that year's TT. He concentrated on a joint business venture with Mike Hailwood in South Africa for a time, but returned to active racing in Europe in 1968; but after being runner-up in the 250cc TT of 1969 and while lying third in the 250cc World Championship table, he announced his retirement again. In 1971 he was appointed competition manager of Nortons responsible for preparation and team management of the factory's three-man team. In 1972 he was firmly established as the team manager of the John Player Norton team.

Perris appeared in the TT Races in 1955 (Matchless), 1956 (AJS and Matchless), 1962–1966 inclusive (Suzuki), 1968 (Suzuki), 1969 and 1971 (Suzuki and Yamaha). His best placings during these years were second in the Lightweight (125) in 1963, second in the Lightweight (250) of 1969, third in the Lightweight (250) of 1965 and third in the Senior of 1971. In addition to his second position in the 125cc World Championship of 1965, Frank Perris was third on a Norton in the 500 World Championship of 1961.

PETTY, Ray J. A.

One of the leading and most well known British motor-cycle tuners during the 1960s, Ray Petty was always closely associated with short circuit road racers Derek Minter and John Cooper. Petty tuned both Minter's and Cooper's Nortons during some of their most successful periods of racing.

He also prepared machines ridden with success by such established names as Dan Shorey, Frank Perris, Hugh Anderson and Tom Phillis. Machines prepared by this Hampshire tuner have lapped the Isle of Man at over 100 mph, won many British championships, the important Race of the Year in 1962 and 1965, figured prominently in the World Championships, and dominated the home circuits for many years in the 350 and 500cc classes. In 1966 Petty machines recorded 43 firsts, 31 seconds and 30 thirds, set up three lap records and secured the 350 and 500cc British titles.

Petty is a former racer who competed on the Isle of Man every year from 1948–54 inclusive. His best performance was in 1953 when he came seventh on a Norton in the lightweight (250) TT.

PICKRELL, Ray

Like so many other British road racers, Ray Pickrell's early experience was on a 500cc Manx Norton and he was to score his major triumphs on big bikes. Born 1938 in London, Pickrell won four TTs between 1967 and 1972, all in 750cc events. His successful years on the Isle of Man were 1968 (first on a Norton in the Production 750), 1971 (first on a Triumph in the Production 750), and 1972 when he won both the Production 750 and the Formula 750 races on Triumphs, the latter with a record lap at 105.68 mph on the Triumph Trident. He was also the only rider to beat Cal Rayborn in the 1972 Anglo-American match races, but in a crash at Mallory Park that same year he suffered serious injuries. Pickrell's early success on home circuits were with the big Norton twins prepared by Kent tuner Paul Dunstall and it was on one of Dunstall's machines that Pickrell came close to a 100-mph TT lap at his first attempt. An easy going rider, he never showed any desire to contest the classics, nor in making racing a full time career. He has also been active in other F750 events like the Superbike Championship and the John Player Transatlantic Trophy races. He was second in the former in 1971 and 1972 and in 1971 won the Thruxton 200-miler.

TT wins

1968: Production 750 (Norton).
1971: Production 750 (Triumph.
1952: Production 750 (Triumph) and Formula 750 (Triumph).

POMEROY, Jim

This American moto cross star gained a particular distinction by becoming the first American to win a European moto cross Grand Prix in 1973 when he won the 250cc event in Spain on his European debut.

PONS, Patrick

French road-racing star Patrick Pons, born in Paris, died in August 1980 from injuries sustained when he came off his 500cc Yamaha at Becketts Corner during the British Grand Prix at Silverstone. He was 28 years old and in March 1980 had won the prestigious Daytona 200. He had been the No. 1 rider for the French-based Gauloises team for several years. He became the first Frenchman to win a motorcycling World Championship when, in 1979, he took the Formula 750 title.

POPE, Noel B.
One of the legendary speed men of the Brooklands era, Noel Pope was the last man to establish solo and sidecar records at the famous Weybridge circuit. His ability at speed events was outstanding. He began racing in 1933 and rode on the Isle of man in 1934–39 inclusive and again in 1947 and 1948 on Velocette and Norton machines. His best performances were in 1936 when he was fifth in the Senior on a Norton and in 1948 (fifth again on a Norton). He gained everlasting fame with his outer circuit lap record at Brooklands in July 1939 when he averaged 124.51 mph on a supercharged 1000cc Brough Superior. Before that he had gained Brooklands Gold Stars for 100 mph laps in the 500cc, 1000cc and sidecar classes, received the first double Gold Star for 120 mph lap and raised the outer circuit sidecar record to 106.6 mph. Both his lap records were standing when racing at the track ended. He made a bid for the world outright speed record at Bonneville Salt Flats in 1949 when the blown 996cc Brough-Superior-Jap was fully streamlined. When the machine was blown off course, Pope was fortunate to survive the 150 mph crash after being catapulted through the roof of the cockpit.

Noel Pope died in 1971 when 61 years old.

PROVINI, Tarquinio
This fine Italian racer was prominent between the mid-1950s and the mid-1960s, concentrating successfully on lighter machinery. He was an intelligent rider, extremely adept at braking and accelerating, and especially good in wet conditions. He rode a variety of machines but reached his greatest success on Mondial and MV. Although he entered his first TT in 1955, it was not until 1957 that he gained prominence, capturing the 125cc World Championship and becoming runner-up in the 250cc class. He also took the lightweight (125) TT that year. All successes were on Mondial. He gained the 250cc world title in 1958 and also won the 250 TT. Both victories were on MV machines. His other results are as follows: 1959 – second in both the 125 and 250cc classes of the World Championship and a double TT victory (125 and 250cc), all MV mounted. 1960 – third in 250 TT on a Morini. 1963 – second in the 250cc World Championship on a Morini. Provini had opportunities to ride the heavier, more glamorous machinery, but he persistently declined and perhaps forfeited some of the recognition his fine riding warranted as a result.

World Champion
1957: 125cc (Mondial).
1958: 250cc (MV).

TT wins
1957: 125cc (Mondial).
1959: 125cc (MV) and 250cc (MV).

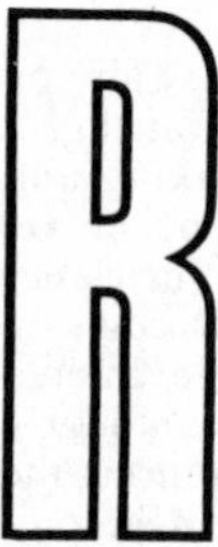

RACE OF THE YEAR
The Race of the Year takes place at Mallory Park, normally in September and was for many years the richest road race in the U.K. It attracts an international entry and most of the star riders. It was first held in 1958. In 1979 it took place at Oulton Park for the first time. (*See* MALLORY PARK AND OULTON PARK.)

RATHMELL, Malcolm
One of the most important trials riders of the present time Malcolm Rathmell (born Yorkshire 1950) was European and British Trials Champion riding Bultaco in 1974. After switching to Spanish rival factory Montesa in December 1974 his declared aim was to become European ("World") Champion again, this time on Montesa. After three years with Bultaco Rathmell's switch to Montesa was surprising. A move was anticipated, perhaps to a Japanese factory; or Puch, or Ossa. A contract with Suzuki GB was on the cards before he concluded his new contract with Montesa, which was for a period of three years.

Rathmell began riding competitively at 16 on a BSA C15 trials machine and mixed trials with scrambling in his early days. By 1968 he was receiving some support from Triumph, after which he signed for Greeves. Moto cross was still strong in Rathmell's mind when he signed for Bultaco in 1970, but after finishing fourth in the ISDT on a factory-loaned machine the way ahead became clearer. He concentrated on trials riding in 1971 and in 1974 secured the world title in Switzerland. In the European Trials Championship Rathmell was runner-up to Mick Andrews in 1971 and 1972 and was third in 1973. (*See also* TRIALS.)

RAYBORN, Calvin
Cal Rayborn, one of America's most successful road racers, died in December 1973 when a borrowed 500cc air cooled Suzuki he was racing in New Zealand crashed at 120 mph. At the time of his death he was the holder of the world motor-cycle speed record and in many quarters was considered to be America's leading road racer.

Rayborn (born 1940) lived at Woodside, California. He started his racing career as a dirt track rider, though he was always much more at home in road races, and was a team member for Harley-Davidson. On two occasions he came third in the American National Championships (1968 and 1969) and was also the winner at Daytona in these two years. He was regarded as one of America's greatest riders over the mile. He enjoyed competing in Europe and is well remembered in Britain for his sensational riding in his debut in the Anglo-American match races in 1972. On unfamiliar circuits he tied with Ray Pickrell as the top scorer with three wins from six races, his victories being at Brands Hatch, Mallory Park and Oulton Park. He was second in the remaining three races.

His career began in 1958, but after a crash at Riverside, California, Rayborn quit the sport, returning as a novice entrant in 1961, becoming an "expert" in 1964.

In 1970 Harley-Davidson made an attempt on the world speed record with a 1,480cc V-twin streamliner. Rayborn was the pilot and escaped injury when it crashed at 150 mph. After the machine had been repaired he set a new record at 265.487 mph. At the inquest after his death it was established that the 500cc Suzuki had seized and that he had died from head injuries. It was his first outing on a 500cc Suzuki.

READ, Philip William
Born in Luton in 1939, Phil Read is one of the most successful of Britain's road racers and an impressive World Champion numerous times over. As a youngster he attended Silverstone with his father, and came from a motor-cycle background, both his father and mother being enthusiasts. He bought his first bike, a 250cc side-valve Matchless, when he was only thirteen.

His first race was at the first ever motor-cycle race meeting at Mallory Park on 13th May 1956 and he registered his first win the following year at Castle

Combe, when he won a non-experts race astride a 350cc BSA. His first appearance on the Isle of Man was in 1960 when he won the Manx Senior on a Norton. The following year he won a TT at his first attempt – the Junior event – on a Bill Lacey Norton. His first experience of Grand Prix competition came in 1961 in Holland, but his first classic victory was not until 1964 when he won the French Grand Prix, also taking lap and race records.

It was the beginning of an outstanding career which has brought Phil Read numerous World Championships and has kept him at the top of international motor-cycle racing longer than any other British rider. He was virtually the only rider to remain, from the exclusive group of "continental circus" riders of the 1960s with lucrative works contracts, to contest the Classics in the 1970s and, even after the middle of the decade was as formidable on heavier machinery as he was in the 1960s on the two-stroke Yamahas.

Read scored his first major successes on Norton in the early 1960s and in 1963 he was selected by Geoff Duke to ride one of the Gilera 4s when the former World Champion came forward with his ambitious and enterprising scheme intended to stop the invincible combination of MV and Hailwood. That was in 1963 and it was unsuccessful. His greatest achievements, however, came in the years 1964 to 1968 when he led the all-conquering Yamaha team. In those five years Read brought the Japanese factory their first World Championship and added three more. He continued to ride with success his own Yamahas after the factory retired from racing, later joining the John Player Norton team briefly before signing for MV Augusta for the 1973 season.

In 1971 Read became the world's most successful 250cc Grand Prix racer. Between 1949, when the World Championship series began, and 1971 he recorded 25 wins in this class and his total number of GP victories totalled 36. By the beginning of 1974 he had secured six World Championships and had become one of the most successful and prolific riders of all time. At the beginning of 1974 Read signed a two-year contract with MV Agusta, which seemed to assure his continued professional career in racing until the end of 1975. It was doubtful, however, because of MVs lack of a Formula 750 race machinery, that he would compete in the lucrative American meetings.

Following his debut win on the Norton in the Junior TT of 1961, Phil Read competed on the Isle of Man every year (except for 1970) until 1972, and scored five firsts, four seconds and one third place. His criticism of the TT races became more pronounced after 1972 and thereafter he refused to take part. While most of his outstanding rides on the Island were on Yamaha he has also been seen there on Norton, Bultaco, Gilera, AJS, Matchless, Benelli and MV. His versatility is well known and his transition from the peak of success on the two-stroke Yamahas in the Sixties to the formidable MV in the 500cc class, where he scored immediate and impressive wins which culminated in two World Championships in succession, is a feat perhaps not achieved to quite that extent by any other rider.

Strong minded and outspoken, Phil Read has also been at the heart of some of the most fierce arguments in the sport. His bitter feud with Yamaha team-mate Bill Ivy in the Sixties, which also brought out into the open the controversial issues of riding to team orders, and his well-publicised rows with Agostini in 1973, following Read's signing for MV, were extensively reported and made headlines in the sport.

The incidents with Ivy, in 1968, earned him the title of Read the Rebel and, as he was to admit, constituted the most notorious period of his career. It was to be his last season as a works rider for Yamaha, since they were planning to withdraw at the end of the year, and it was clear that it would be Read's final chance to regain the 250cc world crown which Hailwood had won from him. Yamaha's idea at the beginning of the season was for Bill Ivy to win the 250 events whenever possible and for Read to take the 125cc title. Read obeyed these orders until the Czech Grand Prix at Brno in July. Then he decided to ignore them and said he told Ivy of his intentions. In a storm of argument and controversy the battle of the Yamahas was a sensational swan song for the Japanese factory. Read went on to become double World Champion.

Read's excellent record in the mid-sixties was against the most formidable opposition and included riders of the outstanding merit of Mike Hailwood and Jim Redman. His World Championship wins in 1964–65 were on the twin-cylinder air-cooled Yamahas and mainly against Redman, but on the more difficult to handle four-cylinder Yamaha in 1966–67 he found the going even harder against the competition of Mike Hailwood. In 1967 he lost the championship only by virtue of the rules. Both he and Hailwood finished the season on 50 points, but Hailwood's five wins to Read's four was enough to give Hailwood the title. He was already a world champion when he decided to leave England in 1965 to become managing director of Yamaha Marine Ltd, the sole concessionaire for Yamaha boats in the UK, operating from Guernsey. After some years he returned to England to live at Oxshott, Surrey, and to be managing director of Phil Read International.

His successful switch from the two-stroke Yamahas to the 500 MV is one of the most interesting aspects of his career. A liaison between the Luton rider and the Italian factory had been tentatively mooted way back in 1968, when Read became available following Yamaha's original withdrawal, but in the end they signed Bergamonti. After the Italian rider's fatal crash at Riccioni, MV once more became interested in the possibility of signing Read and the latter had some rides on MV during 1972 and was offered a contract for 1973. In 1973 Yamaha attacked the 500cc class with new four-cylinder machines which Read, after five years with the Japanese factory, considered to be potential winners. At this time Read had joined Agostini in the MV team, and must have been something of the underdog since Ago had given the illustrious Italian factory twelve world titles in the previous six years. A series of unusual circumstances, however, suddenly made Read favourite for the 500cc world title. First, Yamaha team rider Saarinen was killed at Monza and the Japanese factory withdrew from the championship. Second, Agostini ran into his worst form for years, and Read surprisingly found himself well set to take the 500 World Championship at his first attempt.

Phil Read made the most of his opportunities and went on to take the 500cc World Championship on MV in 1973 in convincing fashion with a total number of 108 points. He repeated his success in 1974 with a total number of 82 points, with Bonera, also on an MV, in second place with 69 points.

Read's winning of the world 500cc crown ended a seven-year reign by MV team-mate Agostini, who, curiously, was soon to move to Yamaha. And in winning the championship Read brought the title back to Britain for the first time since Hailwood's last victory in 1965. Read completed an astonishing year of success in 1973 by winning the lucrative Race of the Year at Mallory Park at the eleventh attempt!

Successes include

World Championships

1962: third in 500cc (Norton).
1964: first in 250cc (Yamaha) and third in 500 (Matchless).
1965: first in 250cc (Yamaha).
1966: second in 250cc (Yamaha).
1967: second in 125cc (Yamaha).
1968: first in 125cc (Yamaha) and first in 250cc (Yamaha).
1971: first in 250cc (Yamaha).
1973: first in 500cc (MV).
1974: first in 500cc (MV).

TT Races

1961: first in Junior TT (Norton).
1963: third in Senior (Gilera).
1964: second in Junior (AJS).
1965: first in lightweight 125cc (Yamaha) and second in Junior (Yamaha).
1966: second in lightweight 125cc (Yamaha).
1967: first in lightweight 125cc (Yamaha) and second in lightweight 250cc (Yamaha).
1968: first in lightweight 125cc (Yamaha).
1971: first in lightweight 250cc (Yamaha).
1972: first in lightweight 250cc (Yamaha).

At the Czech Grand Prix of 1974 Read registered his 50th Grand Prix victory by winning the 500cc event. The breakdown is ten wins in the 125cc class, 27 (250cc), four (350cc) and nine (500cc). He was also declared *Motor Cycle News* "Man of the Year" in 1974. **In 1973 Read moved to MV Agusta and that year, and in 1974, secured the 500cc World Championship. He was runner-up to Agostini (Yamaha) on the MV in 1975. Read received the MBE in 1979.**

REDMAN, James A.
Jim Redman's career coincided with the Japanese-dominated days of the 1960s and it was with the foremost Japanese factory team of the day, Honda, that he gained his major triumphs. He dominated the 250cc class in 1962-63 and the 350cc class from 1962 to 1965, capturing six World Championships and receiving the MBE (awarded in 1964).

Redman had the reputation for being the cool calculated professional. A stylish rider, he never travelled faster than was necessary to win, and had a keen appreciation of his own value.

Though British born, Redman rode for Rhodesia, having gone there in 1952 when he was eighteen. He got involved helping to prepare John Love's Formula 3 Cooper-Norton and in return borrowed Love's Triumph to race. He soon became prominent in Rhodesia and after collecting the 350cc title there, set his sights on Europe.

His debut in Britain was at Brands Hatch in 1958, where he finished in the first three against such outstanding riders as Mike Hailwood, Bob McIntyre, Derek Minter and Alastair King. In spite of this promising start he made little impact in Europe and returned to Rhodesia, disillusioned, in 1959 to retire from racing. But in spirit he never retired and in 1960 he returned to Britain for just one more chance to make his name in racing. He was determind to secure a works contract and had ambitions to join the East German MZ team when Gary Hocking moved on to MV, but while the MZ boss Walter Kaaden professed interest he never made Redman a definite offer.

His big chance came through an accident to Tom Phillis, who crashed while practising for the Dutch TT of 1960. With Phillis' team mate Tanaguchi also injured, Honda were two riders short and Phillis recommended Redman to the Honda team manager. As a result he was given the chance to ride the 125cc Honda at Assen and, because of good practice times and a mix-up over fuel regulations, the 250cc Honda as well. He finished in fourth place in the 125cc event and was seventh in the 250 race. Further good results followed during that season and when Honda decided to launch their all-out attack in Europe in 1961, Jim Redman was a natural choice as a founder member of their team.

In 1962 he was both 350cc and 250cc World Champion and repeated this double triumph in 1963. After that, against the ultra-fast Yamaha lightweights of Phil Read, the Honda was no match, but Redman continued virtually unbeatable in the 350 class securing the 350cc championship for Honda again in 1964/65. He achieved the remarkable record of six world championships in four years and won the 350cc world crown four times in succession.

Redman's rides on the isle of Man were between 1958 and 1965. His early performances there were on Norton machines, mainly in the Senior and Junior TTs, his best performance being in 1959 when he was placed seventh in the FI (350) event. Once he signed for Honda his record on the Isle of Man was outstanding:

1961: third lightweight (250) and fourth lightweight (125)
1962: second lightweight (250) and fifth lightweight (125)
1963: first Junior TT, first lightweight (250) and sixth lightweight (125)
1964: first Junior TT, first lightweight (250) and second lightweight (125)
1965: first Junior TT, and first lightweight (250)

He also won numerous Grands Prix and was a cornerstone of the Continental Circus of the sixties. He became team leader of one of the most powerful works teams in the history of the sport. Once Honda had become established in Europe there was little real challenge for the Japanese factory and Jim Redman, until Read and the very quick Yamahas moved in. Then the battle for supremacy of the 250cc class between Redman and Honda and Read and Yamaha which started at the beginning of 1964 produced some of the most brilliant riding and epic duels of the decade, culminating in 1964 in Yamaha's first world title. Because of Read's intervention Redman just failed to equal John Surtees' record of three double world championship wins in succession, though he was the first man to win the 350cc title more than three times.

Redman (born in Greenford in 1931) retired in 1966 when Honda quit the sport and returned to Rhodesia. While some may regard him as uncommunicative and distant as a champion, his exceptional talent and outstanding record are there for all to see. Intelligent, shrewd, knowledgeable, he was cautious and sensible on the track, never taking unnecessary risks and one of the toughest negotiators of a contract the sport has known. For these reasons he perhaps lacked some of the glamour and excitement of some of his contemporaries, though his supreme mastery of the 350cc class especially, during the stirring 1960s, was never in question.

World Champion:
1962: 350cc (Honda).
1963: 350cc (Honda) and 250cc (Honda)
1964: 350cc (Honda).
1965: 350cc (Honda)

TT wins:
1963: 250cc (Honda) and Junior (Honda).
1964: 250cc (Honda) and Junior (Honda).
1965: 250cc (Honda) and Junior (Honda).

RIDERS STRIKES

The two outstanding occasions of road racers refusing to take part in Grand Prix events were at the Dutch TT of 1955 when half the field withdrew after one lap of the 350cc race, because of poor start money, and at the West German Grand Prix of May 1974 at the Nurburgring when all the leading solo stars due to appear refused to ride because of alleged inadequate safety precautions. Although the Nurburgring results stood, the organiser of the event was banned from all motor-racing activities until the end of the year, and the West German federation was fined some £3,000 (20,000 Swiss francs). In 1979 every prominent Grand Prix rider boycotted the Belgian Grand Prix on the grounds that the new shortened Francorchamps circuit was unfit to race on.

ROBB, Tommy H.

One of Northern Ireland's most frequent and successful road racers, Tommy Robb was only sixteen when he won his first race and the 197cc trials James he used was soon modified for grass track racing and scrambling. That was in 1951. He turned to road racing in 1955 and was soon establishing his presence, winning the 200cc class at the Cookstown and the Killinchy 150 at Dundrod. After Tommy's potential had been spotted by Belfast agent Toby Hurst, he received sponsorship on a 175 MV. In 1957 he joined Geoff Monty and was soon riding a variety of machines including AJS, Matchless, Norton and Ducati.

By 1959 Robb was riding a 250 MZ at the Italian Grand Prix and came sixth. After successfully riding Bultacos in early-season meetings in 1960, he was seriously injured in the TT of that year, but by 1961 was riding successfully again, taking the 500cc Irish championship.

For Tommy Robb 1962 was an excellent year. He was signed by Honda, won the 250cc Ulster Grand Prix and took the 50cc and 125cc first-ever Japanese Grands Prix. In the World Championships he was third in both the 125cc and 350cc classes. Two years later Robb lost his Honda contract and returned to Bultacos, supplemented by a works Yamaha for some classic events. In 1966 he exceeded Bob McIntyre's five year old Honda-four lap record at the Leinster 200. After his membership of several works teams he became one of the most successful private entrants, finishing fourth in the 500cc World Championship of 1970 on a single-cylinder Seeley.

Robb celebrated his twenty-first year of riding in 1971 and was then said to be on the verge of retirement. Yet his greatest moment was yet to come. In 1973, after 15 years and more than 40 races on the Isle of Man, and at 38 years of age, he won the 125cc lightweight TT. Robb showed a fine sense of sportsmanship in his career and was well liked and respected. His first appearance in the TT Races was in 1958 on an NSU, when he finished eighth. His best performances in succeeding years, in addition to his victory in 1973, were as follows:
1962: second in 125cc and third in 50cc on Honda;
1963: fifth in 250cc and seventh in 125cc on Honda;
1967: third in 50cc (Suzuki) and second in 250cc (Bultaco);
1968: fourth in 125cc (Bultaco);
1971: third in Production 250cc (Honda).

ROBERT, Joel

One of the most famous riders in moto-cross, Joel Robert (born Belgium 1943) became the youngest world moto-cross champion when he won the title for the first time in 1964. He was only 20 years 8 months. A volatile, larger-than-life character, Robert's first competition machine was a 500cc trials Matchless. He started racing in 1959 and in 1960 won the Belgian Junior moto-cross title. He competed internationally for the first time in 1961 and experienced his first Grand Prix win in 1964, the Belgian 250cc GP. That year he gained the World 250cc Moto-cross Championship. His incredible record includes six World Championships. more than 40 Grands Prix wins and by 1972 he had won Grands Prix in every European country in the series. He rode for CZ but switched to Suzuki in 1969. In the early days he rode a Greeves machine. Later came a 350cc Jawa and then a 250cc CZ and it was with support from this factory that he won his first world title.

Extrovert Joel Robert, self-confessed smoker, drinker and enjoyer of the good life, is a fine showman and one of the greatest crowd-pullers in moto-cross. An individualist, he can be temperamental and has been at the centre of more than one 'incident' – like the time he flung down his machine and staged a one-man sit down strike.

Robert's peak years were probably the late 1960s. After winning that first world title in 1964, he was beaten by Victor Arbekov in 1965. Torsten Hallman beat him in 1966 and 1967. His determination to regain the 250cc crown was great at the start of 1968 and with typical confidence and audacity he declared: "Everything is on my side." With a CZ contract that provided additional incentive toward winning the title, the flamboyant style of Robert quickly built up points in his favour. He gained the title that year and to demonstrate his exceptional talent he was 250cc World Champion again in 1969, 1970, 1971 and 1972. Robert's victory in 1971 made him the most crowned World Champion in moto-cross history. His win in the Finnish Grand Prix in August that year secured him the title for the fifth time, Torsten Hallman being his closest rival with four world championships to his credit. Robert's 1964, 1968 and 1969 titles were on CZ machinery, those in 1970 and 1971 on Suzukis. He won the title yet again on the Suzuki in 1972. Without doubt a phenomenal moto-cross rider of exceptional talent, Joel Robert's record at international level is outstanding: 250cc World Champion in 1964; runner-up in 1965, 1966 and 1967; World Champion in 1968, 1969, 1970, 1971 and 1972.

ROBERTS, Kenny

This gifted American racer had a sensational rise to the top in his home country and only four years after entering his first professional race he was America's National Champion. He has all the dash and style of a modern hero, with the trappings of a business manager and public relations adviser. Roberts, from Northern California, first rode a motor cycle at 15 and was soon established as a racer of note in the amateur ranks in his own area. In his first year of really competitive racing he collected the top novice title. From the beginning Roberts declared goal was the National Championship and by 1971 he was well on the road to achieving it. In that year he gained the junior (then amateur) national title with a record nine victories, three more than any previous Junior had won. But for mechanical failures it is likely that Roberts would have gained the national title in 1972, for he was leading for the first half of the season. He finished in fourth position. In 1973 he crowned a sensational season by taking the national title with a record 2014 points. At 22 years of age he is also the youngest rider ever to earn the Grand National Championship and during the season he finished in the top three 13 times out of 25 starts, scoring points in 21 out of the 25 races.

Roberts moved out of America to race for the first time in 1974 and almost won at Imola at his first attempt. In the same year he was included in the American team for the Anglo-American Match Race Series. On his 700cc Yamaha he created a minor sensation by winning four of his six races.

Determined and dedicated Kenny Roberts has become one of the all-time greats of American racing. His success in 1973 was Yamaha's first winning of the American National Championship. He was American champion again in 1974.

In the later 1970s, Kenny Roberts became one of the most exciting and successful racers in Europe and in 1978 secured the 500cc World Championship, the first American to win a World Championship in road racing and the first American to win an international motor cycle title since Jack Milne took the speedway World Championship in 1937. He was also the leading rider to campaign for a breakaway 'World Series' for the top riders as a reaction to what he felt were insufficient rewards for riders through the FIM-organized World Championships. He secured the 500cc World Championship again in 1979 and yet again in 1980.

ROBINSON, John

John Robinson was active in motor-cycle racing as a sidecar passenger in the 1960s. He was most famous through his partnership with the Swiss sidecar ace Fritz Scheidegger during the latter's most successful years.

In 1966 Robinson was involved with Scheidegger in one of the sport's major sensations. After winning the sidecar TT by less than one second the A-CU ruled the victory out of order and disqualified them for an alleged infringement of the fuel regulations. It took many months of effort and appeal before they were reinstated as winners. In their first 1967 appearance in Britain at Mallory Park the BMW outfit crashed into the barrier at the hairpin. Scheidegger was killed and Robinson was seriously injured and announced his immediate retirement.

ROMERO, Gene

One of the most notable road racers in the United States Gene Romero, a Mexican-American from San Luis Obispo, was America's National Racing Champion riding Triumphs in 1970 and for a number of years has finished well up in the placings: seventh in 1968, second in 1969, second again in 1971, third in 1972 and seventh in 1973. After five years with Triumph Romero switched to Yamaha in 1974 and in March captured the hour record at 150.66, 5.83 mph faster than Mike Hailwood's record set ten years earlier, on a Yamaha TZ 750 at the Daytona circuit. Born in 1948 Romero has ridden many outstanding races including seconds in the Daytona 200 in 1970 and 1971 on 750 Triumph. In 1974 he won the important Ontario classic, his first road race victory. He was first in the initial leg and second in the second leg. In 1975 he won the important Daytona 200 riding a Yamaha at an average of 106.45 mph.

RUDGE

Rudge-Whitworth was a well known British machine which distinguished itself on the Isle of Man during the early 1930s, during the boom for British bikes between the wars. They had 250, 350 and 500 competition models using a single cylinder motor with four valves. Although a Rudge machine had been placed second in the Senior TT of 1913 and the following year won the event at an average speed of 49.49 mph, the factory's greatest days were 1930-35 and in particular 1930, when they took the first two places in the Senior and first three places in the Junior. In 1931 a Rudge machine was first and second in the lightweight TT, a feat they duplicated in 1932, adding a second and third in the Junior. In 1933, with Norton so strong in the Senior and Junior events, Rudge only achieved a third place in the lightweight class, but came back strongly in this category in 1934 (taking first, second and third) and 1935 (second and third).

Although four-valve heads had been a Rudge-Whitworth speciality since 1924, it was not until they introduced their radials – four valves radially disposed in a hemispherical combustion chamber and operated by two pushrods and six rockers – that they began to have success. The design in 1930 however was untried and the Coventry firm took a gamble by making three such machines for H. G. Tyrell Smith, Ernie Nott and Graham Walker to ride in the 1930 Junior TT. The team had hardly any spares and during practice had to spread out their meagre resources as best they could as problems arose. But on the day, Rudge machines were supreme in this Junior event and they scored a dramatic success. Early on Tyrell Smith went ahead and never lost the lead. After four laps Nott and Walker began moving up and were in second and third places at the start of the final lap. They finished in these positions, with Nott establishing the fastest lap at 72.2 mph. Tyrell Smith's 71.08 was a race record. Afterwards, Tyrell Smith's engine was found to have a broken inlet-valve spring, and Ernie Nott's a broken exhaust valve spring. The piston bosses on all three engines were cracked – Graham's piston being cracked almost all the way down. Earlier Rudge's designer George Hack had estimated that the pistons would last eight laps and he was right ... just! In Walker's case one more lap would probably have seen him out of the race; but for all that, no design had achieved a more sensational debut. With a brand new design, virtually untried, Rudge had dominated the Junior

TT, and at a time when inter-factory competition was high. For Rudge on the Isle of Man, 1930 was an immaculate year for Wally Handley and Graham Walker took first and second places in the Senior.

A 250cc version of this remarkable Rudge was built for the following year and helped Graham Walker to victory, with Tyrell Smith second and Nott once again setting up the fastest lap at 71.73 For several more years the radial Rudges were able to uphold the proud tradition of the pushrod engine against the emerging dominance of overhead camshafts, but their success in the 350cc TT of 1930 was to be the last time a pushrod type of engine was to win the Junior TT.

Rudge-Whitworth found the cost of racing a heavy burden. The factory was reorganised in 1933 and after being heavily committed to racing for seven years, the company abandoned its racing policy. Graham Walker, Ernie Nott and Tyrell Smith formed a syndicate to keep Rudge in the racing picture, which they did for a couple of years. Manufacture of Rudge machines continued until 1939, but the marque was not revived after the war.

RUTTER, A.

Tony Rutter (born 1941) became Britain's fastest road racer in May 1973 when he clocked an incredible 112.44 mph on the third lap of the 350cc event of the North-West 200 in Northern Ireland. It was on the 9.714 mile Portstewart-Coleraine-Portrush circuit in Londonderry. Rutter set the record on a 350cc twin-cylinder water-cooled Yamaha and averaged 110.56 mph for the new '200' circuit. Tony Rutter's first experience of competitive racing came on the short circuits of Britain, his debut being at Brands Hatch on a 350cc BSA Gold Star in 1962. He quickly became one of the United Kingdom's leading short circuit road racers and in 1971 won the 350cc British Championship on a Yamaha sponsored by Bob Priest. In 1972 he was with the John Player Norton team for a while but the association was not a happy one and he soon left. He has been a regular competitor on the Isle of Man, his first appearance in the TTs being in 1965 on a Norton. In 1972 he was second on a Yamaha to Agostini in the Junior TT. He also raced his first 100 mph lap – 100.9 mph. His big successes in the TTs were in 1973 and 1974 when he won the Junior event on the Yamaha. In 1973 he lapped at 104.22 mph to make him the fastest privately entered rider in TT history and in 1974 he reached 104.44 mph to establish a race record.

TT wins:
1973: Junior (Yamaha).
1974: Junior (Yamaha).

SAARINEN, Jarno

There is little doubt that, had not Jarno Saarinen been killed at Monza in 1973, he would have become one of the most successful international racers of all time. He had already established a formidable reputation at the time of his death and was showing no sign that the development of his racing career was in any way likely to be halted. Indeed, his style and success on the very fast Yamaha was already posing a threat to Agostini and Read and, in addition to his Grand Prix victories, he had commanding success in Britain at Silverstone, Scarborough and Mallory Park.

Born 1946 at Turku, Finland, Saarinen was a University graduate and Finland's first-ever World Champion. He began racing motor cycles in 1963 on ice with a 150cc Puch, switching to road racing in 1964, though it was not until towards the end of the 1960s that he began to make an impact in Europe. He finished fourth in the 250cc World Championship of 1970, even though he elected to miss a number of rounds in order to take a degree in mechanical engineering. In 1971 he finished second in the 350cc class and third in the 250 series. He became 250cc World Champion in 1972.

Saarinen was an exciting personality and the major new sensation in the 1970s. He typified a new breed of continental rider who were tending to succeed on European circuits previously dominated by Britain. His brilliant riding was largely responsible for hoisting European racing out of its indifference in the early 1970s and many experts believe he would undoubtedly have become one of the world's greatest riders of all time. His superb balance on a race machine was developed from his early experience on ice in Finland. In 1965 he became the Finnish Ice Racing Champion.

In 1970, and again in 1972, lack of financial support almost brought a premature end to Saarinen's career. On the first occasion the Yamaha importers in Helsinki came to his rescue and the offer of works Yamahas on the second occasion kept him racing. His first big impression in Britain was at Silverstone in 1971 when he got close to robbing Agostini of the limelight in the 350 event. Two important victories over the Italian in 1972 were little short of startling and he won the Race of the Year at Mallory Park on a 350 Yamaha, ahead of an impressive entry of 750cc machinery. It was ironic that during the year in which he had experienced so much success he had thoughts of retirement. "I want to live to be an old man," he said, asserting that only a big-money offer from one of the major factories would keep him in the sport in 1973. By that time, however, Saarinen was hot property and he continued to ride Yamahas. In 1973 he was devastating. He had already won the world's two major races, at Daytona and Imola, and was leading both the 250 (with three victories) and the 500cc (with two successes) World Championship when he was killed instantly on the first lap of the 250cc race at Monza. The crash, in the Italian Grand Prix, was one of the worst tragedies in the history of grand prix racing. It was the attraction of a new four-cylinder Yamaha with full factory support with the object of gaining the 500 world title that had kept him racing.

Perhaps the most outstanding performances in Britain by the remarkable Finn were at Silverstone in August 1972, lapping at almost 107 mph to become the fastest racer on British short circuits. Saarinen crowned wins in earlier 250cc and 350cc races with victory in the all-comers event at the John Player international meeting. He set a new lap record at Silverstone of 106.65 mph.

World Champion:
1972: 250cc (Yamaha).

SACHSENRING

Home of the East German Grand Prix, the Sachsenring is a natural road circuit situated near Dresden. The course takes in the town of the same name and incorporates a variety of large bends and twists and although the road surface is by no means as good as it might be, the circuit is generally recognised as being good for riders. Enormous crowds of 200,000 are drawn to the Sachsenring for the occasion of the East German Grand Prix and, coming from almost all parts of East Germany, there are plenty of attractions and sideshows to entertain them during the night preceding the race. The length of the circuit is 5.43 miles. It was used in pre-war days for the German Grand Prix. Sachsenring was last used for the World Championships in 1972.

SANDFORD, C. C.
Cecil Sandford was a works rider with six factories in the 1950s. He started grass track riding and scrambling in 1947 and graduated after a couple of years to road racing. He was the first rider to win a world championship (in 1952) on an MV. He was also the first Briton to win the 125 world title. Five years later he became the first Briton to win the 250cc world title. With wins in the TT and the Ulster Grand Prix and places in the other rounds he won a hard fought series on a Mondial. In addition to MV and Mondial, Cecil Sandford rode for AJS, Guzzi, Velocette and DKW. He retired as 250cc world champion in 1957. He appeared in the TT Races for the first time in 1950. He won the lightweight 125cc TT on an MV in 1952 and the lightweight 250cc TT on a Mondial in 1957.

World Champion:
1952: 125cc (MV).
1957: 250cc (MV).

TT wins:
1952: 125cc (MV).
1957: 250cc (Mondial).

SAND RACING
A comparatively recent form of racing which includes events rather like speedway or grass track performed on the beach. Corners are often included in the course along with straights in events which can be anything from a few miles up to 50 miles.

SCARBOROUGH
The Oliver's Mount circuit at this North Yorkshire seaside town projects something of the rugged atmosphere and historic quality of the TT Races themselves and is indeed described by many riders as one of the few remaining real road circuits. Popular in the 1950s through regular appearances there of such famous riders as John Surtees, Geoff Duke and Bob McIntyre, it lost some of its prestige and standing in the 1960s, but came more to prominence again in 1974 with the Oliver's Mount International which included a round of the Superbike Championship. It has been repeatedly threatened by rising costs and falling attendances and seemed on the verge of closure at the end of the 1960s, when Scarborough Racing Circuits Ltd was set up to carry out a rescue operation. The circuit, which includes such well known hairpins as Mount, Mountside and Mere, has a lap distance of 2.4 miles and is claimed by some riders to be excessively dangerous, though other riders dispute this. Plans were in hand in 1974 to widen the narrowest part of the circuit leading to Quarry Hill by two feet and to provide a lay-by for stranded riders.

Address:
Scarborough Racing Circuit Ltd, 17 Pavilion Square, Scarborough, Yorkshire.

SCHEIDEGGER, Fritz
An outstanding sidecar champion of the 1960s, Scheidegger (born Switzerland 1930) broke the four-year run of world championship successes of West Germany's Max Deubel when he took the title for the first time on his BMW outfit with 32 points against Deubel's 26 in 1965. He had been runner up the previous year and third in 1963. Scheidegger retained his world title in 1966 and after close season illness, a temporary retirement resulting from an alleged infringement of fuel regulations on the Isle of Man in 1966, he decided to contest the world championship for the last time in 1967 in an attempt to gain the title for the third time running. As a warm up to the 1967 season, Scheidegger appeared at the Easter meeting at Mallory Park and after recording the fastest lap, crashed when going into the hairpin and was killed.

Before turning to sidecars Scheidegger had been impressive as a solo rider and was Swiss 350cc and 500cc champion in 1957. Much respected in the sport, Scheidegger first appeared in the TTs in 1959, taking third place. He was second in 1961, '63 and '65, and won the sidecar TT in 1966. His victory was disputed and four hours after the race the A-CU disqualified him because of alleged fuel regulation infringements. He declared that unless his disqualification was rescinded he would never race again. Scheidegger's appeal was turned down by an international jury in Douglas. Later the Swiss Racing Federation took up his case. They appealed to the FIM. Some six months after the race a meeting of RAC stewards in London gave his case a further hearing and he was reinstated as winner.

SCHWARZEL, Werner
This West German sidecar ace is noted for his determined bid in 1974 to break the stranglehold which BMW had exerted for so long on the World Sidecar Championships. Piloting his Konig outfit, with Karl Kleis as passenger, he ended the season in second place, just two points short of champions Enders and Englehardt (Busch BMW). Schwarzel first raced with a BMW outfit in West German junior events in 1970. With Kleis he entered a number of World Championship events in 1973 with the Konig outfit and made his first real bid for international honours in 1974.

SCOTT
Founded by Alfred Angus Scott in 1908, the Scott motor cycle company supported the TTs unfailingly for twenty years, winning the Senior TT in 1912 and 1913, being second in 1924, third in 1922 and 1928, fourth in 1922 and fifth in 1925. In 1910 a Scott two-stroke machine competed in the TT – the first time a two-stroke had competed in these races.

Scott's early machines were of quite advanced design and were made by the Jowett Motor Company to the originator's own specifications, which included a parallel twin two-stroke engine of 333cc capacity with each cylinder separate and air-cooled and with its own crank chamber. The cylinder heads, however, were water cooled. A number of changes were made during the early years with the introduction in 1913 of a large rotary distribution valve.

Applebee's twin success of 1912 in winning the Senior TT and establishing the fastest lap was duplicated in 1913 by H. O. Wood, who in 1914 seemed set to do it all again, breaking his own lap record in the early stages by setting up a new figure of 53.50 mph, but he slowed down later. Scott machines reappeared in the Isle of Man in 1921, and in 1922 Harry Langman finished third in the Senior. A year later he seemed set to win the reintroduced sidecar event, but crashed on the third and final lap while in the lead.

The company's last significant success was in 1928 when T. L. Hatch secured third place in the Senior TT. Scotts were also raced at Brooklands, a special supercharged model ridden by Joe Wright in 1927 in solo and sidecar form. The original Scott company went into voluntary liquidation in 1950.

SCOTT TRIAL
The Scott is a classic time-and-observation event held late every year on the north Yorkshire moors around Richmond *(see also* TRIALS). It is a tough, demanding test made especially arduous because it is decided on time, as well as through observed sections. It is a one-day trial extending to more than 60 miles and takes place exclusively over rugged country terrain, unlike the International Six-Days Trial, for instance, which includes road mileages. In the Scott the fastest rider sets the standard time and every other rider has marks deducted on the basis of extra time taken to complete the course. The Scott traverses a complex route over difficult terrain and incorporates some 60 observed sections. Over these observed sections marks are dropped for deficiencies – five for a stop, three for repeated footing, one for a single dab. The event attracts around 180 starters including top trials exponents. Sammy Miller won the Scott seven times in 12 years. Because of the time factor the Scott demands a high degree of riding skill and it is essential for the successful rider to be able to assess sections at a glance. It is an extremely popular event. The Scott Trial began as a closed annual event for Scott employees at their Saltaire, Yorkshire, factory, but became an open event for the first time in 1920.

Winners since 1962:
1962, S. H. Miller; 1963, S. H. Miller; 1964, W. Wilkinson; 1965, A. J. Lampkin; 1966, A. R. C. Lampkin; 1967, S. H. Miller; 1968, S. H. Miller; 1969, S. H. Miller; 1970, S. H. Miller; 1971, M. C. Rathmell; 1972, R. M. Shepherd; 1973, M. C. Rathmell; 1974, R. Edwards; 1975, M. C. Rathmell; 1976, M. C. Rathmell; 1977, H. M. Lampkin; 1978, H. M. Lampkin; 1979, M. C. Rathmell; 1980, M. C. Rathmell; 1981, H. M. Lampkin.

SCOTTISH SIX-DAYS' TRIAL

This famous trial is an observation and time event held annually in Scotland. It starts and finishes in Edinburgh and is based on Fort William. It is extremely vigorous and like all trials provides a severe test over rough terrain for both rider and machine. It was first held in 1909 and is the only observation event in the world to be run over six days, though a time element is also involved. A specified time for each section of the course is included, though the overall time schedule is reasonably slow. It is the most important event in Britain. From its inception to 1927 no individual awards were made. Awards of gold medals and silver cups were made to all competitors who returned a specified minimum number of marks forfeited. The sidecar classification was abandoned after 1960. The first Japanese machine victory was in 1974 with Mick Andrews' win on the 250cc Yamaha.

Individual winners since 1947:

1947: best solo B. H. M. Viney (AJS); best sidecar H. R. Taylor (Ariel).
1948: best solo B. H. M. Viney (AJS); best sidecar H. Tozer (BSA).
1949: best solo B. H. M. Viney (AJS). No sidecars.
1950: best solo L. A. Ratcliffe (Matchless); best sidecar H. Tozer (BSA).
1951: best solo G. J. Draper (BSA). No sidecars.
1952: best solo J. V. Brittain (Royal Enfield). No sidecars.
1953: best solo B. H. M. Viney (AJS). No sidecars.
1954: best solo L. A. Ratcliffe (Matchless). No sidecars.
1955: best solo J. V. Smith (BSA). No sidecars.
1956: best solo G. L. Jackson (AJS). No sidecars.
1957: best solo J. V. Brittain (Royal Enfield). No sidecars.
1958: best solo G. L. Jackson (AJS); best sidecar J. S. Oliver (BSA).
1959: best solo R. S. Peplow (Triumph); best sidecar P. W. Roydhouse (Norton).
1960: best solo G. L. Jackson (AJS); best sidecar S. T. Seston (BSA).
1961: best solo G. L. Jackson (AJS); best sidecar event abandoned.
1962: best solo S. H. Miller (Ariel).
1963: best solo A. J. Lampkin (BSA).
1964: best solo S. H. Miller (Ariel).
1965: best solo S. H. Miller (Bultaco).
1966: best solo A. Lampkin (BSA).
1967: best solo S. H. Miller (Bultaco).
1968: best solo S. H. Miller (Bultaco).
1969: best solo W. Wilkinson (Greeves).
1970: best solo M. Andrews (Ossa).
1971: best solo M. Andrews (Ossa).
1972: best solo M. Andrews (Ossa).
1973: best solo M. Rathmell (Bultaco).
1974: best solo M. Andrews (Yamaha).
1975: best solo M. Andrews (Yamaha).
1976: best solo M. Lampkin (Bultaco).
1977: best solo M. Lampkin (Bultaco).
1978: best solo M. Lampkin (Bultaco).
1979: best solo M. Rathmell (Montesa).
1980: best solo Y. Vesterinen (Montesa).
1981: best solo G. Burgat (SWM).

SCRAMBLING

See also Moto Cross

Scrambling, or Moto Cross as it is also known, particularly on the Continent, began in the early 1920s as a development of trials riding. From disorganised and impromptu beginnings Scrambling in Britain became a hectic and exciting all-year round business for the top riders. Television did much to publicise and popularise scrambling and the BBC initially, with their Grandstand series of events, and later ITV, helped to capture an increasing following. Though Britain originated scrambling it is even more popular on the Continent with tens of thousands of fans regularly following the events held in France, Sweden, Belgium and other countries. France was the continental country to first promote moto cross with highly successful meetings on the outskirts of Paris in the immediate postwar period and the Moto Cross des Nations was appropriately held in France in 1966.

The A-CU Scrambles Star contest, originated by Harry Baughan, began in 1951. In 1960 it was divided into two classes, 250cc and 500cc. A sidecars category was added in 1965. Based on the World Championship system, riders gained points in specified events throughout the season. These competitions developed into the British Moto-Cross Championships in 1968. A recent change was the scrapping at the end of the 1974 season of the separate 250cc and 500cc classes. Replacing them was a single class for machines of 176cc-500cc capacity to form the British Moto-Cross

Championship. Vic Allan, the 28-year old Scottish rider, became the first man to win both 250cc and 500cc classes in the same year in 1974. British riders who have been outstandingly successful in scrambling include Jeff Smith, Dave Bickers, John Banks, the Lampkin brothers, Bryan Goss, Arthur Browning, Derek and Don Rickman, Bryan Wade, John Avery, Andy Robertson, Vic Eastwood, Malcolm Davis, Vic Allan and Graham Noyce. Machines which have dominated British scrambling are BSA in the 500cc class, with Jeff Smith, and Greeves in the 250cc class, with Dave Bickers.

Results:

A-CU Stars – 500cc:
1951: Geoff Ward.
1952: John Avery.
1953: Geoff Ward.
1954: Geoff Ward.
1955: Jeff Smith.
1956: Jeff Smith.
1957: not awarded, petrol rationing (Suez crisis).
1958: Dave Curtis.
1959: Arthur Lampkin.
1960: Jeff Smith.
1961: Jeff Smith.
1962: Jeff Smith.
1963: Jeff Smith.
1964: Jeff Smith.
1965: Jeff Smith.
1966: Dave Bickers.
1967: Jeff Smith..

A-CU Stars – 250cc:
1960: Dave Bickers.
1961: Arthur Lampkin.
1962: Dave Bickers.
1963: Dave Bickers
1964: Dave Bickers.
1965: Dave Bickers.
1966: F. K. Mayes.
1967: A. Clough.

A-CU Stars – Sidecars:
1965: Roy Price.
1966: H. L. Crane.
1967: H. L. Crane.

British Championships:
1968: J. Banks (500cc), M. Davis (250cc), M. Guilford (sidecars).
1969: J. Banks (500cc), B. Wade (250cc), M. Guilford (sidecars).
1970: B. Goss (500cc), M. Davis (250cc), B. Nash (sidecars).
1971: J. Banks (500cc), B. Wade (250cc), A. Wilkins (sidecars).
1972: B. Wade (500cc), A. Robertson (250cc), J. Turner (sidecars).
1973: J. Banks (500cc), M. Davis (250cc), B. Wade (125cc), N. Thompson (sidecars).
1974: V. Allan (500cc), V. Allan (250cc), B. Wade (125cc), N. Thompson (sidecars).
1975: J. V. Allan (solo) and N. Thompson/D. Beavis (sidecar).
1976: G. Noyce (solo) and T. Good/J. Rixon (sidecar).
1977: G. Noyce (solo) and J. Elliott/G. Skeates (sidecar).
1978: G. Noyce (solo) and N. Thompson/G. Withers (sidecar).
1979: G. Noyce (solo) and T. Good/B. Williams/J. Rixon (sidecar).
1980: G. Mayes (solo) and T. Good/B. Williams (sidecar).
1981: M. Rathmell (solo) and J. Gaskell/ H. Wood (sidecar).

SEELEY, Colin

One of Britain's most successful sidecar racers, Seeley was prominent in the 1960s, winning many races at circuits in the UK and on the continent. His biggest impact on the World Championships was in 1964 and 1966 when he was third on each occasion, driving BMW. On the Isle of Man his best results were in 1962 (third on a Matchless), 1964 (second with the FCSB) and 1967, his last appearance on the Island (third on the BMW). He began in sidecars with a 1000cc Vincent road machine, then came solo scrambling, hill climbs, sprints and grass track riding. In 1960 he raced a Manx Norton sidecar with Wally Rawlings as passenger, a combination which lasted some six years. Later came a Matchless outfit. Through the influence of the late Florian Camathias, Seeley had the opportunity to use BMW machines and as a result still considers the Dutch Grand Prix victory of 1964 as his best performance when he led from start to finish, also establishing new average race and lap records. The need to devote time to his own motor cycle business and lack of "works" rides restricted his participation in the World Championships. Later, Seeley took over control of the AMC concern – manufacturing rights, spares, tools, etc. of the 7R, Manx and G50, and after producing frame designs for the Yamaha, Commando, Suzuki, Trident and Kawasaki, became joint managing director of Motor Racing Developments.

SHEENE, Barry

Perhaps the most famous of the younger generation of superstars, Barry Sheene (born London 1950) is the son of well-known former rider Frank Sheene and the brother-in-law of Paul Smart. At seventeen he was riding his father's Bultacos and made his racing debut a year later, in 1968, almost immediately showing considerable talent and potential. He took the British 125cc Championship in 1970 and in 1971, at his first attempt and on a privately entered Suzuki twin, almost succeeded in winning the 125cc World Championship, Angel Nieto denying him the distinction in the final round. His first Grand Prix victory was in Belgium in 1971 during his first-ever visit to Spa when he averaged more than 110 mph.

In February 1972 he joined Yamaha's factory team, but the outcome was disappointing and he joined the Suzuki GB team in 1973 when his career once more took a significant step forward. He won the FIM Formula 750cc championship, the British Superbike championship and the Shellsport 500cc title. Also in 1973 he set a new absolute motor-cycle record for the Montjuich circuit at 78.04 mph, took the King of Brands title and was voted Man of the Year in the annual poll run by *Motor Cycle News*. He continued riding Suzuki works machines in 1974 finishing in sixth position in the 500cc World Championship. Sheene's pop-star image makes him a popular rider at all circuits and especially among teenage girl enthusiasts, of which he has the biggest following of any racer. Tipped by several observers as the next Hailwood, Sheene has outstanding ability and emerged as one of the most successful riders in the world in the late 1970s and early 1980s.

In August 1974 Barry Sheene won Britain's first Grand Prix, at Silverstone. On his 750 Suzuki-3 he knocked four-fifths of a second off the lap record for the 2.93 mile circuit and for the first 20 laps averaged 106.22 mph, making this the fastest motor-cycle race ever held at Silverstone.

In 1975 Barry Sheene looked a good prospect for both the 500cc World Championship and the Formula 750 Championship, but a spectacular crash during practice at Daytona followed by other less serious injuries at Mallory Park and Cadwell Park robbed him of the possibility of both titles.

His 175 mph crash at Daytona received huge publicity and largely as a result of Barry Sheene, motor-cycle racing received more attention from television and newspapers in 1975/early 1976 than at any time in the past. It seemed that Sheene was always in the news.

Sheene recovered from his serious injuries of 1975 in a remarkably short time and was quick to show he had lost none of the old flair and skill. He was immediately in the news again, winning the 500cc Dutch TT, setting up a new lap record of 135.75 mph in Belgium and gaining victory and a new lap record in the 500cc Swedish Grand Prix.

It could well be argued that in 1975 and the early part of 1976 Barry Sheene was the World's Number 1 motor cycle road racer, taking both his measure of success and his impact on racing into account.

Sheene's success in Grand Prix racing led him to his first World Championship in 1976 when he took the 500cc class by a commanding margin. He repeated his success in 1977 gaining maximum points in six rounds.

SIDECARS

Spectacular, and one of the most gruelling forms of motor-cycle sport, sidecar racing has taken place since the early days and was first introduced into the TT programme in 1923. After 1925 it disappeared and was not again included until 1954, since when it has been a regular feature. In 1949, when the FIM introduced their new-style World Championships, a sidecar class was included and has remained ever since.

Douglas and Norton machines figured prominently in the early sidecar results, but in the years leading up to the outbreak of the Second World War, and in the immediate postwar years, the sport was dominated by Britain in the form of Eric Oliver. On his Norton Watsonian combination, Oliver secured for Britain the World Sidecar Championship four times between 1949 and 1953, with Cyril Smith maintaining Britain's supremacy with the championship of 1952. With the remarkable reliability of the German BMW machine, ideally suited for competition in sidecar events, the sport's most outstanding record was started in 1954 when Noll of West Germany captured the title for BMW, with the Norton outfits of Oliver and Smith relegated to second and third places. The following year (1955) the World Sidecar Championship was totally dominated by BMW who secured first (Faust), second (Noll) and third (Schneider) places. In the most astounding record in the history of motor-cycle racing, BMW were to take the first three places in the world championships twelve times in thirteen years so that between 1955 and 1967 the only other machine to appear in the results was the Norton of Britain's Pip Harris, with a third place in 1956. The first serious challenge to Eric Oliver and Cyril Smith's Nortons were the Gilera fours of Frigerio and Milani in the early 1950s and, later, the first attack on the BMWs domination came towards the end of the 1960s. Helmut Fath had captured the world title for the German factory in 1960, but in the following year he was badly injured and during a long convalescence he made plans for a 500cc four-cylinder engine to challenge BMW. Fath lived in a village named Ursenbach and he called his new engine URS. He first raced it in 1965 but performance was disappointing. Over the next three years he improved his engine to the point where it developed more than 70 hp at 13,500 rpm and with it in this form Fath took the world title in 1968, though Enders recaptured the Championship the following year. With Britain so long absent in world sidecar honours it is as well to record and remember 1953 when Oliver and Smith were first and second and, along with Switzerland's Haldemann, piloted Norton outfits into the first three places.

The World Sidecar Championship has been monopolised by German drivers of whom one of the greatest has been Max Deubel, who took the world title four times, 1961-64. Other top German drivers include Faust, Schneider, Hillebrand, Auerbacher, Schauzu, Enders and Luthringshauser. The only non-German drivers who have made an impact on the class at an international level are Eric Oliver, Florian Camathias and Fritz Scheidegger, both of Switzerland. Scheidegger took the World Championship in 1965-66 and although Camathias did not win the title (he was second in 1962-63 – his best listings in the World Championships) he is acknowledged as having contributed much to the design of the sidecar outfit with his extremely low-to-the-ground sidecar. In more recent times Klaus Enders has been exceptional. This West German specialist has so far (end 1974) won the World Championship six times, in 1967, 1969-70, 1972-74.

The doyen of British sidecar racers remains to this day the incomparable Eric Oliver, but other British racers to make their mark in sidecar events are Pip Harris (third in the World Championships of 1956 and 1960), Colin Seeley (third in 1964 and 1966), Bill Boddice, Chris Vincent, Terry Vinicombe, Mick Boddice and the Boret Brothers.

In the mid-1960s the greatest controversy to surround sidecar racing in the UK occurred when Owen Greenwood started competing in his Mini-racer at British circuits. The argument centred around what many considered to be the Mini-racer's unfair advantage, for although it had been built to comply with the regulations, it looked more like a small car than a sidecar outfit. This controversial three-wheeler won more than sixty events, including two British Championships, before Greenwood stopped competing with it.

The argument about three-wheelers similar to Greenwood's machine taking part in events alongside traditional sidecars is raised periodically, generally when, as was the case with Greenwood, the three-wheeler driver does well; but so far as the British Championships are concerned no separate category has yet been established and sidecars and three-wheelers can take part in the same events.

Because sidecar racing does not offer such obvious returns to the manufacturers it has not acquired the status of the solo classes, in spite of its obvious popularity among the crowds, but in Britain a major boost to sidecar racing came in 1974 with the *Motor Cycle* International Sidecar Championship, a series of races held at eight major international meetings held on Motor Circuit Developments courses. The inaugural winner was Bill Currie on an 850 Weslake with Kenny Arthur as passenger.

The early forms of racing sidecars were firstly a motor cycle with a side-car attached by swivel joints. They did not form a rigid unit so that steering at speed was indeed a job for the expert. The tendency for the side-wheel to lift when taking bends at speed was always present and the passenger's role was vital to keep the combination steady.

Design development took place seriously after the Second World War, with Oliver and Haldemann in the forefront of work which produced the rigid sidecar ensemble and the kind of "outfits" of today, with the machine and the sidecar considered as one complete unit. The unstable openwork chargers of pre-war days bear little resemblance to the sophisticated streamline outfits of today, though the skills and close understanding of sidecar teams to race their outfits at around 100 mph remain.

The most controversial figure in sidecar racing in recent years emerged in 1978 when Switzerland's Rolf Biland created a storm with his Yamaha-powered Beo outfit. The objections were that the revolutionary design, which had twin-driven wheels with the engine mounted between them, allowed the passenger to sit in a seat so that he did not have to do the usual acrobatics. But the outfit did not contravene the FIM rules. However, after Biland had won the World Sidecar Championship in 1978 his outfit was banned by the FIM "on the grounds of safety", but within a few weeks the ban was lifted after an FIM extraordinary meeting had decided to run two sidecar championships in 1979, one for traditional outfits and the other for those incorporating innovations like sidecar wheel steering and hub centre steering.

The idea of two separate categories was later abandoned. Britain's 'big stars' of recent years have been George O'Dell, who was World Champion in 1977 and Jock Taylor, World Champion in 1980.

SILVERSTONE

This famous Northamptonshire circuit is situated near Towcester, 15 miles south-west of Northampton on the A43. Its Grand Prix circuit is 2.927 miles and its club circuit 1.608 miles, and the venue is used for international, national and club racing. It became the home of the first British Grand Prix in 1974. It is one of the premier racing circuits in Britain and was among the first of a crop of former airfields to be converted into race tracks at the end of the Second World War. Silverstone was established in 1948, during which year the British Motor Cycle Racing Club organised a successful motor-cycle meeting there. Looking for a circuit to take over from the defunct Brooklands, Bemsee settled on Silverstone for their regular Hutchinson 100 meeting and the first "Hutch" was held there in 1949. It moved from Silverstone in 1965. During the 1950s Silverstone was a popular motor-cycle racing circuit and attracted all the stars of the day, including Geoffrey Duke, John Surtees, John Hartle, Bob McIntyre, Mike Hailwood and Derek Minter. For five years from 1965 Silverstone, always important as a car racing circuit, lost much of its interest in bikes. An inspired plan by the *Daily Express* which aimed to bring big-time motor-cycle racing back to Silverstone in 1970 ran into sponsorship problems, but the following year (1971) the circuit reopened for motor-cycle racing with a full-blooded International. The event was also significant because it witnessed the return to motor-cycle racing of Mike Hailwood after two years' absence, riding a Yamaha, and brought Agostini to Silverstone for the first time. At this A-CU meeting, sponsored by John Player with *Daily Express* support, every lap record was broken before a crowd of 27,000, the biggest ever to see motor-cycle racing at Silverstone. It was also at this event that the sensation of the early 1970s, Jarno Saarinen, made his debut in Britain. With annual major meetings sponsored by John Player, Silverstone's status quickly grew in motor-cycle racing. In 1972 the big Silverstone meeting was dominated by Saarinen. In the 350cc event on the Yamaha he produced a new record lap of 104.33 mph and in the 250cc event he, along with Rodney Gould and Phil Read, all exceeded the previous 350cc record. In the all-comers' race the "Flying Finn" outpaced the crop of 750cc machines and on his 350cc Yamaha created a new outright lap record at fractionally under 107 mph to become at that time the fastest motor-cycle racer in Britain.

For the track's 25th anniversary in 1973 big plans were made for the John Player meeting at Silverstone (August 11-12) including the introduction of the new F750 Championship to Britain. Among an impressive entry was Phil Read, making his first British appearance since becoming World 500cc Champion.

The weekend's outstanding racing was witnessed by a crowd of 45,000 – which set the seal on Silverstone's successful return as a motor-cycle circuit. This came at the end of 1973 when news was received that Silverstone had been granted Grand Prix status and that the first British Grand Prix would be staged there in 1974 as a British round of the FIM Formula 750 series. This first-ever British Grand Prix in August 1974 at Silverstone was a major success for Barry Sheene. He won on the works 750cc Suzuki-3 and also won the 500cc race. He achieved a new lap record of 107.74 mph on the 750cc. Altogether, and before another huge crowd of 45,000, six new lap records and eight new race records were set up. The sidecar record was lifted to within three-tenths of a second of the 100 mph mark by the Boret brothers.

Silverstone is the traditional home of racing in Britain and took over from Brooklands when the famous Surrey circuit was not reopened after the Second World War. Originally run by the RAC, the lease of Silverstone was taken over by the British Racing Drivers Club in 1952, whose ownership of the circuit was established in 1970. The circuit has been continually developed and improved over the years. Run in a clockwise direction, the start-finish line is on the straight between Woodcote Corner and Copse. After Copse there is Maggotts, Becketts, Hangar Straight, Stowe, Club, Abbey Curve and Woodcote.

A major development programme was begun at Silverstone at the end of 1974. A new pit area costing £120,000 and stretching from Woodcote to Copse was to be constructed in readiness for the 1975 racing season. This was to be the first stage of a £1 million project to develop Silverstone into a major leisure centre. The start-finish line was scheduled to be moved some 100 feet forward and away from the exit from Woodcote. Silverstone's fine sweeping corners makes it an extremely fast circuit – the fastest in the United Kingdom for cars and exceeded only by the Portstewart-Coleraine-Portrush circuit in Northern Ireland for motor cycles.

In 1965, when the Hutch moved to Brands Hatch, Derek Minter and John Hartle shared the Silverstone lap record at 100.74 mph. When big-time motor cycle racing returned to Silverstone in 1971 Paul Smart set a new lap record on a Triumph-3 at 104.95 mph.

Silverstone became the home of the British Grand Prix, a round in the FIM Formula 750 Prize in 1976, won that year by Victor Palomo (Yamaha).

British Grand Prix results:

1979: 125cc A. Nieto (Minarelli); 250cc K. Ballington (Kawasaki); 350cc K. Ballington (Kawasaki); 500cc K. Roberts (Yamaha); B2A R. Biland/K. Waltisperg (Schmid Yamaha); B2B A. Michel/M. Burkard (Seymaz-Yamaha).

1980: 125cc L. Reggiani (Minarelli); 250cc K. Ballington (Kawasaki); 350cc A. Mang (Kawasaki); 500cc R. Mamola (Suzuki); Formula 1 G. Crosby (Suzuki); sidecar D. Jones (Yamaha).

1981: 125cc A. Nieto (Minarelli); 250cc A. Mang (Kawasaki); 350cc A. Mang (Kawasaki); 500cc J. Middelburg (Suzuki); Formula 1 R. Haslam (Honda); sidecar R. Biland (LCR Yamaha).

SIMMONDS, Dave A.

A prominent British rider of light machinery in the 1960s, Dave Simmonds inherited a love of motor cycles from his family and the story goes that his mother gave his father a 350cc Douglas for a wedding present. Dave, unassuming and trained as an electrical engineer, started racing in 1960 on a 50cc Itom but began to be noticed after obtaining a 50cc Tohatsu engine. The Japanese firm were impressed and supplied the Simmonds family (including Dave's two race-going brothers) with 50cc and 125cc racers. After encouraging performances Simmonds rode ex-works Hondas successfully and, towards the end of 1966, came the offer to ride a works Kawasaki. He was British 125cc Champion in 1965 and in 1969 took the 125cc World Championship on a Kawasaki which was almost four years old. In the TT races he rode Tohatsu, Greeves, Honda and Kawasaki, but did not have the best of fortunes and often suffered retirements. His career ended tragically in October 1972 when a caravan belonging to Australian road racer Jack Findlay blew up in the paddock area of the Rungis race meeting which had taken place a few hours earlier. As a result of the explosion the former 125cc World Champion was fatally injured, just a few days before his

32nd birthday.

SIMPSON, Jimmy H.
One of Britain's illustrious team of TT riders during the 1920s and '30s, Jimmy Simpson won the TT only once (the lightweight of 1934 on a Rudge), but in the 10 races in which he finished from 1922–1934, on only two occasions was he outside the first three. He was second four times and third four times. He is particularly remembered for the speed "milestones" he achieved. He was the first rider to complete a TT race lap at 60 mph, 70 mph and 80 mph as follows: 60 mph, Junior of 1924 on an AJS. 70 mph, Senior of 1926 on an AJS. 80 mph, Senior of 1932 on a Norton. Altogether he made eight fastest laps in his twelve years of TT racing, his record breaking Norton lap in 1932 being taken at 81.50 mph. He rode Scott (1922), AJS (1923–1928), Norton (1929–1934) and Rudge (1934). He competed every year from 1922 to 1934 and came fifth in the sidecar TT of 1925 on an AJS. He joined the Norton works team in 1929 and in 1930 became the world's fastest road racer with a record lap of 84.63 mph in the Ulster Grand Prix. His sole TT victory was achieved in his final year of TT competition. The Jimmy Simpson Trophy, a special award for riders who are fastest round the TT course, was started in 1948. He died in December 1981, aged 83. (See also TT RACES.)

SMART, Paul A.
Paul Smart (born 1943) began racing in 1965 on a 125cc Bultaco at Brands Hatch and achieved his first win at the Kent circuit on a 125cc Honda that same year. In 1966, racing Cotton and Greeves, he won the *Motor Cycle News* championship for 250cc machines and, also that year, competed for the first time on the Isle of Man, retiring on the second lap of the Manx 250cc race while in second place. He achieved his first international success when he partnered Reg Everett in 1969 and on a 250cc Vic Camp Ducati took the Barcelona 24-hour race. In 1970, with Tom Dickie as co-rider on the works Triumph, he won the Bol d'Or 24-hour race. Smart's career is closely linked to 750cc racing and he has ridden works Triumph, Ducati, Kawasaki and Suzuki machines. He was in the British team in the first Anglo-American match series in 1971. He was second in the Thruxton 200-mile that year. Perhaps his most notable ride in 1971 was at Daytona where, on the works Triumph, he set the fastest practice lap though mechanical failure put him out of the race when in the lead. When Triumph moved out of racing in early 1972 Smart joined Bob Hansen's Kawasaki team in America. That year he won the Imola 200, on a Ducati, and the Ontario Champion Spark Plug Classic on a Seeley Kawasaki, two of the richest races in the international calendar.

In Britain in 1972 he won the F750 Hutchinson 100 on the Ducati and was second in the Race of the Year and Race of the South events on the Seeley Kawasaki. He was with Kawasaki for one season only and for 1973 moved on to Suzuki and in Britain that year is remembered for his fine riding at Silverstone. He is typical of the new breed of successful road racer developed from the closer links, through 750cc racing, which now exist between the USA and Britain. He commuted regularly between the two countries. In September 1974 he crashed heavily at Mallory Park and broke both legs.

Paul Smart's first TT was in 1967 on a Norton when he came second in the Production 750 race. He was second again in the same race in 1969 and in 1970 was third in the Junior event on a Yamaha.

In general economies announced at the end of 1974 Suzuki axed Smart from their team, leaving him at that time without a works ride in 1975. He is now retired from racing.

SMITH, Don
One of the great characters of the British trials scene, Don Smith began trials riding in 1953 on a 350cc Ariel and was later with Greeves. He gained two unofficial European titles with Greeves in 1964 and 1967. With Montessa, he gained an official European title in 1969. For two years he left trials to ride speedway for West Ham. A great ambassador for trials, Smith signed with Kawasaki in 1973 to master-mind their attack on the "world" and British trials championship.

SMITH, Jeff Vincent
Regarded by many authorities as Britain's best-ever moto cross star, Jeff Smith received the MBE in the New Year honours lists of 1970, the first motor-cycle sportsman outside road-

racing to be so honoured. It was a fitting tribute to almost twenty years of dedication to trials and scrambling. At sixteen years of age Smith had already won a gold medal in the 1951 International Six Days Trial on a Norton and thirteen years later he took his first 500cc world moto cross title after a gruelling five months battle through fourteen Grands Prix and against the tough opposition of the then reigning world champion Rolf Tibblin. It was an outstanding fight for the younger Tibblin started with four successive Grands Prix wins. Smith, at 31, was competing on a BSA considered to be not fully raceworthy. Jeff Smith's doggedness was part of his immense strength in the sport for at the time of his world victory riders from the Continent had dominated the championship for eight years and Smith had been after the title for a decade. He won his second World Championship the next year, but lost it in 1966, following injury and back trouble, also forfeiting the British title after eight successive years. But in 1967 he took the British 500cc championship for the ninth time at the age of 33.

Jeff Smith was born in Colne, Lancashire, but lived for much of his career life in Streetley, near Birmingham. A qualified engineer, he turned to scrambling at 20 and spent almost the whole of his career as a member of the BSA team. By 1965 he had won eight A-CU Scrambles Stars, was five times the leader of a winning British team in the Moto Cross des Nations and three times winner of the British Experts Trial. Seldom spectacular he was one of the best "thinkers" in the business. An outstanding tactician and a dogged fighter, Jeff moved in the early 1970s and at the end of his long and distinguished career to Canada to take up the post of senior development engineer with the Bombardier company of Valcourt, Quebec Province.

SNETTERTON

The Snetterton race circuit is situated in Norfolk, 10 miles north-east of Thetford on the A11, and is one of a number of former airfield circuits established in Britain. The first races were held there in 1952 with a view to turning it into a race track. The first motor-cycle meeting took place in 1953 and the first International meeting in 1954, following which the Snetterton Motor Racing Club was formed. It became the venue for international, national and club racing. The length of the longer circuit is 2.71 miles extending from the start line to the right-hander at Riches, to Sear and on through the Norwich Straight to the hairpin, back to the Esses, Coram Curve and Russell, returning to the start line. A shorter 1.9 mile circuit was opened there in March 1974 using much of the old course but cutting directly across from Sear to the Esses. The first race to take place on the new circuit was the British Motor Cycle Racing Club's opening meeting of their 13-event 1974 season, on 2nd March 1974. In October 1974 some alteration was made at the Esses of the 1.9 mile circuit when the fast sweeping left-hander was considerably tightened and followed by a tight right-hander. The alterations made the circuit a little longer and slower, but safer, giving better run-off areas in the event of a crash. It was intended that the new circuit be used for most of Snetterton's racing, though the important Race of Aces annual event would remain on the longer circuit. On 25th August 1974, Snetterton became the third mainland circuit to be lapped at over 100 mph, the others being Silverstone and Brooklands, at a meeting during which every motor cycle lap record for the course except the 125cc was broken. Barry Ditchburn on a Yamaha TZ750 was the first rider to lap at over 100 mph (100.16 mph) and later, at the same meeting, Mick Grant riding a three-cylinder Kawasaki raised this to 101.20 mph.

Address: Snetterton Circuit Ltd., Snetterton, Norwich, NOR 10X.

SPA

The famous Spa circuit situated near Francorchamps in Belgium is 4.3 miles long and is extremely fast with many of the bends capable of being taken at speeds in excess of 120 mph. Other than the two hairpins at La Source, just before the start-finish, and Stavelot at the extreme end of the circuit, the course presents more a test of courage than intricate skill though there are one or two tricky corners. It is the rider with the fastest machine who often wins. The start is downhill and the road, which extends through forest, climbs nearly 500 feet in two miles on the back stretches. The roads are broad and the circuit has wide, sweeping corners, the outstanding Burmenville being taken nowadays (1981) at more than 140 mph. The setting is very picturesque, though there are not too many viewing places for spectators. (See also BELGIAN GRAND PRIX.)

SPANISH GRAND PRIX

The Spanish Grand Prix takes place at the Montjuich circuit in Barcelona one year and the new Jarama circuit, of recent construction, in Madrid the next. The Jarama circuit, created mainly for car racing, was first used for a motorcycle Grand Prix in 1969. It is a winding circuit with a very good surface. The Montjuich venue (see separate entry) is a natural road circuit set in the magnificent Montjuich park. At Montjuich in 1974 Grand Prix riders threatened to walk out unless first aid and emergency services were improved. A two-hour meeting between riders and organisers following an incident in the opening 250cc race was necessary before the remainder of the programme could be held. Racing was halted for more than two hours.

Results:

1950: 125cc N. Pagani (Mondial); 350cc T. L. Wood (Velocette); 500cc N. Pagani (Gilera); sidecars A. Milani (Gilera).

1951: 125cc G. Leoni (Mondial); 350cc T. L. Wood (Velocette); 500cc U. Masetti (Gilera); sidecar E. S. Oliver (Norton).

1952: 125cc E. Mendogni (Morini); 500cc R. L. Graham (MV); sidecar E. S. Oliver (Norton).

1953: 125cc A. A. Coppeta (MV); 250cc E. Lorenzetti (Guzzi); 500cc F. K. Anderson (345 Guzzi).

1954: 125cc T. Provini (Mondial); 350cc F. K. Anderson (Guzzi); 500cc R. H. Dale (MV).

1955: 125cc L. Taveri (MV); 500cc H. R. Armstrong (Gilera); sidecar W. Faust (BMW).

1956: not run.

1957: 125cc C. Ubbiali (MV); 500cc J. Surtees (MV); sidecar O. Scmidt (BMW).

1958: 125cc C. Ubbiali (MV); 250cc C. Ubbiali (MV); 500cc J. Surtees (MV).

1959: 125cc R. Fargus (Ducati); 500cc P. Ferbrache (Matchless); sidecar F. Scheidegger (BMW).

1960 125cc L. Taveri (Honda); 500cc J. A. Redman (Norton); sidecar F. Camathias (BMW).

1961: 125cc T. E. Phillis (Honda); 250cc G. Hocking (MV); sidecar H. Fath (BMW).

1962: 50cc H. G. Anscheidt (Kreidler); 125cc K. Takahashi (Honda); 250cc J. A. Redman (Honda); sidecar M. Deubel (BMW).

1963: 50cc H. G. Anscheidt (Kreidler); 125cc L. Taveri (Honda); 250cc T. Provini (Morini); sidecar M. Deubel (BMW).

1964: 50cc H. G. Anscheidt (Kreidler); 125cc L. Taveri (Honda); 250cc T. Provini (Benelli); sidecar F. Camathias (Gilera).

1965: 50cc H. R. Anderson (Suzuki); 125cc H. R. Anderson (Suzuki); 250cc P. W. Read (Yamaha); sidecar M. Deubel (BMW).

1966: 50cc L. Taveri (Honda); 125cc W. D. Ivy (Yamaha); 250cc S. M. B. Hailwood (Honda); 350cc S. M. B. Hailwood (Honda).

1967: 50cc H. G. Anscheidt (Suzuki); 125cc W. D. Ivy (Yamaha); 250cc P. W. Read (Yamaha); sidecars G. Auerbacher - E. Dein (BMW).

1968: 50cc H. G. Anscheidt (Suzuki); 125cc S. Canellas (Bultaco); 250cc P. W. Read (Yamaha); 500cc G. Agostini (MV).

1969: 50cc A. Toersen (Kreidler); 125cc C. Van Dongen (Suzuki); 250cc S. Herrero (Ossa); 350cc G. Agostini (MV); 500cc G. Agostini (MV).

1970: 50cc G. Canellas (Derbi); 125cc A. Nieto (Derbi); 250cc K. Andersson (Yamaha); 350cc A. Bergamonti (MV); 500cc A. Bergamonti (MV).

1971: 50cc J. de Vries (Kreidler); 125cc A. Nieto (Derbi); 250cc J. Saarinen (Yamaha); 350cc T. Lansivuori (Yamaha); 500cc D. Simmonds (Kawasaki).

1972: 50cc A. Nieto (Derbi); 125cc K. Andersson (Yamaha); 250cc R. Pasolini (Aermacchi); 350cc B. Kneubuhler (Yamaha); 500cc C. Mortimer (Yamaha).

1973: 50cc J. de Vries (Kreidler); 125cc C. Mortimer (Yamaha); 250cc J. Dodds (Yamaha); 350cc A. Celso Santos (Yamaha); 500cc P. W. Read (MV).

1974: 50cc H. van Kessel (Van Veen

Kreidler); 125cc B. Grau (Derbi); 250cc J. Dodds (Yamaha); 350cc V. Palomo (Yamaha).

1975: 50cc A. Nieto (Kreidler); 125cc P. Pileri (Morbidelli); 250cc W. Villa (Harley-Davidson); 350cc G. Agostini (Yamaha).

1976: 50cc A. Nieto (Bultaco); 125cc P. Bianchi (Morbidelli); 250cc G. Bonera (Harley-Davidson); 350cc K. Ballington (Yamaha).

1977: 50cc A. Nieto (Bultaco); 125cc P. Bianchi (Morbidelli); 250cc T. Katayama (Yamaha); 350cc M. Rougerie (Yamaha).

1978: 50cc E. Lazzarini (Kreidler); 125cc E. Lazzarini (MBA); 250cc G. Hansford (Kawasaki); 500cc P. Hennen (Suzuki).

1979: 50cc E. Lazzarini (Kreidler); 125cc A. Nieto (Minarelli); 250cc K. Ballington (Kawasaki); 350cc K. Ballington (Kawasaki); 500cc K. Roberts (Yamaha).

1980: 50cc E. Lazzarini (Kreidler); 125cc P. Bianchi (MBA); 250cc K. Ballington (Kawasaki); 500cc K. Roberts (Yamaha).

1981: 50cc R. Tormo (Bultaco); 125cc A. Nieto (Minarelli); 250cc A. Mang (Kawasaki); sidecar R. Biland/K. Waltisperg (Yamaha).

SPEEDWAY

Generally accepted to have had its origins in the United States as early as 1902, Speedway has experienced its ups and downs and has graduated from rather haphazard, fairground type beginnings, to a sophisticated, professional sport which captures a vast audience. In Britain it became popular originally as dirt track racing and was well established before the Second World War. Television pushed it into the doldrums for almost a decade, but it re-emerged stronger and more popular than ever in the late 1960s with weekly attendances in Britain reaching some 350,000 at 40 tracks.

Speedway witnessed its beginnings when motor cyclists in the United States took over the horse-trotting tracks, but the closed-circuit race at the New South Wales Agricultural Show in Australia is generally put forward as the identifiable beginnings of the new sport. In Australia dirt-track racing became very popular. It was first seen in Britain in 1927, when the Camberley Club organised an event on the Military Ground in Camberley Heath. It was reported as the first dirt track meeting in England. Held over a quarter mile sandy circuit, the course incorporated two straights and two corners.

Later that year the South Manchester Motor Club held a meeting at Droylsden, said to be the first held in the North of England. There was a large attendance in spite of poor weather. London's first dirt track meeting is generally recognised as the event organised by the Ilford Club at the Kings Oak High Beech on Sunday, 19th February 1928. The track, based on a square with rounded corners, was cinder surfaced, hard and firm. One side of the track formed an almost continous curve. Some 20,000 spectators accommodated on both the inside and outside of the track, saw the spectacle.

So far, British dirt track racing differed from the sport in the United States and Australia in that the cinder surfaces were hard and did not permit the wholesale broadsiding, or power sliding, which characterised the sport abroad. This situation changed on 7th April 1928, with the opening at High Beech, Essex, of the first licenced Speedway in Britain. Since the Ilford Club meeting of two months before, the surface had been remade, retaining fences had been constructed to separate the competitors from the spectators, and there were now pits and seating accommodation. The event was an enormous success. Speedway was on its way. For the first time in Britain was seen the type of broadsiding which now so characterises the sport. About 3,000 people were expected. Over ten times that number came to see the Australian ace Billy Galloway give a spectacular demonstration. Within months regular meetings were being held in various parts of the country and soon some fifty tracks were operating. On 5th May 1928, at Stamford Bridge, the first evening meeting under floodlighting was held.

The first speedway leagues were formed in 1929 – twelve clubs in the southern league and thirteen in the northern league, but the ups and downs which were to become part of the history of speedway in Britain, were soon apparent. After such a dramatic debut, the number of clubs had dwindled to seven within five seasons, and all the original northern clubs had disbanded. An almost parallel situation developed during the

1950s. In 1951, in the remarkable postwar boom in the sport, there were almost 40 tracks being used frequently. The competition was in three divisions as follows: *Division 1:* Belle Vue, Birmingham, Bradford, Bristol, Harringay, New Cross, Wembley, West Ham and Wimbledon. *Division 2:* Coventry, Cradley Heath, Edinburgh, Fleetwood, Glasgow (Ashfield), Glasgow (White City), Great Yarmouth, Halifax, Leicester, Liverpool, Motherwell, Newcastle, Norwich, Oxford, Sheffield, Southampton and Walthamstow. *Division 3:* Aldershot, Cardiff, Exeter, Ipswich (non-league track), Long Eaton, Plymouth, Poole, Rayleigh, St Austell, Swindon and Wolverhampton. Yet within just six years the three thriving leagues had been reduced to one, consisting of only eleven clubs: Belle Vue, Bradford, Coventry, Ipswich, Leicester, Norwich, Oxford, Rayleigh, Southampton, Swindon and Wimbledon. Discounting newly formed clubs in the British League, only Belle Vue, Oxford, Swindon and Wimbledon have operated continuously since their formation.

Improved administration and variations in the rules and conditions governing the sport have brought much more stability to speedway over the years. No longer is it possible for one team to dominate and monopolise as did Belle Vue in the 'thirties, Wembley in the 'forties and Wimbledon in the 'fifties. While the strong continued to grow more strong, the weaker clubs were driven out. In contrast, in the first three years of British League racing, there were three different champions: West Ham, Halifax and Swindon. The financial arrangement of speedway nowadays gives a cut in the overall prosperity of the sport to the weaker teams as well as to the strong. The growth of speedway at an international level has also given it more security, and the interest taken by the Eastern European countries since 1957 has provided a further tonic. Also retarding the development of speedway as a competitive event has been the domination for almost thirty years of the extraordinarily successful JAP machine. This was out-of-line with motor-cycle sport generally, which had gained its strength as much for its demonstration as a contest between different makes of machine as between men. The challenge to JAP by Jawa with the Eso machines, built in Prague, Czechoslovakia, added further to speedway's interest. The first major setback to the JAP machine in the world championships came in 1966 when Barry Briggs won the title in Sweden riding an Eso.

The early 1930s are recognised as speedway's barnstorming days – the first era in Britain of flying cinder and trailing broadsides. Riders from Australia and America first drew the crowds, but soon British and European riders began to make an impact. The first world championship was held under the auspices of the FIM at Wembley in September 1936 with riders from Australia, Sweden, New Zealand, Germany, Canada, France, America, Denmark, Britain, Spain and South Africa taking part. After tieing on points, Australian Lionel Van Praag won the run-off against Britain's Eric Langton. The 1937 World Championship was won by Jack Milne of the United States and Bluey Wilkinson regained the honours for Australia in 1938. These early events were world championships for individual riders and although classified as having world status, it was not until 1949, when the world championships were restarted after the war, that they became official. Immediately Britain's prowess was shown, Tommy Price bringing England her first international honours. There is a further world championship in speedway, for teams representing countries. These team championships began in 1960 and up to 1970 there were six Swedish victories, four Polish and one British.

Speedway is now the second largest spectator sport in Britain. The British League has two divisions and teams gain two points for a match win and one for a draw. Matches comprise thirteen races of four laps each, with two riders from each team competing for the points: 3 for first, 2 for second and 1 for third. Races take place promptly one after the other building up with points for each team to give a match result. Races are run anticlockwise over a half mile to a lap course, and for a distance of two to three miles. Enthusiasts are able to see their favourite riders at close quarters and on a regular basis and it is not surprising in such circumstances that a "fan-following" has developed for the most flourishing performers. The box-office element has been encouraged, as in road racing for instance, by coloured racing leathers and identifying coloured helmets. The season in Britain begins in March or April and closes at the end of October. The Speedway Control Board is affiliated to the Auto-Cycle Union and operates from 31 Belgrave Square, London SW1X 8QJ.

Speedway tracks in Britain were established at: Belle Vue (Manchester), Coatbridge, Coventry, Cradley Heath, Exeter, Hackney, Halifax, Ipswich, King's Lynn, Leicester, Newport, Oxford, Poole, Sheffield, Swindon, Wimbledon, Wolverhampton, and Barrow, Berwick, Birmingham, Boston, Bradford, Canterbury, Crewe, Eastbourne, Ellesmere Port, Hull, Long Eaton, Peterborough, Scunthorpe, Sunderland, Teesside (Middlesbrough), Workington, Stoke, Weymouth and Rye House (Hoddesdon, Herts).

Riders

One of the great immediate postwar speedway characters in Britain was Split Waterman, who turned to speedway in 1947 after sand racing. His cavalier personality obscured a fine skill on the track which brought him many honours, but never a world title. He came closest in 1951 when Australia's Jack Young beat him. Peter Craven is also recognised as one of the greatest riders of all time. He took the title for Britain in 1962. The following year he was killed while racing in Edinburgh. In later years the sport was dominated for almost a decade by star riders Ove Fundin of Sweden, and New Zealand's Barry Briggs. Briggs won his first world championship in 1957, repeating his success in 1958. Always close to ultimate honours, he secured the world championship again in 1964-66. Briggs began riding in 1951 and moved to Britain in 1952. At first he was clumsily unsuccessful. He rode initially for Wimbledon, then New Cross. His sensationally successful career was already well advanced when he joined the Swindon team in 1963. He is perhaps the outstanding example of a speedway rider making a major impact on the world outside the sport. His widespread fame has brought him recognition in national popularity polls and he was honoured with the MBE in 1973.

A keen rival to Briggs was the Swede, Ove Fundin. In 1967 Fundin won the World Championship title for the fifth time, he alone at that point having won more world titles than Briggs. Fundin (born 1933 at Tranas, Sweden), was also second from 1957 to 1959 and third in 1962, 1964 and 1965, an outstanding record.

In more recent years Ivan Mauger (pronounced Major) (born Christchurch, New Zealand 1939) has been one of the brightest stars. He is the only rider to secure three successive world championships – 1968-70 – and he won the title again in 1972 and was second in 1973. Mauger began his British speedway career in 1957 at Wimbledon. He was with Newcastle from 1963 to 1968, when he joined Belle Vue. He moved to Exeter in 1973 and helped to bring them the British League Championship the following year. Birmingham were champions of Division 2.

Ole Olsen became Denmark's first world motor sport champion when he became World Speedway Champion in 1971. Olsen (born 1946 at Haderslav, Denmark) first appeared in Britain in 1966 and in 1971 was also winner of the Nordic Championship.

Jerzy Szczakiel's achievement in 1973 in becoming World Champion marked the first occasion in the history of speedway that the championship had gone behind the Iron Curtain. More than 100,000 spectators watched the 24-year old Pole snatch the title from holder Ivan Mauger in a run-off for first place.

In Britain the early Southern and Northern Leagues existed for three years, the National League replacing them in 1932. The most successful team in the National League was the Wembley Lions, who won the title eight times: 1932, 1946-47, 1949-53. The National League was discontinued in 1965 when the British League was formed. Belle Vue won this league three times in succession (1970-72). A National Trophy Knock Out Competition was introduced in 1931. Belle Vue have been most successful in this competition with ten victories (to 1973): 1933-34-35-36-37, 1946-47, 1949, 1958, 1973.

British speedway had an excellent year in 1974. At the Slaski Stadium in Katawise, Poland, the English squad won the World Cup Final with the best score they had made in the competition, beating Sweden, Poland and Russia. England, unbeaten in international meetings throughout 1974, won ten races and were second in the remaining six to reach 42 points, two more than their previous best in this competition, at Wembley in 1962. England's team was Collins, Louis, Jessop and Simmons. Heading a new generation of British speedway stars, 20-year-old Peter Collins became the European Speedway Champion in 1974. Collins, from Cheshire, and Belle Vue moved into speedway via grass track racing. He is the first home competitor to win a major individual championship since Peter Craven, also of Belle Vue, took the World title in 1962.

Machines

For almost forty years speedway has been dominated by two makes of machines – JAP, who monopolised the sport for close on thirty years, and Jawa, with their Iso machines. The machines are similar in design and power having only one gear. Engines are limited to 500cc and are fuelled with methanol. Lean and greyhound-looking, speedway bikes have no brakes, control coming from the use of clutch lever and throttle. The 'no brakes' rule was started as a safety measure to prevent a leading rider braking fiercely and running the risk of precipitating a pile-up of oncoming riders. Speedway bike frames have no suspension.

SPEEDWAY – INDIVIDUAL WORLD CHAMPIONSHIP

1936: Lionel Van Praag
1937: Jack Milne
1938: Bluey Wilkinson
1949: Tommy Price
1950: Fred Williams
1951: Jack Young
1952: Jack Young
1953: Fred Williams
1954: Ronnie Moore
1955: Peter Craven
1956: Ove Fundin
1957: Barry Briggs
1958: Barry Briggs
1959: Ronnie Moore
1960: Ove Fundin
1961: Ove Fundin
1962: Peter Craven
1963: Ove Fundin
1964: Barry Briggs
1965: Bjorn Knutsson
1966: Barry Briggs
1967: Ove Fundin
1968: Ivan Mauger
1969: Ivan Mauger
1970: Ivan Mauger
1971: Ole Olsen
1972: Ivan Mauger
1973: Jerzy Szczakiel
1974: Anders Michanek
1975: Ole Olsen
1976: Peter Collins
1977: Ivan Mauger
1978: Ole Olsen
1979: Ivan Mauger
1980: Michael Lee
1981: Bruce Penhall

SPEEDWAY – TEAM WORLD CHAMPIONSHIP

1960: Sweden
1961: Poland
1962: Sweden
1963: Sweden
1964: Sweden
1965: Poland
1966: Poland
1967: Sweden
1968: Great Britain
1969: Poland
1970: Sweden
1971: Great Britain
1972: Great Britain
1973: Great Britain
1974: England
1975: England
1976: Australia
1977: England
1978: Denmark
1979: New Zealand
1980: Great Britain
1981: West Germany

SPENCER, Freddie

This sensational American road racer made his debut on British circuits in 1980 and although still a teenager rode so fast and with such flourish that he was immediately labelled a potential champion. He caught the imagination of British fans with some scintillating riding in the Easter Transatlantic Race Series, but he was not able to compete seriously in the world championships during 1980. He is a rider of immense promise.

SPONSORS

Motor cycle racing benefits enormously from the support it receives from individual private sponsors, generally men with businesses in the trade or with a true love of the sport, who provide financial backing and/or machines for promising or established riders. These sponsors are the backbone of the sport in Britain providing racing with an additional "depth" in good times, and being its virtual saviours when factories and trade companies withdraw support from racing through financial or other considerations. Over the years Britain has benefited from the support of numerous sponsors. They are too many to give a comprehensive list but among perhaps the most prominent have been Tom Arter, Sid Lawton, Reg Dearden, Tom Kirby, the Dugdales, Padgets, Geoff Monty and Paul Dunstall.

SPRINTING

One of the earliest forms of motor-cycle racing, sprinting (or record breaking) was popular in the early 1900s but lost ground between the wars, only to revive more strongly than ever after the war when disused wartime airfields became ideal venues for the sport. The idea is to cover a short established distance as quickly as possible and acceleration is therefore fundamental to the sport. Various sprint distances are established – a popular distance for instance being 440 yards – and for record attempts two runs are made, one in each direction, within a time limit of 30 minutes. There are rigid controls maintained on the extent and nature of the improvement work that can be done on a machine during that time. Entries are governed by engine capacity and speeds are high, well over 100 mph at 440 yards and as much as 170-180 mph over one kilometre.

Sprinting in the United Kingdom is carried out under the rules and regulations of the A-CU. The National Sprint Association (23 Berwick Road, Walthamstow, London E17) was founded in 1958, following which sprinting made outstanding progress. Sprinting, though still perhaps a Cinderella of motor-cycle sport, is gaining rapidly in popularity and in addition to the speeds, and high-powered acceleration, much of the attraction and excitement rests in the specialised machines, often of unique and extraordinary design, which help to give sprinting its "larger-than-life" atmosphere.

Speeds over the years have increased in spectacular fashion, as the record books show.

Legendary post-war characters in the world of sprinting include such famous names as George Brown, Fred Cooper and Alf Hagon. More contemporary names include Dennis Norman, Des Heckle, Angus McPhail, who pilots a cyclecar 3-wheeler, and Paul Windross. Such is the enthusiasm and ingenuity of dedicated sprint men that new records appear to be established almost every other weekend. At Drachten, northern Holland, in August 1980, the Dutch superstar Henk Vink became the first man outside America to crack the eight-second barrier for the quarter mile on his Kawasaki-powered machine.

SPRINTING - BRITISH NATIONAL RECORDS

Quarter Mile - Standing Start

Class	Driver	Machine	sec	mph
Category A1 (Solo Motorcycles)				
50cc	R. J. Sullivan	Meurs-Kreidler	16.25	55.38
75cc	R. Sullivan	Beeline Sondel Yamaha	17.16	52.44
100cc	W. Cowling	Beeline Yamaha	15.385	58.49
125cc	D. Heckle	Rotax	12.655	71.11
175cc	P. Irons	Montaco	12.905	69.74
250cc	M. Hand	Honda	10.50	85.71
350cc	M. Hand	Honda	10.255	87.76
500cc	D. Houghton	Triumph	09.59	93.84
750cc	K. Parnell	Triumph	09.505	94.68
1,000cc	M. Butler	Norton	09.60	93.75
1,300cc	D. Lecoq	Dragwaye	09.69	92.87
2,000cc	J. Hobbs	Westlake	09.165	98.19
Category A2 (Solo Scooters)				
250cc	F. Willingham	Lambretta	14.505	62.04
Category B1 and B2 (Sidecars)				
250cc	A. Reynard	Reynard	14.61	61.60
350cc	N. Hyde	Triumph	13.643	65.9678
500cc	N. Hyde	Triumph	12.645	71.17
750cc	P. Harman	Triumph	11.69	76.98
1,000cc	N. Hyde	Triumph	11.51	78.19
1,300cc	A. Brown	Vincent	11.746	76.6218
Category B3 (Cyclecars)				
250cc	C. Wilson	Trikat Yamaha	14.855	60.58

Class	Driver	Machine	sec	mph
350cc	M. Ellis	Armstrong Suzuki	12.96	69.44
500cc	S. Whitton	Triovad	12.58	71.54
750cc	D. Green	Macon-Triumph	12.66	71.09
1,000cc	T. Kimber-Smith	Triumph	12.705	70.83
1,300cc	A. MacPhail	McCoy-Ford	10.515	85.59
2,000cc	J. Morrison	Fiat	13.765	65.38
3,500cc	T. Kimber-Smith	Moneybox	12.94	69.55

Quarter Mile – Flying Start

Category A1 (Solo Motorcycles)

Class	Driver	Machine	sec	mph
50cc	R. Sullivan	Meurs Kreidler	09.795	91.88
75cc	R. Sullivan	Beeline Sondel Yamaha	10.44	86.20
100cc	W. Cowling	Beeline Yamaha	08.545	105.32
125cc	R. Sullivan	Meurs Yamaha	07.11	126.58
175cc	P. Irons	Montaco	07.575	118.81
250cc	M. Hand	Honda	06.405	140.51
350cc	J. Balchin	BSA	06.225	144.57
500cc	R. Daniel	Triumph	05.525	162.89
750cc	T. Sidebottom	Morgo Triumph	05.41	166.35
1,000cc	R. Daniel	RDS Triumph	04.69	191.89
1,300cc	F. Cooper	Cooper-Triumph	04.74	189.87
2,000cc	P. Windross	Triumph Bi-Motor	04.795	187.69

Category A2 (Solo Scooters)

Class	Driver	Machine	sec	mph
250cc	F. Willingham	Willingham-Lambretta	09.355	96.20

Category B1 and B2 (Sidecars)

Class	Driver	Machine	sec	mph
250cc	A. Reynard	Royal Enfield	08.2355	109.28
350cc	N. Hyde	Triumph	07.470	120.4819
500cc	D. Harmsworth	Triumph	06.735	133.63
750cc	J. McKiernan	Triumph	06.919	130.0766
1,000cc	A. Brown	Vincent	06.135	146.6992
1,300cc	G. Brown	Vincent	05.8885	152.8402

Category B3 (Cyclecars)

Class	Driver	Machine	sec	mph
250cc	C. Wilson	Trikat	07.555	119.12
350cc	A. Garwood	Yamaha	07.865	114.43
500cc	S. Whitton	Triovad	07.225	124.56
750cc	D. Green	Macon-Triumph	07.3205	122.94
1,000cc	R. Vane	Vincent	06.945	129.58
1,300cc	A. MacPhail	McCoy-Ford	06.975	129.03
2,000cc	J. Morrison	Fiat	07.32	112.95
3,500cc	T. Kimber-Smith	Moneybox	06.51	138.24

One Kilometre – Standing Start

Category A1 (Solo Motorcycles)

Class	Driver	Machine	sec	mph
50cc	R. J. Sullivan	Meurs-Kreidler	33.89	66.00
75cc	R. Sullivan	Beeline Sondel Yamaha	33.415	66.94
100cc	W. Cowling	Beeline Yamaha	29.375	76.14
125cc	D. Heckle	Padgett Yamaha	25.06	89.25
175cc	P. Irons	Montaco	25.27	88.52
250cc	M. Hand	Honda	21.71	103.03
350cc	J. Balchin	BSA	20.125	109.62
500cc	D. Houghton	Triumph	18.19	122.97
750cc	C. Richards	CRS Triumph	18.415	121.47
1,000cc	J. Hobbs	Triumph	18.22	122.77
1,300cc	D. Lecoq	Dragwaye	18.80	118.98
2,000cc	B. Jones	Dragwaye	22.37	99.99

Class	Driver	Machine	sec	mph
Category A2 (Solo Scooters)				
250cc	F. Willingham	Lambretta	28.555	78.33
Category B1 and B2 (Sidecars)				
250cc	A. Reynard	Reynard	28.295	79.05
350cc	N. Hyde	Triumph	26.373	84.8191
500cc	D. Harmsworth	Triumph	22.275	100.42
750cc	N. Hyde	Triumph	21.87	102.27
1,000cc	N. Hyde	Triumph	21.285	105.09
1,300cc	G. Brown	Vincent	21.6225	103.4395
Category B3 (Cyclecars)				
250cc	C. Wilson	Trikat Yamaha	26.365	84.84
350cc	Miss I. Scargill	AJS	29.725	75.25
500cc	A. MacPhail	Macon-Triumph	24.5735	91.0303
750cc	D. Green	Macon-Triumph	24.61	90.89
1,000cc	T. Kimber-Smith	Triumph	25.605	87.36
1,300cc	R. Ward	Mogimp	26.475	84.49
2,000cc	J. Morrison	Fiat	27.26	82.05
3,500cc	T. Kimber-Smith	Moneybox	23.76	94.17

One Kilometre – Flying Start

Class	Driver	Machine	sec	mph
Category A1 (Solo Motorcycles)				
50cc	R. Sullivan	Meurs Kreidler	24.395	91.69
75cc	R. Sullivan	Beeline Sondel Yamaha	25.77	86.80
100cc	W. Cowling	Beeline-Yamaha	21.23	105.36
125cc	R. Sullivan	Yamaha	17.87	125.17
175cc	P. Irons	Montaco	18.875	118.51
250cc	R. Thorpe	Padgett-Yamaha	17.155	130.3955
350cc	J. Balchin	BSA	15.135	147.79
500cc	R. Daniel	Triumph	13.785	162.27
750cc	N. Hyde	Triumph	13.515	165.51
1,000cc	R. Daniel	RDS Triumph	11.87	188.45
1,300cc	F. Cooper	Cyclotron	11.94	187.34
2,000cc	B. Jones	Dragwaye	20.775	107.67
3,500cc	T. Kimber-Smith	Moneybox	16.19	138.16
Category A2 (Solo Scooters)				
250cc	F. Willingham	Willingham	22.30	100.30
Category B1 and B2 (Sidecars)				
250cc	A. Reynard	Reynard	20.335	110.00
350cc	E. J. Hurley	Manx Dragster	20.1155	111.210
500cc	D. Harmsworth	Triumph	16.685	134.06
750cc	N. Hyde	Triumph	14.83	150.83
1,000cc	N. Hyde	Triumph	13.825	161.80
1,300cc	G. Brown	Vincent	14.9395	149.7327
Category B3 (Cyclecars)				
250cc	C. Wilson	Trikat Yamaha	18.94	118.10
350cc	A. Garwood	Yamaha	18.69	119.68
500cc	S. Whitton	Triovad	17.895	125.00
750cc	D. Green	Macon-Triumph	17.885	125.07
1,000cc	R. Vane	Vincent	17.695	126.41
1,300cc	O. Greenwood	Mini-Special	18.0905	123.6524
2,000cc	J. Morrison	Fiat	17.635	126.84
3,500cc	T. Kimber-Smith	Moneybox	16.19	138.16

Class	Driver	Machine	sec	mph
One mile – Standing Start				
Category A1 (Solo Motorcycles)				
50cc	R. J. Sullivan	Meurs-Kreidler	48.23	74.64
75cc	R. Sullivan	Beeline Sondel Yamaha	49.305	73.01
100cc	W. Cowling	Beeline Yamaha	43.23	83.27
125cc	D. Heckle	Padgett Yamaha	36.54	98.52
175cc	P. Irons	Montaco	37.00	97.29
250cc	M. Bull	Yamaha	32.66	110.22
350cc	T. Duckworth	Brighouse Yamaha	31.135	115.62
500cc	D. Houghton	Triumph	27.21	132.30
750cc	P. Windross	Triumph	28.165	127.81
1,000cc	J. Hobbs	Triumph	26.395	136.398
1,300cc	G. Brown	Vincent	27.9795	128.6656
Category A2 (Solo Scooters)				
250cc	A. Willingham	Lambretta	44.195	81.45
Category B1 and B2 (Sidecars)				
250cc	A. Reynard	Reynard	42.13	85.44
350cc	A. Garwood	Bailey Yamaha	38.31	93.97
500cc	N. Hyde	Triumph	34.64	103.9260
750cc	N. Hyde	Triumph	32.015	112.44
1,000cc	G. Brown	Vincent	30.3465	119.0869
1,300cc	G. Brown	Vincent	31.057	115.9158
Category B3 (Cyclecars)				
250cc	Miss I. Scargill	Starmaker	41.375	87.009
350cc	A. Garwood	Yamaha	37.235	96.68
500cc	A. MacPhail	Macon-Triumph	36.31	99.1462
750cc	D. Green	Macon-Triumph	36.235	99.10
1,000cc	R. Vane	Vincent	36.68	98.14
1,300cc	O. Greenwood	Mini Special	37.4235	96.1962
2,000cc	J. Morrison	Fiat	36.59	98.38
3,500cc	T. Kimber-Smith	Moneybox	34.00	105.88
One Mile – Flying Start				
Category A1 (Solo Motorcycles)				
50cc	R. J. Sullivan	Meurs-Kreidler	39.40	91.37
75cc	To be established			
100cc	K. White	Beeline Yamaha	41.74	86.24
125cc	D. Heckle	Padgett Yamaha	29.725	121.11
175cc	P. Irons	Montaco	30.545	117.858
250cc	S. Woods	Yamaha	28.745	125.2391
350cc	B. Moore	Yamaha	27.915	128.96
500cc	J. Hobbs	Triumph	23.145	155.54
750cc	P. Windross	Triumph	21.69	169.97
1,000cc	P. Tait	Triumph	23.530	152.99
1,300cc	F. Cooper	Cooper-Triumph	19.66	183.11
Category A2 (Solo Scooters)				
250cc	F. Osgerby	Lambretta	38.685	93.05
Category B1 and B2 (Sidecar)				
250cc	A. Reynard	Royal Enfield	32.3925	111.13
350cc	A. Garwood	Bailey Yamaha	30.715	117.20
500cc	To be established			
750cc	N. Hyde	Triumph	24.445	147.26
1,000cc	N. Hyde	Triumph	25.41	141.67
1,300cc	G. Brown	Vincent	28.0735	128.234

Class	Driver	Machine	sec	mph
Category B3 (Cyclecars)				
250cc	Miss I. Scargill	Starmaker	33.315	108.059
350cc	A. Garwood	Yamaha	30.815	116.82
500cc	C. Wilson	Yamaha	40.35	89.21
750cc	D. Green	Macon-Triumph	29.921	120.31
1,000cc	R. Vane	Vincent	29.79	120.84
1,300cc	H. Beart	Morgan-Blackburne	35.44	101.58
2,000cc	J. Morrison	Fiat	29.29	122.90
3,500cc	T. Kimber-Smith	Moneybox	26.21	137.35

STARTING
A number of starts can be used. *Flying Start:* speed up to the starting line is not restricted. *Rolling Start:* speed up to the starting line is restricted. *Standing Start:* machines are stationary and engines are not started until the order to start is given. *Clutch Start:* machine is stationary until the order is given, but engines are running. *Individual Start:* riders start singly. *Mass Start:* riders start together. *Le Mans Start:* on the order riders run across the track to their machines, start up and move away. *Interval Start.*

STASTNY, Frantisek
Frank Stastny (born Prague 1927) was perhaps the most famous road racer to come from Czechoslovakia. He started racing as a pedal cyclist in 1943 and by 1946 was a member of the national team. In the 1950s he represented his country as a speed skater. He became interested in motor cycling in 1947 and made his racing debut on a Norton in 1948. After a spell in the army, Stastny joined the Jawa factory as a worker and a rider at the start of an association which lasted 17 years. After riding the double overhead camshaft twin 350 Jawas from 1956, he scored a number of important victories on the then new four-cylinder two stroke, including the Ulster Grand Prix of 1965. He never won a world championship but was second to Gary Hocking in the 350cc class of 1961. Stastny suffered severe racing accidents in 1963 and 1964 and in 1970 crashed with serious spinal injuries while racing in his home country.

SUNBEAM
This famous British machine had an outstanding record during the early days of motor cycle racing and was the last pushrod, two-valve single to win a Senior TT, in 1929. Sunbeam's first major success in the TTs came in 1920 with a victory in the Senior event by T. C. De La Hay, with G. Dance registering the fastest lap at 55.62 mph. In 1922 Sunbeam again won the Senior, ridden by Alec Bennett, who set the fastest lap at 59.99 mph. Sunbeam were next, and finally, successful in 1928 and 1929 with superbly engineered 493cc singles of conventional layout. Charlie Dodson was the rider in each case.

SUPERBIKE CHAMPIONSHIP
In the wake of the popularity of Formula 750 racing in the USA and its potentially increasing influence in the UK, the magazine *Motor Cycle News* introduced their Superbike Championship in 1971 when six major international meetings were held. The series was sponsored by Motor Circuit Developments at their tracks at Brands Hatch, Mallory Park, Oulton Park and Snetterton. 750cc Triumphs and BSAs dominated with Percy Tait and Ray Pickrell winning most of the races.

It is the policy of *Motor Cycle News* to attract sponsors for each of the Superbike rounds and it is now the richest championship on the home circuits. The series has done much to help raise the status of 750cc road racing in Britain.

Results:

1971: first Percy Tait (750 Triumph) 99 points; second Ray Pickrell (750 BSA) 93 points, third Charles Sanby (750 Kuhn Commando) 40 points.

1972: first John Cooper (750 Triumph) 112 points; second Ray Pickrell (750 Triumph) 84 points; third Peter Williams (750 John Player Norton) 57 points.

1973: first Barry Sheene (Suzuki) 85 points; second Peter Williams (John Player Norton) 85 points third Paul Smart (Suzuki) 59 points.

1974: first Barry Sheene (Suzuki) 135

21 BOB LEPPAN (*extreme left*) with his team and the remarkable Gyronaut X-1 projectile at Bonneville Salt Flats in 1966. Bob established a new AMA-endorsed World Speed Record of 245.6 mph.

22 Speedway World Champion in 1980 was MICHAEL LEE, the first British champion since Peter Craven's triumph in 1976.

23 RANDY MAMOLA, America's young road racing sensation, who took the World Championships by storm in 1980 and '81.

24 One of the most gifted riders of his day and generally accepted as perhaps the finest rider never to win a world title, Bob McIntyre had outstanding success on a variety of machines.

25 A trials rider of extraordinary talent, Sammy Miller is seen on his 250cc Bultaco in the Scott Trial of 1968, which he won. He was 250cc British Champion, effectively, for eleven years from 1959.

26 The Norton team of 1932: Jimmy Guthrie (31), Jimmy Simpson (15), Tim Hunt (25) and Stanley Woods (29). Woods achieved a TT double that year, with Guthrie and Simpson in second and third places in the Senior.

27 ERIC OLIVER on the 499cc Norton Sidecar combination and with passenger Lorenzo Dobelli racing at Silverstone in 1951. Oliver was World Sidecar Champion in 1949, '50, '51 and '53.

28 RENZO PASOLINI worked at the Aermacchi factory in Italy and in 1964 was a member of the works team. In 1966 he was third in the 350cc World Championship. After a spell with Benelli, Pasolini returned to Aermacchi in 1971 (when this picture was taken) and later rode Harley-Davidson.

29 August 1949 and Noel Pope is seen on his special purpose Brough Superior JAP. On this machine, fully streamlined, Pope attemped to take the world speed record that year but was unsuccessful, surviving a 150 mph crash.

30 Phil Read races the MV ahead of the field in the French Grand Prix of 1974. Read, one of the most enduring of champions, won his first world title in 1964, and was 500cc World Champion a decade later.

31 Spearhead of Honda's brilliant successes in the 1960s, Jim Redman is seen (55) with Provini (24) and Grassetti (10).

32 Yamaha ace Kenny Roberts racing at Daytona in 1975. He was World Champion in 1978, '79 and '80.

33 The phenomenal Joel Robert, brilliant moto-cross rider. He won his first world title in 1964 and added five more in as many years from 1968. Probably the most outstanding 250cc moto-cross racer of all time.

34 Finland's Jarno Saarinen with the impressive trophy after winning Mallory Park's 1972 Race of the Year.

35 Swiss sidecar racer Fritz Scheidegger, with passenger John Robinson, on their way to victory in the TT of 1966. Dramatically, Scheidegger was later disqualified for an alleged infringement of fuel regulations and was only reinstated winner after appeals made through the Swiss Federation.

36 The sensation of the 1970s – BARRY SHEENE, the cockney rider with the international following – obliges the autograph hunters.

37 JEFF SMITH, one of Britain's most succesful moto-cross riders of all time in the 500cc class. In 1967 he took the British 500cc championship for the ninth time, at the age of 33. He was World Champion in 1964 and 1965.

38 The British team which won the SPEEDWAY Team World Championship for the first time in 1968. The captain, Barry Briggs (*centre with trophy*) led a team which finished with forty points, ten points ahead of runners-up Sweden.

39 JOCK TAYLOR, sidecar World Champion 1980, with passenger Benga Johansson of Sweden, in action with the championship winning 498cc Fowler Yamaha sidecar outfit.

40 STANLEY WOODS, the most outstanding rider of his time. His record of ten TT wins was not bettered for 28 years, and after more than 30 years has been improved upon only by Hailwood and equalled only by Agostini.

points; second Stan Woods (Suzuki) 76 points; third Paul Smart (Suzuki) 54 points.

1975: first Mick Grant (Kawasaki) 92 points; second Barry Ditchburn (Kawasaki) 84 points; third Barry Sheene (Suzuki) 72 points.

1976: first Barry Sheene (Suzuki) 176 points; second Mick Grant (Kawasaki) 155 points; third Barry Ditchburn (Kawasaki) 96 points.

1977: first Barry Sheene (Suzuki) 118 points; second Mick Grant (Kawasaki) 97 points; third Pat Hennen (Suzuki) 95 points.

1978: first Barry Sheene (Suzuki) 136 points; second Dave Potter (Yamaha) 100 points and Mick Grant (Kawasaki) 100 points; fourth Barry Ditchburn (Yamaha) 76 points.

1979: first Dave Potter (Yamaha) 166 points; second Ron Haslam (Yamaha) 163 points; third Roger Marshall (Yamaha) 108 points.

1980: first Dave Potter (Yamaha) 202 points; second Roger Marshall (Yamaha) 136 points; third Keith Huewen (Yamaha) 124 points.

1981: first Ron Haslam (Honda) 144 points; second Kork Ballington (Kawasaki) 111 points; third Wayne Gardner (Kawasaki) 96 points.

SUPERCHARGER

A supercharger is a rotating pump used for increasing the quantity of mixture delivered to an engine. It is often referred to as a 'blower'. Before the Second World War superchargers were used in Grand Prix racing, but their ban after the war put a brake on the progress of the two-stroke power unit which did not make its revival, though when it came it was dramatic, until the 1960s. Superchargers are still used in sprinting.

SUPPLEMENTARY REGULATIONS

Supplementary Regulations support the GCRs of the Auto-Cycle Union and form the detailed specification for any particular competitive event.

SURTEES, Jack

Jack Surtees (born 1901) died from a heart attack in 1972. Father of famous motor-cycle racing champion John Surtees, Jack began sidecar racing in 1935 with a 500cc B14 Excelsior/Jap. He later changed to the 596 OHC Norton that gained him, with Frank Lilley, nine home championships up to 1947. He retired in 1952.

SURTEES, John

The exceptional success of John Surtees if confirmed by the record books for he is the only man (1974) to have become a world champion in both motor-cycle racing and car racing. He was one of the youngest of champions and by the time he was 25 had won five world titles and six TTs. In 1958-59 he established the astonishing record of winning all of the 25 World Championship events he contested. Though there were undoubtedly more popular champions (for he was disinclined to socialise and enjoyed limited appeal with the crowds) Surtees' dedication and supreme professionalism as a motor-cycle racer brought him widespread admiration and most of the honours the sport can provide. He was certainly one of the most devoted racers . . . and one of the most successful. The preparation of his own Nortons and the unfailing dedication when he was with MV was an outstanding example. He suffered during his spell with MV, as Agostini was later to suffer, because the Italian machine had no serious competitor once Gilera and Guzzi moved out of racing; many of Surtees' triumphs had therefore a somewhat hollow ring to them. For this reason his outstanding record of seven world titles has perhaps not received the full recognition his outstanding riding so obviously deserved. Somewhat ironically, it is his earlier spell as a works rider for Norton that he is perhaps most remembered by the racing enthusiast, though in terms of racing honours this period compares hardly at all with his time astride the MV.

John Surtees (born Surrey, 1934) received encouragement from his father, Jack, who had a motor-cycle business in Croydon and was also an accomplished grass-track sidecar racer. For a time John was passenger for his father, but his individual career began during his apprenticeship in engineering with Vincents when he rode the famous single-cylinder Vincent Grey Flash. It was on Vincent machinery that he enjoyed some early success at Brands Hatch in 1951, winning his first race there when only seventeen. He later bought a 500 Manx Norton and showed so much promise that in 1955 he joined the Norton works team. In 1954-55 he competed in the TTs on Nortons, his best performance being in the Junior of 1955 when he finished fourth. On the short circuit Surtees was by now supreme and he became the uncrowned 'king' at Brands Hatch and retained this distinction until he moved on to race cars and Derek Minter took over at the famous Kent circuit.

Surtees racing is always closely linked with that of John Hartle for they were together in the same team at Norton and, once the factory retired from racing, they often competed against each other on prototype production models. Later still they were together again in the MV team. Surtees joined MV in 1956 and achieved dramatic success. He immediately won the Senior TT of that year; and the 500cc World Championship! In the following four years he finished first in the TTs five times, was second twice and fourth once. He became double (350cc and 500cc) World Champion in 1958, 1959 and 1960 – an astonishing record. In the annual poll run by *Motor Cycle News* Surtees was "Man of the Year" in 1958 and again in 1959.

John Surtees was very much an individual and it is claimed that other riders knew him little better than did the spectators. Quiet and modest, he had exceptional ability as a mechanic and had the capacity to sort out engine problems. It was a disappointment that the other Italian factories were not seen after 1957 for in the seasons leading up to 1958, Surtees had been applying his knowledge and know-how in an effort to improve the MVs and much of his skill had been incorporated in the 1958 models. One of Surtees' greatest pre-MV rides was in the Ulster GP of 1955 when he almost snatched victory from the works Guzzis, mechanical failure putting him out of the race towards the end. His first rides for MV were against the faster and more successful Gileras of Geoff Duke and Bob McIntyre. It was at the Ulster GP again, this time in 1960 and approaching the end of Surtees' motor-cycle career, that he rode a memorable race. It was a battle with John Hartle, riding a Norton, which produced the drama. Surtees had mechanical trouble and was forced into the pits for repairs, allowing Hartle to move considerably ahead. Once on the road again, Surtees pursued Hartle with such speed and skill that he broke the lap record for the Dundrod circuit a number of times and only just failed to catch Hartle. And that same year, his last as a competitor in the TT, he showed his outstanding talent by producing a second lap speed of 104.08 mph, the fastest lap of the day and almost 3 mph faster than his fastest of the year before.

Surtees first car drives came in 1959 and it was no real surprise when he moved completely over to four wheels, at the end of 1960, where he was again to become a world champion. Surtees received an MBE for his services to motor-cycle racing.

World Champion:
1956: 500cc (MV).
1958: 500cc (MV) and 350cc (MV).
1959: 500cc (MV) and 350cc (MV).
1960: 500cc (MV) and 350cc (MV).

TT wins:
1956: Senior (MV).
1958: Senior (MV) and Junior (MV).
1959: Senior (MV) and Junior (MV).
1960: Senior (MV).

SUZUKI

This famous Japanese factory, with headquarters at Hamamatsu, came to racing prominence in the 1960s after Honda had begun to show the way. After specialising in textiles (the postwar recession in which dictated they look around for other types of manufacture and switched their attention to motor cycles), Suzuki produced their first model in 1954. Within fourteen years they had become the world's biggest manufacturer of two-stroke machines. Throughout their long and significant contribution to racing in the 1960s, Suzuki were to remain faithful to the two-stroke.

They first entered classic racing in 1960 but their 125cc twins, with piston-controlled inlets, were well outclassed. The following year, with machines which were a close copy of MZ 125cc and 250cc racers (but on which the East German factory had cured certain faults) they were hardly more successful and it was not until the 50cc class of the World Championship was established in 1962 that Suzuki made an impact, Ernst Degner winning on the Isle of Man and in three other classics to bring Suzuki their first world championship. Degner, after defecting to West Germany from the East, had gone to Japan and joined the Suzuki team. His previous role as rider and engineer with East Germany's MZ factory had obviously been of value to Suzuki, though in the beginning his knowledge and expertise was not reflected in race results in the 125cc class. Although later versions of the 125cc were to be successful it was with the 50cc machines, derived from the 125, which enabled Suzuki to dominate this new class right from the beginning. Degner's World Championship in 1962 had been achieved with comparative ease and in 1963 Suzuki, in both the 50cc and 125cc classes were devastating. The 50cc Suzuki of 1962 was an air-cooled single with one rotary valve and with a minimum of development was to prove much too good for the strong Honda challenge which was to come in that class in 1965. But in 1963, in the lightweight 125cc TT, Anderson, Perris and Degner secured first, second and third places and Itoh and Anderson produced a one/two in the 50cc TT. Anderson went on to collect both 50cc and 125cc world titles and Degner was placed third in the 50cc class. Itoh's TT Suzuki victory, incidentally, was the first to be recorded by a Japanese rider in the TT.

For 1964, with developing confidence acquired from their 1963 successes, Suzuki produced an extremely powerful 250cc, four-cylinder two-stroke to challenge Honda, but discovered that producing a world beater required more than adding a pair of cylinders to the front of the 125, however successful the latter. The four cylinders were placed in a square, each requiring a feed by rotary valve. The cylinder block was water-cooled and it had a six-speed gearbox. Disappointingly the machine was constantly beset with mechanical problems and overheating. These were never completely sorted out and the "square fours" best TT performance was Frank Perris's third place in the 1965 lightweight 250cc race. With their smaller machines, however, Suzuki continued to do well. In 1964 they once again collected the 50cc World Championship, for the third year running, and Hugh Anderson secured third place in the 125cc class. Anderson also won the 50cc TT that year. Other results during this outstanding period in Suzuki history are as follows:

World Championships:

1965: 125cc first (Anderson) and second (Perris), and 50cc third (Anderson).

TT races: 50cc second (Anderson) and third (Degner), and Lightweight 250cc third (Perris).

1966: World Championships: 50cc first (Anscheidt)

TT races: 50cc third (Anderson) and Lightweight 125cc third (Anderson).

1967: 50cc first (Anscheidt), second (Katayama) and third (Graham) and 125cc third (Graham).

TT races: 50cc first (Graham), second (Anscheidt) and third (Robb), and lightweight 125cc second (Graham).

At the end of 1967, with 50cc racing declining in importance, Suzuki, like Honda, announced their retirement from full-scale racing. The cost of development had by this time reached such proportions that their decision was probably inevitable. The 50cc single had been replaced by the twin and a three-cylinder machine was said to be in preparation - but was never raced. The 50cc Suzuki twin by 1967 had a top speed of about 118 mph on the Spa circuit. In 1968, however, Anscheidt kept Suzuki's name in the World Championship race on a 50 twin which he had kept for his own use, and ended the season 50cc World Champion for the third time running. For the remainder of the 1960s the Suzuki name was kept alive in the Classics by the success of ex-factory machines, bought by private riders. The German rider Dieter Braun was second in the 125cc World Championship of 1969, with Holland's Van Dongen third; and Braun secured the 125cc Championship in 1970. In 1971 Barry Sheene rode a 125cc Suzuki into second place in the World Championships.

Suzuki returned to prominence in the 1970s with their major attention directed to the US market and the big American races like the Daytona 200, building 500cc and 750cc racers derived from standard models. In 1974 came the 500cc square four racers, which proved more reliable than the earlier 250cc square fours, as a prelude to a major attack on the 500cc title in 1975. In Britain the enterprising Suzuki GB concessionaires have enjoyed considerable success since the formation of their racing team in

1973. Barry Sheene and Stan Woods made a major impact in the major home races in 750 and 750-type racing and Sheene was European F750 champion in 1973. Sheene first rode the 500cc Suzuki racer in 1971.

Suzuki have also been extremely active in other branches of motor cycle sport, including endurance events and moto cross. They were the first Japanese factory to take an interest in moto cross, their first prototype machines appearing in 1965, but further development was necessary before a completely new engine for their 250cc machine found them ready to contest the big-time seriously. Top Swedish rider Olle Petterson, who had been engaged to race, prepare and develop the Suzuki moto-cross machine, finished third overall in the World Championship in 1969. After signing top rider Joel Robert, the Japanese factory won their first World title in 1970. By 1975 they secured six world championships in moto-cross, principally with the help of Joel Robert, who added two more titles, and Roger De Coster who gained the 500cc moto-cross world titles for Suzuki in 1971/72. The 376cc RN 72 factory Suzuki used by De Coster had a bore and stroke of 83mm x 73mm and was claimed to develop 39 bhp. With widespread use of titanium and other lightweight materials, the machine weighed only 198 lbs, which was within the permissible minimum for 1973. It was a development of the successful 250cc Suzukis first seen in 1965. The final version ridden by Joel Robert to give Suzuki their third successive World Championship gave 30 bhp with revs peaking at 7200. Weight was 185lb. Both De Coster's and Robert's machines had five-speed gearboxes.

More recent results:

World Championships:

1970: first (D. Braun) in 125cc;
1971: second (B. Sheene) in 125cc, and second (K. Turner) and third (R. Bron) in 500cc;
1973: first (B. Sheene) in F750.
1976: first (B. Sheene) in 500cc; second (T. Lansivuori) in 500cc and next nine positions all held by Suzuki riders;
1977: first (B. Sheene) in 500cc;
1980: second (R. Mamola), third (M. Lucchinelli), fourth (F. Uncini) and fifth (G. Rossi) in 500cc.
1981: first (M. Lucchinelli) and second (R. Mamola) in 500cc.

TT Races:

1970: first (F. Whiteway) in Production 500cc and third (S. Woods) in Production 500cc and third (S. Woods) in Production 250cc;
1971: third (A. Cooper) in Production 500cc;
1972: third (J. Findlay) in Formula 750, first (S. Woods) in Production 500cc and third (E. Roberts) in Production 250cc;
1973: first (J. Findlay) in 500cc.
1977: first (P. Read) Senior TT.
1978: first (T. Herron) Senior TT.
1979: first (M. Hailwood) Senior TT.
1980: first (G. Crosby) Formula 1.
1981: first (G. Crosby) Formula 1, first (M. Grant) and third (J. Newbold) Senior, first (G. Crosby) and second (M. Grant) Classic.

SWEDISH GRAND PRIX

The Swedish Grand Prix takes place on the Anderstorp circuit which is situated near a small aerodrome. It is one of the most modern circuits in Europe. In 1974 Kent Andersson became the first Swedish rider to win a road racing world championship and he secured the title at the Swedish Grand Prix at Anderstorp in July.

Results:

1971: 50cc A. Nieto (Derbi). 125cc B. Sheene (Suzuki). 250cc R. Gould (Yamaha). 350cc G. Agostini (MV); 500cc G. Agostini (MV).
1972: 50cc J. de Vries (Kreidler); 125cc A. Nieto (Derbi); 250cc R. Gould (Yamaha); 350cc G. Agostini (MV); 500cc G. Agostini (MV).
1973: 50cc J. de Vries (Kreidler); 125cc B. Jansson (Maico); 250cc D. Braun (Yamaha); 350cc T. Lansivuori (Yamaha); 500cc P. W. Read (MV).
1974: 50cc H. van Kessel (Kreidler); 125cc K. Andersson (Yamaha); 250cc T. Katayama (Yamaha); 350cc T. Lansivuori (Yamaha); 500cc T. Lansivuori (Yamaha); Open 750cc C. Mortimer (Yamaha).
1975: 50cc E. Lazzarini (Piovaticci); 125cc P. Pileri (Morbidelli); 250cc W. Villa (Harley-Davidson); 500cc B. Sheene (Suzuki).

1976: 50cc A. Nieto (Bultaco); 125cc P. Bianchi (Morbidelli); 250cc T. Katayama (Yamaha); 500cc B. Sheene (Suzuki).
1977: 50cc R. Tormo (Bultaco); 125cc A. Nieto (Bultaco); 250cc M. Grant (Kawasaki); 350cc T. Katayama (Yamaha); 500cc B. Sheene (Suzuki).
1978: 125cc P. Bianchi (Minarelli); 250cc G. Hansford (Kawasaki); 350cc G. Hansford (Kawasaki); 500cc B. Sheene (Suzuki).
1979: 125cc P. Bianchi (Minarelli); 250cc G. Rossi (Morbidelli); 500cc B. Sheene (Suzuki); sidecars J. Taylor/B. Johansson (Yamaha).
1980: No World Championship races.
1981: 125cc R. Tormo (Sanvanero); 250cc A. Mang (Kawasaki); 500cc B. Sheene (Yamaha); sidecars R. Biland/K. Waltisperg (LCR Yamaha).

SWISS GRAND PRIX

Held on a circuit just outside Berne, the Swiss Grand Prix used to be an important event before the introduction of the World Championships in 1949 and for a number of years afterwards counted towards the Championships. The Swiss were sensitive to the dangers of racing and for some time in the 1950s there had been pressure from various sources to discontinue the Grand Prix. The Le Mans car disaster in 1955 settled the issue and the Swiss Grand Prix ended in 1954. It was first held in 1924 and was noted for the emphasis it placed on sidecar racing.

The programme normally included 500cc, 350cc, 250cc and sidecar events.

A Swiss Grand Prix was included in the 750cc World Championship in 1979, but because of the Swiss Government's ban on road racing, the round took place in France at the Paul Ricard circuit near Marseilles. Winner was Johnny Cecotto on a Yamaha.

Results (500cc only) since 1924:
1924: G. Walker (Sunbeam);
1927: S. Woods (Norton);
1928: W. Handley (Motosacoche);
1931: S. Woods (Norton);
1932: S. Woods (Norton);
1933: A. Hunt (Norton);
1934: J. Simpson (Norton);
1935: J. Guthrie (Norton);
1936: J. Guthrie (Norton);
1937: J. Guthrie (Norton);
1938: H. Daniell (Norton);
1947: O. Tenni (Guzzi);
1948: H. Daniell (Norton);
1949: L. Graham (AJS);
1950: L. Graham (AJS);
1951: F. Anderson (Guzzi);
1952: J. Brett (AJS);
1953: G. Duke (Gilera);
1954: G. Duke (Gilera).

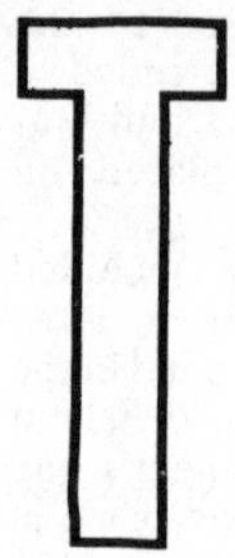

TAIT, Percy

Percy Tait (born 1929) was one of the most enduring of British road racers. He competed in his first road race in 1951 riding a Frank Baker Triumph in the 250cc race at the Hutchinson 100 meeting at Silverstone. He finished second. Twenty years later he was still riding competitively and with remarkable success and in 1971 won the *MCN* Superbike Series, the Bol d'Or 24-hour race (with Ray Pickrell), the Thruxton 500 mile race (with Dave Croxford) and the 750cc British Championship. Throughout his long career Percy Tait concentrated on British circuits. Riding a BSA in the 500cc Clubman's TT of 1954 he finished in sixth position. That year, in the Isle of Man for the Manx Grand Prix, he finished ninth in the Junior event and was lying third in the Senior when he had to retire with stripped bevel gears. He was riding a Bob Foster Norton. He first appeared in the TT Races in 1955 riding an AJS in the Junior TT and a Norton in the Senior, which he crashed at speed near Hillberry. He was a Triumph rider for most of his career and in 1974 finished fourth in the 750cc TT.

TAVERI, Luigi

Prominent in the 1950s and 1960s, Taveri was one of the finest road racers to come from Switzerland. Small, he had an excellent style and a most professional approach to racing. He was a regular competitor in Grands Prix and off the circuit had a happy-go-lucky approach to life. In the World Championships Taveri has a remarkable record. With MV he was in the first three on five occasions in six years, and once also on a Ducati, but his greatest achievements came in the 1960s riding Hondas. He was 125cc World Champion in 1962, '64 and '66 and in the first three in 50cc, 125cc and 250cc racing on four other occasions. On the Honda he finished third in the 350cc class in 1963.

World Championships:

1956: third (MV) in 125cc and second (MV) in 250cc.
1957: second (MV) in 125cc.
1958: third (Ducati) in 125cc.
1960: third (MV) in 250cc.
1961: third (Honda) in 125cc.
1962: World Champion (Honda) 125cc and third (Honda) in 50cc.
1963: second (Honda) in 125cc and third (Honda) in 350cc.
1964: World Champion (Honda) in 125cc.
1966: World Champion (Honda) in 125cc and third (Honda) in 50cc.

TAYLOR, Jock

Jock Taylor won the World Sidecar Championship in 1980, clinching the title with a second place at the Marlboro British Grand Prix at Silverstone in August, the penultimate round of the championship. He became Scotland's first motor-cycle world champion, despite riding for eight laps with a punctured rear tyre. His passenger was Benga Johansson of Sweden.

TECHNICAL DEVELOPMENT

Over the years, technical development has changed classic racing machines out of all recognition. And that development has largely been shaped by the formulae laid down by the international governing body, the Federation Internationale Motocycliste.

To analyse technical development step-by-step and make-by-make would fill this encyclopaedia from cover to cover. A more practical approach – and one that gives a clearer overall picture – is to trace the trends that have flowed from formula changes.

As we do this, however, we shall see another influence at work besides the framework of regulations. That is the calibre of designers as reflected in their different approaches to their problem.

The shrewder brains recognise that there are no specific prizes for horsepower or top speed. The winner is the man who completes the course first – or, in the case of interval starts (as in the Isle of Man TT), in the shortest time. And this involves other factors besides power.

Less shrewd designers concentrate on

the engine, producing spectacular power regardless of weight and bulk, then drape the rest of the machine round it like an afterthought. This approach is wholly justified in the smallest class (50cc). There the machine is flat out for practically the whole of the race, so engine power is all-important, provided weight and windage are kept to a minimum.

But, at the other end of the capacity scale, riders have often had an embarrassing surplus of power (hence weight and bulk) to the detriment of other crucial qualities. For a given level of power, for example, weight hampers acceleration, climb and braking, while bulk hampers speed and handling.

Cornering speeds go up as the centre of gravity comes down – and wide engines have to be mounted high for adequate cornering clearance. All of which shows that a successful machine must be as light, low and slim as possible.

In the 1950s, Moto-Guzzi's brilliant race chief, Ing Giulio Carcano (the greatest exponent of this approach), refined the analysis still further. He established that, of three machines having the same power/weight ratio but different all-up weights (including rider and fuel), the lightest, hence least powerful, was invariably fastest round a give-and-take circuit, and favourite with the riders – although the heaviest (and most powerful) had the highest top speed.

What gave the light machine its edge was its faster and more effortless cornering and the rider's greater confidence in his ability to wrestle with it should the need arise. As a result of this confidence, he rode consistently nearer to the machine's limit of handling.

A logical outcome of this sort of thinking is "horses for courses". And had Moto-Guzzi not pulled out of racing at the end of 1957 (along with other Italian factories) Carcano would have tried fielding his enormously successful 216-lb flat singles on the more tortuous circuits, and his much more powerful water-cooled vee-eights on those with a predominance of long straights.

In the beginning, racing machines were hotted-up versions of standard models, mostly singles. In the face of indisputable engineering logic, multi-cylinder engines were at first allowed a larger total capacity than singles.

The multis were thought to be inherently unreliable and under-developed. But as they took advantage of their greater power potential, the capacity bonus was whittled away step by step.

Two-strokes, however, were thought to have an unfair advantage in their double rate of firing. So their actual capacity was multiplied by 1.25 for classification purposes. If they were so bold as to have two cylinders (like the Scott) the penalty was a 1.33 multiplication!

But the two-stroke penalty went the way of the multi-cylinder bonus. And by the time the First World War interrupted racing, fixed capacity classes were established for two-stroke and four-stroke, single and multi alike.

This was thought to put all designers on an equal footing. That it failed to do so was clearly shown by the dominance of supercharged machines (both two-stroke and four-stroke) just before the Second World War; the eclipse of four-stroke singles and twins by high-revving fours, fives and sixes in the 1960s; and the widespread superiority of two-strokes more recently still.

Even in the 1920s and 1930s it was no secret that multis had a greater power potential. But the single had long been the industry's bread and butter, and several able engineers (notably Joe Craig at Norton) lavished such intensive development on it that it seemed unassailable.

In the mid-1930s, however, Husqvarna and Moto-Guzzi chalked some ominous writing on the wall with their extremely fast vee-twins. Indeed, the Moto-Guzzi 120-degree twin heralded the eventual demise of both the single-cylinder engine and the unsprung frame when Stanley Woods won the 1935 Senior TT from Jimmy Guthrie (Norton). But the single shrugged off the challenge.

Supercharging was another obvious road to more power. But here, too – except for a couple of blown singles (the most difficult type to supercharge) from Velocette and Moto-Guzzi in the early 1930s – the advantage was virtually ignored until Germany and Italy realised the political prestige to be derived from grand-prix supremacy.

From then on, they put a lot of money and effort into developing blown multis. Yet it was not until these machines had a substantial advantage in speed and power that they were able to depose the unblown single.

Partly this was due to the single's high pitch of development (double overhead camshafts and high bore/stroke ratios were already fashionable) but mostly it was because a lot of the power of the blown multis was offset by the superior handling of the singles.

Much of the weight of the big single-cylinder engines was in the flywheels. Even with an upright installation, the slim crankcase could be slung very low between the bottom frame tubes. Hence the centre of gravity was low and could be made exceptionally so if the cylinder was installed horizontally. The handling of the singles was a byword.

The blown BMWs, on the other hand, with their cylinders across the frame for shaft drive, were not nearly so manageable. This was due partly to their necessarily high engine installation, but also to engine torque reaction in a transverse plane (particularly when changing down) and to gyroscopic precession of the crankshaft and flywheel, especially on jarring bumps.

In common with four-stroke multis, pre-war two-strokes never came into their own until supercharged, notably by DKW. This was because there was then only a scanty understanding of the inlet and exhaust resonances on which today's unblown two-strokes rely so heavily for their phenomenal power.

The first machine to dethrone the big single was the BMW blown twin – its most telling performance being Georg Meier's victory in the 1939 Senior TT, backed up by Jock West in second place. But its supremacy was shortlived. Predictably, in engineering terms, it was soon outclassed by the supercharged Gilera four, with water cooling, on which Dorino Serafini won the 1939 European 500cc championship.

In a bid to restore British supremacy, Velocette, though comparative paupers, designed The Roarer – a 496cc blown parallel twin that bypassed the BMW's handling bothers.

To keep the rear tyre free from chain oil, it had shaft drive, hence a longitudinal crankshaft. But torque and precession reactions were both neutralised by having two crankshafts (one for each cylinder) geared together and so rotating in opposite directions.

A 100-per-cent balance factor gave near-perfect engine balance and initial tests were extremely promising. But the war came too soon for it to be raced.

One of the cornerstones of Honda's classic supremacy in the 1960s was the pent-roof four-valve cylinder head, subsequently copied by MV Agusta and Jawa. Yet four-valve heads were tried in the 1920s and 1930s, only to give best to two-valvers.

Easily the most successful pre-war four-valver was the Rudge, first with parallel pairs of valves in a pent-roof head, then with all valves radially disposed and operated by a complex arrangement of two pushrods and six rockers. Both layouts had spectacular TT successes.

Excelsior took the radial layout a stage farther in the Mechanical Marvel, with a separate carburettor for each inlet valve and operation by two high camshafts, a pair of pushrods and four rockers. But a lone TT win was their sole reward. And in all three classes concerned (250, 350 and 500cc) two-valvers reasserted themselves, largely through the persistence of such men as Joe Craig and the use of double overhead camshafts to reduce valve-gear reciprocating masses.

It is ironical that one of the intrinsic benefits of the four-valve layout is the lightest possible reciprocating masses. But nobody exploited this before Honda, who made the most of it by using double overhead camshafts. In conjunction with smaller and smaller cylinders, this enabled them to get more power through higher peak revs, together with more reliability through making the valve gear practically immune to overrevving.

The pre-war four-valvers exploited only the combustion advantages of the layout. These are a larger valve opening area, increased turbulence from converging gas streams, a more compact combustion space and a much shorter flame travel from a central plug. Honda went even better by incorporating large squish segments front and rear.

The post-war ban on supercharging robbed BMW and Gilera of the tremendous power advantage that was the basis of their pre-war dominance. Since the development of unblown multis had scarcely begun, the ban amounted to a new lease of life for the single. This type was already well advanced in development for power and its superior handling enabled it to remain competitive until the multi had again established a considerable power advantage.

The big British singles (Norton and AJS) seized their opportunity by boosting power in two ways. First, they increased their brake mean effective pressure (that is the effectiveness of each individual engine cycle). Second they raised their peak rpm.

The bmep was substantially raised by painstaking attention to port shapes and downdraught angles, valve sizes and included angles, inlet and exhaust resonances, squish forms and surface/volume ratios. Peak revs were raised by higher bore/stroke ratios and cam forms designed to match valve spring characteristics.

Moto-Guzzi extended the single's competitiveness even further, winning the last five world 350cc championships they contested against fours with a substantial power advantage. As a consequence of their horizontal cylinder layout, they had the steepest downdraught angle, the lowest centre of gravity and the smallest frontal area.

Equally important, they slashed weight to an incredible degree (going to such lengths as using unpainted magnesium fairings, 10mm plugs and single-coil valve springs) and built a full-scale wind tunnel to develop the most efficient streamlining ever seen in road racing.

In the 125cc class, Ducati struck a new note by getting away from valve springs altogether. Their triple-knocker desmodromic valve operation gave such benefits in peak revs and mechanical safety that they trounced the haughty double-knocker MVs and might well have started a new trend had not Honda resurrected the four-valve layout.

First machine to put the unblown multi firmly on the world-championship map was the 250cc double-ohc NSU Rennmax parallel twin of 1953 and 1954. Its 39 bhp at 11,500 rpm put it streets ahead of its rivals, while valve control up to 15,000 rpm made it virtually unburstable. Tunnel-developed streamlining boosted its speed, while its spine frame and leading-link fork made for impeccable handling.

In the bigger classes, once Geoff Duke joined them from Norton to perfect their handling, the Gilera fours took over – followed on their withdrawal by very similar MV Agustas. Most noticeable difference was that the Gileras had central plugs (recessed and firing the mixture through narrow slots) whereas those in the MV were inclined outward in the conventional way.

Contemporary with these fours was the Moto-Guzzi vee-eight, water cooled because of the masking of the rear cylinder block, yet weighing only 280lb. Unusual features included valves seating directly in the aluminium heads, split roller big ends, and big-end lubrication by oil squirted into annular grooves in the flywheels (as in the NSU Rennmax).

Absence of valve-seat inserts was a feature of the massive 350cc Bianchi parallel twin, too – a classic example of over-emphasis on the engine to the detriment of the machine as a whole. Lino Tonti's obsession with friction saving led to the use of bearings within bearings in the camshaft gear train. As a result the bike was far too cumbersome to get the best out of its creditable 48 bhp.

Despite the success of the Gilera and MV fours, it was Honda who succeeded in slimming transverse multis so drastically as to make fours, fives and sixes little wider than singles and twins. To meet the challenge once Honda moved up into the 350cc class, MV slimmed their bikes by switching to three cylinders. But after Honda's withdrawal (in 1967) they subsequently reverted to four cylinders to try to match the Yamaha two-strokes for speed.

In broad outline the history of the racing two-stroke has passed through the same three phases as that of the four-stroke multi. These are: first, its dependence on supercharging, at comparatively low engine speeds, for its pre-war successes; second, its consequent slump when blowing was banned; third, its long climb back to full competitiveness (through ultra-high rpm).

From the start, the symmetry of the two-stroke's port timing was seen as an obstacle to competitive power – even with supercharging, which DKW used right from their racing debut in 1925. Six years later, they bypassed the bottleneck with their split-single layout.

In this, two cylinder bores had a common combustion chamber. The exhaust ports were in the rear bore, the transfers in the front. The connecting rods were articulated, with the exhaust piston on the main rod and the transfer piston on a smaller rod hinged in a boss near the main big-end eye. That way the exhaust ports not only opened before the transfers but closed before them, too, allowing much better cylinder filling.

The supercharger took various forms. First, it was a large-diameter, short-stroke horizontal piston, breathing through a reed valve. But valve breakage limited engine speed to 4,700 rpm. Next, a vertical pumping piston fed through a cylindrical rotary valve. With 30 bhp at 6,000 to 7,000 rpm, this version was enormously successful (as well as deafening) and Ewald Kluge pulverised the opposition in the 1938 lightweight (250cc) TT. Its atrocious 22 mpg, however, necessitated an enormous tank if too much time was not to be squandered in refuelling.

Another form of blowing (on catalogue models) was an auxiliary piston which moved forward (downward in some versions) as the working pistons moved upward, so increasing the breathing capacity of the crankcase. Transfer was conventional.

Shortly after Kluge's success, the piston-type supercharger on the works engines gave way to an eccentric-vane type, feeding the crankcase and ordinary transfer passages. Power leaped to 40 bhp and a 350cc was made, too. But dreams of invincibility were shattered by the outbreak of war.

With blowing subsequently outlawed, much greater pains were taken to harness the resonances in the inlet and exhaust tracts. The aim was to cram as much gas as possible into the crankcase, scavenge the cylinder thoroughly and transfer the fresh charge without too much loss to the exhaust.

DKW were soon back with a 125cc single, then a 250cc parallel twin, with a cylindrical rotary valve in the crankcase. But results were disappointing, so they put a third cylinder in place of the horizontal valve, made the capacity 350cc and switched to piston-controlled induction. For a time the bike was practically a match for the championship-winning Moto-Guzzi singles.

But meanwhile the seeds of the two-stroke's future glory were being sown by MZ in East Germany. There, Ing Walter Kaaden got away from symmetrical inlet timing by using a rotary disc valve in the crankcase wall. Painstaking development soon led to a basic formula that has yet to be improved.

Besides the disc valve and highly resonant tracts, the formula boils down to one or more auxiliary transfer ports (opposite the exhaust), a large squish band in the head, and square or slightly oversquare cylinder dimensions. Original purpose of the auxiliary transfer port was to pass some cool oily gas over the overheated, under-oiled small end. But an unexpected bonus was a 10 per cent power boost.

The Japanese were quick to copy the MZ formula, pour money into it and refine it with pumped water cooling, auxiliary oiling and energy transfer ignition. For higher revs and smaller heat problems, they went to smaller cylinders. As a result, Suzuki and Yamaha proved a match for Honda and won many world titles.

Because of the side-facing carburettors, the cylinders could be coupled no more than two abreast. And the most successful disc-valve two-strokes were the spectacular Yamaha 125 and 250cc vee-fours, which were virtually a brace of parallel twins driving a common transmission gear.

Invincible in 1968, they were then outlawed by the FIM's misguided restriction to two cylinders and six gears, which dropped development to a much lower key. Suzuki subsequently revived the four-cylinder layout in the 500cc class, where the restriction did not apply. But most racing two-strokes in the next decade were variants of catalogue models, with piston-controlled induction and cylinders arranged two, three and four abreast. Not until the late 1970s did Kawasaki give design a fillip with disc-valve 250 and 350cc tandem twins, after which they and Yamaha followed Suzuki's highly successful lead with 500cc square fours.

The sidecar class was the last to fall to two-stroke power, for the simple reason that the BMW layout gave such a low centre of gravity (for drifting), low overall height (for minimum drag), ideal cylinder cooling and reliable transmission.

Except for streamlining, where the FIM outlawed frontal fairings for solos in 1958, development of cycle parts has been dictated largely by engineering considerations.

Frame design has shown the least logic. Front forks have progressed from girders (first with friction dampers, then progressive snubber springs) to telescopics – despite the apparent advantages of leading links (as on the Moto-Guzzis).

Plunger rear springing (a simple adaptation from rigid frames) has given way to hydraulically damped pivoted forks, with triangulation gaining ground under the names of cantilever and monoshock (though used by Moto-Guzzi and Vincent before the Second World War).

Drum brakes progressed from single to double leading shoes for more power, then to discs to resist fade. But most spectacular of all, with the exception of engine development, has been progress, mostly since 1950, in the high-grip tyres without which all other development would be hamstrung.

THRUXTON

This popular racing circuit, first opened on Easter Monday 1950, is situated in Hampshire, four miles west of Andover on the A303. It is used for international, national and club racing. The length of the original circuit was 1.89 miles and during its first few years it was raced both clockwise and anti-clockwise. A lap was increased in 1953 to 2.76 miles, a year in which the British Championships were held there. It became the home of the 500-mile Grand Prix d'Endurance, forerunner of the *Motor Cycle* International 500-mile Grand Prix. The first Commonwealth Trophy meeting was held there, but deterioration of the circuit resulted in its closure in 1966. It was reopened in 1968 to a length of 2.356 miles and a width of 48 feet, and the 500-miler returned to Thruxton in 1969 after being run at Castle Combe and Brands Hatch. Recent winners are as follows:

1973: R. Butcher and N. White (750 Norton) 82.57 mph.
1974: B. Ditchburn and K. Ballington (750 Kawasaki) 86.33 mph.
1975: A. Vial and J. Luc (1000 Kawasaki) 87.47 mph.
1976: C. Huguet and R. Ruiz (940 Honda) 89.95 mph.
1977: S. Woods and C. Williams (997 Honda) 86.97 mph.

The European Endurance Grand Prix was held at Brands Hatch in 1978, on the 2.6136-mile circuit (238 laps) and was won by C. Williams and S. Woods (998 Honda RCB) at 90.46 mph.

The Endurance Series was given World Championship status for 1981 and the British round was held at Donington Park. It was won by Hervé Moineau and Richard Hubin on a Suzuki at 80.12 mph.

TRIALS

see also International Six-Days Trial, The Scottish Six-Days Trial and the Scott Trial.

The trial is one of the oldest forms of motor-cycle sport and derives from the desire of early riders to test their machines, one against the other, to establish reliability, manoeuvreability and hill-climbing performance. The organised reliability trial springs from these origins. Early events were unsophisticated and straightforward; and establishing the winners was easy: those who finished the course, generally over roads and hills, within a prescribed time received an award. As machines improved, however, something more was required to establish the winners and "observed sections" were introduced. Points were lost for stopping in these special sections. To keep pace with improving machine technology and rider skills, these observed sections were made more difficult and this, in turn, helped to develop machines specifically for trials and riders who concentrated on this form of motor-cycle sport. In time the emphasis shifted: reliability of machine was taken more and more for granted and the real test in trials, as dictated by the number of points forfeited, was the extent to which a rider had to put a foot (or feet) on the ground to keep him upright or help him along.

To do well in trials requires a great deal of skill, controlled riding, a sensitive feeling for balance and a kind of sixth-sense unity with the machine.

The most prestigeous event in the trials calendar – the International Six-Days Trial (see separate item) – was established by Britain in 1913 and developed along different lines, time schedules between check points now forming the basis of marking with points quickly mounting against the riders for excess time. Another important event, the Scottish Six-Days Trial (see separate entry) has also a time element, riders having to be on time at a number of checks.

Yorkshire's one-day Scott Trial (see

separate entry) is reputedly one of the toughest events in the world, decided on observation and speed over a 65-mile route.

The majority of trials are one-day events over a course of about 30 or 40 miles which incorporates many observed sections. Time is not altogether important, though riders can be penalised for taking longer than their set time over the entire course. In the observed sections points are lost for a variety of infringements including a machine or rider receiving outside assistance, when boundary markers are not observed, the rider is forced to dismount, the machine stops or any part of the rider touches the ground. This is called footing and for it within a section penalty marks are collected as follows: one for touching the ground once, another mark for a second "footing" and three marks for "footing" in excess of two. After successfully negotiating a special section riders move on quickly to the next one, since it is only necessary to keep within a generous time schedule.

Apart from the major international events there are many important national trials and a British Championship taken over a series of meetings (see results below). In Britain Sammy Miller (see separate entry) and Gordon Jackson are riders who have become legends in the sport far beyond home shores. Malcolm Rathmell, the British and European trials champion in 1974, later became one of the biggest names in the sport (see separate entry).

The sport is fiercely demanding and trials courses are over rough terrain which includes rocks, ruts, paths, forest tracks, fords; and riders become artists as they fight the hazards in order to remain on their machines, standing high on footrests or applying weight to the rear wheel to re-establish grip.

Spain has produced some of the best trials machines – Ossa, Bultaco and Montesa, though Japan, through Yamaha, Suzuki, Honda and Kawasaki, has become prominent in the sport in more recent years.

Results:

A-CU Stars:

1950: P. H. Alves (solo); H. Tozer (sidecars).
1951: W. Nicholson (solo); H. Tozer (sidecars).
1952: W. Nicholson (solo); F. Wilkins (sidecars).
1953: J. V. Smith (solo); F. Wilkins (sidecars).
1954: J. V. Smith (solo); A. J. Humphries (sidecars).
1955: G. L. Jackson (solo); A. J. Humphries (sidecars).
1956: J. V. Brittain (solo); F. Darrieulat (sidecars).
1957: Cancelled through petrol rationing.
1958: G. L. Jackson (solo); F. Darrieulat (sidecars).
1959: S. H. Miller (solo); A. Pulman (sidecars).
1960: S. H. Miller (solo); A. Pulman (sidecars).
1961: S. H. Miller (solo); P. Wraith (sidecars).
1962: S. H. Miller (solo); R. J. Langston (sidecars).
1963: S. H. Miller (solo); R. J. Langston (sidecars).
1964: S. H. Miller (solo); R. J. Langston (sidecars).
1965: S. H. Miller (solo); R. J. Langston (sidecars).

British Champions:

1966: S. H. Miller (solo); R. J. Langston (sidecars).
1967: S. H. Miller (solo); C. A. Morewood (sidecars).
1968: S. H. Miller (solo); C. A. Morewood (sidecars).
1969: S. H. Miller (solo); R. G. Bradley (sidecars).
1970: G. Farley (solo); R. G. Bradley (sidecars).
1971: G. Farley (solo); R. Round (sidecars).
1972: M. Rathmell (solo); R. Round (sidecars).
1973: H. M. Lampkin (solo); J. Mathews (sidecars).
1974: M. Rathmell (solo); J. Mathews (sidecars).

A newly-formed World Championship began in 1975 with fourteen rounds, best eight to count. Rounds were held in Northern Ireland, Belgium, Spain, Britain, France, Poland, Italy, Canada, America, Finland, Sweden, Switzerland, West Germany and Czechoslovakia.

World Champion:

1975: H. M. Lampkin (Bultaco).
1976: Y. Vesterinen (Bultaco).
1977: Y. Vesterinen (Bultaco).

1978: Y. Vesterinen (Bultaco).
1979: B. Schreiber (Bultaco).
1980: U. Karlsson (Montesa).
1981: G. Burgat (SWM).

TRIUMPH
This famous British machine was originally the product of the Triumph Engineering Company Ltd., at Meriden, near Coventry, the Meriden works still functioning (and making Triumph machines) as a workers' cooperative into 1975, after Government intervention and following the intention of Norton Villiers Triumph to close down the works. For most of motor cycle racing's long history Triumph had an undistinguished record of success in Grand Prix and TT events, even though they figured in the results of the early TTs, Marshall and Hulbert gaining a second and third place in the Singles class of the very first TT in 1907, and Jack Marshall winning the same race the following year. Third places in 1909-10 and second places in 1912 and 1922 were to follow, though that was to end Triumph's success in TTs until 1967, when the Production TTs were introduced.

Since then, through the successful Bonneville, and Trident models, Triumph machines have an impressive record in the larger capacity 750cc and 500cc Production TTs. Triumph engines have also been important power sources for numerous world record attempts, the success of Johnny Allen in 1955, Bill Johnson in 1962 and Bob Leppan in 1966 being outstanding ultimate examples. Towards the end of the 1960s and into the 1970s the British motor-cycle industry revived an interest in racing with the growing emphasis on production machine racing and Formula 750 events and Triumph machines, along with Norton and BSA, were in the vanguard of this assault, significant beyond the Isle of Man.

Triumphs have a magnificent record on the Isle of Man since the Production TT was introduced in 1967. John Hartle won the 750 Production TT of that year and in 1968 Ray Knight won the 500cc Production event on a Triumph Daytona. In 1971 a Triumph Bonneville with Malcolm Uphill took the 750 Production TT, an event which Uphill again won in 1970 on a Trident. Results in the TT since then:

1971: first (A. Jefferies) in the Formula 750 class and first (R. Pickrell) and second (A. Jefferies) in the Production 750 TT;
1972: first (R. Pickrell) and second (A. Jefferies) Formula 750cc; first (R. Pickrell) and third (D. Nixon) Production 750 TT; second (R. Bowler) Production 500 TT.
1973: third (A. Jefferies) Formula 750; first (A. Jefferies), second (J. Williams) and third (D. Nixon) Production TT.
1974: first (M. Grant) Production 1000cc TT.

Triumphs have also consistently finished in events like the Bol d'Or and the Hutchinson 100. The workers' cooperative continued to operate at Meriden, though was substantially in debt, and in 1980 there was some talk of a liaison with a Japanese manufacturer. (*See also* BSA and NORTON).

TT COURSE
The TT Mountain Course of 37¾ miles incorporates over 200 bends and is acknowledged to be one of the most arduous and most gruelling circuits for both man and machine in the world. The course details are as follows: from the start to Bray Hill, Quarter Bridge, Braddan Bridge (2 miles), Union Mills, Glen Vine, Crosby, Highlander, Greeba Castle, Greeba Bridge, Ballacraine, Ballig Bridge, Doran's Bend, Laurel Bank, Glen Helen, Sarah's Cottage (10 miles), Cronk-y-Voddy (11 miles), Handley's Bends, Barregarrow, Kirk Michael, Rhencullen, Ballaugh Bridge (17 miles), Quarry Bends, Sulby Straight, Sulby Bridge (20 miles), Ginger Hall, Kerrowmoar, Glentramman, Churchtown, Milntown, Ramsey, Ramsey Hairpin, Waterworks, Gooseneck, Guthrie's Memorial, East Mountain Gate, Black Hut, Verandah (30 miles), Bungalow, Brandywell, Windy Corner, Keppel Gate, Kate's Cottage (34 miles), Gregny-baa, Brandish Corner, Hillberry (36 miles), Cronk-ny-Mona, Signpost Corner, Governor's Bridge and Depots (37¾ miles). The ascent coming out of Ramsey extends for about five miles and reaches its peak of 1400 feet just beyond East Mountain Gate and the descent back to the Depots begins at Brandywell and covers some 6½ miles.

TT DOUBLES
The exclusive club of riders who have

scored TT doubles in the Senior and Junior classes in the same year is as follows: Tim Hunt (1931), Stanley Woods (1932-33), Jimmy Guthrie (1934), Geoff Duke (1951), Ray Amm (1953), Bob McIntyre (1957), John Surtees (1958-1959), Mike Hailwood (1967), Giacomo Agostini (1968-70 and 1972).

TT (TOURIST TROPHY) RACES

There are few who would dispute the claim that the TT Races on the Isle of Man historically constitute the greatest series of road races in the world. Certainly, the emergence in the 1920s of Britain as a dominant force in motor cycle racing can be directly attributable to their establishment. It was on an Isle of Man course acknowledged as the most demanding and exacting of all that British motor cycles were developed to lead the world; and riders of immense potential were able to gain their experience and riding skills.

The TTs are also the most adventurous and historic of road races, their foundings manifest in the labour pains of motor-cycle racing itself. There had been races before, of course; but until the establishment of the TT Races in 1907, British aspirants to motor-cycle honours were hampered by restrictions in the United Kingdom which did not permit the closure of public roads for racing purposes. On the continent of Europe there were no such restrictions and motor-cycle racing was flourishing as early as the turn of the century with stirring inter-city marathons, fearsome races which culminated in the ill-fated Paris-Madrid event of 1903. These were thundering affairs open to both motor cars and motor cycles and by the time the 1903 event reached Bordeaux the marathon race was abandoned, a number of spectators having been killed and injured as cars and machines emerged at speed through giant dust clouds over the pot-holed, spectator-lined roads.

Next came the more moderate International Cup Races, in France in 1904-5 and Austria in 1906. Shabbily organised with regulations which meant little and results disputed, the first was little short of a total shambles and the results were annulled. The second was better controlled, but the third again evoked much dissatisfaction and controversy (*see* INTERNATIONAL CUP RACES) and the International Cup Races were thus discontinued.

It was in the period and atmosphere of the International Cup Races that the TTs were born. British manufacturers and riders found these European events extremely unsatisfactory. They placed too much emphasis on the performance of highly specialised *racing* machines (as opposed to the normal road-going touring bike) and were badly organised, ill-controlled and threw up "doubtful" results. Yet a 20 mph speed limit in the UK, combined with restrictions which denied the possibility of closing roads for racing purposes, forced British riders and factories to compete on the continent. How else could pioneer manufacturers gain the opportunity to test and develop their machines over long periods of top speed running on roads; or riders develop their racing skills and courage?

Facilities nearer home were desperately needed, a want also felt some years before by pioneer car racers and manufacturers. As early as 1904 Lord Raglan, the Governor of the Isle of Man, had invited the RAC to stage trials for the famous Gordon Bennett Cup car races on a closed roads course in the Island. To facilitate this a Bill was rushed through the Island's Tynwald Parliament, the RAC using a 52-mile course which incorporated much of the usable roads on the island. When the Auto-Cycle Club (later to become the Auto-Cycle Union) decided to send a team to take part in the International Cup Races of 1905 they looked to the Isle of Man as a location for the holding of their trials. A closed roads circuit extending 15.8 miles was agreed upon, taking in Tynwald Green, St John's, Ballacraine, Kirkmichael, Peel and back to St John's.

Later, in an atmosphere of disillusionment with continental racing, the idea developed for an event for touring machines on a circuit in the British Isles, with the Isle of Man as a likely venue. The idea was further promoted in a toast made by journalist Etienne Boileau at the A-CC dinner in January 1907. Such a race, for machines "similar to those sold to the public" eventually took place by courtesy of the Manx authorities on 28th May 1907 over what became known as the St John's circuit. Freddie Straight, first secretary of the Auto-Cycle Club, produced provisional regulations which classified machines as single or twin cylinders; there was no capacity limit and no weight limit. Obligatory were efficient silencers, ordinary type saddle and mudguards, and two-inch tyres. Pedalling gear was permitted. Fuel was restricted on the basis of 90 mpg for the singles and 75 mpg for the twins. The "short course" used for the International Cup Race trials two years before was adopted for the race, competitors lapping ten times to give a total distance of 158 miles. There was a compulsory ten-minute "rest" stop for every competitor after the completion of five laps and riders were set off in pairs at one-minute intervals. The English-based Marquis de Mouzilly St Mars agreed to provide a trophy – a copy of the Montagu Trophy used for the Isle of Man car races and featuring a figure of Mercury, the God of Speed, on a winged wheel – for the winner of the single-cylinder class and Dr Hele-Shaw presented an award for the winner of the twin cylinder class. As the race was expressly for touring machines with restricted fuel consumption, it was labelled the Tourist Trophy, the name being taken from the existing car event. And so the first TT race took place.

There were 25 starters – 18 on single cylinder machines and 7 on twins. Almost half that number completed the course. Machines competing included Matchless, Rex, Triumph, Norton, Vindec, Bat and Kerry. The single-cylinder race was held first, the first riders away being Frank Hulbert and Jack Marshall. The famous Collier Brothers, H. A. and C. R., were the next pair away. After taking the lead on the first lap, Charlie Collier was the eventual winner on his pedal-assisted Matchless.

His average speed was 38.23 mph and he registered 94.5 mpg, comfortably over the minimum of 90. In the twin-cylinder class Rem Fowler on a Peugeot-powered Norton led from Billy Wells on a Vindec on the first lap, but mechanical trouble on the second lap dropped Fowler behind. He revived soon afterwards and went on to win at 36.22 mph, below the single-cylinder average though Fowler's fastest lap of 42.91 mph was more than 1 mph better than Collier's. By later standards this initial TT was primitive in the extreme. Road surfaces were bad, there were no pits or pit signals, the start was made from a pub yard at St John's and riders, dressed in ordinary motor-cycle clothing of long leather coat or raincoat and back-to-front caps, were embellished around their waists and chests with spare belts and inner tubes. Pedalling gear was essential and the obligatory tool kits were many times necessary. Competitors learned of their progress as they puffed and pedalled up Creg Willys from supporters running alongside.

A row after the race centred on pedals, Jack Marshall's followers claiming that he would have won had they been barred. They further asserted that as the TT was supposed to be a *motor*-cycle race, pedalling should not be permitted. Collier enthusiasts countered by claiming it was natural and sensible for their man to have eased off to save wear on the engine, since he was so far ahead of other competitors. For 1908 pedals were indeed barred and a touch of irony was that this time Jack Marshall won, with Charlie Collier in second place. Other than the banning of pedals, the only change was a reduction in petrol consumption, singles now required to average 100 mpg and twins 80 mpg, and a switching of the races from May to September. The need for well-organised marshals had become obvious following the 1907 races and for 1908 marshals for the first time were sworn in as special constables by the Governor of the Island. The event was even more popular, there being 36 starters, with a decided swing to twin-cylinder machines of which there were 21 against the 15-single-cylinder, belt-driven entries. The "twins" included two four-cylinder machine entries. Marshall's winning average was 40.4 mph and his fastest lap, 42.48 mph. His petrol consumption was 117.6 mph! The multi-cylinder race was won by Harry Reed riding a Dot machine at 38.59 mph. Although Jack Marshall made the fastest lap for both races, Rem Fowler's previous year's record of 42.91 mph was not beaten.

For the 1908 TT two major changes took place: fuel restrictions were abandoned, along with the two machine-categories, though some restriction on engine capacity was introduced. With petrol cheap, the fuel economy consideration was regarded as somewhat irrelevant and, since the twin-cylinder machines had not demonstrated any unreasonable advantage over the singles in the two previous TTs, it was felt that they could all race together, the overall winner receiving the Tourist Trophy. Engine capacities were limited to 500cc for the single-cylinder entries and 750cc for the twins. The results of the race were to show that the singles had been unfairly handicapped and adjustments were made for 1910. Entries for the 1909 race went up to almost 60, about half of them being twins, and this time it was the other racing Collier, Charlie, who finished as winner. His average for the ten laps on his Matchless was 49.00 mph and he turned in a record lap of 52.27 mph – 9.36 mph better than Rem Fowler's record of 1907. Lee Evans on an Indian was second and Newsome on a Triumph third. It was in 1909 that the first public prize-giving took place, in the Palace Ballroom, with the Governor making the presentations.

A new circuit, to become famous as the Mountain Course (*see below and* TT COURSE), was established in 1911, but it would be an injustice to those redoubtable Collier brothers to pass over 1910, for Charlie won his second TT with Harry second some five minutes behind, both on the twin-cylinder Matchless machines. Winner Charlie's average was 50.63 mph, but the record lap was relinquished by Harry in favour of Bowden on a Bat at 53.15 mph. This 1910 TT marked the end of the first stage in the development of the Isle of Man races. In the short space of just four years the record average speed had been increased from 38.23 mph to 50.63 mph and the fastest lap from 42.91 mph to 53.15 mph. For British riders and manufacturers, the TT Races were already proving their worth.

The Mountain Course

By 1911 improvement in the design and performance of motor cycles was such that a more arduous test of man and machine was felt to be desirable and the initial St John's course gave way to the Mountain Course, then basically as it is today. In 1911, however, it was 37½ miles in length (against the present 37¾ miles), and much of the circuit was simply earth and stones rolled together, giving plenty of dust in dry weather and mud in the wet. Road conditions varied enormously. The best sections were little better than minor roads, others were cart tracks which would in no way glorify a motocross course of today. Wandering cattle and sheep were by no means an unfamiliar sight as riders roared past. The short course had served the sport well and largely as a result of the races over it, the motor-cycle industry was experiencing a boom. Progress was to be well maintained during the four years remaining over the Mountain Course before the outbreak of the First World War, with significant advances being made in both speed and reliability. The course was a severe test of endurance for both rider and machine and provided a challenge to be found irresistible by an increasing number of enthusiasts. A record number of 104 entries for the first Mountain Course event in 1911 was double that of 1910 and for the first time there were Senior (for singles up to 500cc and twins up to 585cc) and Junior (singles 300cc and twins 340cc) races. The Senior race, over five laps, attracted 64 competitors, including 24 twin-cylinder machines. The Junior event had 34 entries, of which 17 were twin-cylinder machines, and was run over four laps. Two official pits at Ramsay and Douglas were the refuelling points, silencers were not compulsory during the races, but were for practice, and pushing or wheeling the machine in the direction opposite to that of the race was not permitted. The races were switched to the end of June. P. J. Evans on a Humber twin won the earlier Junior event and the Senior brought the first outstanding victory for foreign machinery – the American Indian machines occupying first, second and third positions, though ridden by British competitors. This year witnessed the first disqualification – Charlie Collier, who finished second in the Senior being eliminated for taking on fuel unofficially – and the first fatality when during practice Victor Surridge crashed on his Rudge on the Glen Helen section.

The twin-cylinder machines having dominated the races so far, it was obvious that the singles were too severely handicapped and for 1912 the A-CU decided on one engine size for each race, irrespective of the number of cylinders, thus setting the pattern for today: Senior 500cc and Junior 350cc. The races, as in 1911, were held on the last Friday in June and the first Monday in July. For the first time in the history of the TT there was a decrease in the number of entries; 49 for the Senior event and 25 for the Junior. The weather only added to the falter in TT progress apparent in 1912 for it was very wet and with most machines using direct belt-drive, belt-slip was prevalent. It was to be the first of two consecutive Senior wins for the Scott machine, for Applebee was first home at an average speed of 48.69 mph and had a fastest lap of 49.44 mph. But however optimistically the 1912 TTs were judged, there was little doubt that the races had suffered a temporary setback. Entries were alarmingly down from 104 to 74, speeds in the Senior had advanced only fractionally and had been slower in the Junior, and the eighteen firms who had competed in 1911 and who were absent in 1912 were not wholly compensated for by the ten new firms who had entered.

While pessimists began to write off the TT Races, a number of innovations for 1913 were being worked out by the A-CU. Major changes were that races would be substantially longer and held over two days split as follows: Juniors to do two laps on the morning of day 1; Seniors to cover three laps in the afternoon. On the second day the survivors from the earlier races, or 75 per cent of the starters, whichever were the smaller, would compete together, the Junior competitors wearing blue waistcoats and the Seniors red. The A-CU took the machines into custody immediately following the end of the first day's races and no work was allowed to be done on them until the start of the second day. The races were brought forward almost a month and took place on Wednesday and Friday, 4th and 6th June. The changes worked wonders and Tom Loughborough, to whom the 1912 races had been a disappointing baptism to what was to become 34 years of secretaryship of the A-CU, was a much happier man. Entries doubled with 104 for the Senior race and 44 for the Junior. The Senior event boosted 32 different makes and the Junior 16. Honours in the Senior category again were taken by Scott, when H. Wood averaged 48.27 mph and also recorded the fastest lap at 52.12 mph.

The last TTs before the outbreak of war witnessed a reversal to the usual one-day-one-race system, crash helmets of an approved type were made compulsory, doubtless resulting from a large number of crashes in 1913 and the death of the leading Rudge competitor, T. Bateman. The dates for the race in 1914 were moved to 19th and 21st May and the sole petrol depot, at Douglas, had been properly equipped with pits. Again the races attracted strong following with 49 entries in the Junior (five more than in the previous year) and 111 in the Senior (against 104 in 1913). For the first year since the inception of the TT races a victory by a single-cylinder machine looked a possibility, with new AJS machines with side-valve engines and four speeds viewed as distinct favourites. The Junior event, won by E. Williams on an AJS with C. Williams also on an AJS in second place, was marred by the fatal accident to F. J. Walker. In the Senior event Cyril Pullin on the single-cylinder Rudge was the victor. Although the singles had proved themselves on the day it should not be forgotten that in the Junior race the ill-fated Walker was in the lead on his Royal Enfield twin until a third lap puncture delayed him. After completing repairs he set off in chase and in spite of a couple of falls finished in third position – an outstanding ride. It was after the finishing line had been crossed, and probably as a result of exhaustion and fatigue, that he crashed into the barrier and was killed. In the 1914 races Tim Wood on a Scott recorded a new fastest lap record in the Senior reaching 53.50 mph. To the Scott therefore went the distinction of setting up the fastest lap in all of the first four Mountain Course races.

Early Machines

Historically interesting, the machines entered in the early TT Races reflect the early development of the motor-cycle industry in Britain and, as it has already been noted, twin-cylinder machines took the honours until the singles first victory in 1914. In 1908 nearly all of the 36 starters rode single-gear models with direct belt-drive. For the first Mountain Junior race in 1911 there were six Humber twins, five NSUs (three singles and two twins), three New Hudson singles and three Alcyon singles from France. Also represented were AJS, Enfield, Matchless, Moto-Reve and Zenith-Gradua. Nearly all the machines had variable gears, popular type being the three-speed hub with direct belt-drive. The Enfields, though, had two speeds with all-chain drive and the Douglases two-speed countershaft boxes with chain and belt drive. The only single-gear machines in the race came from abroad.

In the Senior event of 1911 almost one third of the total entry, in contrast to the Junior race, rode single-gear machines and the majority had direct belt-drive. There were nine Triumphs and nine Rudges in the list, seven Matchlesses and five Indians. The then American champion and legendary figure Jake de Rosier led the Indian entry. The water-cooled Scotts were interesting as the smallest twins in the Senior event, with a capacity of 543cc. Although lacking a little speed on the straights they were said to be excellent to hold on corners and generally handled well.

For the 1912 races all the machines in the Junior race had moved up to near the 350cc limit, though there were three Singers at 299cc. And in the Senior race were entered two Junior models, though the remainder were all near the 500cc limit, the Scott twins at 486cc being the smallest. In the Junior, Douglas and Humber had five entries each followed by NSU with four, Singer three, Alcyon, Forward and NUT (two each), Ivy and OK (one each). Included in the ten makes absent from the previous year's entry were Enfield, Matchless, New Hudson and Zenith. In the Senior event of 1912 there were five newcomers, including a team of Regals, though Triumphs headed the entry with nine – all as "private owner" entries. Indians had five machines there. Rudge were not entered officially, though four private owners were mounted on the new Rudge multis. Among the eight firms who dropped out were Premier, Bat and Ariel.

In 1913 the entries included AJS and Enfield again, after their absence in 1912, and several new names included Levis and Veloce. A strong Douglas team of 13 on the flat twins headed the entry in the Junior. There were 32 different makes entered for the Senior of 1913 and though three makes withdrew, including the well-known Rex, newcomers included BSA, Ariel, Rover and Brough. Rudge and Triumph had twelve machines each and BSA and Indians had eight each. Rudge and Triumph returned as manufacturer entries.

In the Junior entry list of 1914 there were twelve Douglas machines, nine Enfields and five NUTs and AJSs, the latter with side-valve engines, but with four speeds, the four ratios being obtained by double primary-chain drive and a dog clutch, together with a two-speed countershaft gearbox. In the Senior there were thirty manufacturer entries. Indian and BSA had eight apiece, with seven each for Rudge and Triumph. There were six Scotts and six Zeniths, five Premiers and four Ariels, James', Matchlesses and NUTs. On one of the three new Sunbeams was H. R. Davies, who was to become one of the most famous TT riders of all time.

Between the Wars

Although the first mountain circuit TT witnessed the first foreign victory in the races – the rugged American Indian machines with their two-speed, chain-drive transmissions finishing in the first three places in the Senior event of 1911 – it was the demands made by the new course, with the gruelling climb and descent of Mount Snaefell, that forced the development of British machinery. It was during those last years before the war that the TT Races stimulated an exciting, growing enthusiasm for motor-cycle racing in Britain while curiously at the same time, interest on the Continent waned.

In 1920 it was seen that an enforced lapse of five war years had done nothing to dampen the British enthusiasm for the TTs and once again they became the central arena for successes which quickly developed into a Golden Age of motor-cycle racing for Britain. Manufacturers clamoured for the publicity and prestige of winning races and dominating the scene was the Isle of Man mountain course. When racing restarted it almost immediately became the standard by which other circuits were judged. The demands it made developed the type of rider and machine which for nearly twenty years were to dominate motor cycle racing in Europe.

Not only the TTs themselves, but the half dozen or so Grands Prix in Europe, were won repeatedly, almost up to the outbreak of the Second World War, by British machines developed over the mountain course and ridden by a cluster of British riders whose technique and daring resulted from regular competition in the TT. Sunbeam, AJS, Rudge, Velocette and, of course, Norton were names which became world famous, along with riders like Stanley Woods, Jimmy Simpson, Graham Walker, Freddie Frith, Harold Daniell, Jimmy Guthrie, Wal Handley and Alec Bennett:

and in spite of consistent challenge from the Continent, these supreme days for Britain continued for well over a decade.

By the mid-1930s however, the situation was markedly changing with the Italians and Germans challenging strongly. Guzzi, offering stiff competition to Norton in 500cc events, were making a successful impact, along with Benelli and the extremely fast supercharged two-strokes of the German DKW factory, in the lightweight category. A further threat in the Senior events was the 500cc twin-cylinder BMW from Germany and in 1939 there came a major milestone in TT history when Georg Meier won the Senior race and thus became the first foreign rider on a foreign machine to win this event. By then Continental factories, helped by government funds allocated in a drive for national prestige, had provided winners in all three solo classes.

A glance at the list of comprehensive results given elsewhere will quickly show how extensive was British domination of the TT Races between the wars. Norton alone between 1931 and the outbreak of war collected fourteen Tourist Trophies. The prestige and reputation of the races were never higher. The fastest average speed in the Senior rose from 51.48 mph in 1920 to 89.38 mph in 1939, while in the same period the fastest lap timing increased from 55.62 mph to 90.75 mph.

It was during the early years following the war that the TT races settled down into a regular festival of racing and "TT Week" became an annual pilgrimage for an increasing number of enthusiasts. Regular changes were made, of both major and minor importance, some successful, others not. The course itself was slightly enlarged for 1920 and, including the Governor's Bridge section, was now 37¾ miles in length. The start and finish, with the Grandstand of course, were moved to the Glencrutchery Road. A private telephone line was laid round the circuit so that marshals were able to report the arrival of each rider. On receipt of such news Boy Scouts were able to adjust the markings on large scoreboards which had been put up at the Grandstand to help spectators follow the progress of the race.

It was also in 1920 that, in acknowledgement of the increasing popularity of the 250cc class, a separate race within the Junior event was held. *Motor Cycle* provided a cup for the best performance by a lightweight machine. The following year, with the country settling down after the war, the TTs attracted twice the number of entries of 1920 with 68 in the Senior and 65 in the Junior; in the latter there were 21 lightweight machines. Little wonder that in 1922 the lightweights were given a separate race of their own. A significant winner in the Senior race of 1921 was Howard Davies, who became the first rider to win the Senior event on a 350cc machine. His average speed of 54.50 mph brought him home some 2¼ minutes ahead of the best 500. It was a fine year for AJS who also finished first, second and third in the Junior 350cc class.

The first Lightweight TT proper was in 1922 and was won by Geoff Davison on a Levis at 49.89 mph average. It was to be the last two-stroke TT victory until 1938.

In 1923 there came a further development with the introduction of the first Sidecar TT, incorporated into the race programme, as the A-CU explained, by popular demand. Entries for the year's races once again established a record, totalling 177. Eight different makes were represented in the fourteen competitors in the sidecar event. Biggest sensation was Yorkshireman Freddie Dixon's remarkable banking sidecar Douglas outfit which leaned over to the right or left as required. Dixon reckoned it was very much faster than a rigid-frame and on high-speed left-handers was capable of increasing the safe speed by as much as ten or fifteen miles an hour. He won the race, with Norton riders Walker and Tucker in second and third places.

The 1923 results were also noteworthy for the first inclusion of the great Stanley Woods, who won the Senior at an average of 55.55 mph and was to go on to complete ten TT victories, a record which lasted until the heyday of Hailwood.

In 1924 the programme was extended to include five races, with the addition of an Ultra-lightweight TT for machines with a capacity limit of 175cc. This race further wrote itself into TT history by the use, for the first time, of a massed start. Porter on a New Gerrard was first home (51.20 mph average) and also recorded the fastest lap at 52.61 mph. The five-race programme was maintained for 1925, after which it was reduced to three, lack of support eliminating the Ultra-lightweight and Sidecar TTs until 1951, when the Lightweight 125cc event was introduced, and 1954, when the sidecar TT returned, though an unsuccessful attempt to revive the Sidecar event had been made in 1933.

Among a number of notable events which charted the progress of the races through the twenty series of races between the wars were the following:

1924: first lap at more than 60 mph (Jimmy Simpson, 64.24 mph, 350cc AJS).
1926: a Guzzi, the first Italian machine to appear in the races, won the Lightweight TT, but rider Pietro Ghersi was disqualified because his declaration card gave a different make of plug from the one he used.
1926: dope fuel banned and petrol-benzole only allowed.
1926: first TT victory by an overhead camshaft machine (Alec Bennett's Velocette).
1926: first lap at more than 70 mph (Jimmy Simpson, 70.43 mph, 500cc AJS).
1927: first broadcast commentaries by the BBC.
1927: Alec Bennett rides the first Norton ohc to victory in the Senior event.
1928: for the first time, roads are closed during practice as well as during the races. The change resulted from a number of accidents which culminated in the death of Archie Birkin, when he crashed into a lorry.
1930: Rudge, at their first attempt in the Junior TT, gain first, second and third places.
1931: first lap at more than 80 mph (Jimmy Simpson, 80.82 mph, 500cc Norton).
1931: Graham Walker gains his first, and only, TT victory.
1931: Tim Hunt (Norton) becomes the first rider to win the Junior and Senior races in the same year.
1932: Stanley Woods (Norton) wins both Junior and Senior TTs.
1934: Jimmy Simpson gains his first, and only, TT victory in his thirteenth and final year of TT competition.
1934: Jimmy Guthrie (Norton) wins both Junior and Senior TTs.
1935: first Continental victory in the Senior – Stanley Woods (Guzzi).
1937: Omobono Tenni becomes the first foreign rider to win a TT (Lightweight) on a Guzzi.
1937: first lap at more than 90 mph (Freddie Frith, 90.27 mph, Norton).
1938: Harold Daniell's 91.00 mph lap was to stand until 1950.

Postwar Years

The almost absolute supremacy of British machines and British riders in the TT Races had witnessed the first tiny erosions as early as 1936, with DKW in the lightweight event, and then Guzzi, and in 1939 the auspicious victory by Georg Meier, constituting the first victory by a foreign rider on a foreign machine, in the Senior, was significant writing on the wall even if, as was the case, the Norton factory had given up competition temporarily to concentrate on war preparations.

For a remarkably long time after the TTs were restarted in 1947, helped by the postwar ban on superchargers, the reliability of the single-cylinder British bike kept the UK ahead of the world on the Isle of Man. In the first postwar TT for instance, Norton took first and second in the Senior, and Velocette first, second and third in the Junior, with a third in the Senior. In these two classes Britain held on tenaciously, surrendering the lightweight class earlier. Here, Guzzi moved immediately to the front, taking the Lightweight TT in the first three postwar races. By this time, 1949, there was no doubt about the developing power in motor-cycle racing of the Italians and it was not long before the speed and thrust of Gilera and then MV was to end the long and glorious reign of Britain in the Senior event. Reg Armstrong's third place in the Senior of 1953 on a Gilera was the first real sign and when Geoffrey Duke switched to Gilera the outcome was anticipated. The inevitable happened in 1955 when Gilera secured first and second places in the Senior and Guzzi first and third in the Junior. The lightweight class was already foreign dominated by MV, Mondial and NSU.

By this time Britain's pre-war power, vested especially in Velocette and Norton, had virtually disappeared. Velocette did not support an official works team in the postwar years and Norton, together with AJS, gave full works support in an international way for the last time in 1954. And so the exciting reign of Italy, with Guzzi, Gilera, MV and Mondial, had begun. Through much of the remainder of the fifties, the Italians carried all before them until the retirement of Gilera, Guzzi and Mondial in 1957 left a vacuum, into which Norton machines briefly fitted, until the emergence of first Honda, then Yamaha and Suzuki in the huge-investment days of the 1960s. A string of British tuners including people like Steve Lancefield, Tom Arter, Joe Potts, Tom Kirby and Ray Petty, were able to keep Manx Nortons and the Matchless G50s alive long after the factories had given up racing. Ridden by a group of stalwart British riders these die-hard machines were ever-ready to take over on the infrequent occasions when the Italian and Japanese entries faltered.

In the fifties and sixties the TT continued as a world focal point for motorcycle racing and various changes were made during the postwar years. Machines entered for the immediate postwar TTs were raced on "pool" petrol and it was not until 1950 that petrol-benzole was once more available and speeds began to move up dramatically, with most of the pre-war records falling. This coincided with the first of the "featherbed" frame Nortons, ridden to success by Geoff Duke and Artie Bell. A 125cc Lightweight TT was re-introduced in 1951 and a sidecar TT in 1954, at which point the 10.79 Clypse Circuit was opened in an attempt to cater more easily for the lower number of entries in these two, and (in 1955) also the 250cc class. It used some of the Mountain Circuit and provided massed starts. Use of the Clypse course was, however, abandoned after 1959, the increasing interest resulting in a return to the Mountain Course with a complete programme.

In the 1950s there was a trend towards full frontal streamlining, hiding the riders more and more from the view of spectators. In 1958 full frontal streamlining was banned, a popular move with spectators and safer indeed for the riders, who were endangered by big fairings during strong crosswinds, though the effect of the ban was to reduce speeds.

Starting in 1960 was the pattern for future TT weeks with two races taking place in each of three days. The races in 1961 were significant for three reasons: Mike Hailwood became the first rider to win three TTs in a week; and Honda dominated the lightweight classes and took the first five places in both the 125cc and 250cc classes. In the Senior TT every one of the 45 machines which finished were British – 24 Nortons, 14 Matchlesses, five AJSs and two BSAs. This, of course, was before the days of Honda in the Senior and after the retirement from racing of the Italian factories. Hocking on the MV retired. A 50cc event was introduced in 1962 with Suzuki (first) and Honda occupying second and third positions. In 1959 a standard production machine race (Formula 1) was tried out for 350 and 500cc machines, the idea being immediately abandoned, not to reappear until the Diamond Jubilee of the TT in 1967, which incorporated three production machine TT events, for 750cc, 500cc and 250cc machines. In 1968 two categories of the Sidecar TT (for 500cc and 750cc outfits) were established, this year there being no fewer than ten different events. The 50cc TT was dropped for 1969. A Formula 750cc TT was begun in 1971.

The 125cc TT was dropped from the programme, then reinstated, in both 1973 and 1974, but with time fully allocated for 1975, there appeared little hope of a similar reprieve.

With the 90-mph lap established by Freddie Frith before the war, it was not long after the re-start of the races that speculation rose over the possibility of the first 100 mph lap. In the mid-fifties this particular landmark had almost been reached and in 1955 Geoff Duke was actually announced over the loudspeakers as having achieved the distinction on the third lap of the Senior on his Gilera; but then a correction was announced. Duke had reached 99.97 mph! The record was finally achieved, appropriately, during the Golden Jubilee TT Races of 1957 when Bob McIntyre became the first man to lap the circuit at more than 100 mph. His time of 22 mins 23.2 secs was equivalent to 101.12 mph. Only three years later in 1960 John Surtees and John Hartie became the first riders to record an *average* time for the race in excess of 100 mph – both on MVs at 102.44 (Surtees) and 100.44 (Hartle). To Derek Minter goes the distinction of being the first man to lap the Mountain Circuit at over 100 mph on a single cylinder machine – a record he achieved on his Lancefield Norton in 1960. Other outstanding speed occasions include Mike Hailwood's average of 100.60 mph on a Manx Norton (1961), Agostini's standing start lap of 108.38 mph (1967) and Bill Ivy's lap of 100.32 mph on the 125cc Yamaha (1968).

After the sensational domination by the Japanese in the 1960s, the Production TT was to lead the way back for Britain, not in the established Grand Prix classes, but in the new Formula 750 racing, where a new generation of British machinery had come about as a result of production events. The development of 750cc racing decided the A-CU to adopt the F750 TT of 1974 as its main event – and out went the Production race which had started it all. But it was revived in 1974 as a 1000cc event.

The first F750 TT in 1971 was won by Tony Jefferies on a Triumph Trident at 102.85 average. Winners since then have been Ray Pickrell on a Triumph in 1972, Peter Williams on a Norton in 1973 and Charlie Mortimer on a Yamaha in 1974. In spite of predictions to the contrary, and Peter Williams challenging to within an ace of it, the TT lap record of 108.77 mph set up by Mike Hailwood on a 500cc Honda in 1967 was still intact after the TTs of 1975.

The developing importance of F750 racing in the TTs was suggested in the summer of 1974, when the A-CU announced the distinct possibility of a two-leg F750 TT for 1975. But when the 1975 programme was announced towards the end of the year, a 300cc–1000cc six-lap open-to-all free-formula TT replaced the F750 race.

In recent years the TT races have been increasingly criticised by many of the world's top riders and this came to a head in the 1970s. Even in the 1960s, home circuit experts like John Cooper and Derek Minter declared that the rewards on the Isle of Man were inadequate and from a financial point of view made it not worth their while to compete. More bitter condemnation was levelled at the TTs in the early 1970s with riders of the calibre of Read, Agostini, Gould and others coming out strongly against the dangers of the Mountain Course. The TTs, as a world championship occasion, seemed to live from year to year under a growing call for a shorter road course which would be safer.

The A-CU's reply to this growing criticism was to increase the prize money and to remind everyone that the Mountain Course was still the most challenging circuit and the TT still the greatest series of road races in the world. The A-CU Chairman Norman Dixon declared: "The TT has become known as the classic of the classics. Since 1911 these races have been regarded by the connoisseur as the supreme test of rider and machine, so much so that there can be very few, if any, road racing world champions who did not graduate on the Isle of Man." Prize money for the 1975 series was fixed at £15,650, a 15 per cent increase on the 1974 figure which was itself a record. Also arranged were additional prizes of £50 for each rider who qualified for the seven races.

But in spite of these moves, the threat to the world status of the TTs grew. The FIM's racing commission drew up a list of circuits which did not meet their new stringent safety requirements and in it included the Isle of Man Mountain Course. Then, in the autumn of 1974, the FIM made the first definite moves to drop the TTs from the classics calendar, in the face of considerable pressure to abandon true road race circuits in favour of track races of the type on which the majority of world championship events are now held. The claim was that as speeds had increased, circuits like that on the Isle of Man had become too dangerous. The idea, expected to be confirmed in the spring of 1975, was to continue in that year with 250, 350, 500 and sidecar events counting for the World Championship, but from 1976, the TT Races would not be included in the World Championship programme.

Even with the loss of world championship status, the TT races appeared in no danger in themselves. Indeed, the FIM indicated that in such circumstances they would recognise the TT in a special manner with an FIM Supreme Road Race, or a similar title, and would contribute a special prize from FIM funds to the TT Races. It was also suggested that the TT Races could become a vital round in a new-look road racing world championship series since the A-CU were said to be considering co-operating with other organisers of events held on true road courses to start their own championship series. These could include the Yugoslav, Finnish and Czech Grands Prix; the

Nurburgring, where the West German Grand Prix is held on alternate years; and the Ulster Grand Prix.

In spite of the absence of some of the top international racers – including Phil Read and Giacomo Agostini – the 1974 TTs attracted a record number of visitors.

In April 1976 the anticipated withdrawal of World Championship status from the TT Races was announced. The decision of the Bureau Centrale, chief policy-making committee of the FIM, indicated that in 1977 the TT would be granted special status. Ironically, it was Phil Read, who had voiced much criticism of the TT Races and had assisted therefore in their demise as a World Championship event, who was the surprise hero of the 1977 races. He returned to the Island and won the Senior TT on a Suzuki and also the TT Formula 1 race, a new class, on an 820cc Honda.

Despite its loss of World Championship status, the TT races proved they were more than just a series of motor-cycling events. The Isle of Man in June continued to be an inescapable pilgrimage for thousands, helped in 1978 by the return of undoubtedly the greatest motor bike personality of modern times, Mike Hailwood.

And it was Hailwood, on what he said was positively his last appearance as a competitor on the Isle of Man, who stole the limelight with a dramatic performance on a Suzuki in the Senior event. He scored a magical runaway victory, his fourteenth on the Island, with a staggering new class record of 114.02 mph only 3.2 seconds outside Mick Grant's absolute record set on a Kawasaki the year before.

A new overall lap record for the Mountain Course was established in 1980 by Joey Dunlop on a 750cc Yamaha, who broke Mick Grant's previous record on lap five of the six-lap event and on the final lap beat his own new record with a record lap of 115.22 mph.

See also GRAND PRIX RACING; TECHNICAL DEVELOPMENT.

Year	RACE Class	Miles	Rider	Machine	Time hms	Speed mph	Fastest Laps	Time ms	Speed mph
1907	**Twins**	158⅛	1 H. Rem Fowler	Norton	4.21.53	36.22	H. Rem Fowler	22.06	42.91
			2 W. H. Wells	Vindec	4.53.04	32.21	Norton		
			3 W. M. Heaton	Rex	5.11.04	28.50			
	Singles	158⅛	1 C. R. Collier	Matchless	4.08.08	38.22	H. A. Collier	23.05	41.81
			2 J. Marshall	Triumph	4.19.47	37.11	Matchless		
			3 F. Hulbert	Triumph	4.27.50	35.89			
1908	**Twins**	158⅛	1 H. Reed	D.O.T.	4.05.58	38.59	W. H. Bashall	22.27	42.25
			2 W. H. Bashall	B.A.T.	4.08.15	37.18	B.A.T.		
			3 R. O. Clark	F. N.	4.11.03	36.19			
	Singles	158⅛	1 J. Marshall	Triumph	3.54.50	40.49	J. Marshall	22.20	42.48
			2 C. R. Collier	Matchless	3.57.07	40.01	Triumph		
			3 Sir R. Arbuthnot	Triumph	4.07.57	38.22			
1909		158½	1 H. A. Collier	Matchless	3.13.37	49.01	H. A. Collier	18.05	52.27
			2 G. L. Evans	Indian	3.17.35	47.28	Matchless		
			3 W. F. Newsome	Triumph	3.31.10	45.88			
1910		158⅛	1 C. R. Collier	Matchless	3.07.24	50.63	H. H. Bowen	17.51	53.15
			2 H. A. Collier	Matchless	3.12.45	48.61	B.A.T.		
			3 W. Creyton	Triumph	3.17.58	46.28			
1911	**Senior**	187½	1 O. C. Godfrey	Indian	3.56.10	47.63	F. Philipp	44.52	50.11
			2 C. B. Franklin	Indian	3.59.52	46.81	Scott		
			3 A. Moorhouse	Indian	4.05.34	45.39			
	Junior	150	1 P. J. Evans	Humber	3.37.07	41.45	P. J. Evans	53.24	42.00
			2 H. A. Collier	Matchless	3.46.20	40.09	Humber		
			3 H. J. Cox	Forward	3.55.56	38.23			
1912	**Senior**	187½	1 F. A. Applebee	Scott	3,51.08	48.69	F. A. Applebee	45.31	49.44
			2 J. R. Haswell	Triumph	3.57.57	46.41	Scott		
			3 H. A. Collier	Matchless	4.01.56	44.89			
	Junior	150	1 W. H. Bashall	Douglas	3.46.59	39.65	E. Kickham	53.53	41.76
			2 E. Kickham	Douglas	3.51.36	37.58	Douglas		
			3 H. J. Cox	Forward	4.06.29	34.27			
1913	**Senior**	262½	1 H. O. Wood	Scott	5.26.18	48.27	H. O. Wood	43.10	52.12

			2 W. F. Newsome	Douglas	5.09.30	43.69	N.U.T.		
			3 H. C. Newman	Ivy Green	5.23.06	41.57			
1914	**Senior**	225	1 C. G. Pullin	Rudge	4.32.48	49.49	H. O. Wood	42.16	53.50
			2 {H. R. Davies	Sunbeam	4.39.12	48.50	Scott		
			2 {O. C. Godfrey	Indian	4.39.12	48.50			
	Junior	187½	1 E. Williams	A.J.S.	4.06.50	45.58	E. Williams	47.18	47.57
			2 C. Williams	A.J.S.	4.11.34	44.88	A.J.S.		
			3 F. J. Walker	Royal Enfield	4.19.55	43.72			
1920	**Senior**	226½	1 T. C. De La Hay	Sunbeam	4.22.23	51.48	G. Dance	40.53	55.62
			2 D. M. Brown	Norton	4.26.15	51.00	Sunbeam		
			3 W. R. Brown	Sunbeam	4.32.27	49.68			
	Junior 350c.c.	187½	1 C. Williams	A.J.S.	4.37.57	40.74	E. Williams	44.06	51.36
			2 J. Watson-Bourne	Blackburne	4.47.07	39.10	A.J.S.		
			3 J. Holroyd	Blackburne	4.47.37	39.09			
	Junior 250c.c.	187½	1 R. O. Clark	Levis	4.55.37	38.30	R. O. Clark	52.37	43.00
			2 G. Kuhn	Levis	—	35.61	Levis		
			3 F. W. Applebee	Levis	—	31.00			
1921	**Senior**	226½	1 H. R. Davies	350cc A.J.S.	4.09.22	54.50	F. G. Edmond	40.08	56.40
			2 F. W. Dixon	Indian	4.11.35	54.02	Triumph		
			3 H. Le Vack	Indian	4.12.06	53.91			
	Junior 350cc	187½	1 E. Williams	A.J.S.	3.37.23	52.11	H. R. Davies	41.04	55.15
			2 H. R. Davies	A.J.S.	3.41.10	51.20	A.J.S.		
			3 T. M. Sheard	A.J.S.	3.49.09	49.42			
	Junior 250cc	187½	1 D. G. Prentice	New Imperial	4.12.37	44.61	B. Kershaw	49.07	46.11
			2 G. S. Davison	Levis	—	44.33	New Imperial		
			3 W. G. Harrison	Velocette	—	43.14			
1922	**Senior**	226½	1 A. Bennett	Sunbeam	3.53.02	58.31	A. Bennett	37.46	59.99
			2 W. Brandish	Triumph	4.00.22	56.52	Sunbeam		
			3 H. Langman	Scott	4.02.14	56.09			
	Junior	187½	1 T. M. Sheard	A.J.S.	3.26.38	54.75	H. Le Vack	40.07	56.46
			2 G. Grinton	A.J.S.	3.37.17	53.00	New Imperial		
			3 J. Thomas	Sheffield Henderson	3.47.28	50.00			
	Light-weight	187½	1 G. S. Davison	Levis	3.46.56	49.89	W. L. Handley	44.24	51.00
			2 D. Young	Rex-Acme	4.00.17	47.12	O.K.		
			3 S. J. Jones	Velocette	4.01.31	46.90			

Year	RACE Class	Miles	Rider	Machine	Time hms	Speed mph	Fastest Laps	Time ms	Speed mph
1923	**Senior**	226½	1 T. M. Sheard	Douglas	4.04.43	55.55	J. Whalley	37.54	59.74
			2 G. M. Black	Norton	4.06.26	55.14	Douglas		
			3 F. W. Dixon	Indian	4.07.02	55.00			
	Junior	226½	1 S. Woods	Cotton	4.03.47	55.73	J. Simpson	38.00	59.59
			2 H. F. Harris	A.J.S.	4.06.16	55.16	A.J.S.		
			3 A. H. Alexander	Douglas	4.09.35	54.43			
	Light-weight	226½	1 J. A. Porter	New Gerrard	4.21.37	51.93	W. L. Handley	41.58	53.95
			2 H. Le Vack	New Imperial	4.26.19	51.01	O.K.		
			3 D. Hall	Rex-Acme	4.34.20	49.53			
	Sidecar	113¼	1 F. W. Dixon	Douglas	2.07.48	53.15	H. Langman	41.24	54.69
			2 G. W. Walker	Norton	2.09.26	52.50	Scott		
			3 G. H. Tucker	Norton	2.10.27	52.07			
1924	**Senior**	226½	1 A. Bennett	Norton	3.40.24	61.64	F. W. Dixon	35.31	63.75
			2 H. Langman	Scott	3.41.51	61.23	Douglas		
			3 F. W. Dixon	Douglas	3.45.46	60.17			
	Junior	226½	1 K. Twemlow	New Imperial	4.04.21	55.67	J. H. Simpson	35.05	64.54
			2 S. Ollerhead	D.O.T.	4.07.26	54.91	A.J.S.		
			3 H. R. Scott	A.J.S.	4.09.01	54.55			
	Light-weight	226½	1 E. Twemlow	New Imperial	4.05.03	55.44	E. Twemlow	38.51	58.28
			2 H. F. Brockbank	Cotton	4.17.05	52.85	New Imperial		
			3 J. Cooke	D.O.T.	4.18.33	52.54			
	Ultra Light-weight	113¼	1 J. A. Porter	New Gerrard	2.12.40	51.20	J. A. Porter	43.02	52.61
			2 F. G. Morgan	Cotton	2.17.11	49.51	New Gerrard		
			3 C. Stead	Cotton	2.17.39	49.34			
	Sidecar	151	1 G. H. Tucker	Norton	2.56.31	51.31	F. W. Dixon	42.32	53.23
			2 H. Reed	D.O.T.	3.26.46	43.80	Douglas		
			3 A. Tinkler	Matador	3.33.03	42.49			
1925	**Senior**	226½	1 H. R. Davies	H.R.D.	2.25.25.8	66.13	J. H. Simpson	32.50	68.97
			2 F. A. Longman	A.J.S.	3.29.10	64.95	A.J.S.		
			3 A. Bennett	Norton	3.30.08	64.65			
	Junior	226½	1 W. L. Handley	Rex-Acme	3.28.56.4	65.02	W. L. Handley	34.23	65.89

			3 K. Twemlow	New Imperial	4.03.19	55.83			
	Ultra-Light-weight	151	1 W. L. Handley	Rex-Acme	2.49.27	53.45	W. L. Handley	41.52	54.12
			2 C. W. Johnston	Cotton	2.53.54	52.08	Rex-Acme		
			3 J. A. Porter	New Gerrard	2.57.40	50.98			
	Sidecar	151	1 L. Parker	Douglas	2.44.01.8	55.22	F. W. Dixon	39.36	57.18
			2 A. E. Taylor	Norton	2.45.58	54.57	Douglas		
			3 G. Grinton	Norton	2.46.45	54.31			
1926	Senior	264½	1 S. Woods	Norton	3.54.39.8	67.54	J. H. Simpson	32.09	70.43
			2 W. L. Handley	Rex-Acme	3.59.00.4	66.31	A.J.S.		
			3 F. A. Longman	A.J.S.	4.00.03.4	66.03			
	Junior	264¼	1 A. Bennett	Velocette	3.57.37	66.70	A. Bennett	32.56	68.75
			2 J. H. Simpson	A.J.S.	4.08.02	63.90	Velocette		
			3 W. L. Handley	Rex-Acme	4.10.06	63.37			
	Light-weight	264¼	1 C. W. Johnston	Cotton	4.23.16.4	60.20	P. Ghersi	35.49	63.12
			2 F. G. Morgan	Cotton	4.47.30.4	55.15	Guzzi		
			3 W. Colgan	Cotton	4.56.05	53.53			
1927	Senior	264¼	1 A. Bennett	Norton	3.51.42	68.41	S. Woods	31.54	70.90
			2 J. Guthrie	New Hudson	4.00.04	66.02	Norton		
			3 T. Simister	Triumph	4.01.03	65.75			
	Junior	264¼	1 F. W. Dixon	H.R.D.	3.55.54	67.19	W. L. Handley	32.44	69.18
			2 H. J. Willis	Velocette	4.04.39	64.78	Rex-Acme		
			3 J. H. Simpson	A.J.S.	4.04.52	64.33			
	Light-weight	264¼	1 W. L. Handley	Rex-Acme	4.10.22	63.30	A. Bennett	35.08	64.45
			2 L. Arhangeli	Guzzi	4.18.52	61.22	O.K.-Supreme		
			3 C. T. Ashby	O.K.-Supreme	4.19.24	61.10			
1928	Senior	264¼	1 C. J. P. Dodson	Sunbeam	4.11.40	62.98	J. H. Simpson	32.20	67.94
			2 G. E. Rowley	A.J.S.	4.18.41	61.27	A.J.S.		
			3 T. L. Hatch	Scott	4.20.18	60.89			
	Junior	264¼	1 A. Bennett	Velocette	3.50.52	68.65	A. Bennett	32.13	70.28
			2 H. J. Willis	Velocette	3.56.00	67.16	Velocette		
			3 K. Twemlow	D.O.T.	4.08.57	63.67			
	Light-weight	264¼	1 F. A. Longman	O.K.-Supreme	4.11.59	62.90	F. A. Longman	35.08	64.45
			2 C. S. Barrow	Royal Enfield	4.29.01	58.92	O.K.-Supreme		
			3 E. Twemlow	D.O.T.	4.29.26	58.83			

Year	RACE Class	Miles	Rider	Machine	Time hms	Speed mph	Fastest Laps	Time ms	Speed mph
1929	**Senior**	264¼	1 C. J. P. Dodson	Sunbeam	3.39.59	72.05	C. J. P. Dodson	30.47	73.55
			2 A. Bennett	Sunbeam	3.44.47	70.51	Sunbeam		
			3 H. G. Tyrell-Smith	Rudge	3.45.37	70.25			
	Junior	264¼	1 F. G. Hicks	Velocette	3.47.23	69.71	F. G. Hicks	31.55	70.95
			2 W. L. Handley	A.J.S.	3.48.45	69.29	Velocette		
			3 A. Bennett	Velocette	3.49.97	68.97			
	Light-weight	264¼	1 S. A. Crabtree	Excelsior	4.08.10	63.87	P. Ghersi	35.49	63.12
			2 K. Twemlow	D.O.T.	4.13.25	62.55	Guzzi		
			3 F. A. Longman	O.K.-Supreme	4.16.33	61.78			
1930	**Senior**	264¼	1 W. L. Handley	Rudge	3.33.30	74.24	W. L. Handley	29.41	76.28
			2 G. W. Walker	Rudge	3.36.49	73.10	Rudge		
			3 J. H. Simpson	Norton	3.38.01	72.70			
	Junior	264¼	1 H. G. Tyrell-Smith	Rudge	3.43.00	71.08	G. E. Nott	31.21	72.20
			2 G. E. Nott	Rudge	3.43.35	70.89	Rudge		
			3 G. W. Walker	Rudge	3.43.58	70.77			
	Light-weight	264¼	1 A. J. Guthrie	A.J.S.	4.04.56	64.71	W. L. Handley	33.52	66.86
			2 C. W. Johnston	O.K.-Supreme	4.07.23	64.07	Rex-Acme		
			3 C. S. Barrow	O.K.-Supreme	4.09.27	63.54			
1931	**Senior**	264¼	1 P. Hunt	Norton	3.23.28	77.90	J. H. Simpson	28.01	80.82
			2 A. J. Guthrie	Norton	3.24.57	77.34	Norton		
			3 S. Woods	Norton	3.27.36	76.35			
	Junior	264¼	1 P. Hunt	Norton	3.34.21	73.94	P. Hunt	30.05	75.27
			2 A. J. Guthrie	Norton	3.37.26	72.90	Norton		
			3 G. E. Nott	Rudge	3.39.01	72.37			
	Light-weight	264¼	1 G. W. Walker	Rudge	3.49.47	68.98	G. E. Nott	31.34	71.73
			2 H. G. Tyrell-Smith	Rudge	3.52.13	68.26	Rudge		
			3 E. A. Mellors	New Imperial	3.57.08	66.84			
1932	**Senior**	264¼	1 S. Woods	Norton	3.19.40	79.38	J. H. Simpson	27.47	81.50
			2 A. J. Guthrie	Norton	3.21.59	78.47	Norton		
			3 J. H. Simpson	Norton	3.22.13	78.38			
	Junior	264¼	1 S. Woods	Norton	3.25.25	77.16	S. Woods	28.48	78.62
			2 W. L. Handley	Rudge	3.27.35	76.36	Norton		

	weight		2 G. W. Walker	Rudge	3.46.13	70.07	Rudge		
			3 W. L. Handley	Rudge	3.46.53	69.86			
1933	Senior	264¼	1 S. Woods	Norton	3.15.35	81.04	S. Woods	27.22	82.74
			2 J. H. Simpson	Norton	31.17.07	80.41	Norton		
			3 P. Hunt	Norton	3.17.43	80.16			
	Junior	264¼	1 S. Woods	Norton	3.23.00	78.08	S. Woods	28.35	79.22
			2 P. Hunt	Norton	3.23.07	78.03	Norton		
			3 A. J. Guthrie	Norton	3.26.56	76.59			
	Light-weight	264¼	1 S. Gleave	Excelsior	3.41.23	71.59	S. Gleave	31.11	72.62
			2 C. J. P. Dodson	New Imperial	3.43.43	70.85	Excelsior		
			3 C. H. Manders	Rudge	3.49.08	69.17			
1934	Senior	264¼	1 A. J. Guthrie	Norton	3.23.10	78.01	S. Woods	28.08	80.49
			2 J. H. Simpson	Norton	3.30.35	75.27	Husqvarna		
			3 W. F. Rusk	Velocette	3.36.19	73.27			
	Junior	264¼	1 A. J. Guthrie	Norton	3.20.14	79.16	A. J. Guthrie	28.16	80.11
			2 J. H. Simpson	Norton	3.20.23	79.10	Norton		
			3 G. E. Nott	Husqvarna	3.26.02	76.93			
	Light-weight	264¼	1 J. H. Simpson	Rudge	3.43.50	70.81	J. H. Simpson	30.45	73.64
			2 G. E. Nott	Rudge	3.47.07	69.76	Rudge		
			3 G. W. Walker	Rudge	3.54.13	67.67			
1935	Senior	264¼	1 S. Woods	Guzzi	3.07.10	84.68	S. Woods	26.10	86.53
			2 A. J. Guthrie	Norton	3.07.14	84.65	Guzzi		
			3 W. F. Rusk	Norton	3.09.45	83.53			
	Junior	264¼	1 A. J. Guthrie	Norton	3.20.16	79.14	W. F. Rusk	28.19	79.96
			2 W. F. Rusk	Norton	3.21.22	78.71	Norton		
			3 J. H. White	Norton	3.22.42	78.19			
	Light-weight	264¼	1 S. Woods	Guzzi	3.41.29	71.56	S. Woods	30.31	74.19
			2 H. G. Tyrell-Smith	Rudge	3.44.17	70.67	Guzzi		
			3 G. E. Nott	Rudge	3.48.30	69.37			
1936	Senior	264¼	1 A. J. Guthrie	Norton	3.04.43	85.80	S. Woods	26.02	86.98
			2 S. Woods	Velocette	3.05.01	85.66	Velocette		
			3 F. L. Frith	Norton	3.07.35	84.49			
	Junior	264¼	1 F. L. Frith	Norton	3.17.46	80.14	F. L. Frith	27.38	81.94
			2 J. H. White	Norton	3.23.16	77.97	Norton		
			3 E. A. Mellors	Velocette	3.23.25	77.91			

Year	RACE Class	Miles	Rider	Machine	Time hms	Speed mph	Fastest Laps	Time ms	Speed mph
1936 cont.	**Light-weight**	264¼	1 A. R. Foster 2 H. G. Tyrell-Smith 3 A. Geiss	New Imperial Excelsior D.K.W.	3.33.22 3.38.34 3.38.37	74.28 72.51 72.49	S. Woods D.K.W.	29.43	.76.20
1937	**Senior**	264¼	1 F. L. Frith 2 S. Woods 3 J. H. White	Norton Velocette Norton	2.59.41 2.59.56 3.08.44	88.21 88.09 83.97	F. L. Frith Norton	25.05	90.27
	Junior	264¼	1 A. J. Guthrie 2 F. L. Frith 3 J. H. White	Norton Norton Norton	3.07.42 3.10.17 3.12.00	84.43 83.29 82.54	F. L. Frith & A. J. Guthrie Norton	26.35	85.18
	Light-weight	264¼	1 O. Tenni 2 S. Wood 3 E. R. Thomas	Guzzi Excelsior D.K.W.	3.32.06 3.32.43 3.36.36	74.72 74.50 73.17	O. Tenni Guzzi	29.08	77.72
1938	**Senior**	264¼	1 H. L. Daniell 2 S. Woods 3 F. L. Frith	Norton Velocette Norton	2.57.50.6 2.58.05.8 2.58.07.4	89.11 88.99 88.98	H. L. Daniell Norton	24.52.6	91.00
	Junior	264¼	1 S. Woods 2 E. A. Mellors 3 F. L. Frith	Velocette Velocette Norton	3.08.30 3.12.20 3.12.27	84.08 82.40 82.35	S. Woods Velocette	26.33	85.30
	Light-weight	264¼	1 E. Kluge 2 S. Wood 3 H. G. Tyrell-Smith	D.K.W. Excelsior Excelsior	3.21.56 3.33.05 3.35.16	78.48 74.38 73.62	E. Kluge D.K.W.	28.11	80.35
1939	**Senior**	264¼	1 G. Meier 2 J. M. West 3 F. L. Frith	B.M.W. B.M.W. Norton	2.57.19 2.59.39 3.00.11	89.38 88.22 87.96	G. Meier B.M.W.	24.57	90.75
	Junior	264¼	1 S. Woods 2 H. L. Daniell 3 H. Fleischmann	Velocette Norton D.K.W.	3.10.10 3.10.38 3.12.05	83.19 83.13 82.51	H. L. Daniell Norton	26.38	85.05
	Light-weight	264¼	1 E. A. Mellors 2 E. Kluge 3 H. G. Tyrell-Smith	Benelli D.K.W. Excelsior	3.33.26 3.37.11 3.40.23	74.25 72.97 71.91	S. Woods Guzzi	28.58	78.16
1947	**Senior**	264¼	1 H. L. Daniell						

			3 J. A. Weddell	Velocette	3.28.07	76.15			
	Light-weight	264¼	1 M. Barrington	Guzzi	3.36.26.6	73.22	M. Cann	30.17	74.78
			2 M. Cann	Guzzi	3.37.10.8	72.97	Guzzi		
			3 B. Drinkwater	Excelsior	3.45.57	70.14			
1948	**Senior**	264¼	1 A. J. Bell	Norton	3.06.31	84.97	O. Tenni	25.43	88.06
			2 W. Doran	Norton	3.17.16	80.34	Guzzi		
			3 J. A. Weddell	Norton	3.19.11.2	79.56			
	Junior	264¼	1 F. L. Frith	Velocette	3.14.33.6	81.45	F. L. Frith	27.28	82.45
			2 A. R. Foster	Velocette	3.19.12.6	79.55	Velocette		
			3 A. J. Bell	Norton	3.20.50.6	78.91			
	Light-weight	264¼	1 M. Cann	Guzzi	3.30.49	75.18	M. Cann	29.31	76.72
			2 R. H. Pike	Rudge	3.40.33.4	71.86	Guzzi		
			3 D. St. J. Beasley	Ecelsior	3.54.09	67.68			
1949	**Senior**	264¼	1 H. L. Daniell	Norton	3.02.18.6	86.93	A. R. Foster	25.14	89.75
			2 R. St. J. Lockett	Norton	3.03.52.4	86.19	Guzzi		
			3 E. Lyons	Velocette	3.05.22	85.50			
	Junior	264¼	1 F. L. Frith	Velocette	3.10.36	83.15	F. L. Frith	26.53	84.23
			2 E. Lyons	Velocette	3.11.08	82.92	Velocette		
			3 A. J. Bell	Norton	3.11.49	82.62			
	Light-weight	264¼	1 M. Barrington	Guzzi	3.23.13.2	77.96	R. H. Dale &	28.09	80.44
			2 T. L. Wood	Guzzi	3.23.25.8	77.91	T. L. Wood		
			3 R. H. Pike	Rudge	3.37.42.6	72.79	Guzzi		
1950	**Senior**	264¼	1 G. E. Duke	Norton	2.51.45.6	92.27	G. E. Duke	24.16	93.33
			2 A. J. Bell	Norton	2.54.25.6	90.85	Norton		
			3 R. St. J. Lockett	Norton	2.55.22.4	90.37			
	Junior	264¼	1 A. J. Bell	Norton	3.03.35	86.33	A. J. Bell	25.56	86.49
			2 G. E. Duke	Norton	3.04.52	85.73	Norton		
			3 H. L. Daniell	Norton	3.07.56	84.33			
	Light-weight	264¼	1 D. Ambrosini	Benelli	3.22.58	78.08	D. Ambrosini	27.59	80.91
			2 M. Cann	Guzzi	3.22.58.2	78.07	Benelli		
			3 R. A. Mead	Velocette	3.29.38	75.60			
1951	**Senior**	264¼	1 G. E. Duke	Norton	2.48.56.8	93.83	G. E. Duke	23.47	95.22
			2 W. Doran	A.J.S.	2.53.19.2	91.44	Norton		
			3 W. McCandless	Norton	2.55.27	90.33			

Year	RACE Class	Miles	Rider	Machine	Time hm's	Speed mph	Fastest Laps	Time ms	Speed mph
1951 cont.	**Junior**	264¼	1 G. E. Duke	Norton	2.56.17.6	89.90	G. E. Duke	24.47	91.38
			2 R. St. J. Lockett	Norton	2.59.35	88.25	Norton		
			3 J. Brett	Norton	3.00.22.4	87.87			
	Light-weight 250cc	151	1 T. L. Wood	Guzzi	1.51.15.8	81.39	F. K. Anderson	27.03	83.70
			2 D. Ambrosini	Benelli	1.51.24.2	81.29	Guzzi		
			3 E. Lorenzetti	Guzzi	1.55.00	78.75			
	Light-weight 125cc	75½	1 W. McCandless	Mondial	1.00.30	74.85	W. McCandless	30.03	75.34
			2 C. Ubbiali	Mondial	1.00.52.4	74.38	Mondial		
			3 G. Leoni	Mondial	1.03.19.8	71.52			
1952	**Senior**	264¼	1 H. R. Armstrong	Norton	2.50.28.4	92.97	G. E. Duke	23.52	94.88
			2 R. L. Graham	M.V.	2.50.55	92.72	Norton		
			3 W. R. Amm	Norton	2.51.31.2	92.40			
	Junior	264¼	1 G. E. Duke	Norton	2.55.30.6	90.29	G. E. Duke	24.53	91.00
			2 H. R. Armstrong	Norton	2.56.57.8	89.55	Norton		
			3 R. W. Coleman	A.J.S.	2.58.12.4	88.93			
	Light-weight 250cc	151	1 F. K. Anderson	Guzzi	1.48.08.6	83.82	B. Ruffo	26.42	84.82
			2 E. Lorenzetti	Guzzi	1.48.40.8	83.36	Guzzi		
			3 S. Lawson	Guzzi	1.49.43.2	82.54			
	Light-weight 125cc	113¼	1 C. C. Sandford	M.V.	1.29.54.8	75.54	C. C. Sandford	29.46	76.07
			2 C. Ubbiali	Mondial	1.31.35	74.16	M.V.		
			3 A. L. Parry	Mondial	1.34.02.6	72.22			
1953	**Senior**	264¼	1 W. R. Amm	Norton	2.48.51.8	93.85	W. R. Amm	23.15	97.41
			2 J. Brett	Norton	2.49.03.8	93.74	Norton		
			3 H. R. Armstrong	Gilera	2.49.16.8	93.62			
	Junior	264¼	1 W. R. Amm	Norton	2.55.05	90.52	W. R. Amm	24.40	91.82
			2 K. T. Kavanagh	Norton	2.55.14.6	90.44	Norton		
			3 F. K. Anderson	Guzzi	2.57.40.6	89.41			
	Light-weight 250cc	151	1 F. K. Anderson	Guzzi	1.46.53	84.73	F. K. Anderson	26.29	85.52
			2 W. Haas	N.S.U.	1.47.10	84.52	Guzzi		
			3 S. Wunsche	D.K.W.	1.51.20	81.34			

			2 G. E. Duke	Gilera	1.43.52.6	87.19	Norton		
			3 J. Brett	Norton	1.45.15.2	86.04			
	Junior	188¾	1 R. Coleman	A.J.S.	2.3.41.8	91.51	W. R. Amm	23.56	94.61
			2 D. Farrant	A.J.S.	2.05.34	90.15	Norton		
			3 R. D. Keeler	Norton	2.05.43.6	90.03			
	Light-weight 250cc	113¼	1 W. Haas	N.S.U.	1.14.44.4	90.88	W. Haas	24.49.4	91.22
			2 R. Hollaus	N.S.U.	1.15.28.6	89.99	N.S.U.		
			3 H. R. Amstrong	N.S.U.	1.15.31.8	89.92			
	Light-weight 125cc	114	1 R. Hollaus	N.S.U.	1.33.03.4	69.57	R. Hollaus	9.03.4	71.53
			2 C. Ubbiali	M.V.	1.33.07.4	69.52	N.S.U.		
			3 C. C. Sandford	M.V.	1.37.35.8	66.35			
	Sidecar	114	1 E. Oliver	Norton	1.34.00.2	68.87	E. Oliver	9.09	70.85
			2 F. Hillebrand	B.M.W.	1.35.56.2	67.48	Norton		
			3 W. Noll	B.M.W.	1.39.16.4	65.22			
1955	**Senior**	264¼	1 G. E. Duke	Gilera	2.41.49.8	97.93	G. E. Duke	22.39	99.97
			2 H. R. Armstrong	Gilera	2.43.49	96.74	Gilera		
			3 K. T. Kavanagh	Guzzi	2.46.32.8	95.16			
	Junior	264¼	1 W. A. Lomas	Guzzi	2.51.38.2	92.33	W. A. Lomas	24.03.2	94.13
			2 R. Mcintyre	Norton	2.52.38.2	91.79	Guzzi		
			3 C. C. Sandford	Guzzi	2.53.02.2	91.59			
	Light-weight 250cc	97	1 W. A. Lomas	M.V.	1.21.38.2	71.37	W. A. Lomas	8.52	73.13
			2 C. C. Sandford	Guzzi	1.22.29.4	70.63	M.V.		
			3 H. P. Muller	N.S.U.	1.26.21.6	67.47			
	Light-weight 125cc	97	1 C. Ubbiali	M.V.	1.23.38.2	69.67	C. Ubbiali	9.02.2	71.65
			2 L. Taveri	M.V.	1.23.40.2	69.64	M.V.		
			3 G. Lattanzi	Mondial	1.25.53	67.84			
	Sidecar	97	1 W. Schneider	B.M.W.	1.23.14	70.01	W. Noll	9.00	71.93
			2 W. G. Boddice	Norton	1.26.58.6	66.69	B.M.W.		
			3 P. V. Harris	Matchless	1.28.22	65.94			
1956	**Senior**	264¼	1 J. Surtees	M.V.	2.44.05.8	96.57	J. Surtees	23.09.4	97.79
			2 J. Hartle	Norton	2.45.36.6	95.69	M.V.		
			3 J. Brett	Norton	2.46.54.2	94.96			
	Junior	264¼	1 K. T. Kavanagh	Guzzi	2.57.29.4	89.29	K. T. Kavanagh	24.18.8	93.15
			2 D. Ennett	A.J.S.	3.02.07.4	87.02	Guzzi		
			3 J. Hartle	Norton	3.04.48.6	85.75			

Year	RACE Class	Miles	Rider	Machine	Time hms	Speed mph	Fastest Laps	Time ms	Speed mph
1956 cont.	**Light-weight 250cc**	97	1 C. Ubbiali 2 R. Colombo 3 H. Baltisberger	M.V. M.V. N.S.U.	1.26.54.0 1.29.02.6 1.29.24.6	67.05 65.43 65.17	H. Baltisberger N.S.U.	9.21.6	69.17
	Light-weight 125cc	97	1 C. Ubbiali 2 M. Cama 3 F. Gonzalez	M.V. Montesa Montesa	1.24.16.8 1.29.19.2 1.35.18.8	69.13 65.24 61.13	C. Ubbiali M.V.	9.09.8	70.65
	Sidecar	97	1 F. Hillebrand 2 P. V. Harris 3 W. Boddice	B.M.W. Norton Norton	1.23.12.2 1.23.47.8 1.26.19.2	70.03 68.71 67.50	W. Noll B.M.W.	9.01.6	71.12
1957	**Senior**	302	1 R. McIntyre 2 J. Surtees 3 R. N. Brown	Gilera M.V. Gilera	3.02.57.0 3.05.04.2 3.09.02.0	98.99 97.86 95.81	R. McIntyre Gilera	22.23.2	101.12
	Junior	264¼	1 R. McIntyre 2 K. Capbell 3 R. N. Brown	Gilera Guzzi Gilera	2.46.50.2 2.50.29.8 2.51.38.2	94.99 92.95 92.34	R. McIntyre Gilera	23.14.2	97.42
	Light-weight 250cc	107½	1 C. C. Sandford 2 L. Taveri 3 R. Colombo	Mondial M.V. M.V.	1.25.25.4 1.27.12.4 1.27.21.8	75.80 74.24 74.10	T. Provini Mondial	8.18.00	78.00
	Light-weight 125cc	107½	1 T. Provini 2 C. Ubbiali 3 L. Taveri	Mondial M.V. M.V.	1.27.51.0 1.28.25.0 1.30.37.8	73.69 73.22 71.44	T. Provini Mondial	8.41.8	74.44
	Sidecar	107½	1 F. Hillebrand 2 W. Schneider 3 F. Camathias	B.M.W. B.M.W. B.M.W.	1.30.03.4 1.30.54.8 1.32.18.2	71.89 71.21 70.14	F. Hillebrand B.M.W.	8.55.4	72.55
1958	**Senior**	264¼	1 J. Surtees 2 R. H. F. Anderson 3 R. N. Brown	M.V. Norton Norton	2.40.39.8 2.46.06.0 2.46.22.2	98.63 95.40 95.25	J. Surtees M.V.	22.30.4	100.58
	Junior	264¼	1 J. Surtees 2 D. V. Chadwick 3 G. B. Tanner	M.V. Norton Norton	2.48.38.4 2.52.50.6 2.53.06.4	93.97 91.68 91.54	J. Surtees M.V.	23.43.4	95.42
	Light-weight	107½	1 T. Provini 2 C. Ubbiali	M.V. M.V.	1.24.12.0 1.24.20.2	76.89 76.77	T. Provini M.V.	8.06.2	79.90

	Light-weight 125cc	107½	1 C. Ubbiali	M.V.	1.28.51.2	72.86	C. Ubbiali	8.44.0	74.13
			2 R. Ferri	Ducati	1.29.04.4	72.68	M.V.		
			3 D. V. Chadwick	Ducati	1.30.27.8	71.56			
	Sidecar	107½	1 W. Schneider	B.M.W.	1.28.40.0	73.01	W. Schneider	8.44.4	74.07
			2 F. Camathias	B.M.W.	1.29.47.2	72.11	B.M.W.		
			3 J. Beeton	Norton	1.35.34.8	67.73			
1959	**Senior**	264¼	1 J. Surtees	M.V.	3.00.13.4	87.94	J. Surtees	22.22.4	101.18
			2 A. King	Norton	3.05.21.0	85.50	M.V.		
			3 R. Brown	Norton	3.10.56.4	83.00			
	Junior	264¼	1 J. Surtees	M.V.	2.46.08.0	95.38	J. Surtees	23.19.2	97.08
			2 J. Hartle	M.V.	2.49.12.2	93.65	M.V.		
			3 A. King	Norton	2.49.22.6	93.56			
	Light-weight 250cc	107½	1 T. Provini	M.V.	1.23.15.8	77.77	T. Provini	8.04.2	80.22
			2 C. Ubbiali	M.V.	1.23.16.2	77.76	M.V.		
			3 D. Chadwick	M.V.	1.26.52.4	74.52			
	Light-weight 125cc	107½	1 T. Provini	M.V.	1.27.25.2	74.06	L. Taveri	8.38.0	74.99
			2 L. Taveri	M.Z.	1.27.32.6	73.95	M.Z.		
			3 S. M. B. Hailwood	Ducati	1.29.44.0	72.15			
	Sidecar	107½	1 W. Schneider	B.M.W.	1.29.03.8	72.69	W. Schneider	8.49.8	73.32
			2 F. Camathias	B.M.W.	1.31.06.8	71.05	B.M.W.		
			3 F. Scheidegger	B.M.W.	1.33.16.2	69.42			
	Formula I 500cc	113¼	1 R. McIntyre	Norton	1.09.28.4	97.77	R. McIntyre	23.01.0	98.35
			2 R. N. Brown	Norton	1.10.39.0	96.14	Norton		
			3 T. Shepherd	Norton	1.10.54.4	95.79			
	Formula I 350cc	113¼	1 A. King	A.J.S.	1.11.45.4	94.66	A. King	23.45.6	95.27
			2 R. H. F. Anderson	Norton	1.12.05.2	94.23	A.J.S.		
			3 S. M. B. Hailwood	Norton	1.12.27.8	93.73			
1960	**Senior**	226½	1 J. Surtees	M.V.	2.12.35.2	102.44	J. Surtees	21.45.0	104.08
			2 J. Hartle	M.V.	2.15.14.2	100.44	M.V.		
			3 S. M. B. Hailwood	Norton	2.18.11.6	98.29			
	Junior	226½	1 J. Hartle	M.V.	2.20.28.8	96.70	J. Surtees	22.49.4	99.20
			2 J. Surtees	M.V.	2.22.24.2	95.39	M.V.		
			3 R. McIntyre	A.J.S.	2.22.50.4	95.11			
	Light-weight 250cc	188¾	1 G. Hocking	M.V.	2.00.53.0	93.64	C. Ubbiali	23.42.8	95.47
			2 C. Ubbiali	M.V.	2.01.33.4	93.13	M.V.		
			3 T. Provini	Morini	2.01.44.6	92.98			

Year	RACE Class	Miles	Rider	Machine	Time hms	Speed mph	Fastest Laps	Time ms	Speed mph
1960 cont.	**Light-weight 125cc**	113¼	1 C. Ubbiali	M.V.	1.19.21.2	85.60	C. Ubbiali	26.17.6	86.10
			2 G. Hocking	M.V.	1.19.41.0	85.24			
			3 L. Taveri	M.V.	1.21.07.6	83.72			
	Sidecar	113¼	1 H. Fath	B.M.W.	1.20.45.8	84.10	H. Fath B.M.W.	26.23.4	85.79
			2 P. V. Harris	B.M.W.	1.22.10.2	82.66			
			3 C. Freeman	Norton	1.28.07.2	77.08			
1961	**Senior**	226½	1 S. M. B. Hailwood	Norton	2.15.02.0	100.60	G. Hocking M.V.	22.03.6	102.62
			2 R. McIntyre	Norton	2.16.56.4	99.20			
			3 T. E. Phillis	Norton	2.17.31.2	98.78			
	Junior	226½	1 P. W. Read	Norton	2.22.50.0	95.10	G. Hocking M.V.	22.41.0	99.80
			2 G. Hocking	M.V.	2.24.07.8	94.25			
			3 R. B. Rensen	Norton	2.25.03.0	93.65			
	Light-weight 250cc	188¾	1 S. M. B. Hailwood	Honda	1.55.03.6	98.38	R. McIntyre Honda	22.44.0	99.58
			2 T. E. Phillis	Honda	1.57.14.4	96.56			
			3 J. A. Redman	Honda	2.01.36.2	93.09			
	Light-weight 125cc	113¼	1 S. M. B. Hailwood	Honda	1.16.58.6	88.23	L. Taveri Honda	25.35.6	88.45
			2 L. Taveri	Honda	1.17.06.0	88.09			
			3 T. E. Phillis	Honda	1.17.49.0	87.28			
	Sidecar	113¼	1 M. Deubel	B.M.W.	1.17.29.8	87.65	M. Deubel B.M.W.	25.44.0	87.97
			2 F. Scheidegger	B.M.W.	1.18.02.6	87.03			
			3 P. V. Harris	B.M.W.	1.19.40.4	85.26			
1962	**Senior**	226½	1 G. Hocking	M.V.	2.11.13.4	103.51	G. Hocking M.V.	21.24.4	105.75
			2 E. Boyce	Norton	2.21.06.2	96.27			
			3 F. J. Stevens	Norton	2.21.09.4	96.24			
	Junior	226½	1 S. M. B. Hailwood	M.V.	2.16.24.2	99.59	S. M. B. Hailwood M.V.	22.17.2	101.58
			2 G. Hocking	M.V.	2.16.29.8	99.52			
			3 F. Stastny	Jawa	2.23.23.4	94.74			
	Light-weight 250cc	226½	1 D. W. Minter	Honda	2.20.30.0	96.68	R. McIntyre Honda	22.51.2	99.06
			2 J. Redman	Honda	2.22.23.6	95.40			
			3 T. Phillis	Honda	2.26.15.6	92.87			
	Light-weight	113½	1 L. Taveri	Honda	1.15.34.2	89.88	L. Taveri	25.07.0	90.13
			2 T. Robb	Honda	[illegible]	[illegible]			

	50cc	75½	1 E. Degner	Suzuki	1.00.16.4	75.12	E. Degner	29.38.6	75.32
			2 L. Taveri	Honda	1.00.34.4	74.75	Suzuki		
			3 T. Robb	Honda	1.00.47.6	74.48			
	Sidecar	113¼	1 C. Vincent	B.S.A.	1.21.16.4	83.57	M. Deubel	24.57.6	90.70
			2 O. Kolle	B.M.W.	1.21.53.8	82.93	B.M.W.		
			3 C. J. Seeley	Matchless	1.22.01.8	82.90			
1963	**Senior**	226½	1 S. M. B. Hailwood	M.V.	2.09.48.4	104.64	S. M. B. Hailwood	21.16.4	106.41
			2 J. Hartle	Gilera	2.11.01.8	103.67	M.V.		
			P. W. Read	Gilera	2.15.42.2	100.10			
	Junior	226½	1 J. A. Redman	Honda	2.23.08.2	94.91	J. A. Redman	22.20.8	101.30
			2 J. Hartle	Gilera	2.29.58.2	90.58	Honda		
			3 F. Stastny	Jawa	2.31.20.6	89.76			
	Light-weight 250cc	226½	1 J. A. Redman	Honda	2.23.13.2	94.85	J. A. Redman	23.17.0	97.23
			2 F. Ito	Yamaha	2.23.40.4	94.55	Honda		
			3 W. A. Smith	Honda	2.29.05.2	91.12			
	Light-weight 125cc	113¼	1 H. R. Anderson	Suzuki	1.16.05.0	89.27	H. R. Anderson	24.47.4	91.32
			2 F. F. Perris	Suzuki	1.17.25.0	87.74	Suzuki		
			3 E. Degner	Suzuki	1.17.31.6	87.61			
	50cc	113¼	1 M. Itch	Suzuki	1.26.10.6	78.81	E. Degner	28.37.2	79.10
			2 H. R. Anderson	Suzuki	1.26.37.4	78.40	Suzuki		
			3 H. G. Anscheidt	Kreidler	1.26.42.0	78.33			
	Sidecar	113¼	1 F. Camathias	F.C.S.	1.16.51.0	88.38	F. Camathias	25.19.0	89.42
			2 F. Scheidegger	B.M.W.	1.17.29.2	87.66	F.C.S.		
			3 A. Birch	B.M.W.	1.21.17.6	83.52			
1964	**Senior**	226½	1 S. M. B. Hailwood	M.V.	2.14.33.8	100.95	S. M. B. Hailwood	22.05.0	102.51
			2 D. Minter	Norton	2.17.56.6	98.47	M.V.		
			3 F. Stevens	Matchless	2.20.54.6	96.40			
	Junior	226½	1 J. Redman	Honda	2.17.55.4	98.50	J. Redman	22.28.0	100.76
			2 P. W. Read	A.J.S.	2.25.09.6	93.58	Honda		
			3 M. A. Duff	A.J.S.	2.25.21.4	93.46			
	Light-weight 250cc	226½	1 J. Redman	Honda	2.19.23.6	97.45	P. W. Read	22.46.2	99.42
			2 A. Shepherd	M.Z.	2.20.04.6	96.67	Yamaha		
			3 A. Pagani	Paton	2.37.35.8	86.20			
	Light-weight 125cc	113¼	1 L. Taveri	Honda	1.13.43.0	92.14	L. Taveri	24.12.2	93.53
			2 J. Redman	Honda	1.13.46.0	92.08	Honda		
			3 R. Bryans	Honda	1.14.28.2	91.22			

Year	RACE Class	Miles	Rider	Machine	Time hms	Speed mph	Fastest Laps	Time ms	Speed mph
1964 cont.	**50cc**	113¼	1 H. R. Anderson	Suzuki	1.24.13.4	80.64	H. R. Anderson	27.54.2	81.13
			2 R. Bryans	Honda	1.25.14.8	79.68	Suzuki		
			3 I. Morishita	Suzuki	1.25.15.4	79.67			
	Sidecar	113¼	1 M. Deubel	B.M.W.	1.16.13.0	89.12	M. Deubel	25.15.4	89.63
			2 C. Seeley	F.C.S.B.	1.18.17.6	86.76	B.M.W.		
			3 G. Auerbacher	B.M.W.	1.20.26.2	84.45			
1965	**Senior**	226½	1 S. M. B. Hailwood	M.V.	2.28.09.0	91.69	S. M. B. Hailwood	23.48.2	95.11
			2 J. Dunphy	Norton	2.30.28.8	90.28	M.V.		
			3 M. Duff	Matchless	2.34.12.0	88.09			
	Junior	226½	1 J. Redman	Honda	2.14.52.2	100.72	S. M. B. Hailwood	22.00.6	102.85
			2 P. W. Read	Yamaha	2.16.44.4	99.35	M.V.		
			3 G. Agostini	M.V.	2.17.53.4	98.52			
	Light-weight 250cc	226½	1 J. Redman	Honda	2.19.45.8	97.19	J. Redman	22.37.0	100.09
			2 M. Duff	Yamaha	2.23.26.4	94.71	Honda		
			3 F. Perris	Suzuki	2.24.32.0	93.99			
	Light-weight 125cc	113¼	1 P. W. Read	Yamaha	1.12.02.6	94.28	H. R. Anderson	23.34.6	96.02
			2 L. Taveri	Honda	1.12.08.4	94.15	Suzuki		
			3 M. Duff	Yamaha	1.12.23.6	93.83			
	50cc	113¼	1 L. Taveri	Honda	1.25.15.6	79.66	L. Taveri	28.00.4	80.83
			2 H. R. Anderson	Suzuki	1.26.08.8	78.85	Honda		
			3 E. Degner	Suzuki	1.28.10.0	77.04			
	Sidecar	113¼	1 M. Deubel	B.M.W.	1.14.59.8	90.57	M. Deubel	24.39.6	91.80
			2 F. Scheidegger	B.M.W.	1.15.13.8	98.11	B.W.W.		
			3 G. Auerbacher	B.M.W.	1.20.26.2	84.45			
1966	**Senior**	226½	1 S. M. B. Hailwood	Honda	2.11.44.8	103.11	S. M. B. Hailwood	21.08.6	107.07
			2 G. Agostini	M.V.	2.14.22.6	101.09	Honda		
			3 C. R. Conn	Norton	2.22.26.8	95.37			
	Junior	226½	1 G. Agostini	M.V.	2.14.40.4	100.87	G. Agostini	21.57.6	103.09
			2 P. J. Williams	A.J.S.	2.24.46.6	93.83	M.V.		
			3 C. R. Conn	Norton	2.26.45.4	92.56			
	Light-	226½	1 S. M. B. Hailwood	Honda	2.13.26.0	101.79	S. M. B. Hailwood	21.42.4	104.29

	Light-weight 125cc	113¾	1 W. Ivy	Yamaha	[illegible]	[illegible]			
			2 P. W. Read	Yamaha	1.10.03.2	96.96	Yamaha		
			3 H. R. Anderson	Suzuki	1.10.09.2	96.82			
	50cc	113¼	1 R. Bryans	Honda	1.19.17.2	85.66	R. Bryans	26.10.2	85.66
			2 L. Taveri	Honda	1.20.08.4	84.74	Honda		
			3 H. R. Anderson	Suzuki	1.21.41.0	83.14			
	Sidecar	113¼	1 F. Scheidegger	B.M.W.	1.14.50.0	90.76	M. Deubel	24.42.4	91.63
			2 M. Deubel	B.M.W.	1.14.50.8	90.75	B.M.W.		
			3 G. Auerbacher	B.M.W.	1.16.52.4	88.35			
1967	**Senior**	226.4	1 S. M. B. Hailwood	Honda	2.08.36.2	105.62	S. M. B. Hailwood	20.48.8	108.77
			2 P. J. Williams	Arter Matchless	2.16.20.0	99.64	Honda		
			3 S. Spencer	Lancefield Norton	2.17.47.2	98.59			
	Junior	226.4	1 S. M. B. Hailwood	Honda	2.09.45.6	104.68	S. M. B. Hailwood	21.00.8	107.73
			2 G. Agostini	M.V. Agusta	2.12.48.8	102.28	Honda		
			3 D. Woodman	M.Z.	2.20.53.6	96.41			
	Light-weight 250cc	226.4	1 S. M. B. Hailwood	Honda	2.11.47.6	103.07	S. M. B. Hailwood	21.39.8	104.50
			2 P. W. Read	Yamaha	2.13.06.4	102.05	Honda		
			3 R. Bryans	Honda	2.16.27	99.55			
	Light-weight 125cc	113.2	1 P. W. Read	Yamaha	1.09.40.8	97.48	P. W. Read	23.00.8	98.36
			2 S. Graham	Suzuki	1.09.44.2	97.40	Yamaha		
			3 A. Motohashi	Yamaha	1.11.49.6	94.56			
	50cc	113.2	1 S. Graham	Suzuki	1.21.56.8	82.89	S. Graham	26.34.4	85.19
			2 H. G. Anscheidt	Suzuki	1.22.58.0	81.86	Suzuki		
			3 T. Robb	Suzuki	1.38.02.0	69.28			
	Production 750cc	113.2	1 J. Hartle	Tri. Bonneville	1.09.56.8	97.10	J. Hartle	23.07.8	97.87
			2 P. Smart	Duns. Dominator	1.11.48.0	94.60	Triumph Bonneville		
			3 A. J. Smith	B.S.A. Spitfire	1.15.42.0	89.73			
	Production 500cc	113.2	1 N. Kelly	Velo Thrux. Venom	1.15.33.8	89.89	N. Kelly	24.52.6	91.01
			2 K. Heckles	Velo Thrux. Venom	1.16.11.6	89.15	Velo Thruxton		
			3 D. J. Nixon	Triumph T.100	1.19.48.0	85.11	Venom		
	Production 250cc	113.2	1 W. A. Smith	Bultaco Metralla	1.16.38.2	88.63	W. A. Smith	25.19.4	89.41
			2 T. Robb	Bultaco Metralla	1.16.38.6	88.62	Bultaco Metralla		
			3 B. Smith	Suzuki	1.18.43.2	86.29			

Year	RACE Class	Miles	Rider	Machine	Time hms	Speed mph	Fastest Laps	Time ms	Speed mph
	Sidecar 500cc	113.2	1 S. Schauzu	B.M.W.	1.14.40.6	90.96	G. Auerbacher	24.41.2	91.70
			2 K. Enders	B.M.W.	1.14.59.2	90.58	B.M.W.		
			3 C. Seeley	B.M.W.	1.17.15.6	87.92			
1968	**Senior**	226.4	1 G. Agostini	M.V. Agusta	2.13.39.4	101.63	G. Agostini	21.34.8	104.91
			2 B. A. Ball	Seeley	2.22.08.4	95.57	M.V. Agusta		
			3 B. J. Randle	Petty-Norton	2.22.08.8	95.56			
	Junior	226.4	1 G. Agostini	M.V. Agusta	2.09.38.6	104.78	G. Agostini	21.12.2	106.77
			2 R. Pasolini	Benelli	2.12.19.6	102.65	M.V. Agusta		
			3 W. A. Smith	Honda	2.22.58.6	95.02			
	Light-weight 250cc	226.4	1 W. D. Ivy	Yamaha	2.16.24.8	99.58	W. D. Ivy	21.27.4	105.51
			2 R. Pasolini	Benelli	2.18.36.8	98.00	Yamaha		
			3 H. Rosner	M.Z.	2.22.56.4	95.04			
	Light-weight 125cc	113.2	1 P. W. Read	Yamaha	1.08.31.4	99.12	W. D. Ivy	22.34.0	100.32
			2 W. D. Ivy	Yamaha	1.09.27.8	97.78	Yamaha		
			3 K. Carruthers	Gates Honda	1.18.21.2	86.69			
	50cc	113.2	1 B. Smith	Derbi	1.33.10.4	72.90	B. Smith	30.46.0	73.44
			2 C. M. Walpole	Honda	1.40.59.6	67.26	Derbi		
			3 E. L. Griffiths	Honda	1.42.36.0	66.20			
	Produc-tion 750cc	113.2	1 R. Pickrell	Duns. Dominator	1.09.13.2	98.13	R. Pickrell	22.46.6	99.39
			2 B. Nelson	Norton Atlas	1.11.47.2	94.62	Dunstall Dominator		
			3 A. J. Smith	B.S.A Spitfire	1.12.23.8	93.82			
	Produc-tion 500cc	113.2	1 R. Knight	Triumph Daytona	1.15.23.6	90.09	R. L. Knight	24.52.2	91.03
			2 J. Blanchard	Velocette Thruxton	1.16.41.2	88.58	Triumph Daytona		
			3 D. J. Nixon	Triumph Daytona	1.16.44.4	88.52			
	Produc-tion 250cc	113.2	1 T. E. Burgess	Ossa	1.17.53.4	87.21	T. E. Burgess	25.45.4	87.89
			2 G. E. Leigh	Bultaco Metralla	1.19.41.8	85.23	Ossa		
			3 B. Smith	Thompson Suzuki	1.19.45.0	85.17			
	Sidecar 500cc	113.2	1 S. Schauzu	B.M.W.	1.14.34.2	91.09	K. Enders	24.00.0	94.32
			2 J. Attenberger	B.M.W.	1.15.55.2	89.47	B.M.W.		
			3 H. Luthringhauser	B.M.W.	1.17.32.6	87.60			
	Sidecar [illegible]	113.2	1 T. Vinicombe	Kirby-B.S.A.	1.19.07.4	85.85	C. Vincent	25.25.0	89.11

			2 A. J. Barnett	Kirby-Metisse	2.18.12.6	98.28	M.V.		
			3 T. Dickie	Kuhn-Seeley	2.18.44.2	97.92			
	Junior	226.4	1 G. Agostini	M.V. Agusta	2.13.25.4	101.81	G. Agostini	21.46.0	104.00
			2 B. Steenson	Aermacchi	2.23.36.4	94.60	M.V.		
			3 J. Findlay	Beart-Aermacchi	2.24.41.2	93.89			
	Light-weight 250cc	226.4	1 K. Carruthers	Benelli	2.21.35.2	95.95	K. Carruthers	22.51.8	99.01
			2 F. Perris	Crooke Suzuki	2.24.59.4	93.69	Benelli		
			3 S. Herrero	Ossa	2.26.21.0	92.82			
	Light-weight 125cc	113.2	1 D. A. Simmonds	Kawasaki	1.14.34.6	91.08	D. A. Simmonds	24.29.0	92.46
			2 K. Carruthers	Aermacchi	1.20.27.2	84.43	Kawasaki		
			3 R. J. G. Dickinson	Honda	1.21.10.6	83.67			
	Produc-tion 750cc	113.2	1 M. Uphill	Tri. Bonneville	1.07.55.4	99. 99	M. Uphill	22.33.2	100.37
			2 P. Smart	Nor. Commando	1.08.21.2	99.37	Triumph Bonneville		
			3 D. Pendlebury	Tri. Bonneville	1.10.16.2	96.66			
	Produc-tion 500cc	113.2	1 W. G. Penny	Honda CB450	1.17.01.6	88.18	T. Dunnell	24.55.2	90.84
			2 R. L. Knight	Triumph Daytona	1.17.30.4	87.64	Kawasaki		
			3 R. W. Baylie	Triumph Daytona	1.19.04.0	85.90	Mach 3		
	Produc-tion 250cc	113.2	1 A. M. Rogers	Ducati Mach 1	1.21.03.8	83.79	C. S. Mortimer	26.35.6	85.13
			2 F. Whiteway	Suzuki T20	1.21.33.4	83.29	Ducati Mach 3		
			3 C. S. Mortimer	Ducati Mach 3	1.22.49.6	82.01			
	Sidecar 500cc	113.2	1 K. Enders	B.M.W.	1.13.27.0	92.48	K. Enders	24.27.8	92.54
			2 S. Schauzu	B.M.W.	1.14.39.4	90.99	B.M.W.		
			3 H. Fath	U.R.S.	1.15.00.0	90.56			
	Sidecar 750cc	113.2	1 S. Schauzu	B.M.W.	1.15.36.8	89.83	S. Schauzu	24.35.4	92.06
			2 P. M. Brown	B.S.A.	1.19.18.2	85.65	B.M.W.		
			3 L. W. Currie	L.W.C.	1.23.07.4	81.72			
1970	**Senior**	226.4	1 G. Agostini	M.V.	2.13.47.6	101.52	G. Agostini	21.30.0	105.29
			2 P. J. Williams	Arter Matchless	2.18.57.0	97.76	M.V.		
			3 W. A. Smith	Kawasaki	2.21.07.6	96.26			
	Junior	226.4	1 G. Agostini	M.V.	2.13.28.6	101.77	G. Agostini	21.39.0	104.56
			2 A. J. Barnett	Aermacchi	2.18.23.8	98.16	M.V.		
			3 P. Smart	Padgett-Yamaha	2.20.08.8	96.93			
	Light-weight 250cc	226.4	1 K. Carruthers	Yamaha	2.21.19.2	96.13	K. Carruthers	23.05.4	98.04
			2 R. Gould	Yamaha	2.24.54.0	93.75	Yamaha		
			3 G. Bartusch	M.Z.	2.26.58.4	92.43			

Year	RACE Class	Miles	Rider	Machine	Time hms	Speed mph	Fastest Laps	Time ms	Speed mph
1970 cont.	**Light-weight 125cc**	113.2	1 D. Braun	Suzuki	1.16.05.0	89.27	D. A. Simmonds	24.52.2	90.90
			2 B. Jansson	Maico	1.18.28.4	86.56	Kawasaki		
			3 G. Bartusch	M.Z.	1.19.02.8	85.93			
	Produc-tion 750cc	188.65	1 M. Uphill	Triumph Trident	1.55.51.0	97.71	P. J. Williams	22.38.4	99.99
			2 P. J. Williams	Norton Commando	1.53.52.6	97.69	Norton Commando		
			3 R. Pickrell	Norton Commando	1.58.05.2	95.86			
	Produc-tion 500cc	188.65	1 F. Whiteway	Suzuki T500 II	2.05.52.0	89.94	F. Whiteway	24.57.0	90.75
			2 G. Pantall	Triumph Daytona	2.07.20.0	88.90	Suzuki T500 II		
			3 R. L. Knight	Triumph Daytona	2.07.20.4	88.89			
	Produc-tion 250cc	188.65	1 C. Mortimer	Ducati Mk III	2.13.23.4	84.87	C. Mortimer	26.25.6	86.71
			2 J. Williams	Honda CB250	2.13.29.0	84.80	Ducati Mk II		
			3 S. Woods	Suzuki T250	2.14.40.6	84.06			
	Sidecar 500cc	113.2	1 K. Enders	B.M.W.	1.13.05.6	92.93	K. Enders	24.08.2	93.79
			2 S. Schauzu	B.M.W.	1.14.56.4	90.64	B.M.W.		
			3 H. Luthringshauser	B.M.W.	1.16.58.0	88.25			
	Sidecar 750cc	113.2	1 S. Schauzu	B.M.W.	1.15.18.0	90.20	K. Enders	24.30.6	92.37
			2 P. Brown	B.S.A.	1.19.00.4	85.97	B.M.W.		
			3 E. Leece	L.M.S.	1.23.50.2	81.02			
1971	**Senior**	226.4	1 G. Agostini	M.V.	2.12.24.4	102.59	G. Agostini	21.35.4	104.86
			2 P. J. Williams	Arter-Matchless	2.18.03.0	98.40	M.V.		
			3 F. Perris	Suzuki	2.20.45.4	96.51			
	Junior	188.65	1 A. Jefferies	Yamsel	2.05.48.6	89.98	P. Read	22.33.2	100.37
			2 G. Pantall	Padgett-Yamaha	2.06.25.0	89.55	Yamaha		
			3 W. A. Smith	Honda	2.07.04.8	89.09			
	Light-weight 250cc	150.92	1 P. Read	Yamaha	1.32.23.6	98.02	P. Read	22.37.2	100.08
			2 B. Randle	Yamaha	1.34.27.6	95.87	Yamaha		
			3 A. J. Barnett	Yamsel	1.35.02.0	95.29			
	Light-	113.19	1 C. Mortimer	Yamaha	1.20.54.0	83.96	C. Mortimer	26.00.2	87.05

	750cc		2 R. Pickrell 3 P. J. Williams	750cc B.S.A. 750cc Norton	1.06.28.0 1.07.06.2	102.18 101.22	750cc Triumph		
	Produc- tion 750cc	150.92	1 R. Pickrell 2 A. Jefferies 3 R. Heath	Triumph Trident Triumph Trident B.S.A. Rocket 3	1.30.30.2 1.32.03.0 1.33.17.4	100.07 98.38 97.08	P. Williams 750cc Norton	22.24.0	101.06
	Produc- tion 500cc	150.02	1 J. Williams 2 G. Penny 3 A. Cooper	Honda CB 450 Honda CB 450 Suzuki T500	1.39.28.8 1.41.39.6 1.44.32.8	91.04 89.09 86.63	J. Williams Honda CB450	24.45.4	91.45
	Produc- tion 250cc	150.92	1 W. A. Smith 2 C. Williams 3 T. Robb	Honda CB 250 Yamaha YDS 7 Honda CB 250	1.47.43.6 147.52.0 1.49.47.6	84.14 84.04 82.49	C. Williams Yamaha YDS 7	26.44.8	84.64
	Sidecar 500cc	113.19	1 S. Schauzu 2 G. Auberbacher 3 A. Butscher	B.M.W. B.M.W. B.M.W.	1.19.47.8 1.18.53.2 1.23.32.6	86.21 86.10 81.31	G. Auerbacher B.M.W.	25.56.2	87.27
	Sidecar 750cc	113.19	1 G. Auerbacher 2 A. J. Sansum 3 R. Williamson	B.M.W. Triumph W.H.B. Weslake	1.18.12.0 1.22.20.2 1.22.35.0	86.86 82.50 82.25	S. Schauzu B.M.W.	24.13.6	93.44
1972	Senior	226.38	1 G. Agostini 2 A. Pagani 3 M. Grant	M.V. M.V. Padgett-Yamaha	2.10.34.4 2.18.25.8 2.20.00.0	104.02 98.13 97.03	G. Agostini M.V.	21.28.8	105.39
	Junior	188.65	1 G. Agostini 2 T. Rutter 3 M. Grant	M.V. Yamaha Padgett-Yamaha	1.50.56.8 1.55.21.4 1.56.01.0	102.03 98.13 97.57	G. Agostini M.V.	21.54.4	103.34
	Light- weight 250cc	150.92	1 P. W. Read 2 R. Gould 3 J. Williams	Yamaha Yamaha Yamaha	1.30.51.2 1.32.19.6 1.33.16.4	99.68 98.09 97.09	P. W. Read Yamaha	22.30.0	100.61
	Light- weight 125cc	113.19	1 C. Mortimer 2 C. Williams 3 W. Rae	Yamaha Johnson-Yamaha Maico	1.17.38.2 1.24.23.0 1.25.39.8	87.49 80.49 79.29	C. Mortimer Yamaha	24.59.6	90.58
	Formula 750cc	188.65	1 R. Pickrell 2 A. Jefferies 3 J. Findlay	Triumph Triumph Suzuki	1.48.36.0 1.49.28.4 1.55.07.4	104.23 103.46 98.33	R. Pickrell Triumph	21.25.2	105.68
	Produc- tion 750cc	150.92	1 R. Pickrell 2 P. J. Williams 3 D. Nixon	Triumph Norton Triumph	1.30.34.0 1.33.48.8 1.36.18.4	100.00 96.53 94.04	R. Pickrell Triumph	22.16.8	101.61

Year	RACE Class	Miles	Rider	Machine	Time hms	Speed mph	Fastest Laps	Time ms	Speed mph
1972 cont.	**Production 500cc**	150.92	1 S. Woods	Suzuki	1.38.13.3	92.20	S. Woods Suzuki	24.11.0	93.61
			2 R. Bowler	Triumph	1.38.20.6	92.09			
			3 W. A. Smith	Honda	1.46.08.8	91.16			
	Production 250cc	150.92	1 J. Williams	Honda	1.46.08.8	85.32	J. Williams Honda	26.24.4	85.73
			2 C. Williams	Yamaha	1.47.50.2	84.06			
			3 E. Roberts	Suzuki	1.48.56.4	83.14			
	Sidecar 500cc	113.19	1 S. Schauzu	B.M.W.	1.13.57.2	91.85	H. Luthringshauser B.M.W.	24.28.0	92.53
			2 H. Luthringshauser	B.M.W.	1.14.04.6	91.70			
			3 G. Boret	Konig	1.20.27.4	84.43			
	Sidecar 750cc	113.19	1 S. Schauzu	B.M.W.	1.14.40.0	90.97	S. Schauzu B.M.W.	24.47.2	91.33
			2 A. J. Sansum	Triumph	1.17.24.0	87.76			
			3 J. L. Barker	B.S.A.	1.18.41.6	86.32			
1973	**Senior**	226.38	1 J. Findlay	Suzuki	2.13.45.2	101.55	M. Grant	21.40.8	104.44
			2 P. Williams	Arter Matchless	2.14.59.4	100.62			
			3 C. Sanby	Hi-tac Suzuki	2.15.27.6	100.27			
	Junior	188.65	1 T. Rutter	Yamaha	1.50.58.8	101.99	T. Rutter	21.43.2	104.22
			2 K. Huggett	Dugdale Yamaha	1.52.31.6	100.58			
			3 J. Williams	Yamaha	1.52.49.4	100.32			
	Lightweight 125cc	113.19	1 T. Robb	Danfay Yamaha	1.16.23.6	88.90	T. Robb	25.22	89.24
			2 J. Kostwinder	Yamaha	1.17.21.6	87.79			
			3 N. Tuxworth	Yamaha	1.18.27.2	86.56			
	Lightweight 250cc	150.92	1 C. Williams	Johnson Yamaha	1.30.30.0	100.05			
			2 J. Williams	Yamaha	1.30.54.6	99.60			
			3 B. Rae	Padgett Yamaha	1.31.35.4	98.86			
	Formula 750	188.65	1 P. Williams	750 Norton	1.47.19.2	105.47	P. Williams	21.06.2	107.27
			2 M. Grant	750 Norton	1.50.21.6	102.56			
			3 T. Jefferies	750 Triumph	1.50.55.2	102.04			
	Production 750cc	150.92	1 T. Jefferies	Triumph Trident	1.34.41.6	95.62	P. Williams	22.31.2	100.52
			2 J. Williams	Triumph Trident	1.35.24.8	94.90			
			3 D. Nixon	Triumph Trident	1.38.53.6	91.56			

	tion 500cc		2 S. Woods	Suzuki T500R	1.42.55.2	87.98	record		
			3 K. Martin	Kawasaki HIB	1.43.02.8	89.87			
	Production 250cc	150.92	1 C. Williams	Yamaha YDS7	1.50.45.0	81.76	E. Roberts	26.55.8	84.06
			2 E. Roberts	Yamaha YDS7	1.51.27.0	81.24			
			3 T. Robb	Honda CB250	1.53.05.8	80.06			
	Sidecar 500cc	113.19	1 K. Enders/ R. Englehardt	B.M.W.	1.11.32.4	94.93	K. Enders record	23.46.4	96.22
			2 S. Schauzu/ W. Kalauch	B.M.W.	1.14.18.2	91.40			
			3 R. Steinhausen/ K. Scheurer	Konig	1.15.35.4	89.84			
1974	Senior	188.65	1 P. Carpenter	354 Yamaha	1.56.41.6	96.99	C. Williams	22.12.6	101.92
			2 C. Williams	395 Dugdale Yamaha	1.57.31.6	96.31			
			3 T. Rutter	351 Yamaha	1.59.57.4	94.35			
	Junior	188.65	1 T. Rutter	Yamaha	1.48.22.2	104.44	C. Mortimer	21.16.6	106.39
			2 M. Grant	Yamaha	1.50.06.2	102.80			
			3 P. Cott	Yamaha	1.51.47	101.25			
	Lightweight 125cc	113.19	1 C. Horton	Yamaha	1.16.47.0	88.44	A. Hockley/C. Horton	25.29.8	88.78
			2 I. Hodgkinson	Granby Yamaha	1.17.27.0	87.68			
			3 T. Herron	Yamaha	1.18.08.6	86.91			
	Lightweight 250cc	150.92	1 C. Williams	Yamaha	1.36.09.8	94.16	M. Grant	23.08	97.85
			2 M. Grant	Yamaha	1.37.09.2	93.20			
			3 C. Mortimer	Yamaha	1.37.31.2	92.85			
	Formula 750cc	188.65	1 C. Mortimer	350 Yamaha	2.15.07.2	100.52	C. Williams	21.142	106.61
			2 C. Williams	350 Dugdale Yamaha	2.15.15.8	100.41			
			3 T. Rutter	350 Yamaha	2.15.42.6	100.08			
	Production 1000cc	150.92	1 M. Grant	Triumph Trident	1.30.48.0	99.72	M. Grant	22.28.2	100.74
			2 H. Butenuth	B.M.W. R90	1.32.41.0	97.70			
			3 H. Dahne	B.M.W. R90	1.33.20.6	97.01			
	Production 500cc	150.92	1 K. Martin	Kawasaki	1.36.28.6	93.85	K. Martin	23.46.6	95.21 record
			2 A. Rogers	Triumph T100T	1.36.58.0	93.38			
			3 P. Gurner	B.S.A. B50	1.38.14.4	92.17			
	Production	150.92	1 M. Sharpe	Yamaha RD 250	1.44.09.2	86.94	E. Roberts	25.35.0	88.48
			2 E. Roberts	Yamaha RD 250	1.44.11.6	86.90			
			3 B. Rae	Suzuki GT	1.45.22.6	85.93			

Year	RACE Class	Miles	Rider	Machine	Time hms	Speed mph	Fastest Laps	Time ms	Speed mph
1974 cont.	**Sidecar 500cc**	113.19	1 H. Luthringshauser/ H. Hahn	B.M.W.	1.13.36.2	92.27	J. Gawley/ K. Birch	24.14.8	93.36
			2 G. O'Dell/ B. Boldison	Konig	1.18.46.4	86.21			
			3 M. Hobson/ J. Armstrong	Hamilton Yamaha	1.19.35.0	85.33			
	Sidecar 750cc	113.19	1 S. Schauzu/ W. Kalauch	B.M.W.	1.10.18.4	96.59	R. Steinhausen/ K. Scheurer	23.03.4	98.18
			2 H. Luthringshauser/ H. Hahn	B.M.W.	1.13.52.2	90.93			
			3 M. Horspole/ G. Horspole	Weslake	1.16.30.6	88.76			
1975	**Senior**	226.38	1 M. Grant	Kawasaki	2.15.27.6	100.27	M. Grant	21.59.6	102.93
			2 J. Williams	390 Yamaha	2.15.58.8	99.88			
			3 C. Mortimer	351 Danfay Yamaha	2.18.22.8	98.15			
	Junior	188.65	1 C. Williams	Dugdale Maxton Yamaha	1.48.24.4	104.38	A. George Vesco Yamaha	21.17.8	106.29
			2 C. Mortimer	Danfay Yamaha	1.49.51.0	103.04			
			3 T. Herron	Yamaha	1.50.35.4	102.35			
	Light-weight 250cc	150.92	1 C. Mortimer	Danfay Yamaha	1.28.57.8	101.78	D. Chatterton	21.59.4	103.54
			2 D. Chatterton	Chat Yamaha	1.28.20.0	101.36			
			3 J. Williams	Yamaha	1.29.42.2	100.94			
	1000cc Open Classic	226.38	1 J. Williams	350 Yamaha	2.08.56.8	105.33	M. Grant 750 Kawasaki	20.36.8	109.82
			2 P. Tait	750 Yamaha	2.12.54.4	102.19			
			3 C. Sanby	750 Yamaha	2.13.28.4	101.76			
	Produc-tion Handicap	377.30	1 D. Croxford/ A. George	750 Triumph	4.01.17.2	99.60	A. George	22.01.0	102.82
			2 C. Mortimer/ B. Guthrie	250 Yamaha	4.03.43.6	86.43			
			3 S. Griffiths/ D. Williams	750 Triumph	4.06.04.4	97.54			
	(Overall Placings. Times include handicaps)								
	Sidecar 500cc	113.19	1 R. Steinhausen/ J. Huber	Konig	1.10.47.0	95.94	M. Hobson/ G. Russell	23.24.4	96.71

			3 D. Greasley/ C. Holland	Yamaha	1.12.04.6	94.22			
	Sidecar 1000cc	113.19	1 S. Schauzu/ W. Kalauch	560 BMW	1.09.37.0	97.55	S. Schauzu/ W. Kalauch	22.47.6	99.31
			2 D. Greasley/ C. Holland	700 Yamaha	1.10.33.0	96.26			
			3 G. Boret/N. Boret	680 Shellsport Renwick Konig	1.13.30.6	92.38			
1976	**Senior**	226.38	1 T. Herron	351 Yamaha	2.09.10.0	105.15	J. Williams Suzuki	20.09.8	112.27
			2 I. Richards	352 Yamaha	2.09.13.4	105.11			
			3 B. Guthrie	354 Danfay Yamaha	2.09.33.0	104.84			
	Junior	188.65	1 C. Mortimer	Yamaha	1.46.00.2	106.78	T. Rutter	20.49.6	108.69
			2 T. Rutter	Yamaha	1.46.70.0	106.66			
			3 B. Guthrie	Yamaha	1.49.01.8	103.81			
	Light-weight 250cc	150.92	1 T. Herron	Yamaha	1.27.26.8	103.55	T. Herron	21.27.8	105.47
			2 T. Katayama	Yamaha	1.27.52.2	103.05			
			3 C. Mortimer	Danfay Yamaha	1.28.43.2	102.06			
	1000cc Open Classic	226.38	1 J. Williams	750 Suzuki	2.05.33.0	108.18	J. Williams	20.32.4	110.21
			2 A. George	750 Yamaha	2.06.57.8	106.98			
			3 T. Rutter	350 Yamaha	2.08.19.6	105.84			
	Produc-tion Handicap	377.3	1 B. Simpson/ C. Mortimer	250 Yamaha	4.05.09.8	87.00	R. Nicholls 900 Ducati	21.5.7	103.12
			2 T. Rutter/D. Hughes	250 Suzuki	4.06.37.8	86.46			
			3 F. Rutter/M. Poxon	500 Honda	4.08.15.4	91.18			
	(Overall Placings. Times include handicaps)								
	Sidecar 500cc	113.19	1 R. Steinhausen/ J. Huber	Busch Konig	1.10.26.0	96.42	S. Schauzu/ W. Kalauch ARO	23.10	97.50
			2 R. Greasley/ C. Holland	Chell Yamaha	1.10.59.8	95.65			
			3 M. Hobson/M. Burns	Ham Yamaha	1.11.09.6	95.43			
	Sidecar 1000cc	113.19	1 M. Hobson/M. Burns	750 Ham Yamaha	1.09.27.8	97.77	M. Hobson/M. Burns	22.38.8	99.96
			2 S. Schauzu/ W. Kalauch	750 BMW	1.10.12.4	96.73			
			3 D. Greasley/ C. Holland	700 Chell Yamaha	1.10.50.6	95.86			

Year	RACE Class	Miles	Rider	Machine	Time hms	Speed mph	Fastest Laps	Time ms	Speed mph
1977	**Senior**	188.65	1 P. W. Read	497 Suzuki	1.45.48.4	106.98	P. W. Read Suzuki	20.34.6	110.02
			2 T. Herron	384 Yamaha	1.47.06.6	105.67			
			3 E. Roberts	347 Yamaha	1.48.34.4	104.25			
	Junior 250cc	113.19	1 C. Williams	Yamaha	1.08.10.0	99.63	I. Richards	22.18.8	101.45
			2 I. Richards	Yamaha	1.08.18.8	99.41			
			3 T. Herron	Yamaha	1.09.23.0	97.88			
	1000cc Open Classic	226.38	1 M. Grant	747 Kawasaki	2.02.37.4	110.76	M. Grant	20.04.04 (outright record)	112.77
			2 C. Williams	347 Yamaha	2.06.04.2	107.74			
			3 E. Roberts	348 Yamaha	2.08.03.0	106.07			
	Schweppes Jubilee 1000cc	150.92	1 J. Dunlop	746 Yamaha	1.23.10.6	108.87	J. Dunlop	20.24.4	110.93
			2 G. Fogarty	738 Suzuki	1.24.02.2	107.75			
			3 S. Tonkin	347 Yamaha	1.24.31.0	107.14			
	Formula 1	150.92	1 P. W. Read	820 Honda	1.33.19.6	97.02	P. W. Read	22.15	101.74
			2 R. Nicholls	860 Ducati	1.33.58.0	96.36			
			3 I. Richards	810 Honda	1.36.46.0	95.55			
	Formula 2/3	150.92	1 A. Jackson	550 Honda	1.31.8.0	99.36	A. Jackson	22.22.8	101.15
			2 N. Tuxworth	590 Honda	1.32.32.6	97.84			
			3 D. Casement	450 Honda	1.34.58.4	95.34			
	Formula 3	150.92	1 J. Kidson	398 Honda	1.37.04.4	93.28	J. Kidson	52.06	94.81
			2 D. Loan	250 Suzuki	1.38.04.4	92.33			
			3 B. Peters	250 Suzuki	1.42.19.4	88.49			
	Sidecar (1st race)	150.92	1 G. O'Dell/K. Arthur	Windale/Yamaha	1.30.31.2	100.03	G. O'Dell/K. Arthur	22.12	102.80
			2 D. Greasley/ M. Skeels	Chell/Yamaha	1.31.21.2	99.12			
			3 R. Steinhausen/ W. Kalauch	Busch/Konig	1.32.17.4	98.11			
	(2nd race)	150.92	1 M. Hobson/ S. Collins	Yamaha	1.30.47.0	99.745	M. Hobson/ S. Collins	22.15	101.76

Year	Race	Distance	Pos	Rider	Machine	Time	Speed	Fastest lap	Lap time	Lap speed
			2	R. Biland/ K. Williams	Schmid/Yamaha	1.31.46.8	98.66			
			3	R. Steinhausen/ W. Kalauch	Busch/Konig	1.31.50.0	98.60			
1978	**Senior**	226.38	1	T. Herron	Suzuki	2.01.33.4	111.74	P. Hennen Suzuki	19.53.2	113.835
			2	B. Guthrie	Suzuki	2.06.05.4	107.72			
			3	C. Mortimer	349 Yamaha	2.06.48.4	107.11			
	Junior 250cc	188.65	1	C. Mortimer	Yamaha	1.52.28.8	100.63	C. Mortimer	22.10.8	102.06
			2	C. Williams	Yamaha	1.52.57.4	100.20			
			3	T. Herron	Yamaha	1.53.56.4	99.34			
	Schweppes Classic 1000cc	226.38	1	M. Grant	750 Kawasaki	2.00.50.2	112.41	M. Grant	19.48.0	114.33 (outright record)
			2	J. Williams	496 Suzuki	2.01.41.0	111.62			
			3	A. George	738 Yamaha	2.04.10.0	109.39			
	Formula 1	226.38	1	M. Hailwood	860 Ducati	2.05.10.2	108.51	S. B. M. Hailwood	20.27.8	110.63
			2	J. G. Williams	890 Honda	2.08.07.4	106.82			
			3	I. Richards	984 Kawasaki	2.08.26.8	106.01			
	Formula 2/3	150.92	1	A. Jackson	598 Honda	1.31.08.6	99.35	A. Jackson	21.56.0	103.21
			2	D. Mason	600 Honda	1.32.42.0	97.68			
			3	N. Tuxworth	596 Honda	1.34.06.8	96.21			
	Formula 3	150.92	1	B. Smith	398 Honda	1.35.50.8	94.48	B. Smith	23.32.6	95.155
			2	D. Mortimer	250 Yamaha	1.40.31.8	90.07			
			3	J. Stephens	346 Honda	1.40.41.8	89.92			
	Sidecar (1st race)	113.19	1	D. Greasley/ G. Russell	Busch/Yamaha	1.06.44.6	101.75	R. Biland/ K. Williams Beo/Yamaha	21.48.4	103.81
			2	J. Taylor/K. Arthur	Windle/Yamaha	1.07.05.4	101.22			
			3	G. Milton/ J. Brushwood	British Magnum	1.07.53.0	100.04			
	(2nd race)	113.9	1	R. Steinhausen/ W. Kalauch	Seymaz/Yamaha	1.12.30	93.67	R. Steinhausen/ W. Kalauch	23.32.8	96.14
			2	M. Boddice/ C. Birks	Woodhouse/ Yamaha	1.14.13.6	91.49			
			3	J. Taylor/K. Arthur	Windle/Yamaha	1.14.38.6	90.98			

Year	RACE Class	Miles	Rider	Machine	Time hms	Speed mph	Fastest Laps	Time ms	Speed mph
1979	**Senior**	226.38	1 M. Hailwood	Suzuki	2.01.32.4	111.75	M. Hailwood	19.51.2	114.02
			2 T. Rutter	Suzuki	2.03.39.4	109.84			
			3 D. Ireland	Suzuki	2.04.07.2	109.43			
	Junior 250cc	226.38	1 C. Williams	Yamaha	2.09.11.8	105.13	C. Williams	21.11.4	106.83
			2 G. McGregor	Yamaha	2.10.19.6	104.22			
			3 I. Richards	Yamaha	2.10.25.6	104.14			
	1000cc Open Classic	226.38	1 A. George	998 Honda	2.00.07.0	113.08	A. George	19.49.6	114.18
			2 M. Hailwood	500 Suzuki	2.00.10.4	113.03			
			3 C. Williams	350 Yamaha	2.03.29.4	109.99			
	Formula 1	226.38	1 A. George	Honda	2.02.50.6	110.27	A. George	20.02.6	112.94
			2 C. Williams	Honda	2.03.46.2	109.74			
			3 R. Haslam	Honda	2.05.00	108.66			
	Formula 2	150.92	1 A. Jackson	600 Honda	1.29.09.8	101.55	A. Jackson	21.53.6	103.40
			2 R. Bowler	600 Honda	1.30.51.0	99.67			
			3 S. Tonkin	600 Honda	1.31.50.8	98.59			
	Formula 3	150.92	1 B. Smith	250 Yamaha	1.32.33.8	97.82	B. Smith	22.46.8	99.37
			2 R. Hunter	400 Honda	1.37.13.2	93.14			
			3 M. Wheeler	350 Aermacchi	1.39.05.0	91.39			
	Sidecar (1st race)	113.19	1 T. Iveson/ C. Pollington	Yamaha	1.06.29.4	102.14	M. Boddice/ C. Birks Yamaha	21.55.4	103.26
			2 D. Greasley/ J. Parkins	Yamaha	1.06.51.4	101.58			
			3 M. Boddice/C. Birks	Yamaha	1.07.56.2	99.96			
	(2nd race)	113.19	1 T. Iveson/ C. Pollington	Yamaha	1.07.22.6	100.79	R. Steinhausen/ K. Arthur Yamaha	22.09.4	102.17
			2 N. Rollason/ D. Homer	Barton Phoenix	1.08.02.0	99.82			
			3 D. Sevill/ H. Sanderson	Yamaha	1.08.13.0	99.55			

1980	**Senior**	226.38	1	G. Crosby	Suzuki	2.03.52.2	109.65	S. Woods Suzuki	20.19.6	111.37
			2	S. Cull	Suzuki	2.04.45.6	108.87			
			3	S. Ward	Suzuki	2.05.05.2	108.58			
	Junior 250cc	150.92	1	C. Williams	Yamaha	1.28.34.8	102.22	D. Robinson	21.39.4	104.53
			2	D. Robinson	Yamaha	1.28.36.2	102.00			
			3	S. Tonkin	Cotton	1.29.06.6	101.61			
	1000cc Open Classic	226.38	1	J. Dunlop	750 Yamaha	2.00.29.8	112.72	J. Dunlop	19.38.8 (outright record)	115.22
			2	M. Grant	1062 Honda	2.00.50.2	112.40			
			3	R. Haslam	999 Honda	2.03.02.6	110.39			
	Formula 1	226.38	1	M. Grant	999 Honda	2.08.59.8	105.29	S. McClements	21.10.8	106.88
			2	G. Crosby	998 Suzuki	2.09.10.6	105.14			
			3	S. McClements	996 Honda	2.09.12.6	105.12			
	Formula 2	150.92	1	C. Williams	350 Yamaha	1.34.04.0	96.2	C. Williams	23.03.6	98.17
			2	C. Guy	600 Honda	1.36.04.0	94.26			
			3	M. Lucas	600 Honda	1.37.43.6	92.65			
	Sidecar (1st race)	113.2	1	T. Ireson/ C. Pollington	Yamaha	1.09.12.2	98.13	J. Taylor/ B. Johansson	22.20	100.61
			2	J. Taylor/ B. Johansson	Yamaha	1.09.18.2	97.99			
			3	D. Greasley/ J. Parkins	Yamaha	1.10.12.4	96.73			
	(2nd race)	113.19	1	J. Taylor/ B. Johansson	Yamaha	1.05.34.8	103.55	J. Taylor/ B. Johansson	21.20.4 (new record lap)	106.08
			2	T. Ireson/ C. Pollington	Yamaha	1.06.09.8	102.64			
			3	N. Rollason/ D. Homer	Barton Phoenix	1.06.41.8	101.82			
1981	**Senior**	226.38	1	M. Grant	Suzuki	2.07.58.2	106.14	M. Grant	20.05.4	112.68
			2	D. Robinson	Yamaha	2.10.32.4	104.05			
			3	J. Newbold	Suzuki	2.10.58.2	103.77			

Year	RACE Class	Miles	Rider	Machine	Time hms	Speed mph	Fastest Laps	Time ms	Speed mph
	Junior 250cc	226.38	1 S. Tonkin	Armstrong CCM	2.07.53.0	106.21	G. McGregor Kawasaki	20.43.6	109.22
			2 R. Jackson	WLT Yamaha	2.09.15.2	105.08			
			3 C. Williams	Yamaha	2.09.39.0	104.76			
	1000cc Open Classic	226.38	1 G. Crosby	Suzuki	1.59.34.8	113.58	J. Dunlop Honda	19.37.0	115.40
			2 M. Grant	Suzuki	2.00.04.8	113.11			
			3 A. George	Honda	2.02.14.0	111.12			
	Formula 1	226.38	1 G. Crosby	Suzuki	2.01.28.2	111.81	G. Crosby	19.54.6	113.70
			2 R. Haslam	Honda	2.03.29.8	109.98			
			3 J. Dunlop	Honda	2.04.07.6	109.41			
	Formula 2	150.92	1 T. Rutter	Ducati	1.28.51.4	101.91	T. Rutter	21.52.2	103.51
			2 P. Odlin	Honda	1.30.22.8	100.19			
			3 C. Williams	Yamaha	1.31.46.8	98.67			
	Formula 3	150.92	1 B. Smith	Yamaha	1.30.51.4	99.66	B. Smith	22.20.6	101.31
			2 D. Rayborn	Yamaha	1.33.04.2	97.29			
			3 D. Casement	Yamaha	1.34.39.8	95.65			
	Sidecar (1st race)	113.19	1 J. Taylor/ B. Johansson	Yamaha	1.03.27.4	107.02	J. Taylor/ B. Johansson	20.56.2	108.12
			2 M. Boddice/C. Birks	Yamaha	1.06.17.6	102.44			
			3 D. Bayley/R. Bryson	Yamaha	1.08.29.4	99.15			
	(2nd race)	113.19	1 J. Taylor/ B. Johansson	Yamaha	1.04.57.2	104.55	J. Taylor/ B. Johansson	21.03.0	107.54
			2 D. Greasley/ S. Atkinson	Yamaha	1.06.52.2	101.56			
			3 R. Hanks/B. Biggs	Yamaha	1.08.18.6	99.42			

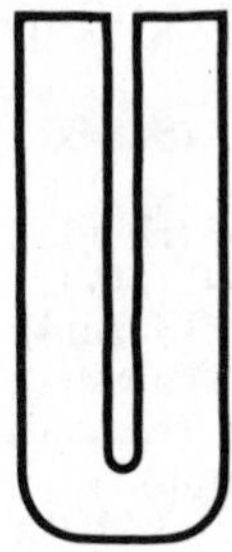

UBBIALI, Carlo

Carlo Ubbiali (born Bergamo, Italy, 1929) was one of the most successful and gifted riders the world has known in the 125cc and 250cc classes. In ten years of competition up to 1960 he was 125cc World Champion six times, runner-up three times, and won more than 30 classic races. In the same period he was 250cc World Champion three times and double World Champion in 1956, 1959 and 1960. He was 20 when he began racing and was soon spotted by Mondial, joining their works team to contest the 125cc class. In 1951, at 22 years of age, he won his first World Championship and remained with Mondial for three years. In 1953 he joined MV Agusta. At first he was unsuccessful with MV against the superior German NSU machines. With the retirement of NSU from world competition there was little opposition for MV and Ubbiali notched six out of a possible ten World Championships and was a TT winner seven times. He was generally acknowledged to be one of motor-cycle racing's most outstanding tacticians, riding with a great deal of guile and craft.

Ubbiali ultimately won the World Championship nine times, a record he held until it was exceeded by Mike Hailwood. He retired from racing in 1960.

Much more recognition at a popular level would have come Ubbiali's way had he contested the more glamorous and newsworthy larger capacity classes and not specialised on the 125 and 250cc categories. But Ubbiali's diminutive stature made him an ideal candidate for the riding of these lighter machines and his calm, untemperamental approach to racing made him one of the most admired and respected characters in the sport. His first appearance in the TT was in 1951 when he was second in the lightweight (125) event and his remarkable record over the next nine years brought him five firsts and seven seconds. In fifteen rides on the Island he retired twice and on only one other occasion was lower than second– being fifth in the lightweight (125) TT of 1959.

Results:

World Champion 125cc: 1951 (Mondial), 1955 (MV), 1956 (MV), 1958 (MV), 1959 (MV), and 1960 (MV).

World Champion 250cc: 1956 (MV), 1959 (MV) and 1960 (MV).

TT Races:

1951: second, lightweight 125cc (Mondial);
1952: second, lightweight 125cc (Mondial);
1953: retired, lightweight 125cc (MV);
1954: second, lightweight 125cc (MV);
1955: first, lightweight 125cc (MV);
1956: first in the lightweight 125cc and lightweight 250cc (MV);
1957: second lightweight 125cc (MV) and retired lightweight 250cc (MV);
1958: first lightweight 125cc (MV) and second lightweight 250cc (MV);
1959: fifth lightweight 125cc (MV) and second lightweight 250cc (MV);
1960: first lightweight 125cc (MV) and second lightweight 250cc (MV).

ULSTER GRAND PRIX

This classic event takes place on Ireland's premier $7\frac{1}{2}$-mile road race circuit at Dundrod (see seperate entry), just outside Belfast. Because of the problems in Northern Ireland there was no Ulster Grand Prix in 1972. Instead, an international race was held at an aerodrome circuit away from Belfast. It returned in 1973, and to Dundrod, but was not a World Championship round. A brave fight against extinction has been waged by the organisers at Dundrod. The race control building was bombed, security along the public roads of the course was a headache, and there were acute financial problems. But the airfield meeting in 1972 and permission by the Stormont Parliament to allow the organisers to charge for admission, helped to improve the financial situation.

In 1969, following the FIM's declaration that all grand prix programmes must include five races, the 125cc race was dropped and 50cc and sidecar events included. Sidecars had not been part of the Ulster programme since 1956 and there had not before been a 50cc event. Because of the Irish troubles the Ulster GP lost its Classic status after 1971.

Results:

1950: 125cc C. Ubbiali (Mondial); 250cc M. Cann (Guzzi); 350cc A. R. Foster (Velocette), 500cc G. E. Duke (Norton).
1951: 125cc W. A. C. McCandless (Mondial); 250cc B. Ruffo (Guzzi); 350cc G. E. Duke (Norton); 500cc G. E. Duke (Norton).
1952: 125cc C. C. Sandford (MV); 250cc M. Cann (Guzzi); 350cc K. T. Kavanagh (Norton); 500cc W. A. C. McCandless (Gilera).
1953: 125cc W. Haas (NSU); 250cc H. R. Armstrong (NSU); 350cc K. H. Mudford (Norton); 500cc K. T. Kavanagh (Norton); sidecar C. Smith (Norton).
1954: 125cc R. Hollaus (NSU); 250cc W. Haus (NSU); 350cc W. R. Amm (Norton); 500cc W. R. Amm (Norton); sidecar E. S. Oliver (Norton).
1955: 250cc J. Surtees (NSU); 350cc W. A. Lomas (Guzzi); 500cc W. A. Lomas (Guzzi).
1956: 125cc G. Ubbiali (MV); 250cc L. Taveri (MV); 350cc W. A. Lomas (Guzzi); 500cc J. Hartle (Norton); sidecar W. Noll (BMW).
1957: 125cc L. Taveri (MV); 250cc C. C. Sandford (Mondial); 350cc K. Campbell (Guzzi); 500cc L. Liberati (Gilera).
1958: 125cc C. Ubbiali (MV); 250cc T. Provini (MV); 350cc J. Surtees (MV); 500cc J. Surtees (MV).
1959: 125cc S. M. B. Hailwood (Ducati); 250cc G. Hocking (MZ); 350cc J. Surtees (MV); 500cc J. Surtees (MV).
1960: 125cc C. Ubbiali (MV); 250cc C. Ubbiali (MV); 350cc J. Surtees (MV); 500cc J. Hartle (Norton).
1961: 125cc K. Takahashi (Honda); 250cc R. McG. McIntyre (Honda); 350cc G. Hocking (MV); 500cc G. Hocking (MV);
1962: 125cc L. Taveri (Honda); 250cc T. H. Robb (Honda); 350cc J. A. Redman (Honda); 500cc S. M. B. Hailwood (MV).
1963: 125cc H. R. Anderson (Suzuki); 250cc J. A. Redman (Honda); 350cc J. A. Redman (Honda); 500cc S. M. B. Hailwood (MV).
1964: 125cc H. R. Anderson (Suzuki); 250cc P. W. Read (Yamaha); 350cc J. A. Redman (Honda); 500cc P. W. Read (Norton).
1965: 125cc E. Degner (Suzuki); 250cc P. W. Read (Yamaha); 350cc F. Stastny (Jawa); 500cc R. Creith (Norton).
1966: 125cc L. Taveri (Honda); 250cc G. Molloy (Bultaco); 350cc S. M. B. Hailwood (Honda); 500cc S. M. B. Hailwood (Honda).
1967: 125cc W. D. Ivy (Yamaha); 250cc S. M. B. Hailwood (Honda); 350cc G. Agostini (MV); 500cc S. M. B. Hailwood (Honda).
1968: 125cc W. D. Ivy (Yamaha); 250cc W. D. Ivy (Yamaha); 350cc G. Agostini (MV); 500cc G. Agostini (MV).
1969: 50cc A. Nieto (Derbi); 250cc K. Carruthers (Benelli); 350cc G. Agostini (MV); 500cc G. Agostini (MV); sidecar K. Enders (BMW).
1970: 50cc A. Nieto (Derbi); 250cc K. Carruthers (Yamaha); 350cc G. Agostini (MV); 500cc G. Agostini (MV); sidecars K. Enders (BMW).
1971: 250cc R. McCullough (Yamsel); 350cc P. J. Williams (MZ); 500cc J. Findlay (Suzuki); sidecar H. Owesle/P. Rutterford (Munch).
1972: Not run.
1973: 250cc J. G. Williams (Yamaha); 350cc J. G. Williams (Yamaha); 500cc J. G. Williams (Yamaha); sidecar D. Keen/D. Houghton (500 Konig).
1974: 250cc A. Hockley (Granby Yamaha); 350cc T. Rutter (Yamaha); 500cc T. Rutter (325 Yamaha); sidecar D. Edgington/T. Sanways (680 Konig).
1975: 250cc A. Rutter (Yamaha); 350cc R. McCullough (Yamsel); 500cc M. Robinson (Yamsel); 1000cc P. Tait (Yamaha); sidecar R. McConnell/G. Stewart (750 Vroom).
1976: 250cc R. McCullough (Yamaha); 350cc R. McCullough (Yamaha); 500cc S. Woods (Suzuki); 1000cc G. Barry (Yamaha).
1977: 250cc T. Herron (Yamaha); 350cc T. Herron (Yamaha); 500cc J. Wil-

liams (Suzuki); 1000cc J. Williams (Yamaha); sidecar M. Boddice/C. Birks (Yamaha).

1978: 250cc T. Herron (Yamaha); 350cc J. Ekerold (Yamaha); 500cc J. Williams (Suzuki); 1000cc T. Herron (Yamaha); sidecar M. Boddice/C. Birks (Yamaha).

1979: 250cc R. McCullough (Yamaha); 350cc D. Robinson (Yamaha); 500cc J. Dunlop (Suzuki); 1000cc J. Dunlop (Yamaha).

1980: 250cc J. Dunlop (Yamaha); 350cc R. McCullough (Yamaha); 500cc D. Robinson (Suzuki); classic J. Dunlop (1000cc Suzuki).

1981: 250cc T. Rutter (Yamaha); 350cc G. McGregor (Yamaha); 500cc G. Lingham (Suzuki); classic R. Haslam (Honda); Formula 1 R. Haslam (Honda); Formula 2 P. Mellor (Yamaha); Formula 3 B. Smith (Yamaha).

VELOCETTE

Included among the small élite group of British racers which shared many of the honours in the years between the wars, Velocette machines were manufactured by the Veloce Company of Birmingham which was established in 1904 and closed in 1971. Velocette is thus one of the earliest makes of British designs and a Velocette "works" machine competed in the TT as early as 1913, when Cyril Pullin finished 22nd in the Junior event. The firm first moved into racing prominence in 1926 (having had two machines retire in the TT of 1925) when Alec Bennett won the Junior TT by more than 10 minutes at a record of 66.70 mph on one of the new single cylinder overhead camshaft machines, an early version of the famous Velocette KTT model which was to gain two further Junior TTs and numerous Continental victories before yielding to the challenge from works' Nortons and Rudges. In 1926 it was significantly superior to anything else in the field.

After Bennett's 1928 TT victory the factory marketed a replica of the winning machines, known as the KTT. Thus Veloce became the first factory to produce an over-the-counter racer, giving road racing opportunities to a great many more riders. It was a major development for until then only those who were able to get the factory-type racers had any chance of success.

It was quite extraordinary that although the KTT engine had been designed in the mid-1920s and remained in its basic form for the next couple of decades (though it went through numerous modifications and had its power increased), it was sufficiently competitive to return strongly to take the Junior TT in 1938-39 and yet again in 1948-49. In the pre-war years a 500 version of the 350 was sufficiently potent for Walter Rusk to bring Velocette a third place in the Senior and Stanley Woods, one of the greatest TT riders of all time, rode the 500 Velocette into second place in the Senior three years in succession, 1936-38;

In an effort to combat the emergence of Continental makes immediately prior to the outbreak of war, Velocette produced an exciting supercharged vertical twin 500cc machine with geared cranks and shaft drive and this machine, known as the Roarer, showed great promise in the hands of Stanley Woods when he practiced it on the Isle of Man; but sadly International events of greater magnitude overtook the project. Immediately after the war Velocette did not support an official works team, though assisted private owners, and this, plus the banning of superchargers by the FIM in 1946, meant that the 500 machine was never raced. The design was such that modification to the new rules would have been difficult and expensive, so Velocette dusted off the unblown singles of 1938 and recaptured that old pre-war Velocette magic in the 350 class. It must be said that circumstances assisted the factory for the KTT design ran more happily on the obligatory "pool" petrol of immediate post-war years than did its major competitors including, perhaps most significant of all, the Manx Norton.

In 1947 Velocette machines occupied all first three places in the Junior TT, Bob Foster winning at 80.31 mph and David Whitworth (second) setting the fastest lap at 81.61 mph. Success continued into 1948 with Frith and Foster coming home first and second. Frith again won in 1949, a year in which he also captured the 350cc World Championship for Velocette with Bob Foster in second place. These "world" victories were achieved on a twin overhead-cam KTT, the result of a special effort of Velocette following the introduction of the World Championship. It was the first year of the World Championships and significant for Velocette for although Foster brought them the 350 world title again in 1950 the KTT design was rapidly becoming outdated and was no match for the all-conquering Nortons of the following year.

Velocette were always known for their versatility and enterprise and during the many years the Veloce Company supported racing they were responsible for many novel and important innovations. As far back as 1924 Veloce, not indifferent to the potential of the two-stroke, were experimenting with timed-valve-induction. I26 they were the first to put the overhead-camshaft on any size of machine and in 1928 came the first positive-stop foot gear change (on Alec Bennett's successful TT machine) recognised as such an advance that the idea was promptly adopted by other factories. There had of course been foot changes before, but mostly from the origins of hand levers, but with a different pedal position for each gear. The 1928 Velocettes introduced the ratchet-type device and so obviously assisted Bennett achieve his TT win at a record 68.65 mph, also recording a lap of 70.28 mph, the first 70 mph lap speed by a 350.

Also in 1928 they were seriously experimenting with pivoted-fork rear springing, though rigid frames continued to be used until 1936, and some years later they introduced what was the forerunner of the modern untriangulated pivoted fork controlled by compressed air and hydraulic damping, much more sophisticated than the plunger systems then generally in use. They also had a hand in the development of the modern racing seat and, of course, made the successful change from single to double overhead camshafts.

In 1928 Velocette 350cc ohc models broke around 50 world records in 350, 500, 750 and 1000cc classes as well as achieving a first, second and fifth in the Junior TT.

In 1936 came the swinging-arm rear-suspension.

Among these many distinctions must be noted Velocette's exceeding of 100 mph, the first 350cc to do so, and the first-ever recorded 100 mph average for 24 hours. In their history they recorded 8 TT wins, 11 seconds and 8 thirds, including the one-two of the Velo Thruxton Venom in the Production 500cc TT of 1967 and the second place in the similar event of 1968.

There is little doubt that Velocettes could have reached greater success in 1930-38 had they concentrated more on "works" machines, but history records that they preferred to apply much of their energies into development of their ohc design as a production racer. This was their policy and it is interesting to note that the 1928 TT winner was introduced virtually unchanged as the KTT model of 1929. While this policy curtailed more lofty victories it should not be forgotten that Velocette machines occupied the first eight places in the Manx Grand Prix of 1930.

By 1936, however, the Veloce Company had sensed the dangers in remaining faithful to their original concept of design and in order to boost prestige their ten-year-old engine incorporated double overhead camshafts for the first time.

In 1949 seven special engines were produced, two each of 350cc and 500cc capacity, for Frith and Bills and the remainder for Bob Foster, David Whitworth and Ernie Thomas racing through private entrants. The engines were of double overhead camshaft design, not too far different from the original 1935 version, though the crankcase and rockerbox castings had been lightened as had the cylinder-head and barrel, now made of light alloy. Freddie Frith won the Junior with Bill Doran, coming in for the injured Ken Bills, taking second place. At this point the 350cc engine was said to peak at around 116 mph in top gear. It was this machine which took Frith to every major Grand Prix that year, bringing him the 350cc world crown.

By 1950 Frith had retired and the Veloce Company faced its first really serious challenge with the introduction of the "featherbed" Norton and a team of Norton riders which included Bell, Daniell and a newcomer named Geoffrey Duke. Although Velocettes were swamped on the Isle of Man Bob Foster took over Frith's mantle and raced Velocettes into a second World Championship in two years.

As a small independent manufacturer determined to avoid being absorbed into a larger combine, and faced with the increasing costs of competition, the difficulties of remaining in racing were obvious. Ambition still ran high within the firm and although it was destined never to be introduced, one of a number of ambitious projects that was started in 1950 was an in-line four to meet the increasing challenge from the Italian MV and Gilera factories. The aim was to have it ready by 1953, but a change in company policy and a lack of outside capital which was now virtually essential to maintain an active interest in racing, brought the project to a premature end. Towards the end of its racing history

Veloce directed interest towards the lightweight class and had three double overhead camshaft models which were really "cut down" versions of the KTT for Bob Foster, Bill Lomas and Cecil Sandford, and there was a new 350 with a five-speed gearbox for Bob Foster; but in neither class was Velocettes able to get among the honours on the Isle of Man. By 1952 their only support was a works 348cc KTT for Cecil Sandford and a 350cc for Les Graham, who had shown promise with consistent riding of a privately entered KTT the previous season. It was a last, and generally unsuccessful fling, for at the end of 1952 it was decided that the firm could no longer support racing and the racing department was closed down.

Included in any account of Velocette's place in racing must be Harold Willis, who in 1927 rode the 350 into second place in the TT, the only Velocette to finish. In the 1930s he became considerably involved with development within the firm and to him, with the late Percy Goodman, a member of the family which founded the firm, goes the credit for the first-ever positive-stop footchange. Willis died in 1939.

VENEZUELAN GRAND PRIX

Results:

1979: 125cc A. Nieto (Minarelli); 250cc W. Villa (Yamaha); 350cc C. Lavado (Yamaha); 500cc B. Sheene (Suzuki).

VESCO, Don

Californian Vesco held the world motor cycle speed record in 1970 and again in 1974. In 1970 he clocked 251.9 mph with a streamlined projectile powered by two 350cc Yamaha road racing engines. He held the record for less than a month, but won it back in 1974, exceeding Cal Rayborn's 265.492 mph with an average for the two mile-runs, one in each direction, of 281.714 mph. Vesco later pushed the record even higher, to 303 mph on a Yamaha in 1975 and, after signing for Kawasaki, to 314.598 mph in 1978.

VILLA, Walter

An Italian from Modena, Villa entered the record books in 1974 when he took Harley-Davidson into the European-based World Championships for the first time. He gained the 250cc world title. His first championship win was in the Italian Grand Prix at Imola in 1974. He later won the Dutch and Finnish Grands Prix. Walter Villa (born 1944) began racing in 1962 and achieved success in Italy, winning five Italian championships, He first made impact in the Grands Prix in 1973 riding Yamahas, finishing second in the Austrian Grand Prix. Villa has ridden a variety of machines but has never had a comprehensive works contract. He had an opportunity to ride Harley-Davidson machines after Bonera left to join MV. Villa was 250cc World Champion again in 1975, when he first became a works rider. In 1976 Villa won his third 250cc world title in succession, clinching the crown in Czechoslovakia.

VINCENT, Chris J.

Britain's most successful sidecar exponent of modern times, Chris Vincent (born 1935) came to notice in 1961 by driving an extremely low sidecar with a great deal of flourish. He switched to sidecar road racing in 1959 after winning the British grass track sidecar championship in 1958. Six times British Champion and A-CU Star winner (1961, 1964-5, 1969-71) Vincent did less well in the TTs when up against the power and reliability of the BMWs. His first TT appearance was in 1960 and after retirements that year and in 1961 he won the event on a BSA in 1962. After many years of success with his own BSA outfits, Vincent raced the the four-cylinder Munch outfit in 1972 and at the Finnish Grand Prix that year he became the first British sidecar driver for eight years to win a World Championship race. Although he has specialised in sidecar racing on road, grass and in speedway, Vincent has also raced solo machines. His best solo performance on the Isle of Man was in 1967 (eighth in the 250cc Production TT on a Suzuki).

VINCENT HRD

This company's racing activity started in 1925 when H. R. Davies won the Senior TT and was second in the Junior on machines of his own manufacture. Freddie Dixon won the 1927 Junior TT on another HRD. In 1928 HRD sold out to Philip Vincent who, after a period of development and the introduction of his now famous spring frame and engine, re-entered the racing scene gaining some success in the Island and demonstrating his spring frame to advantage (the Italians, Japanese and others were later to follow this design into 1975 on their latest works road-racing and scramble machines).

The first of the 1000cc V-twins (the series A) appeared on the racing scene at Donington Park in 1939, ridden by "Ginger" Wood, who established a new petrol-benzole lap record. It was after the war however that the then Vincent HRD company startled the racing world when the totally re-designed 1000cc V-twin appeared all over the world establishing solo and sidecar records culminating in the world's fastest "record" solo at 185 mph and 176 mph – this with a production "Black Lightning" as the 1000cc racer was known, which sold for £500.

The most successful riders of the "big twins" were George Brown (solo) and Ted Davis (sidecar), both of whom worked at the Vincent company, although many riders including John Surtees, who also worked at Vincent's Stevenage factory, rode the 500cc single cylinder racer know as the Grey Flash with considerable success on all the home circuits. In 1952 the Vincent Black Shadow established eight world long-distance records at Montlhery (near Paris) ridden by John Surtees, Ted Davis, Cyril Julian, Phil Heath and several other well known racers of that era. All motor-cycle production ceased in 1955, the year a Vincent took the world absolute record (Wright of New Zealand at 185 mph).

VINICOMBE, Terry

A sidecar racer of note, Terry Vinicombe died in January 1969, aged 31. Winner of the first ever 750cc sidecar TT in the Isle of Man in 1968, Vinicombe was one of Britain's most prominent and successful sidecar racers in the 1960s. In 1964, with John Flaxman as passenger, he was sponsored by Tom Kirby. With Chris Vincent he is regarded as a pioneer of the use of the BSA twin in sidecar racing. He is also remembered for his breaking of the nine-year-old sidecar race record at the Crystal Palace in 1965 (70.80 mph) on a 649 Triumph, when he was already the lap record holder.

WESLAKE

Since Britain lost its dominant role in motor-cycle racing there have been a number of projects announced which had as an objective the building of a British racing engine to give Britain a road racing "world beater". Such was the Weslake project, announced in the 1960s and with which, for a while, champion rider Phil Read was associated. Harry Weslake, the man behind the scheme, had been actively involved in motorcycle racing previously; for the first time during the days of Brooklands and later during the dying days of Norton in 1954-55. The aim in the 1960s was a 75 bhp 500cc twin revving to 11,000 and weighing, complete with five-speed gear box and clutch, under 100lb; and to have it ready within six months. The project received a boost in 1968 when Phil Read subordinated his competitive programme to voluntary service to the Weslake project for testing and racing. But the engine development work was delayed and the first appearance of the Weslake, in Ireland, was not very promising when it suffered lubrication problems during practice for the North West 200. With progress difficult to make, the Weslake "world beater" project faltered and Read, frustrated and impatient - and tempted back into racing with lucrative new-season offers, finally severed his association with it. The "world beater" project never really materialised, though Harry Weslake maintained as recently as 1972 that it had not been abandoned entirely, only shelved. In the meantime Weslake worked on racing engines different from the original "world beater" conception. By 1972 they were offering twin cylinder engines producing in excess of 80 bhp in 750cc form, and became actively involved in road racing, with sidecar specialist Bill Currie racing an outfit powered by a works engine, and people like Colin Seeley, who produced a frame kit for the 750 engine; Ray Petty also became involved. This increasing activity in the sport heightened Weslake's reputation and in 1974 their four-valve single speedway engine was being considered a possible serious contender. Later, sprint expert John Hobbs chose the Weslake eight-valve twin for his new drag bike on which in 1975 he hoped to secure the first Britsh eight-second standing quarter mile. But the "world beater" project for which Weslake first came to prominence in the 1960s had still not come to fruition in 1975. Weslake engines later became very successful in both speedway and grass track.

WEST GERMAN GRAND PRIX

The West German Grand Prix has had a number of homes. The early Hockenheim circuit, near Heidelberg, extended to 4.80 miles and as early as 1957 Bob McIntyre set a lap record of 129.55 mph on a 500cc Gilera. The circuit, consisting basically of two straights and two hairpins, offered little scope for a rider to employ his skills and it was generally the rider with the fastest machine who won. It was not a particular favourite with the riders of the day and there were few regrets when the West German Grand Prix moved to Solitude.

This 7.09 miles course situated near Stuttgart was preferable from both a rider's and a spectator's point of view. It was slower than Hockenheim and set in beautiful forest country.

Perhaps the most famous of all the West German circuits is the Nurburgring, accepted by many riders to be the most complicated. Situated near Adenau in the neighbourhood of Koblenz, it is 14.17 miles long and includes many corners, hairpins, bankings and gradients. It incorporates 170 corners and, together with changes of camber and surface, is undoubtedly a rider's circuit. For a number of years the German Grand Prix was run on the south loop of the circuit, the north loop being used for the first time in 1970. A walk-out of Grand Prix Stars took place at the Nurburgring in 1974 as a protest against what they alleged to be inadequate safety protection. The West German Grand Prix is now held alternately at Hockenheim, revised in 1966 and again in 1970, and the Nurburgring.

Results:

1952: 125cc W. Haas (NSU): 250cc R. Felgenheier (DKW): 350cc H. R. Armstrong (Norton): 500cc H. R. Armstrong (Norton): sidecar C. Smith (Norton).

1953: 125cc C. Ubbiali (MV): 250cc W. Haas (NSU): 350cc C. Bandirola (MV): 500cc W. Zeller (BMW).

1954: 125cc R. Hollaus (NSU): 250cc W. Haas (NSU): 350cc W. R. Amm (Norton): 500cc G. E. Duke (Gilera): sidecar W. Noll (BMW).

1955: 125cc C. Ubbiali (MV): 250cc H. P. Muller (NSU): 350cc W. A. Lomas (Guzzi): 500cc G. E. Duke (Gilera): sidecar W. Faust (BMW).

1956: 125cc R. Ferri (Gilera): 250cc C. Ubbiali (MV): 350cc W. A. Lomas (Guzzi): 500cc H. R. Armstrong (Gilera): sidecar W. Noll (BMW).

1957: 125cc C. Ubbiali (MV): 250cc C. Ubbiali (MV): 350cc L. Liberati (Gilera): 500cc L. Liberati (Gilera): sidecar F. Hillebrand (BMW).

1958: 125cc C. Ubbiali (MV): 250cc T. Provini (MV): 350cc J. Surtees (MV): 500cc J. Surtees (MV): sidecar W. Schneider (BMW).

1959: 125cc C. Ubbiali (MV): 250cc C. Ubbiali (MV): 350cc J. Surtees (MV): 500cc J. Surtees (MV): sidecar F. Camathias (BMW).

1960: 250cc G. Hocking (MV): 500cc J. Surtees (MV): sidecar H. Fath (BMW).

1961: 125cc F. Degner (MZ): 250cc K. Takahashi (Honda): 350cc F. Stastny (Jawa): 500cc G. Hocking (MV): sidecar M. Deubel (BMW).

1962: 50cc E. Degner (Suzuki): 125cc L. Taveri (Honda): 250cc J. A. Redman (Honda): sidecar M. Deubel (BMW).

1963: 50cc H. R. Anderson (Suzuki): 125cc E. Degner (Suzuki): 250cc T. Provini (Morini): 350cc J. A. Redman (Honda): sidecar F. Camathias (BMW).

1964: 50cc R. Bryans (Honda): 125cc J. A. Redman (Honda): 250cc P. W. Read (Yamaha): 350cc J. A. Redman (Honda): 500cc S. M. B. Hailwood (MV): sidecar F. Scheidegger (BMW).

1965: 50cc R. Bryans (Honda): 125cc H. R. Anderson (Suzuki): 250cc P. W. Read (Yamaha): 350cc G. Agostini (MV): 500cc S. M. B. Hailwood (MV): sidecar F. Scheidegger (BMW).

1966: 50cc H. G. Anscheidt (Suzuki): 125cc L. Taveri (Honda): 250cc S. M. B. Hailwood (Honda): 350cc S. M. B. Hailwood (Honda): 500cc J. Redman (Honda): sidecar F. Scheidegger (BMW).

1967: 50cc H. G. Anscheidt (Suzuki): 125cc Y. Katayama (Suzuki): 250cc R. Bryans (Honda): 350cc S. M. B. Hailwood (Honda): 500cc G. Agostini (MV): sidecars K. Enders/R. Engelhardt (BMW).

1968: 50cc H. G. Anscheidt (Suzuki): 125cc P. W. Read (Yamaha): 250cc W. D. Ivy (Yamaha): 350cc G. Agostini (MV): 500cc G. Agostini (MV): sidecars H. Fath/W. Kalauch (URS).

1969: 50cc A. Toersen (Kreidler): 125cc D. A. Simmonds (Kawasaki): 250cc K. Andersson (Yamaha): 350cc G. Agostini (MV): 500cc G. Agostini (MV): sidecars K. Enders/R. Engelhardt (BMW).

1970: 50cc A. Nieto (Derbi): 125cc J. Dodds (Aermacchi): 250cc K. Carruthers (Yamaha): 350cc G. Agostini (MV): 500cc G. Agostini (MV): sidecars G. Auerbacher/H. Hahn (BMW).

1971: 50cc J. De Vries (Kreidler): 125cc D. Simmonds (Kawasaki): 250cc P. W. Read (Yamaha): 350cc G. Agostini (MV): 500cc G. Agostini (MV): sidecars G. Auerbacher/H. Hahn (BMW).

1972: 50cc J. de Vries (Kreidler): 125cc G. Parlotti (Morbidelli): 250cc H. Kanaya (Yamaha): 350cc J. Saarinen (Yamaha): 500cc G. Agostini (MV): sidecars S. Schauzu/W. Kalauch (BMW).

1973: 50cc T. Timmer (Jamathi): 125cc K. Andersson (Yamaha): 250cc J. Saarinen (Yamaha): 350cc T. Lansivuori (Yamaha): 500cc P. W. Read (MB): sidecars K. Enders (BMW).

1974: 50cc I. Emmerich (Kreidler): 125cc F. Reitmaier (Maico): 250cc H. Kassner (Yamaha): 350cc H. Kassner (Yamaha): 500cc E. Czihak (Yamaha): sidecars W. Schwarzel/K. H. Kleis (Konig).

1975: 50cc A. Nieto (Kreidler); 125cc P. Pileri (Morbidelli); 250cc W. Villa (Harley-Davidson); 350cc C. Cecotto (Yamaha); 500cc G. Agostini (Yamaha); sidecar R. Biland/F. Freiburghaus (Seyma).
1976: 50cc A. Nieto (Bultaco); 125cc A. Mang (Morbidelli); 250cc W. Villa (Harley-Davidson); 350cc W. Villa (Harley-Davidson); 500cc G. Agostini (MV Agusta); sidecars W. Schwarzel/A. Huber (Konig).
1977: 50cc H. Rittberger (Kreidler); 125cc P. Bianchi (Morbidelli); 250cc C. Sarron (Yamaha); 350cc T. Katayama (Yamaha); 500cc B. Sheene (Suzuki); sidecars R. Biland/K. Williams (Schmid-Yamaha).
1978: 50cc R. Tormo (Bultaco); 125cc A. Nieto (Minarelli); 250cc K. Ballington (Kawasaki); 350cc T. Katayama (Yamaha); 500cc V. Ferrari (Suzuki); sidecars W. Schwarzel/A. Huber (Fath).
1979: 50cc G. Waibel (Kreidler); 125cc A. Nieto (Minarelli); 250cc K. Ballington (Kawasaki); 350cc J. Ekerold (Yamaha); 500cc W. Hartog (Suzuki); sidecars (BZA) R. Steinhausen/K. Arthur (Yamaha).
1980: 50cc S. Dorflinger (Kreidler); 125cc G. Bertin (Motobecane); 250cc K. Ballington (Kawasaki); 350cc J. Ekerold (Yamaha); 500cc M. Lucchinelli (Suzuki); sidecars J. Taylor/B. Johansson (Yamaha).
1981: 50cc S. Dorflinger (Kreidler); 125cc A. Nieto (Minarelli); 250cc A. Mang (Kawasaki); 350cc A. Mang (Kawasaki); 500cc K. Roberts (Yamaha); sidecars A. Michel/M. Burkard (Yamaha).

(*See also* GERMAN GRAND PRIX; EAST GERMAN GRAND PRIX).

WILLIAMS, Peter J.
Peter Williams is best known as the number one rider in the John Player Norton team in the early and mid 1970s. Born in 1939 and the son of famous AMC race engineer Jack Williams. Peter did not begin racing seriously until 1963, when he was 24. On AJS and Matchless machines, he entered his first TT in 1966 and finished second in the Junior and seventh in the Senior.

Almost always near to success with outstanding rides on the Island (he collected six second places in as many years including two behind Agostini in the Senior), Williams had to wait until 1973 for his first victory when he won the F750 event on the John Player Norton. On an Arter Matchless he came second in the Senior race of that year. It was on the Isle of Man that he clocked 107.27 mph – the third-fastest TT lap at that time. The bespectacled Williams first aspired to a racing career while working for Ford at Dagenham and regularly attended practice sessions at Brands Hatch before buying a Manx 350 and finishing fifth in his first outing, at Snetterton, towards the end of the 1963 season. Throughout his career he has never concentrated on Grand Prix racing, though it was said in the sixties that at one time he was a serious contender for a place in the Honda team alongside Mike Hailwood. He joined John Player Norton and it was as their race team leader and development engineer that he crashed while lying third in the Oulton Park race in August 1974 and was seriously injured, just one day before his 35th birthday. It was while he was recovering from his injuries that John Player pulled out of motor cycle sponsorship and the future of the Norton team was put in doubt.

Something of an academic in motorcycle racing and a fine technical man, Peter Williams, studious looking and British 500cc champion in 1970, made his biggest impact with the John Player Norton team in F750 racing. A careful, thinking rider, Williams has been described as a rider of unpretentious talent and dedication. His achievements in earlier years were often gained in the midst of fierce competition and on outdated single-cylinder machines.

WINDROSS, Paul
In October 1974 32-year-old Paul Windross of York became the fastest man on two wheels in Britain when he recorded 207.9 mph during practice at Elvington on a 1500cc double-Triumph-engined sprint machine. This made him only the third man to reach 200 mph in Britain, Alf Hagon (206.54) in 1968 and Fred Cooper (200.4) in 1972. His aim was to record 200 mph officially in Britain and then to take his machine to Bonneville.

WOODS, Stanley
In the 1920s and 1930s Stanley Woods

became not only the most outstanding rider of his time, but a living legend in a period when motor-cycle racing was bristling with personalities and extreme talent. These were the halcyon, swash-buckling days of British motor-cycle racing, the golden age, and Stanley Woods for most people was the greatest hero of them all. Within 17 years Woods won ten TT races and though this record was established in 1939 it had still in 1980 been bettered only by one man, Mike Hailwood, and equalled by only one other, Agostini! Although he had countless victories elsewhere Woods' career is closely identifiable with the Isle of Man and he competed in 37 TT races. Of these he finished in 21 and was never more lowly placed than sixth. On three occasions he won two TT races in a week.

Stanley Woods was born in Dublin and when only seventeen competed in his first TT as a Cotton works rider. He simply wrote to them and convinced the factory of his ability. In that debut TT he by no means let them down. In spite of his engine catching fire, brake trouble and a push rod flying out, he finished in fifth position. The following year, 1923, and still riding for Cotton he registered his first TT victory, in the Junior event. He completed the course in 4 hours 3 minutes 47 seconds at an average speed of 55.73 mph. In the TTs Woods was to compete on a variety of machines: Scott, New Imperial, Royal Enfield, Norton, Husqvarna, Guzzi, DKW, Velocette.

His fourteen races for Norton brought him five victories, 1932 and 1933 being supreme when he was first in both the Senior and Junior TTs. In three out of four performances he also established the fastest lap. Woods' promise had been brought to the attention of Nortons by a Dublin motor-cycle dealer during the early part of 1926 and in spite of being largely unconvinced that they were doing the right thing, the famous British factory invited Woods to join the team for the Isle of Man that year. His team-mate for the Senior event was the redoubtable Alec Bennett, but it was newcomer Woods who rode to glory, bringing Norton victory in the Senior in his first Norton TT, also establishing a record race speed at 67.54 mph. Stanley Woods remained with Norton for the next seven years, moving to works Guzzi and Husqvarna rides in 1934 and 1935.

His move came following a disagreement with Norton, whose dominance at this point meant that Norton team members were riding more against each other for the honours, rather than against other makes. This inevitably led to Norton riders racing to team orders and when this developed to a "you win this time" routine, Woods decided it was time to quit. As Woods later commented: "It all came to a head at the Ulster in 1933 when Nortons made it clear that I wasn't to win the 500cc class. I did win, as it happens, for Tim Hunt broke down, but I left Nortons and never again rode to team orders." His short spell on foreign machinery was also successful, particularly 1935 when he rode the Italian machine into first place in both the Senior and Lightweight events, establishing fastest laps in each race. In 1936 Woods was recruited by Velocette and from then until the outbreak of war in 1939 he rode for the British factory in Junior and Senior TTs, competing only in the Lightweight event on a DKW in 1936 and Guzzi in 1937 and '39. He retired in both Guzzi races. His record with Velocette was as follows:

1936: second in the Senior and retired in the Junior;
1937: second in the Senior and fourth in the Junior;
1938: second in the Senior and first in the Junior;
1939: fourth in the Senior and first in the Junior.

During these years he set fastest laps in the Senior (86.98 mph) and the Lightweight (76.20 mph on a DKW) of 1936; the Junior (85.35 mph) of 1938 and the Lightweight (78.16 mph on the Guzzi) of 1939.

Unfortunately, the war brought the career of the great Stanley Woods to a premature end. He did not compete again, when racing resumed with the return of peace.

WOODS, Stan V.

This promising young clubman of the late 1960s with the famous name comes from Cheshire and began to do well in northern events on a 350cc BSA Gold Star in 1967. A year later he rode modified 250cc and 350cc Yamahas for Cheshire dealer Hector Dugdale. Riding a Suzuki he became prominent in the 750cc class and was British Champion in 1974, when he also was second in the Superbike Championship. In 1972

Woods won the 500cc Production TT on a Suzuki at an average of 92.20 mph and registered the fastest lap at 93.61 mph. Again on Suzuki he won the 500cc Production event at the Silverstone International in 1973 and the 750cc event at the A-CU International Trophy Meeting at Oulton Park in 1974.

WORLD CHAMPIONS

World title winners since the present championships were started in 1949 and who are not covered with separate entries in this encyclopaedia are as follows: N. Pagani (Italy), B. Ruffo, (Italy), D. Ambrosini (Italy), A. R. Foster (GB), U. Masetti (Italy), E. Lorenzetti (Italy), C. Smith (GB), W. Haas (W. Germany), R. Hollaus (Austria), W. Noll (W. Germany), H. P. Muller (W. Germany), W. Faust (W. Germany), L. Liberati (Italy), F. Hillebrand (W. Germany), W. Schneider (W. Germany), T. Phillis (Australia), M. Deubel (W. Germany), D. Braun (W. Germany), J. de Vries (Holland), H. Owestle (W. Germany), K. Andersson (Sweden), H. van Kessel (Holland), P. Pileri (Italy), R. Steinhausen (W. Germany), P. Bianchi (Italy), M. Lega (Italy), R. Tormo (Spain), E. Lazzarini (Italy), R. Biland (Switzerland), B. Holzer (Czechoslovakia), M. Lucchinelli (Italy), A. Mang (W. Germany), J. Ekerold (South Africa).

WORLD CHAMPIONSHIPS

The World Championships were started in 1949 under the auspices of the FIM. Riders gain points based on performance in a series of Grand Prix events. Since the World Championships were started the system for deciding the winners has changed. In 1949 the first five placed riders gained points – 10 for the winner, then 8, 7, 6 and 5, plus one point for a fastest lap, if this was recorded by a finishing rider. In 1950 the point for the fastest lap was abandoned and points awarded for the first six finishers – 8 points for the winner, then 6, 4, 3, 2, and 1 for sixth place. In 1969 a new system was introduced with a winner receiving 15 points and there were 12 points for the second place rider, 10 for the third, and 8, 6, 5, 4, 3, 2 and 1 point for tenth place. Only half the number of rounds held, plus 1, counted. For instance, if there were 12 Grands Prix in a class, a rider would count only his best seven. More recently this was changed so that all rounds counted towards the championship.

In the later 1970s Suzuki, through riders like Barry Sheene, Tepi Lausivuori, Pat Hennen, Wil Hartog and Marco Lucchinelli, and Yamaha, with Kenny Roberts and Johnny Cecotto, dominated the 500cc class. In the 350cc and 250cc classes Harley-Davidson, Yamaha and then Kawasaki were supreme, while the leading makes in 125cc and 50cc were Bultaco and Morbidelli.

Such is the popularity of motor cycle road racing at international level that over a million people watched the World Championships in 1977. Average attendance at each Grand Prix was almost 87,000.

1949

125cc
1 N. Pagani, Italy (Mondial) 27
2 R. Magi, Italy (Morini) 14
3 U. Masetti, Italy (Morini) 13

250cc
1 B. Ruffo, Italy (Guzzi) 24
2 D. Ambrosini, Italy (Benelli) 19
3 R. Mead, GB (Mead Norton) 13

350cc
1 F. Frith, GB (Velocette) 33
2 R. Armstrong, Ireland (AJS) 18
3 A. R. Foster, GB (Velocette) 16

500cc
1 L. Graham, GB (AJS) 30
2 N. Pagani, Italy (Gilera) 29
3 A. Artesiani, Italy (Gilera) 25

Sidecar
1 E. Oliver, GB (Norton) 26
2 E. Frigerio, Italy (Gilera) 18
3 F. Vanderschrick, Belgium (Norton) 16

1950

125cc
1 B. Ruffo, Italy (Mondial) 17
2 G. Leoni, Italy (Mondial) 14
3 C. Ubbiali, Italy (Mondial) 14

250cc
1 D. Ambrosini, Italy (Benelli) 30
2 M. Cann, GB (Guzzi) 14
3 F. Anderson, GB (Guzzi) 6

350cc
1 A. R. Foster, GB (Velocette) 30
2 G. Duke, GB (Norton) 24
3 L. Graham, GB (AJS) 17

500cc
1 U. Masetti, Italy (Gilera) 28
2 G. Duke, GB (Norton) 27
3 L. Graham, GB (AJS) 17

Sidecar
1 E. Oliver, GB (Norton) 24
2 E. Frigerio, Italy (Gilera) 18
3 H. Haldemann, Switzerland (Norton) 8

1951

125cc
1 C. Ubbiali, Italy (Mondial) 20
2 G. Leoni, Italy (Mondial) 12
3 W. McCandless, Ireland (Mondial) 11

250cc
1 B. Ruffo, Italy (Guzzi) 26
2 T. L. Wood, GB (Guzzi) 21
3 D. Ambrosini, Italy (Benelli) 14

350cc
1 G. Duke, GB (Norton) 40
2 J. Lockett, GB (Norton) 19
3 W. Doran, GB (AJS) 19

500cc
1 G. Duke, GB (Norton) 35
2 Alfredo Milani, Italy (Gilera) 31
3 U. Masetti Italy (Gilera) 21

Sidecar
1 E. Oliver, GB (Norton) 30
2 E. Frigerio, Italy (Gilera) 26
3 Albino Milani, Italy (Gilera) 19

1952

125cc
1 C. Sandford, GB (MV) 28
2 C. Ubbiali, Italy (Mondial) 24
3 E. Mendogni, Italy (Morini) 16

250cc
1 E. Lorenzetti, Italy (Guzzi) 28
2 F. Anderson, GB (Guzzi) 24
3 L. Graham, GB (Velocette) 11

350cc
1 G. Duke, GB (Norton) 32
2 R. Armstrong, Ireland (Norton) 24
3 W. R. Amm, Rhodesia (Norton) 21

500cc
1 U. Masetti, Italy (Gilera) 28
2 L. Graham, GB (MV) 25
3 R. Armstrong, Ireland (Norton) 22

Sidecar
1 C. Smith, GB (Norton) 24
2 Albino Milani, Italy (Gilera) 18
3 J. Drion, France (Norton) 17

1953

125cc
1 W. Haas, W. Germany (NSU) 30
2 C. Sandford, GB (MV) 20
3 C. Ubbiali, Italy (MV) 18

250cc
1 W. Haas, W. Germany (NSU) 28
2 R. Armstrong, Ireland (NSU) 23
3 F. Anderson, GB (Guzzi) 22

350cc
1 F. Anderson, GB (Guzzi) 30
2 E. Lorenzetti, Italy (Guzzi) 26
3 W. R. Amm, Rhodesia (Norton) 18

500cc
1 G. Duke, GB (Gilera) 38
2 R. Armstrong, Ireland (Gilera) 24
3 Alfredo Milani, Italy (Gilera) 18

Sidecar
1 E. Oliver, GB (Norton) 32
2 C. Smith, GB (Norton) 26
3 H. Haldemann, Switz. (Norton) 12

1954

125cc
1 R. Hollaus, Austria (NSU) 32
2 C. Ubbiali, Italy (MV) 18
3 H. P. Muller, W. Germany (NSU) 15

250cc
1 W. Haas, W. Germany (NSU) 32
2 R. Hollaus, Austria (NSU) 26
3 H. P. Muller, W. Germany (NSU) 17

350cc
1 F. Anderson, GB (Guzzi) 32
2 W. R. Amm, Rhodesia (Norton) 22
3 R. Coleman, New Zealand (AJS) 20

500cc
1 G. Duke, GB (Gilera) 32
2 W. R. Amm, Rhodesia (Norton) 20
3 K. Kavanagh, Australia (Norton) 16

Sidecar
1 W. Noll, W. Germany (BMW) 30
2 E. Oliver, GB (Norton) 26
3 C. Smith, GB (Norton) 22

1955

125cc
1 C. Ubbiali, Italy (MV) 32
2 L. Taveri, Switzerland (MV) 26
3 R. Venturi, Italy (MV) 16

250cc
1 H. P. Muller, W. Germany (NSU) 19
2 C. Sandford, GB (Guzzi) 14
3 W. Lomas, GB (MV) 13

350cc
1 W. Lomas, GB (Guzzi) 30
2 R. Dale, GB (Guzzi) 18
3 A. Hobl, W. Germany (DKW) 17

500cc
1 G. Duke, GB (Gilera) 32
2 R. Armstrong, Ireland (Gilera) 26
3 U. Masetti, Italy (MV) 19

Sidecar
1 W. Faust, W. Germany (BMW) 30
2 W. Noll, W. Germany (BMW) 28
3 W. Schneider, W. Germany (BMW) 22

1956

125cc
1 C. Ubbiali, Italy (MV) 32
2 R. Ferri, Italy (Gilera) 14
3 L. Taveri, Switzerland (MV) 12

250cc
1 C. Ubbiali, Italy (MV) 32
2 L. Taveri, Switzerland (MV) 26
3 E. Lorenzetti, Italy (Guzzi) 10

350cc
1 W. Lomas, GB (Guzzi) 24
2 A. Hobl, W. Germany (DKW) 17
3 R. Dale, GB (Guzzi) 17

500cc
1 J. Surtees, GB (MV) 24
2 W. Zeller, W. Germany (BMW) 16
3 J. Hartle, GB (Norton) 14

Sidecar
1 W. Noll, W. Germany (BMW) 30
2 F. Hillebrand, W. Germany (BMW) 26
3 P. V. Harris, GB (Norton) 24

1957

125cc
1 T. Provini, Italy (Mondial) 30
2 L. Taveri, Switzerland (MV) 22
3 C. Ubbiali, Italy (MV) 22

250cc
1 C. Sandford, GB (Mondial) 26
2 T. Provini, Italy (Mondial) 16
3 S. H. Miller, Ireland (Mondial) 14

350cc
1 K. Campbell, Australia (Guzzi) 30
2 R. McIntyre, Scotland (Gilera) 22
3 L. Liberati, Italy (Gilera) 22

500cc
1 L. Liberati, Italy (Gilera) 32
2 R. McIntyre, Scotland (Gilera) 20
3 J. Surtees, GB (MV) 17

Sidecar
1 F. Hillebrand, W. Germany (BMW) 28
2 W. Schneider, W. Germany (BMW) 20
3 F. Camathias, Switzerland (BMW) 17

1958

125cc
1 C. Ubbiali, Italy (MV) 32
2 A. Gandossi, Italy (Ducati) 25
3 L. Taveri, Switzerland (Ducati) 20

250cc
1 T. Provini, Italy (MV) 32
2 H. Fugner, E. Germany (MZ) 25
3 C. Ubbiali, Italy (MV) 116

350cc
1 J. Surtees, GB (MV) 32
2 J. Hartle, GB (MV) 24
3 G. Duke, GB (Norton) 17

500cc
1 J. Surtees, GB (MV) 32
2 J. Hartle, GB (MV) 20
3 R. H. Dale, GB (BMW) 13

Sidecar
1 W. Schneider, W. Germany (BMW) 30
2 F. Camathias, Switzerland (BMW) 26
3 H. Fath, W. Germany (BMW) 8

1959

125cc
1 C. Ubbiali, Italy (MV) 30
2 T. Provini, Italy (MV) 28
3 M. Hailwood, GB (Ducati) 20

250cc
1 C. Ubbiali, Italy (MV) 28
2 T. Provini, Italy (MV) 16
3 G. Hocking, Rhodesia (MZ) 16

350cc
1 J. Surtees, GB (MV) 32
2 J. Hartle, GB (MV) 16
3 R. N. Brown, Australia (Norton) 14

500cc
1 J. Surtees, GB (MV) 32
2 R. Venturi, Italy (MV) 22
3 R. N. Brown, Australia (Norton) 17

Sidecar
1 W. Schneider, W. Germany (BMW) 22
2 F. Camathias, Switzerland (BMW) 22
3 F. Scheidegger, Switzerland (BMW) 16

1960

125cc
1 C. Ubbiali, Italy (MV) 24
2 G. Hocking, Rhodesia (MV) 18
3 E. Degner, E. Germany (MZ) 16

250cc
1 C. Ubbiali, Italy (MV) 32
2 G. Hocking, Rhodesia (MV) 28
3 L. Taveri, Switzerland (MV) 11

350cc
1 J. Surtees, GB (MV) 22

2 G. Hocking, Rhodesia (MV) 22
3 J. Hartle, GB (MV)/Norton) 18

500cc
1 J. Surtees, GB (MV) 32
2 R. Venturi, Italy (MV) 26
3 J. Hartle, GB (Norton/MV) 16

Sidecar
1 H. Fath, W. Germany (BMW) 24
2 F. Scheidegger, Switzerland (BMW) 16
3 P. V. Harris, GB (BMW) 14

1961

125cc
1 T. Phillis, Australia (Honda) 48
2 E. Degner, E. Germany (MZ) 42
3 L. Taveri, Switzerland (Honda) 30

250cc
1 M. Hailwood, GB (Honda) 44
2 T. Phillis, Australia (Honda) 38
3 J. Redman, Rhodesia (Honda) 36

350cc
1 G. Hocking, Rhodesia (MV) 38
2 F. Stastny, Czechoslovakia (Jawa) 30
3 G. Havel, Czechoslovakia (Jawa) 19

500cc
1 G. Hocking, Rhodesia (MV) 48
2 M. Hailwood, GB (Norton/MV) 40
3 F. Perris, GB (Norton) 16

Sidecar
1 M. Deubel, W. Germany (BMW) 30
2 F. Scheidegger, Switzerland (BMW) 28
3 E. Strub, Switzerland (BMW) 14

1962

50cc
1 E. Degner, W. Germany (Suzuki) 41
2 H-G. Anscheidt, W. Ger. (Kreidler) 36
3 L. Taveri, Switzerland (Honda) 29

125cc
1 L. Taveri, Switzerland (Honda) 48
2 J. Redman, Rhodesia (Honda) 28
3 T. Robb, Ireland (Honda) 30

250cc
1 J. Redman, Rhodesia (Honda) 48
2 R. McIntyre, Scotland (Honda) 32
3 A. Wheeler, GB (Guzzi) 19

350cc
1 J. Redman, Rhodesia (Honda) 32
2 M. Hailwood, GB (MV) 20
3 T. Robb, Ireland (Honda) 18

500cc
1 M. Hailwood, GB (MV) 40
2 A. Shepherd, GB (Matchless) 29
3 P. Read, GB (Norton) 11

Sidecar
1 M. Deubel, W. Germany (BMW) 30
2 F. Camathias, Switzerland (BMW) 26
3 F. Scheidegger, Switzerland (BMW) 18

1963

50cc
1 H. Anderson, New Zealand (Suzuki) 34
2 H-G. Anscheidt, W. Ger. (Kreidler) 32
3 E. Degner, W. Germany (Suzuki) 30

125cc
1 H. Anderson, New Zealand (Suzuki) 54
2 L. Taveri, Switzerland (Honda) 38
3 J. Redman, Rhodesia (Honda) 35

250cc
1 J. Redman, Rhodesia (Honda) 44
2 T. Provini, Italy (Morini) 42
3 F. Ito, Japan (Yamaha) 26

350cc
1 J. Redman, Rhodesia (Honda) 32
2 M. Hailwood, GB (MV) 28
3 L. Taveri, Switzerland (Honda) 16

500cc
1 M. Hailwood, GB (MV) 40
2 A. Shepherd, GB (Matchless) 21
3 J. Hartle, GB (Gilera) 20

Sidecar
1 M. Deubel, W. Germany (BMW) 22
2 F. Camathias, Switzerland (BMW) 20
3 F. Scheidegger, Switzerland (BMW) 20

1964

50cc
1 H. Anderson, New Zealand (Suzuki) 38
2 R. Bryans, Ireland (Honda) 30
3 H-G. Anscheidt, W. Ger. (Kreidler) 29

125cc
1 L. Taveri, Switzerland (Honda) 46
2 J. Redman, Rhodesia (Honda) 36
3 H. Anderson, New Zealand (Suzuki) 34

250cc
1 P. Read, GB (Yamaha) 46
2 J. Redman, Rhodesia (Honda) 42
3 A. Shepherd, GB (MZ) 23

350cc
1 J. Redman, Rhodesia (Honda) 40
2 B. Beale, Rhodesia (Honda) 24
3 M. Duff, Canada (AJS) 20

500cc
1 M. Hailwood, GB (MV) 40

2 J. Ahearn, Australia (Norton) 25
3 P. Read, GB (Matchless) 25

Sidecar
1 M. Deubel, W. Germany (BMW) 28
2 F. Scheidegger, Switzerland (BMW) 26
3 C. Seeley, GB (BMW) 17

1965

50cc
1 R. Bryans, Ireland (Honda) 36
2 L. Taveri, Switzerland (Honda) 32
3 H. Anderson, New Zealand (Suzuki) 32

125cc
1 H. Anderson, New Zealand (Suzuki) 56
2 F. Perris, GB (Suzuki) 44
3 D. Woodman, GB (MZ) 28

250cc
1 P. Read, GB (Yamaha) 56
2 M. Duff, Canada (Yamaha) 42
3 J. Redman, Rhodesia (Honda) 34

350cc
1 J. Redman, Rhodesia (Honda) 38
2 G. Agostini, Italy (MV) 32
3 M. Hailwood, GB (MV) 20

500cc
1 M. Hailwood, GB (MV) 48
2 G. Agostini, Italy (MV) 38
3 P. Driver, South Africa (Matchless) 26

Sidecar
1 F. Scheidegger, Switzerland (BMW) 32
2 M. Deubel, W. Germany (BMW) 26
3 G. Auerbacher, W. Germany (BMW) 15

1966

50cc
1 H-G. Anscheidt, W. Germany (Suzuki) 28
2 R. Bryans, Ireland (Honda) 26
3 L. Taveri, Switzerland (Honda) 26

125cc
1 L. Taveri, Switzerland (Honda) 46
2 W. Ivy, GB (Yamaha) 40
3 R. Bryans, Ireland (Honda) 32

250cc
1 M. Hailwood, GB (Honda) 56
2 P. Read, GB (Yamaha) 34
3 J. Redman, Rhodesia (Honda) 20

350cc
1 M. Hailwood, GB (Honda) 48
2 G. Agostini, Italy (MV) 42
3 R. Pasolini, Italy (Aermacchi) 17

500cc
1 G. Agostini, Italy (MV) 36
2 M. Hailwood, GB (Honda) 30
3 J. Findlay, Australia (Matchless) 20

Sidecar
1 F. Scheidegger, Switzerland (BMW) 24
2 M. Deubel, W. Germany (BMW) 20
3 C. Seeley, GB (BMW) 13

1967

50cc
1 H-G. Anscheidt, W. Germany (Suzuki) 30
2 Y. Katayama, Japan (Suzuki) 28
3 S. Graham, GB (Suzuki) 22

125cc
1 W. Ivy, GB (Yamaha) 56
2 P. Read, GB (Yamaha) 40
3 S. Graham, GB (Suzuki) 38

250cc
1 M. Hailwood, GB (Honda) 50
2 P. Read, GB (Yamaha) 50
3 W. Ivy, GB (Yamaha) 46

350cc
1 M. Hailwood, GB (Honda) 40
2 G. Agostini, Italy (MV) 32
3 R. Bryans, Irleland (Honda) 20

500cc
1 G. Agostini, Italy (MV) 46
2 M. Hailwood, GB (Honda) 46
3 J. Hartle, GB (Matchless) 22

Sidecar
1 K. Enders, W. Germany (BMW) 40
2 G. Auerbacher, W. Germany (BMW) 32
3 S. Schauzu, W. Germany (BMW) 28

1968

50cc
1 H-G. Anscheidt, W. Germany (Suzuki) 24
2 P. Lodewijkx, Holland (Jamathi) 17
3 B. Smith, Australia (Derbi) 15

125cc
1 P. Read, GB (Yamaha) 40
2 W. Ivy, GB (Yamaha) 24
3 G. Molloy, New Zealand (Bultaco) 15

250cc
1 P. Read, GB (Yamaha) 52
2 W. Ivy, GB (Yamaha) 52
3 H. Rosner, E. Germany (MZ) 32

350cc
1 G. Agostini, Italy (MV) 32
2 R. Pasolini, Italy (Benelli) 18
3 K. Carruthers, Australia (Aermacchi) 17

500cc
1 G. Agostini, Italy (MV) 48
2 J. Findlay, Australia (Matchless) 34
3 G. Marsovszky, Switz. (Matchless) 10

Sidecar
1 H. Fath, W. Germany (Urs) 27
2 G. Auerbacher, W. Germany (BMW) 22
3 S. Schauzu, W. Germany (BMW) 19

1969

50cc
1 A. Nieto, Spain (Derbi) 76
2 A. Toersen, Holland (Kreidler) 75
3 B. Smith, Australia (Derbi) 69

125cc
1 D. Simmonds, GB (Kawasaki) 90
2 D. Braun, W. Germany (Suzuki) 59
3 C. van Dongen, Holland (Suzuki) 51

250cc
1 K. Carruthers, Australia (Benelli) 89
2 K. Andersson, Sweden (Yamaha) 84
3 S. Herrero, Spain (Ossa) 83

350cc
1 G. Agostini, Italy (MV) 90
2 S. Grassetti, Italy (Yamaha/Jawa) 47
3 G. Visenzi, Italy (Yamaha) 45

500cc
1 G. Agostini, Italy (MV) 105
2 G. Marsovszky, Switzerland (Linto) 47
3 G. Nash, GB (Norton) 45

Sidecar
1 K. Enders, W. Germany (BMW) 60
2 H. Fath, W. Germany (Urs) 55
3 G. Auerbacher, W. Germany (BMW) 40

1970

50cc
1 A. Nieto, Spain (Derbi) 87
2 A. Toersen, Holland (Jamathi) 75
3 R. Kunz, W. Germany (Kreidler) 66

125cc
1 D. Braun, W. Germany (Suzuki) 84
2 A. Nieto, Spain (Derbi) 72
3 B. Jansson, Sweden (Maico) 62

250cc
1 R. Gould, GB (Yamaha) 102
2 K. Carruthers, Australia (Yamaha) 84
3 K. Andersson, Sweden (Yamaha) 67

350cc
1 G. Agostini, Italy (MV) 90
2 K. Carruthers, Aus. (Benelli/Yamaha) 58
3 R. Pasolini, Italy (Benelli) 46

500cc
1 G. Agostini, Italy (MV) 90
2 G. Molloy, New Zealand (Kawasaki) 62
3 A. Bergamonti, Italy (Aermacchi/MV) 59

Sidecar
1 K. Enders, W. Germany (BMW) 73
2 G. Auerbacher, W. Germany (BMW) 62
3 S. Schauzu, W. Germany (BMW) 56

1971

50cc
1 J. de Vries, Holland (Kreidler) 75
2 A. Nieto, Spain (Derbi) 69
3 J. Schurgers, Holland (Kreidler) 42

125cc
1 A. Nieto, Spain (Derbi) 87
2 B. Sheene, GB (Suzuki) 79
3 B. Jansson, Sweden (Maico) 64

250cc
1 P. Read, GB (Yamaha) 73
2 R. Gould, GB (Yamaha) 68
3 J. Saarinen, Finland (Yamaha) 64

350cc
1 G. Agostini, Italy (MV) 90
2 J. Saarinen, Finland (Yamaha) 63
3 K-I. Carlsson, Sweden (Yamaha) 39

500cc
1 G. Agostini, Italy (MV) 90
2 K. Turner, New Zealand (Suzuki) 58
3 R. Bron, Holland (Suzuki) 57

Sidecar
1 H. Owesle, W. Germany (Munch) 69
2 A. Butscher, W. Germany (BMW) 57
3 S. Schauzu, W. Germany (BMW) 57

1972

50cc
1 A. Nieto, Spain (Derbi) 69
2 J. de Vries, Holland (Kreidler) 69
3 T. Timmer, Holland (Jamathi) 50

125cc
1 A. Nieto, Spain (Derbi) 97
2 K. Andersson, Sweden (Yamaha) 87
3 C. Mortimer, GB (Yamaha) 87

250cc
1 J. Saarinen, Finland (Yamaha) 94
2 R. Pasolini, Italy (Aermacchi) 93
3 R. Gould, GB (Yamaha) 88

350cc
1 G. Agostini, Italy (MV) 102
2 J. Saarinen, Finland (Yamaha) 89
3 R. Pasolini, Italy (Aermacchi) 78

500cc
1 G. Agostini, Italy (MV) 105
2 A. Pagani, Italy (MV) 87
3 B. Kneubuhler, Switz. (Yamaha) 57

Sidecar
1 K. Enders, W. Germany (BMW) 72
2 H. Luthringshauser, W. Germany (BMW) 63
3 S. Schauzu, W. Germany (BMW) 62

1973

50cc
1 J. de Vries, Holland (Van Veen Kreidler) 60
2 B. Kneubuhler, Czechoslovakia (Van Veen Kreidler) 51
3 T. Timmer, Holland (Jamathi) 47

125cc
1 K. Andersson, Sweden (Yamaha) 90
2 C. Mortimer, GB (Yamaha) 75
3 J. Schurgers, Holland (Bridgestone) 71

250cc
1 D. Braun, W. Germany (Yamaha) 80
2 T. Lansivuori, Finland (Yamaha) 64
3 J. Dodds, Australia (Yamaha) 58

350cc
1 G. Agostini, Italy (MV) 84
2 T. Lansivuori, Finland (Yamaha) 77
3 P. Read, GB (MV) 56

500cc
1 P. Read, GB (MV) 84
2 K. Newcombe, New Zealand (Konig) 63
3 G. Agostini, Italy (MV) 57

Sidecar
1 K. Enders, W. Germany (BMW) 75
2 W. Schwarzel, W. Germany (Konig) 48
3 S. Schauzu, W. Germany (BMW) 45

1974

50cc
1 H. van Kessell, Holland (Van Veen Kreidler) 90
2 H. Rittberger, W. Germany (Kreidler) 68
3 J. van Zoebroeck, Belgium (Kreidler) 59

125cc
1 K. Andersson, Sweden (Yamaha) 87
2 B. Kneubuhler, Czechoslovakia (Yamaha) 63
3 O. Buscherini, Italy (Malanca) 60
A. Nieto, Spain (Derbi) 60

250cc
1 W. Villa, Italy (Harley-Davidson) 77
2 D. Braun, W. Germany (Yamaha) 58
3 P. Pons, France (Yamaha) 50

350cc
1 G. Agostini, Italy (Yamaha) 75
2 D. Braun, W. Germany (Yamaha) 62
3 P. Pons, France (Yamaha) 49

500cc
1 P. Read, GB (MV) 82
2 G. Bonera, Italy (MV) 69
3 T. Lansivuori, Finland (Yamahi) 67

Sidecar
1 K. Enders, W. Germany (Busch BMW) 66
2 W. Schwarzel, W. Germany (Konig) 64
3 S. Schauzu, W. Germany (BMW) 60

1975

50cc
1 A. Nieto, Spain (Kreidler) 75
2 E. Lazzarine, Italy (Piovaticci) 61
3 J. Van Zeebroek, Belgium (Kreidler) 43

125cc
1. P. Pileri, Italy (Morbidelli) 90
2 P. Bianchi, Italy (Morbidelli) 72
3 K. Andersson, Sweden (Yamaha) 67

250cc
1 W. Villa, Italy (Harley-Davidson) 85
2 M. Rougerie, France (Harley-Davidson) 76
3 D. Braun, W. Germany (Yamaha) 56

350cc
1 J. Cecotto, Venezuela (Yamaha) 78
2 G. Agostini, Italy (Yamaha) 59
3 P. Korhonen, Finland (Yamaha) 48

500cc
1 G. Agostini, Italy (Yamaha) 84
2 P. Read, GB (MV) 76
3 H. Kanaya, Japan (Yamaha) 45

Sidecar
1 R. Steinhausen, W. Germany (Konig) 67
2 W. Schwarzel, W. Germany (Konig) 54
3 R. Biland, Czechoslovakia (Yamaha) 30

1976

50cc
1 A. Nieto, Spain (Bultaco) 85
2 H. Rittberger, Germany (Kreidler) 76
3 U. Graf, Switzerland (Kreidler) 69

125cc
1 P. Bianchi, Italy (Morbidelli) 90
2 A. Nieto, Spain (Bultaco) 67
3 P. Pileri, Italy (Morbidelli) 64

250cc
1 W. Villa, Italy (Harley-Davidson) 90

2 T. Katayama, Japan (Yamaha) 73
3 G. Bonero, Italy (Harley-Davidson) 61

350cc
1 W. Villa, Italy (Harley-Davidson) 76
2 J. Cecotto, Venezuela (Yamaha) 65
3 C. Mortimer, GB (Yamaha) 54

500cc
1 B. Sheene, GB (Suzuki) 72
2 T. Lansivuori, Finland (Suzuki) 48
3 P. Hennen, USA (Suzuki) 46

Sidecar
1 R. Steinhausen, Germany (Busch Konig) 65
2 W. Schwarzel, Germany (Konig) 51
3 H. Schmid, Switzerland (Yamaha) 38

1977

50cc
1 A. Nieto, Spain (Bultaco) 87
2 E. Lazzarini, Italy (Kreidler) 72
3 R. Tormo, Spain (Bultaco) 69

125cc
1 P. Bianchi, Italy (Morbidelli) 131
2 E. Lazzarini, Italy (Morbidelli) 115
3 A. Nieto, Spain (Bultaco) 80

250cc
1 M. Lega, Italy (Morbidelli) 85
2 F. Uncini, Italy (Harley-Davidson) 72
3 W. Villa, Italy (Harley-Davidson) 67

350cc
1 T. Katayama, Japan (Yamaha) 95
2 T. Herron, GB (Yamaha) 56
3 J. Ekerold, South Africa (Yamaha) 54

500cc
1 B. Sheene, GB (Suzuki) 107
2 S. Baker, USA (Yamaha) 80
3 P. Hennen, USA (Suzuki) 67

Sidecar
1 G. O'Dell, GB (Seymaz-Yamaha & Windle-Yamaha) 64
2 R. Biland, Switzerland (Schmid-Yamaha) 56
3 W. Schwarzel, Germany (Aro) 46

Formula 750
1 S. Baker, USA (Yamaha) 131
2 C. Sarron, France (Yamaha) 55
3 G. Agostini, Italy (Yamaha) 45

1978

50cc
1 R. Tormo, Spain (Bultaco) 99
2 E. Lazzarini, Italy (Kreidler) 64
3 P. Plisson, France (ABF) 48

125cc
1 E. Lazzarini, Italy (MBA) 114
2 A. Nieto, Spain (Bultaco/Minarelli) 88
3 P. Bianchi, Italy (Minarelli) 70

250cc
1 K. Ballington, South Africa (Kawasaki) 124
2 G. Hansford, Australia (Kawasaki) 118
3 P. Fernandez, France (Yamaha) 55

350cc
1 K. Ballington, South Africa (Kawasaki) 134
2 T. Katayama, Japan (Yamaha) 77
3 G. Hansford, Australia (Kawasaki) 76

500cc
1 K. Roberts, USA (Yamaha) 110
2 B. Sheene, GB (Suzuki) 100
3 J. Cecotto, Venezuela (Yamaha) 66

Sidecar
1 R. Biland, Switzerland (Beo-Yamaha &TTM-Yamaha) 79
2 A. Michel, France (Seymaz-Yamaha) 76
3 B. Holzer, Switzerland (LCR-Yamaha) 49

Formula 750
1 J. Cecotto, Venezuela (Yamaha) 97
2 K. Roberts, USA (Yamaha) 92
3 C. Sarron, France (Yamaha) 55

1979

50cc
1 E. Lazzarini, Italy (Kreidler) 75
2 R. Blatter, Czechoslovakia (Kreidler) 62
3 G. Waibel, Germany (Kreidler) 31

125cc
1 A. Nieto, Spain (Morbidelli) 120
2 M. Massimiami, Italy (MBA) 53
3 H. Muller, Czechoslovakia (Morbidelli) 50

250cc
1 K. Ballington, South Africa (Kawasaki) 141
2 G. Hansford, Australia (Kawasaki) 81
3 G. Rossi, Italy (Morbidelli) 67

350cc
1 K. Ballington, South Africa (Kawasaki) 99
2 P. Fernandez, France (Yamaha) 90
3 G. Hansford, Australia (Kawasaki) 77

500cc
1 K. Roberts, USA (Yamaha) 113
2 V. Ferrari, Italy (Suzuki) 89
3 B. Sheene, GB (Suzuki) 87

Sidecar B2A
1 R. Biland, Czechoslovakia (Yamaha) 67
2 R. Steinhausen, W. Germany (Yama-

ha) 58
2 R. Greasley, GB (Yamaha) 58

Sidecar B2B
1 B. Holzer, Czechoslovakia (LCR) 72
2 R. Biland, Czechoslovakia (LCR) 60
3 M. Kumano, Japan (Yamaha) 41

1980

50cc
1 E. Lazzarini, Italy (Kreidler) 74
2 S. Dorflinger, Switzerland (Kreidler) 72
3 H. Hummel, Austria (Kreidler) 37

125cc
1 P. Bianchi, Italy (MBA) 90
2 G. Bertin, France (Motobecane) 81
3 A. Nieto, Spain (Minarelli) 78

250cc
1 A. Mang, W. Germany (Kawasaki) 128
2 K. Ballington, South Africa (Kawasaki) 87
3 J.-F. Balde, France (Kawasaki) 59

350cc
1 J. Ekerold, South Africa (Yamaha) 63
2 A. Mang, W. Germany (Kawasaki) 60
3 J.-F. Balde, France (Kawasaki) 38

500cc
1 K. Roberts, USA (Yamaha) 87
2 R. Mamola, USA (Suzuki) 72
3 M. Lucchinelli, Italy (Suzuki) 59

Sidecar
1 J. Taylor, GB (Yamaha) 94
2 R. Biland, Switzerland (Yamaha) 63
2 A. Michel, France (Yamaha) 63

1981

50cc
1 R. Tormo, Spain (Bultaco) 90
2 T. Timmer, Holland (Bultaco) 65
3 S. Dorflinger, Switzerland (Kreidler) 51

125cc
1 A. Nieto, Spain (Minarelli) 140
2 L. Reggiani, Italy (Minarelli) 95
3 P. Bianchi, Italy (MBA) 84

250cc
1 A. Mang, W. Germany (Kawasaki) 160
2 J.-F. Balde, France (Kawasaki) 95
3 R. Freymond, Switzerland (Ad Majora) 72

350cc
1 A. Mang, W. Germany (Kawasaki) 103
2 J. Ekerold, South Africa (Yamaha) 52
3 J.-F. Balde, France (Kawasaki) 49

500cc
1 M. Lucchinelli, Italy (Suziki) 105
2 R. Mamola, USA (Suzuki) 94
3 K. Roberts, USA (Yamaha) 74

Sidecar
1 R. Biland, Switzerland (LCR Yamaha) 127
2 A. Michel, France (Seymaz-Yamaha) 106
3 J. Taylor, GB (Windle Yamaha) 87

WORLD MOTOR CYCLE SPEED RECORD

The history of the world outright speed record is almost as long as the history of motor-cycle racing itself. An early list of achievements, grouped under the heading "World's Motorcycle Maximum Speed Record" begins with W. E. Cook of Great Britain who, in 1909, propelled his 994cc NLG at 75.92 mph. The mantle was then taken over by Charlie Collier who, on Matchless machines, secured the record no fewer than four times in the space of two years: at 80.24 mph and again at 84.89 mph in 1910; and in 1911 at 89.84 mph and 91.23 mph. Earlier in 1911 Jake de Rosier from the USA had improved upon Collier's earlier records when he reached 85.89 mph and 88.77 mph on American Indian machines. In 1914 Britain and the United States combined as Britain's Sydney George urged a 994cc American Indian machine round Brooklands circuit at 93.48 mph on 2nd May.

This Surrey circuit had been the background to much record-breaking activity pre-war and with the war over the chase to be the first to reach 100 mph was on . . . with Brooklands once again at the centre of activity.

Britain's Bert Le Vack edged nearer the historic milestone in 1920 when he reached 94.79 mph on a 998cc Indian, but motor-cycle racers over in America also had their sights set on that magical 100 mph and it was on the famous Daytona Beach in Florida that the distinction of being the first man to travel at more than 100 mph officially on a motor cycle came to Ed Walker. In February 1920 he reached 103.56 mph on a 994cc Indian twin. The record stood for three years, at which time Britain's Freddie Dixon reached 106.8 mph on a Harley-Davidson along the Bois de Boulogne on 9th September 1923.

Dixon's switch to the continent for his record breaking attempt was significant since by now the Brooklands saucer, which had seen so much record-breaking through the years, was no longer the ideal venue for world speed record attempts. Speeds had risen to a point where extra distance to run-in and then pull-up were necessary. Such attempts therefore became virtually impossible in England, where the Government did not permit the temporary closure of roads for such attempts.

Claude Temple brought the curtain down on Brooklands with a new record of 108.48 mph on the 996cc OEC-Temple-Anzani in 1923. During the remainder of the 1920s Britain dominated the world speed record scene with Le Vack, Temple, Baldwin and Wright leap-frogging one another, at the same time taking the record to 134.51. mph by early 1930. On the Brought Superior JAP, Bert Le Vack reached 113.61 mph in 1924 and that same year improved to 119.05 mph. Claude Temple reached 121.41 mph in 1926 and Oliver Baldwin 124.62 mph in 1928.

The year 1930 turned out to be a vintage year for record breaking. New speeds were established on four separate occasions, with Joe Wright of Britain the hero. On an OEC-Temple machine he improved on his own record by reaching 137.32 mph and after seeing Ernst Henne of Germany capture the record at 137.66 mph on a 735cc BMW, showed who was boss later that same year with a remarkable 150.74 mph on his 995cc OEC-Temple-JAP. Two years later, however, Henne came back strongly for Germany and in 1932 took the title again at the start of a decade to be dominated by Germany and Henne.

With British riders and machines in such command in the 1920s, the emergence of Henne as a world record breaker in 1929 took the élite corps of British riders completely by surprise. The attempt had been a closely guarded secret and so shocked by the German victory were Temple and Wright that they immediately responded. Wright arrived at Arpajon to find Henne already there! Wright failed with the OEC-JAP, onto which had been fitted a blower, and Henne, without the stimulus of a new record to beat, went home, satisfied his record was secure. Wright saw his chance, hired the stretch of road privately, and when everyone else had left improved on Henne's record with 137.32 mph.

Within a month, Henne was out again with the BMW and spent two days racing up and down the Bavarian autobahn, finally managing to beat Wright's record by just 0.34 mph.

The Wright-Henne combat continued. Wright went to Cork and in November 1930 really settled the issue with an outstanding two-way average speed of 150.7 mph – well in excess of Henne's best. He held the record for two years, after which Henne's 151.86 mph started the German-Henne domination which lasted, except for a brief period, until the outbreak of war.

The authenticity of the very early records can possibly be challenged and even in the early 1920s there was so much record breaking being done that the picture is confused and obscure. Some of the 100 mph-plus speeds were set in one direction only and timed to the nearest fifth of a second, though there is little doubt that Le Vack's 102.8 mph at Brooklands on 31st October 1922, was a two-way average. Dissension was caused at an early date by the upper capacity limit of 1000cc made by the FICM and there seems little doubt that this was one of the reasons for the breakaway from the European authority of the United States and even into the 1970s the FIM continued to recognise Bill Johnson's 1962 record of 224.5 mph (on a 650cc Triumph), but not the numerous speed records set up later by machines in excess of 1000cc capacity.

Henne's success in 1932 was the beginning of an outstanding epoch of record breaking for Germany which lasted, except for two brief intervals, right up to 19th November 1937. On four occasions Henne improved his own performance, pushing up the record by 21.5 mph to 173.5 mph. All the records were established on BMW machinery. In Hungary in 1932 he added 1.5 mph to Wright's record. Two years later he reached 153 mph. In 1935, on a new stretch of road for record breaking near Frankfurt, he moved the record up to 159 mph on a 735cc BMW. He returned to the Frankfurt road in 1936 and with a fully-streamlined BMW of only 495cc shattered his own record by 10 mph. By this time streamlining had caught on with a vengeance and the picture of Henne wearing a streamlined helmet, the rear part of which tapered way down his back as he crouched over the machine for the record breaking run, became a part of motor cycle history. His speed of 169 mph was extremely impressive and for the first time we saw a fully-enclosed machine – forerunner to the streamlined projectiles which were to gain the world record in post-war years.

A mere recital of Henne's records does him an injustice, for he achieved these records against serious competition, with AJS and Excelsior making special machines for an attack on the record. The first successful challenge to Henne came from Eric Fernihough, a British private racer, who took his powerful supercharged Brough to a new world record of 169.78 mph in 1937. Influenced by Henne's streamlined BMW, Fernihough added a good deal of enclosure to his Brough Superior JAP, but once over in Hungary, he decided to dispense with the fairing and made his successful record bid with the machine almost totally naked of streamlining. Britain held the record for only six months. In October Piero Taruffi took a 492cc Gilera four-cylinder supercharged Rondine-engined machine of unusual design to a stretch of road between Brescia and Bergamo and to the surprise of almost everyone captured the world title for Italy with a speed of 170.5 mph. Henne responded, and the following month at Darmstadt, Germany, recaptured the record on the BMW at 173.6 mph. It was a record which was to remain intact for almost fourteen years, all through the war and until April, 1951, when fellow-German Herz became the first post-war record holder at 180 mph on a NSU.

Britain made a final valiant attempt as the war clouds gathered as Fernihough, determined to win back the title for Britain, made the long trek back to Hungary in the spring of 1938. Heavy winds made the attempt impossible but Fernihough, undeterred, returned in April and paid £150 for the use of the closed road at Gyon. His first sensational run tragically was to be his last. At a speed estimated to be in excess of 180 mph – and well ahead of the existing record – the machine developed a wobble. Fernihough crashed and was killed.

Although it was to be April 1951, before a new world record was established, Britain, once hostilities had ended, quickly made a new attempt with Noel Pope challenging on a supercharged 1000cc Brough Superior. After achieving lap records at Brooklands, his plans were abandoned in 1947 because of lack of sufficient funds, but two years later he set off for America with hopes high. A series of misfortunes and disasters accompanied the attempts and Pope was fortunate to escape with his life, though his machine was wrecked.

In the meantime the Germans had not been idle and in April, 1951 Wilhelm Herz shattered the three-miles-a-minute barrier on the Munich to Ingoldstadt autobahn. His 500cc supercharged NSU twin had streamlining similar to Henne's pre-war BMW, except for an open cockpit. Helped by a five mile run-in and an attempt on the record which could be said was the most scientific to date, Herz nonetheless took two days to secure the record at 180 mph.

There was surprisingly little activity over the next four years and when interest was revived it came from a rather unexpected direction – New Zealand. A 24-year-old New Zealander named Russel Wright bought a 1000cc Vincent HRD which was said to have been exhibited by the British firm at the 1953 Earls Court Show and around the machine had constructed a superb shell which had been designed from pictures of the NSU record breaker. In spite of wheelspin problems, an unsteady second run and generally damp conditions, Wright reached 185 mph to take the world record. The New Zealander claimed that the machine had a near-standard engine, though had racing cylinder heads and larger carburetters. For the first time in almost twenty years the world record was back standing to the credit of a British machine.

Although it was to be more than a year before the FIM officially recognised record was exceeded, attention only one month later was focused on America and the Bonneville Salt Flats as Johnny Allen, in a revolutionary cigar-shaped projectile powered by a Triumph 650cc engine registered 182.45 mph. By this time Bonneville was the mecca of the record breakers and there at the same time as Allen was Wilhelm Herz. In August 1956 he pushed the record up to 189 mph and two days later reached 210 mph, this after Allen, under American Motorcycle Association rules (unfortunately not recognised by the FIM) had put in a couple of runs to establish the unofficial record at 193.72 mph. Herz's latest achievement, established on the NSU which was now fully enclosed, was so well ahead of Allen's timing that he decided to go home, thinking his record was secure. Johnny Allen stayed behind and in a new attempt took the record to 214.17 mph.

Allen's machine had moved motor-cycle record breaking into a new era. No longer did motor cycles look like motor cycles when out to break the world record. They were sophisticated projectiles with glass-fibre shells and small cockpits, into which a new-style of gladiator was wedged. It was sophisticated and scientific, a world apart from the open chargers of twenty years before.

Allen's success also signified the domination of the United States in world record breaking. In September 1962 Bill Johnson, with a 649cc Triumph engine carefully installed in a remarkable machine which one report claimed looked more like one of Malcolm Campbell's early racing cars than a two-wheel record breaker, took the official world speed record to 224.5 mph at Bonneville on 5th September. Four years later, in 1966, Bob Leppan, a 28-year-old Triumph distributor of Detroit, moved into the record books when, during the American Motorcycle Association's speed week at the Bonneville Salt Flats, he piloted his super-streamlined Gyronaut X-1 to a new "world fastest" of 245.67 mph, his faster of the two runs being timed at 247.76 mph. Leppan's machine looked like the ultimate in design technology.

The rift between the American Motorcycle Association (AMA) and the official world authority for motor cycle sport, the Federation Internationale Motorcyliste (FIM) caused real confusion in the quest for the outright speed record. Johnny Allen's record had created a storm of protest and outrage, for although his runs were timed by the AMA (which of course the FIM did not recognise), it was generally agreed that the AMA apparatus was equal to, if not superior, to the FIM's minimum requirements. When NSU asked if Allen's attempt had been staged within FIM rules, the FIM said that Allen's claim to be the holder of the world record would have to be investigated. In April 1957 it was rejected. Then, before increasing pressure, the FIM reopened the investigation two months later. In October that same year the FIM declared the attempt as "no record" so far as they were concerned. Reaction to the decision was sharp and dramatic and Triumph, whose engine had powered Allen's projectile, brought an action against the FIM, which the British company lost. In 1960 the FIM banned Triumph from International (FIM) competition for two years. The curious sequel was that the new official record of 224.57 mph by Bill Johnson in 1962 *was* made under FIM jurisdiction and was, therefore, fully recognised by them, in spite of Johnson's machine having been powered by a 650cc Triumph engine and the record set just before the ending of the FIM ban on the British factory.

Johnson's record still stood at the end of 1975 as the official FIM record, but in America, where almost all the record attempts are now made, there has been intense activity in the ultimate speed event and there exists little concern over the FIM's attitude. Another major difference which opened the gap between the two organisations was the power limit imposed on machines attacking the world speed record by the FIM. Originally it had been 1000cc and was later raised to 1300cc. But by this time, ambition had far outstripped this kind of limitation and Leppan's success in 1966 was, as we have seen, achieved in a machine powered by two 650cc Triumph twin engines.

The trip to Bonneville salt flats for an assault on the world record became an annual pilgrimage for those with ambitions to go fastest of all, though Leppan's success was to remain the fastest until 1970.

There is perhaps no greater prestige for man or factory than the honour of being the fastest in the world and the early 1970s were to see almost continuous activity in this field. Towards the end of 1969 it was no secret that Yamaha's American subsidiary were planning an attack on the absolute world speed record: their aim was to reach 250-plus mph. Leppan was also reported to be actively engaged in plans to improve on his earlier 245.67 mph and there was talk of a Gyronaut X-2, with coupled three-cylinder 750cc Tridents, which he anticipated would take him near to the 300 mph mark. Yamaha claimed first success in September 1970 with Don Vesco, in a fully streamlined projectile powered by two 350cc Yamaha TR2 racing engines running on pump petrol, reaching 251.9 mph. But the record was held for only a short time for in October, veteran AMA racer Cal Rayborn, in the first serious attempt at the record by the Harley-Davidson factory, reached a two-way average of 255.37 mph for the flying mile, after crashing twice during practice runs. The very next day Rayborn tried to do even better, but after clocking over 260 mph one way, his 1480cc engine failed on the return run. Such was the activity in record breaking at this point that even as Rayborn became the fastest man in the world on two wheels, reports were reaching the salt flats that Bob Leppan was on his way and Don Vesco, having learned of Rayborn's success, was hurrying back for a further attempt. Rayborn, knowing that such intense activity was certain to put his record in jeopardy, tried again. With a shorter run-in to the timing strip to avoid overheating, and running on nitromethane fuel, he hoisted the record to 265.49 mph.

Rayborn's new record was to endure for perhaps longer than he had dared to hope. Despite a number of attempts, including a remarkable effort by Honda in the form of their eight-cylinder, twin engined 1500cc Hawk weighing 900 lbs, Cal Rayborn and Harley-Davidson were still holding the record at the end of the Bonneville Speed Week of 1972. Honda had contested the world speed record the previous year when their machine crashed more than ten times in an attempt to take the record. By 1972, however, Norton had moved on to the scene, but that year at Bonneville they were never a threat.

Leppan's 1970 spectacular attempt ended in disaster. After clocking 268 mph through the flying mile (more than 2 mph faster than the record) his Gyronaut X-1 somersaulted end-over-end after being caught by side winds and following the failure of the front suspension. He sustained a badly damaged left arm which was saved by a four-hour operation.

By 1974 the chase was on to break the 300 mph barrier. Denis Manning, the designer of the Harley projectile, was now eager for the record himself as pilot of the exciting Norton streamliner and he and Don Vesco, who had now progressed to a Yamaha fitted with two TZ700 engines, were the two most prolific candidates in the field. In September 1974 Vesco's attempt ended when one of the engines seized, though he managed 245 mph on one motor.

For Britain, Norton's interest in the world speed record recaptured something of the excitement of the great days of the 1920s. Their modern streamliner, 15½ feet long and weighing 900 lb, was powered by two Norton Commando 850cc fuel injected engines and the machine was said to have a staggering 210 bhp. The laminated glass fibre body had been wind tested in California and gave Denis Manning and his second rider Denis Blackwell 120 degrees field of view. The 34 inch high projectile was equipped with two parachutes, a drogue and a main chute, supplemented by a single disc brake on the rear wheel, for stopping purposes. At the time pilot Manning was a Norton-Triumph area sales manager in America.

In the autumn of 1974 both the Norton and Don Vesco's Yamaha were at the salt flats intent on creating a new record. Cal Rayborn's record had now remained intact for almost four years, though tragically he had been killed, while racing, in December 1973. His record was soon to go and it was the Yamaha which finally took the record. The new average speed was 281.714 mph, appreciably ahead of Rayborn's old record of 265.492 mph. During the final quarter mile of the return run Don Vesco touched 287.539 mph. A further attempt to hoist the record nearer 300 mph failed. But he was successful when, with one engine, he set a new FIM record of 234.245 mph for the mile for the 750cc class. This was better than Bill Johnson's previous record with a Triumph at 224 mph, though it was under Vesco's own AMA 750cc record of 251 mph set in 1970.

Meantime the Norton challenge was totally unsuccessful. Denis Manning, having crashed the machine twice in practice, handed over to Boris Murray for the actual attempt, but the machine exploded at about 170 mph, the top centre section of the streamlining being flung into the air. Murray was able to bring the machine to a standstill without crashing. The explosion was caused by a fractured fuel line between the fuel injector pump and the injectors. Later, the Norton did better, achieving a best speed of 271 mph for its two-way run – within just 15 mph of Vesco's new world record.

Don Vesco, with an eight cylinder 1,500cc Yamaha streamliner, finally cracked the 300 mph barrier and in September 1975 set up a new world record of 302.928 mph at Bonneville Salt Flats. He also set a new AMA world record at 303.812 mph.

WORLD MOTOR CYCLE SPEED RECORD HOLDERS

1909 W. E. Cook (GB) NLG	75.92 mph
1910 C. R. Collier (GB) Matchless	80.24 mph
1910 C. R. Collier (GB) Matchless	84.89 mph
1911 Jake de Rosier (USA) Indian	85.38 mph
1911 Jake de Rosier (USA) Indian	88.77 mph
1911 C. R. Collier (GB) Matchless	89.84 mph
1911 C. R. Collier (GB) Matchless	91.23 mph
1914 S. George (GB) Indian	93.48 mph
1920 H. Le Vack (GB) Indian	94.79 mph
1920 E. Walker (USA) Indian	103.77 mph
1923 F. W. Dixon (GB) Harley-Davidson	106.8 mph
1923 C. F. Temple (GB) British Anzani	108.85 mph
1924 H. Le Vack (GB) Brough Superior JAP	113.60 mph
1924 H. Le Vack (GB) Brough Superior JAP	119.05 mph
1925 C. F. Temple (GB) O.E.C.-Temple	121.41 mph
1928 O. M. Baldwin (GB) Zenith-JAP	124.62 mph
1929 H. Le Vack (GB) Brough Superior JAP	129.00 mph
1929 E. Henne (Germany) BMW	134.68 mph
1930 J. S. Wright (GB) O.E.C.-Temple	137.32 mph
1930 E. Henne (Germany) BMW	137.66 mph
1930 J. S. Wright (GB) O.E.C.-Temple JAP	150.70 mph
1932 E. Henne (Germany) BMW	151.86 mph
1934 E. Henne (Germany) BMW	152.90 mph
1935 E. Henne (Germany) BMW	159.1 mph
1936 E. Henne (Germany) BMW	169.00 mph
1937 E. C. Fernihough (GB) Brough Superior JAP	169.78 mph
1937 P. Taruffi (Italy) Gilera	170.5 mph
1937 E. Henne (Germany) BMW	173.67 mph
1951 W. Herz (Germany) NSU	180.00 mph
1955 R. Wright (New Zealand) Vincent HRD	185.00 mph
1955 J. Allen (USA) Triumph	193.72 mph
1955 J. Allen (USA) Triumph	214.17 mph
1956 W. Herz (Germany) NSU	189.00 mph
1956 W. Herz (Germany) NSU	210.64 mph
1962 W. Johnson (USA) Triumph	224.57 mph
1966 R. Leppan (USA) Triumph	245.67 mph
1970 D. Vesco (USA) Yamaha	251.92 mph
1970 C. Rayborn (USA) Harley-Davidson	255.37 mph

1970 C. Rayborn (USA) Harley-Davidson	265.49 mph
1974 D. Vesco (USA) Yamaha	281.71 mph
1974 D. Vesco (USA) Yamaha	234.24 mph
1975 D. Vesco (USA) Yamaha	302.66 mph
1975 D. Vesco (USA) Yamaha	303.82 mph
1978 D. Vesco (USA) Kawasaki	314.36 mph
1978 D. Vesco (USA) Kawasaki	318.60 mph

Note: some records were not officially recognized by the FIM – hence the 'drop' in some speeds from previous records.

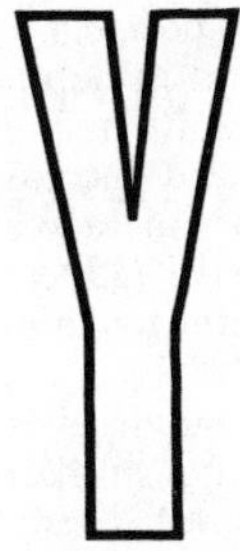

YAMAHA
The leading two-stroke factory in the world and certainly, in the late 1960s and early 1970s, the most prolific name in international competition, Yamaha followed in the wake of Honda into Europe in the 1960s, gaining an eighth position in their debut event, the French Grand Prix of 1961, competing with 125 and 250 air-cooled twins. After a year of intensive work in Japan, the Yamaha technicians achieved much more power in the 250 and sent their challenger, known as the RD 56, back to Europe in 1963. Their efforts met with immediate success.

Fumio Ito won the Belgian Grand Prix against competition from the Honda four and set a new record lap at 117.82 mph. Earlier Ito had averaged 94.85 mph on the Isle of Man to take second place behind Jim Redman. It was a remarkable ride since it was only Ito's second time in the Island. He was second to Redman again at the Dutch TT. The RD 56 was a seven-speed machine with an air-cooled 250 rotary valve engine and it was Yamaha's first twin-cylinder. Ito ended the season by gaining third place in the 250cc World Championship behind Redman and Provini on Honda and Morini respectively. For 1964 Yamaha signed Phil Read and Mike Duff and Read, riding the RD 56, brought them their first World Title that year, the 250cc Championship. He won five Grands Prix during the season and established Yamaha's indisputable place in the vanguard of motor cycle racing. Yamaha did even better in 1965 when Read again brought home the title with Duff, riding a similar Yamaha, in second position. Threatened by Yamaha, Honda responded with a new six-cylinder machine and in the expert hands of Hailwood, Read struggled during 1966 and finally relinquished the title. Honda and Hailwood again were supreme in 1967, but by this time Yamaha were hotting up their challenge. They had produced a new four-cylinder 250 and signed the diminutive Bill Ivy, following a crash by Mike Duff, as team-mate for Read. The four-cylinders were water-cooled and supplied by four rotary valves; the gearbox had eight gears and the initial machine was designed to produce a maximum speed of 149 mph. Although the combination of Read and Ivy failed to pierce the impregnability of Honda and Hailwood, they finished second and third in the 250cc class and, with Ivy capturing the 125cc World Title and Read in second position, the Japanese factory had enjoyed their most successful season so far. In 1968, with Honda having retired from racing, the field was wide open for Yamaha. Read and Ivy made no mistake. With improved machines (the 250 could now reach 155 mph theoretically and the 125cc had been developed along similar lines to the 250 and was an exact replica to give a capability approaching 133 mph) they secured 1st and 2nd (Read and Ivy) in the 125 category and 1st and 2nd (Read and Ivy) in the 250 class. Within the comparatively short space of six years Yamaha had gone from almost total obscurity to world acclaim and the admiration of millions.

Yamaha's story is all the more remarkable when considered against the firm's background and history. It began life as a manufacturer of reed organs in the late 1880s and quickly added the making of pianos. Later it encompassed aircraft propellers. In the 1950s Yamaha turned their attention to the making of motor cycles and earned an award for motor-cycle design for their 125 machine. The first Yamaha racing division was formed in 1960 following encouraging performances in Europe. They were then set to launch an all-out assault on the Grand Prix scene. Their first racing machines were claimed to have been produced in just one year and (whether or not their racing success was in any way responsible) the production of Yamaha motor cycles, according to figures released by the firm, rose from 27,000 in 1958 to 406,000 in 1967 and 450,000 in 1969.

Although Yamaha retired from the Grand Prix scene officially at the end of 1968, they did not withdraw completely from the sport. Their two-stroke twins with two carburettors did well in the hands of private entrants and immediately following 1968 Phil Read continued successfully to compete with his own Yamahas. In 1970 the FIM imposed a new rule, first mooted two years earlier, which limited the number of cylinders in the 250cc category to two and the gearboxes to not more than six-speed. The aim was to discourage the exotic and lavish multis which had been so expensive to the Japanese and had led to their eventual withdrawal from the sport, and to encourage the smaller manufacturers back into racing. This had the effect of bringing Yamaha machinery very much into the picture once more for their TD2 was by far the most competitive racer which could be bought. Recognising the opportunity Yamaha backed Rodney Gould and Kent Andersson with free machines and spares, together with a small contract, though this investment was only a fraction of their commitment during their Grand Prix days. With Yamahas also being ridden by Read and Kel Carruthers, among others, the Japanese factory was again very well represented in the 250cc class and in 1970 they secured first (Gould), second (Carruthers) and third (Andersson) in the World Championship.

Four-stroke machines until now had dominated the larger capacity 500cc class, but times were changing and in the 350cc class the infiltration of the two-strokes was forcing Agostini to ride the MV harder than for years. His major rival was an exciting new personality in the sport from Finland, Jarno Saarinen. Riding for the Yamaha importer in Finland, Saarinen scored two significant victories over Agostini during 1971, finishing in second place in the 350cc World Championship table. With Swedish rider Carlsson giving Yamaha a third place in this class, and Read, Gould and Saarinen riding Yamahas into the first three places in the 250cc class, the Japanese factory had the most successful machines of 1971. In 1972 Saarinen captured the 250cc crown and was second in the 350cc class on Yamaha. Into such a dominating situation had Yamaha machinery moved in 1973 that they achieved a first and second in the 125cc class, first, second, third, fourth, fifth and sixth in the 250cc class, second, fourth, fifth and sixth in the 350cc class, and even a fourth and sixth in the 500cc class. They were even more dominant in depth in 1974 with the following results in the World Championships: first and second (125cc), second to eighth inclusive (250cc), first to seventh inclusive (350cc) and third, fourth and seventh to thirteenth inclusive (500cc).

Over in the USA Yamaha, their eyes cocked towards the vast potential market for their machines there, were already eating into the records by 1971 when Don Vesco made Yamaha the world's fastest two-stroke by breaking records at 251.92 mph on his double-engined 700cc machine. By 1974 the Japanese factory had added the one hour record at a speed of 150.66 mph and had secured three wins in a row (1972/73/74) in the prestigeous Daytona 200. Two ultimate speed records were established by Yamaha (with Don Vesco) in 1974. In the autumn the Yamaha took the outright speed record from Harley-Davidson at a new average for the two runs of 281.714 mph. During the final quarter mile of the return run Don Vesco had got the Yamaha as high as 287.539 mph, but further attempt to hoist the record closer to the 300 mark failed. But he was successful when, with one engine, he set a new FIM record of 234.245 mph for the mile for the 750cc class. On a world-wide basis there was now no other machine to make such an impact as Yamaha.

On the Isle of Man Yamaha first appeared in the results in 1963 when, as already noted, Ito raced second to Redman in the 250cc TT. In 1965 they achieved second in the Junior and 250cc TTs, were first and third in the 125cc event. Results since then:

1966: first and second 125cc.
1967: second 250cc, first and third 125cc.
1968: first 250cc, first and second 125cc.
1970: first and second 250cc.
1971: first and second 250cc, first 125cc, second Production 250cc, second (Padgett-Yamaha) Junior.
1972: third (Padgett-Yamaha) Senior; second and third (Padgett-Yamaha) Junior; first, second and third 250cc; first and second (Johnson-Yamaha) 125cc; second Production 250cc.
1973: first, second (Dugdale-Yamaha) and 3rd Junior, first (Johnson-Yamaha), second and third (Padgett-Yamaha) 250cc, first, second and third 125cc.

1974 first, second (Dugdale-Yamaha) and third F750; first, second (Dugdale-Yamaha) and third Senior; first, second and third Junior· first, second (Granby-Yamaha) and third 125cc. This 1974 performance was one of the most remarkable ever in the history of the TT for a Yamaha machine finished first, second and third in every one of the solo classes.

On November 5, 1975, Yamaha of Japan announced the withdrawal of direct factory participation from the three categories of motor cycle championship competition – road racing, moto cross and trials. The manufacture of production racing machines for private competition was to be continued and plans were made at Yamaha's European headquarters to produce a support programme for European motor cycle competition.

Yamaha machinery has continued to dominate road racing in the second half of the 1970s and in the World Championships alone in the three years 1976–1978, most contenders in the 350cc and 250cc classes were Yamaha-mounted. In 1977 Katayama took the 350cc world title, and in 1978, Roberts the 500cc world title on Yamaha machinery.

YUGOSLAV GRAND PRIX

The Yugoslav Grand Prix was given World Championship status for the first time in 1969. The race takes place on the seafront road circuit at the Adriatic resort of Opatija, near Rijeka. A tricky, twisting 3.7 mile course, Opatija includes two very tight hairpins and a long bend towards the end. Its location helps to give the Yugoslav Grand Prix a holiday flavour.

Results:

1969: 50cc P. Lodewijkx (Jamathi); 125cc D. Braun (Suzuki); 250cc K. Carruthers (Benelli); 350cc S. Grassetti (Jama); 500cc G. Nash (Norton).

1970: 50cc A. Nieto (Derbi), 125cc D. Braun (Suzuki); 250cc S. Herrero (Ossa); 350cc G. Agostini (MV); 500cc G. Agostini (MV).

1972: 50cc J. Bruins (Kreidler); 125cc K. Andersson (Yamaha); 250cc R. Pasolini (Aermacchi); 350cc J. Drapal (Yamaha); 500cc A. Pagani (MV).

1973: 50cc J. de Vries (Kreidler); 125cc K. Andersson (Yamaha); 250cc D. Braun (Yamaha); 350cc J. Drapal (Yamaha); 500cc K. Newcombe (Konig).

1974: 50cc H. van Kessell (Kreidler); 125cc K. Andersson (Yamaha); 250cc C. Mortimer (Yamaha); 350cc G. Agostini (Yamaha).

1975: 50cc A. Nieto (Kreidler); 125cc D. Braun (Morbidelli); 250cc D. Braun (Yamaha); 350cc P. Korhonen (Yamaha).

1976: 50cc U. Graf (Kreidler); 125cc P. P. Bianchi (Morbidelli); 250cc D. Braun (Yamaha); 350cc O. Chevallier (Yamaha).

1977: 50cc A. Nieto (Bultaco); 125cc P. Bianchi (Morbidelli); 250cc M. Lega (Morbidelli); 350cc T. Katayama (Yamaha).

1978: 50cc R. Tormo (Bultaco); 125cc A. Nieto (Minarelli); 250cc G. Hansford (Kawasaki); 350cc G. Hansford (Kawasaki).

1979: 50cc E. Lazzarini (Kreidler); 125cc A. Nieto (Minarelli); 250cc G. Rossi (Morbidelli); 350cc K. Ballington (Kawasaki); 500cc K. Roberts (Yamaha).

1980: 50cc R. Tormo (Kreidler); 125cc G. Bertin (Motobecane); 250cc A. Mang (Kawasaki); sidecar R. Biland/K. Waltisperg (Yamaha).

1981: 50cc R. Tormo (Bultaco); 125cc L. Reggiani (Minarelli); 350cc A. Mang (Kawasaki); 500cc R. Mamola (Suzuki).

Index